LIVING AND ACTIVE

SACRA DOCTRINA

Christian Theology for a Postmodern Age

LIVING AND ACTIVE

Scripture in the Economy of Salvation

TELFORD WORK

WILLIAM B. EERDMANS PUBLISHING COMPANY
GRAND RAPIDS, MICHIGAN / CAMBRIDGE, U.K.

© 2002 Wm. B. Eerdmans Publishing Co.

Wm. B. Eerdmans Publishing Co.
255 Jefferson Ave. S.E., Grand Rapids, Michigan 49503 /
P.O. Box 163, Cambridge CB3 9PU U.K.

Printed in the United States of America

07 06 05 04 03 02   7 6 5 4 3 2 1

Library of Congress Cataloging-in-Publication Data

Work, Telford.
Living and active: Scripture in the economy of salvation / Telford Work.
p.   cm.   — (Sacra doctrina)
Includes bibliographical references.
ISBN 0-8028-4724-2 (alk. paper)
1. Bible — Theology.   2. Bible — Evidences, authority, etc.
I. Title.   II. Series.

BS543.W67   2002
220.1 3 — dc21
                                                    2001040308

www.eerdmans.com

To the disciples at Christian Assembly
and Westmont College
who, in using Scripture,
show that you know intuitively
what I have found myself struggling here
to put in analytical language.
You say more in inflecting one verse
than I can write in an entire book.

Contents

vii

CONTENTS

CONTENTS

Contents

Foreword

Telford Work's *Living and Active* is a book of signal importance for the church's *theological* reflection about Scripture. To explain the reasons for this judgment, it will be useful to sketch — begging the reader's indulgence — a bit of my own intellectual pilgrimage in grappling with the role of the Bible in Christian theology.

As a novice in the study of theology, I spent a long time worrying over the problem of the authority of Scripture. Why should the Bible be treated as normative for the faith and practice of the church? Although this seemed a pressing question on which much depended, I had trouble finding satisfying answers. The arguments of conservative apologists for biblical authority often seemed contrived and unpersuasive, and "mainline" Protestantism — the tradition in which I had been raised — offered little help on this matter. As William Placher has remarked, "Non-fundamentalists' discussions of appeals to the Bible have often consisted principally in ridiculing fundamentalism, without defining any clear alternative to it."[1]

One apologetic strategy I encountered, especially among evangelical writers, was to argue for the authority of Scripture by citing isolated Bible verses. Even apart from the disconcerting logical circularity of such arguments, they fail the test of careful exegesis. Scriptural passages (such as Isa. 55:11, 1 Thess. 2:13, and Heb. 4:12) that refer to "the word of God" are not speaking — at least not in any simple sense — of the canonical text of the Bi-

---

1. William C. Placher, "Is the Bible True?" *The Christian Century* 112 (1995): 924-28; the cited sentence appears on p. 924.

ble. Rather, they are speaking of the word orally proclaimed in a particular setting by a prophet or apostle.[2] Therefore, to invoke these texts in defense of biblical authority entails an act of unacknowledged special pleading, a theological sleight of hand that transmutes statements about the prophetically proclaimed word into doctrines about the subsequently canonized text of the Bible.

Even 2 Tim. 3:16, the cornerstone of many arguments for the authority of the Bible — while it does refer explicitly to "scripture" — will not support the weight of the claims that have often been constructed upon it. The Greek syntax of the sentence favors the translation "Every scripture inspired by God is also useful . . ." (as in the NRSV footnote) rather than "All scripture is inspired by God and useful. . . ." Thus, contrary to the way the verse has often been understood, the text does not categorically assert that all scripture is inspired. Furthermore, the sentence does not say that Scripture is inerrant or even that it is authoritative on all theological questions. Rather, the passage makes a more modest and sturdy affirmation: that every inspired text is "useful for teaching, for reproof, for correction, and for training in righteousness." In other words, Scripture, according to 2 Tim. 3:16, is edifying for the purpose of moral instruction. One might grant this claim but still wonder whether (or how) the text informs theological reflection about the character of God or about christology or eschatology or other theological topics. Finally, and most significantly, when the author of 2 Timothy uses the term "scripture," he is certainly referring to the Old Testament, not the canonical New Testament, which was of course not yet in existence when this letter was written.

In sum, the attempt to buttress the authority of the Bible by prooftexting proves to be theologically vapid and unsatisfactory. Perhaps sensing this unsatisfactoriness, some defenders of biblical authority have appealed to a very different sort of argument, attempting to demonstrate the factual truthfulness of Scripture. The Bible, according to this line of argument, is true because it can be shown to be historically reliable. This project, however, is even more fatally flawed than the prooftexting method, for two reasons. First, it must expend vast energies seeking to explain away internal tensions and contradictions within the biblical narratives. It violently subordinates the untidy particularity of the Scripture we have actually been given to a theoretical ideal of what sort of Scripture God ought to have given us. Second, and equally

---

2. Of course, the term "word of God" in the prologue of John's Gospel refers to Jesus Christ, not to the biblical text. Jesus is the "word" in the metaphorical sense that he is the "uttered" manifestation of God's grace and truth; therefore, he has "exegeted" the invisible God (John 1:17-18).

damning, this apologetic project seeks to justify the authority of the Bible by showing that the Bible somehow conforms to other previously recognized canons of truth. To make this move, however, is to concede tacitly that these other fundamental canons of truth (historical factuality or whatever) are in principle more authoritative than the Bible: if the Bible fails to answer to these higher authorities, its own claim to normative status must be denied.[3] Thus, ironically, some of the staunchest defenders of biblical inerrancy are actually captive to modernist, Enlightenment conceptions of truth and authority.

The recognition of this last point proved pivotal in my own theological pilgrimage. When I read Karl Barth and Hans Frei, however, I discovered a new way of understanding the authority of the Bible: the Bible narrates a world into which we are drawn, a world in which we live and move, a world in which God's word encounters us with power. The biblical narrative reshapes our understanding of "reality." As George Lindbeck has summarized this way of understanding biblical authority, "Intratextual theology redescribes reality within the scriptural framework rather than translating Scripture into extra-scriptural categories. It is the text, so to speak, which absorbs the world, rather than the world the text."[4]

This epistemological revolution, which laid the groundwork for all my subsequent work as a New Testament scholar, has characterized the theological movement that is often called postliberalism. Understanding biblical authority within this model allows us to respect the narrative character of the scriptural witness, and to acknowledge its truth claims, without falling into the characteristic conundrums and rationalistic fallacies of fundamentalism.

Still, nagging problems remain. Two critiques of postliberal hermeneutics are particularly worrisome. On the one hand, some critics allege that the "intratextual" epistemology of this theological perspective lends itself to an uncritical docetism that in effect, if not in intention, denies the extratextual *reference* of biblical language. Does Scripture merely narrate a self-enclosed imaginative world, or does it refer to events that have really occurred within time and space? Much postliberal theology is at best equivocal about such issues.[5]

On the other hand, other critics protest, on quite a different front, that

---

3. It probably goes without saying that an analogous criticism applies to attempts to defend the Bible's truthfulness by appeals to experiential criteria: "The Bible should be believed because it satisfies our psychological or emotional needs."

4. George A. Lindbeck, *The Nature of Doctrine: Religion and Theology in a Postliberal Age* (Louisville: Westminster, 1984), p. 118.

5. See, however, Bruce D. Marshall, "Absorbing the World: Christianity and the Universe of Truths," in Bruce D. Marshall (ed.), *Theology and Dialogue: Essays in Conversation with George Lindbeck* (Notre Dame: University of Notre Dame Press, 1990), pp. 69-102.

some followers of the Frei-Lindbeck school are insufficiently attentive to the ways in which their construals of the Bible's narrative world are tacitly dependent upon the church's classic Trinitarian confessional traditions. In other words, the theological meaning of Scripture cannot simply be read descriptively off the face of the texts, but it must be located within a reading dependent upon the time-honored decisions of the church's ecumenical councils. By disregarding or downplaying the hermeneutical centrality of the church's rule of faith, postliberal theology — in some of its forms — privileges a "New Critical" theory of textual meaning that asserts the presence of certain theological ideas within "the text itself," apart from any actual ecclesial reading community. Such an approach, it is alleged, cannot withstand the postmodern critique that identifies all interpretations as performances of particular readers or communities of readers.[6] On this view, the authority of the Bible is rooted in the church's conventions of reading.

Against this background, the significance of Telford Work's book comes into focus. He has offered us a fresh systematic account of the Christian doctrine of Scripture — "bibliology," as he calls it. This theological reflection is light-years ahead of the usual evangelical apologetics for the authority of the Bible. Rather than falling into fruitless patterns of prooftexting or rationalistic defense, Work has undertaken a constructive theological reflection about "the Bible's relationship with God and its role in God's plan of salvation" (p. 9). Building on the incarnational theology of Athanasius, Work mounts a case for understanding the Bible as a direct manifestation of "the Word's self-involvement in the world." The result is a bold and nuanced account of the Bible as the triune God's instrument of self-revelation.

Although this book was originally written as a dissertation at Duke, under the discerning direction of my colleague Geoffrey Wainwright, it transcends the dissertation genre. Indeed, it is a major piece of constructive theology. Work writes with confidence, depth, and theological maturity, showing how the revelatory function of Scripture is grounded in the trinitarian character of God.

Readers of the book will perceive that Work's account of the Bible's role in "the economy of salvation" avoids the two pitfalls of postliberalism as outlined above. First, he forcefully asserts that Scripture is an instrument of the living God's activity in the world, ensuring that it cannot be understood merely as a self-enclosed, self-referential literary text. Second, Work's vigorous engagement with the church's confessional traditions ensures that his

---

6. For discussion of these problems and related issues, see Stephen E. Fowl, *Engaging Scripture: A Model for Theological Interpretation* (Oxford: Blackwell, 1998).

claims about Scripture as the medium of God's self-disclosure are imbedded in sustained dialogue with the ecclesiologies of various catholic Christian traditions, ranging from Athanasius and Augustine to Barth and von Balthasar. His illuminating comparison of recent battles over biblical authority to the Iconoclastic controversy of the eighth century — including his suggestion that the Seventh Ecumenical Council's understanding of icons provides an analogy for our understanding of Scripture as an instrument of God's action — exemplifies the deep ways in which Work's constructive proposals are consciously grounded in ecclesial tradition. (This aspect of Work's project is particularly interesting since he comes from a background in one of the "new paradigm" postdenominational churches. He could be the first major ecumenical systematic theologian emerging from this new movement; at least, he is the first known to me.) By any measure, this is a remarkable piece of theological work, and it should become a benchmark for subsequent discussion of Scripture's role in the church.

One final observation about *Living and Active* is perhaps in order. This book, like all significant systematic theology, has aims that are profoundly and explicitly pastoral. That is, Work seeks to clarify and sustain the practices through which Scripture nurtures the church. This book will be incomprehensible to those who stand apart from the communities of prayer and praise that God brings into being through the scriptural word. Only those who listen for the word in such communities will grasp the necessity and the extraordinary contribution of this theological labor. At the same time, the value of Work's account of Scripture will be tested — as he would wish — by its capacity to edify such communities. My own judgment is that the edifying power of Work's work is substantial. In 2 Tim. 2:15, we find a charge from Paul to Timothy: "Do your best to present yourself to God as one approved by him, a worker who has no need to be ashamed, rightly explaining the word of truth." All who bear the teaching office in the church necessarily aspire to carry out that charge, and all who read this book closely will be given help and encouragement in the task.

Richard B. Hays
The Center of Theological Inquiry
Princeton, NJ
August 6, 2001

Acknowledgments

Please rejoice with me in my debts, as I list my creditors:

Thanks to my family for the sacrifices you made in uprooting twice, moving even more than twice, relocating for summers and winters, accepting separated friendships, career changes, and countless inconveniences — all for the insecurity of a future career in theology.

Thanks to the Graduate Program in Religion at Duke University for an exceedingly generous five-year fellowship, and thanks to Bill Work and George Barna for providing rare and rewarding employment opportunities. You made it possible not only to complete my theological training, but even to do so while beginning and growing a family.

Thanks to the churches in which I have been involved, particularly Glendale Community Church and Christian Assembly Foursquare Church, for teaching me worship, discipleship, vision, and solid theology in word and deed.

Thanks to Westmont College, for offering an undergraduate context of faithfulness, charity, centeredness, openness, and critical rigor that is (or should be) the envy of the evangelical world. You have won my enduring admiration and loyalty.

Thanks to Alan Padgett and the editorial board of *Sacra Doctrina*, for your willingness to include the work of a young scholar alongside the work of seasoned veterans, and for criticisms and suggestions that substantially improved this project.

Thanks to Geoffrey Wainwright and all my theological mentors at Duke and Fuller Theological Seminary, whose dedication and effort turned me

ACKNOWLEDGMENTS

from the eager but clueless novice I was, into — well, you all are the proper judges of who I am now. My achievements are your achievements, my great ideas are really your great ideas, and my mistakes are my own.

Et soli Deo gloria!

TELFORD WORK
Ash Wednesday, 2001

The Crisis of Scripture

Why?

This project is a long scratch at a persistent itch.

My life has passed through several theological stages, each of which has been characterized by a particular attitude toward the Bible. From an unworried childhood agnosticism, I moved to a somewhat arrogant preadolescent and early-teen atheism, then (thanks to Hal Lindsey's conspiracy theories) to a premillennial, but never fundamentalist, teenage conversion, then to a mainstream evangelicalism near the end of my undergraduate years. Since then my formal theological education has taken me into a more ecumenical, charismatic evangelicalism. Along the line (if *line* is the right term), the idea of the Bible went from being interesting, to mysterious, to a matter of urgency. Through years of training by brilliant and faithful mentors (both pastoral and academic), and through the discipline of this exercise, it has finally become *satisfying* as well.

Fellow sojourners do not always have the same story. Some found themselves unable to trust a text that emerged from "organized religion," and turned to other canons. Some tied their sails to the mast of fundamentalism. Some seminary acquaintances were unable to reconcile evangelical faith with the critical practices they were encountering, despite the efforts of faculty, administrators, and students. These either returned to fundamentalism or, on the rebound, adopted radical alternatives. A Bible study friend lost her brother to the faith when he found out that rabbits do not chew their cud (proving false, in his opinion, the inerrancy of Scripture; cf. Lev. 11:6 and

1

Deut. 14:7). For all the successes — and there were many! — these failures mounted. And as they did, I grew increasingly frustrated with the distance that separated evangelical faith and practice from the findings of modern (then postmodern) biblical criticism. I longed for a language that could span the distance between the two and correct the failures of each. I hungered more and more for a truly satisfying, truly theological, truly sophisticated doctrine of Scripture.

Here, then, is an effort to satisfy my own hunger, and alleviate the hunger of others. It began in Marianne Meye Thompson's introductory course on the Gospels. As an extra credit assignment, she asked us to explain what we mean when we say the Gospels are true. She allowed us five pages, no secondary sources, and only one biblical citation. I discovered I could not answer the question without appealing to ecclesiology. That little appetizer proved how hungry I really was, and showed me where to go for seconds.

The project that follows develops a fully Trinitarian account of Scripture, establishing and exploring its divine and human character and its salvific purpose in its Church setting and beyond. It claims that the Christian Bible, as divine message, historical phenomenon, and physical object, participates in the Trinitarian economy of salvation. It concludes that the Bible is theologically indispensable to the Christian faith, and finds the doctrine of Scripture to norm, inform, enhance, and ground the Church's entire biblical practice (here referring centrally to preaching, but comprehensively to the entire range of practices in which the Church uses Scripture). If not a gourmet meal, it is at least a full one.

My prayer is that it serves several purposes: First, as a guide for faithful Christians, and especially for frustrated, perplexed, and worried students of theology, who want answers to the faithful (and sometimes doubtful) questions that arise when they engage Scripture, or who are tired of academic and confessional languages that seem incommensurable. Second, as a common ground for the polarized academic communities of theologians and biblical scholars, to show each camp that the other offers invaluable resources for its own work. Third, as a teaser for those who want to taste the rich fruit of a deep exercise in the Christian institution of Scripture. Fourth, as a joyful apology for the Christian biblical practices of a Church that increasingly stammers, mumbles, shouts, or changes the subject when asked to defend itself.

We are certainly not the first Christians to have lived in such theological and practical discomfort. Before beginning the exercise, we will be encouraged by considering another crisis that faced a community of persecuted Christians long ago and far away. It is a community nearly forgotten by American evangelicals, who tend to believe they would not have sided with

2

them anyway. That controversy was the Iconoclastic Controversy. We turn to it for more than just company in our misery; it shows that there can be gain in our pain.

Iconoclasm as a Paradigm for Reflection on Scripture

In the eighth century, Leo III, perhaps shaken by the rapid expansion of Islam into Byzantine Orthodox territory under the Umayyads and by the way Christian use of images presented obstacles to the conversion of Muslims and Jews, imposed a ban on images in the empire. Backing up his ban were sophisticated theological arguments against images that had long been available in Christianity, both in its canonical texts and in the work of patristic theologians. The Iconoclasts held the use of images to be heretical for their failure to respect God's transcendence, the two natures of Christ, and their unity in his person. It was not simply the abuse of a defensible practice that was attacked. The practice itself was called abusive, a violation of the depth grammar of Christianity.

The most perceptive Iconodules saw that the Iconoclasts' arguments represented a fundamentally different vision of Christianity than their own. But the Iconoclastic case enjoyed strong biblical and apostolic warrants, and could ground its claims on central Christian theological and practical convictions. An adequate response could not appeal merely to precedent or to settled "catholicity," but had to establish the intrinsic connections between images and the central confessions of the Christian faith.

So John of Damascus and Theodore of Studium responded to the Iconoclasts' arguments with a theology of images grounded in Chalcedonian Christology, in ecclesial pneumatology, and in the eschatology of divinization. John's work laid the theological groundwork for the Second Council of Nicea, which secured support for iconic practices in the Church. Theodore's work answered the Iconoclast counteroffensive and helped finally settle the dispute. Indeed, their iconologies found these practices not just *licit* but *essential* to orthodox Christianity, reaching into the very heart of the Christian faith. From the perspective of the Iconodules and the Seventh Ecumenical Council, heresy had precipitated "the Triumph of Orthodoxy." And so the occasion of Iconoclasm and the Iconodules' theological response to it remain deeply formative for Orthodox theology and practice.

The Second Council of Nicea found images and relics to be analogous in essence to the books of the Gospels. Iconic practice thus followed liturgical practices regarding the nature and use of Scripture, which were far more

3

firmly embedded in all Church traditions. However, just as the earlier heresies had focused the agenda of the fourth and fifth centuries, pushing other items down the Church's list of priorities, so in the East the growing appreciation for iconic practice crowded out attention to the way the Council's reasoning applied to Scripture. The bias persists to this day — far more Orthodox attention is devoted to the quasi-sacramental qualities of images than to such qualities in Scripture. In the West, where images were considered more pragmatically, where Islam was less threatening, and where Iconoclasm did not become a widespread issue until the Reformation, the balance of theological attention remained tilted towards the canonical text. Consequently, Second Nicea's theology of images has rarely been put to much constructive use in Catholic or Protestant theology.

An Era of "Biblioclasm"?

As a thought-experiment, imagine a different scenario: What would have happened had the practice under attack in the eighth century been the use of *Scripture* in the Church? The Bible has been so central to Christian worship from the beginning that the question is nearly inconceivable.[1] Marcion and others had already led Christians to reflect on the boundaries of the canon, but even they had not questioned the divine character and purpose of Scripture. How might the equivalents of John of Damascus or Theodore of Studium — or for that matter, Athanasius, Augustine, or the Cappadocians — have responded on theological grounds to a *wholesale* attack, from *inside* the Church, on the idea and use of Scripture itself?

This is not quite as speculative a question as it sounds, at least in the West, where since the Enlightenment the concept and practice of Scripture have been under unprecedented and sustained stress. From an ever-thickening stack of new hermeneutical proposals to radical uses of the historical-critical method (from both liberal Protestants and fundamentalists) and the "hermeneutics of suspicion," new ways of appreciating the Bible have challenged traditional concepts of Scripture in ways sometimes reminiscent of the era of

---

1. This is the irony of Newman's theory of the development of doctrine: Sometimes the issues that create friction and develop doctrine come from the margins, not the center, of the Christian faith. The result is a shift in the tradition's theological center of gravity: Iconoclasm directed Orthodox attention towards images and away, relatively, from Scripture. Newman supposes all such shifts to be healthy to the tradition, but MacIntyre helps show that the solution to one crisis might possibly weaken the tradition's ability to respond to future crises.

Iconoclasm. "Formerly, people saw nothing but God" in Scripture, says Aidan Nichols. "Now they might see nothing but humans."[2] Protestants in general, and fundamentalists in particular, have been labeled bibliolaters by their rivals. In return, these movements have faulted Catholics, then modernist Protestants, for adopting human traditions that usurped or denied Scripture's divinity. Liberals have been called adoptionists and ebionites, conservatives docetists and monophysites, neo-orthodox Nestorians — not because of their formal Christologies, but because of the Christological implications of their uses of Scripture. These charges and countercharges are reminiscent of the atmosphere in the eighth century.

For all the theological finger-pointing and anathematizing, it is hyperbolic to call the current state of the Church an era of biblioclasm. Iconoclasm was an official state policy, which led to popular revolt, casualties on both sides, and the torture and martyrdom of Iconodule clergy and laity.[3] If there is something like biblioclasm today, it is more an academic than an imperial movement. And, like Iconoclasm, it is still widely opposed by clergy and laity alike. If anything, biblical practice has recently been enjoying a revival, especially in the Roman Catholic tradition. The centuries-long debate over how to read the Bible has spurred the development of theologies of Scripture in a seemingly unprecedented way. Any theological hermeneutics textbook witnesses to the variety of orthodox Christian uses of Scripture. And there is no reason to be entirely negative, or even negative on balance, about developments in biblical practice in the past few centuries. Many of them have genuinely enriched Christian use of Scripture.

Furthermore, biblical practice enjoys an unproblematic place in the lives of many Christians. For them, the mere assertion that the Bible is the Word of God is enough, just as the bumper sticker proclaims: "God said it. I believe it. That settles it."

Yet the apparent simplicity of this assertion dissipates as soon as either "the Bible" or "the Word of God" is given more careful scrutiny.[4] Both terms are essentially contested concepts within the orthodox Christian tradition. On the matter of "Bible," there are the long-standing issues about the nature and boundaries of the canon — which books are "Bible" and which are not,

---

2. Aidan Nichols, *The Shape of Catholic Theology* (Collegeville, Minn.: Liturgical Press, 1991), p. 124.

3. Leonid Ouspensky, *Theology of the Icon,* 2 vols. (Crestwood, N.Y.: St. Vladimir's Seminary Press, 1992), vol. 1, p. 109.

4. And it should. If Trinity, salvation, and Church inform the doctrine of Scripture, then one can hardly expect the various traditions, with their rival accounts of Trinity, salvation, and Church, to agree completely on the meaning of either "Bible" or "Word of God."

and why. These involve the status of the Septuagintal books of the Old Testament, and even the authority of the LXX, Vulgate, King James, and other traditions of translation. There is also the theological significance of tradition-history: For instance, is the story of Jesus and the woman caught in adultery (John 7:53–8:11) canonical, and why or why not? Then there is the tendency, most pronounced in Lutheranism, to adopt radical theological tests for canonicity. Here Luther's subordination of Hebrews, James, Jude, and Revelation within the canon is outmatched by the modern Lutheran hermeneutical suspicion of any text showing traces of "early Catholicism,"[5] or feminist hermeneutical suspicion of any text showing traces of patriarchalism. Both varieties of suspicion claim that the Bible is *not* the Word of God as emphatically as they claim that it is — or, rather, that parts are Word of God, and parts are not. It is hardly inappropriate to call such an attitude biblioclastic.

The predicate, "inspired Word of God," is no simpler than the subject. Inspiration is hardly an uncontested concept. When does it take place, to whom or to what, and what are its effects? And most profoundly, there are the complexities in the relationship between "Word" and "God." How strong is the connection between them? To what extent is the genitive objective, subjective, or even epexegetical? The phrase "Word of God" is intentionally multivalent in Christian usage, referring both to the *logoi* of John 1 and the *logos* of John 1. What is the nature of the analogy between them, if there is any such thing?

So, despite the Bible's apparent strength in the churches, the crisis of Scripture continues. The "Triumph of Orthodoxy" regarding Scripture is yet to come, if it will come at all. Lay people, pastors, theologians, even entire traditions are confused about what the Bible is, and what roles it plays in the life of their communities. They scratch their heads more than ever, wondering how they should be reading their Bibles. They find it difficult to name the Bible's character and work in their churches, let alone the Church at large and the wider world. They adapt only painfully to the conclusions of historical-critical biblical scholarship. Growing groups of Orthodox, Catholics, Protestants, and radicals look back to precritical biblical exegesis for *ressourcement*

---

5. See, for instance, Ernst Käsemann's "Thoughts on the Present Controversy Over Scriptural Interpretation," in *New Testament Questions of Today* (Philadelphia: Fortress, 1969), pp. 274, 277. While the appeal to Christocentricity is most typical of Lutheran doctrines of Scripture, it is one typical Protestant argument against the canonicity of the Apocrypha: "The Apocrypha is not important for doctrine," claims J. I. Packer ("Scripture," in Sinclair B. Ferguson, David F. Wright, and J. I. Packer, eds., *New Dictionary of Theology* [Downers Grove, Ill.: InterVarsity, 1988], p. 628).

and hermeneutical training.[6] Yet these same traditions find themselves unable to adopt or even endorse each other's reading practices. We have yet to hear a modern-day Theodore of Studium deliver the kind of argument that settles the hermeneutical melée, or even establishes boundaries to inform subsequent discussion.

Modern biblioclasm takes on a painfully real existential dimension in the lives of both liberal and conservative Christians exposed to critical biblical methods and conclusions. Even when teachers and pastors explore these carefully and faithfully, students and parishioners can be damaged. Some conservatives lose their faith when their naïve notions of inerrancy are dislodged. Unless such biblical criticisms are justified theologically and not merely empirically, no new doctrine of Scripture takes the place of the old one. Too often, the result is that so-called "bibliolaters" are not reformed into "bibliodules," but turned into new biblioclasts — stripped of their old justifications for faith but not provided with the theological resources they need to appreciate the Bible's true role in the Christian life. And so one demon gives way to seven. In more liberal traditions, students and parishioners with "lower" doctrines of Scripture may experience the same alienation, with or without the shock of abandoning their old epistemologies.

If ours really is something like an era of biblioclasm, then the situation seems grave. Yet the Church remembers the Iconoclastic era as being more of an opportunity than a real threat. Iconoclasm's lasting gift to Christianity was its challenge in the sharpest possible terms concerning the role of images in Christian practice. This challenge was too fundamental to be turned away by anything but a comprehensive ontology and phenomenology of images. John of Damascus and Theodore of Studium are the pioneers of precisely such a systematic iconology. And the Iconodules' case was much more than a mere defense of the status quo. It laid the doctrinal foundations for the flowering of images in Christianity. It gave Christians better reasons, and more reliable guidelines, for using icons.

In our imaginary scenario, where the concept of Scripture itself is at issue, John's and Theodore's work can be paradigmatic for an ontology and practical theology of Scripture. An era of biblioclasm would likely generate a kind of reflection on Scripture that has not yet been necessary in the Church. A critique of the Bible as radical as full-scale biblioclasm would call for much

6. For an influential example among Protestants, see David Steinmetz, "The Superiority of Pre-Critical Exegesis," in *Memory and Mission: Theological Reflections on the Christian Past* (Nashville: Abingdon, 1988), pp. 143-63. Eerdmans' *Ressourcement* series is another example of growing Protestant appreciation for patristic, medieval, and modern Catholic theology and exegesis.

more than a descriptive account of the Bible's importance in Christian traditions. It could not rely on generalized literary or sociological categories like "community" and "canon," but would have to locate these within a thoroughly theological analysis. The Church's defenses of its biblical practices would tend to make Christian convictions about the Bible explicit that have probably been implicit all along.

The result would not be merely an apologetic that would leave Christian biblical practice as it was before the crisis, but constructive Christian reflection on the significance of Scripture — what will here be called, somewhat awkwardly, "bibliology"[7] — that would bear fruit in richer biblical practices and a more profound appreciation of Scripture. It would not merely toy with the margins of bibliology, making claims about trajectories of texts and the boundaries of the canon, but it would frame the entire Christian institution of Scripture according to the relationship between the Triune God and God's inspired Word.

This project is a first stab at such a reflection. It argues that many of the theological resources for a kind of second Triumph of Orthodoxy lie at hand within the *loci* of systematic theology. The full range of Christian theological and practical categories, not just the ones most directly related to texts, can and should inform any adequate Christian doctrine and practice of Scripture. This project makes the case for a fully Trinitarian doctrine of Scripture that articulates the Bible's role in the divine economy of salvation. It establishes the specific divine and human characters of the biblical text. It delineates boundaries for orthodox readings, and shows why some hermeneutical techniques are promising, while others are unpromising and even heretical (in the sense that they inevitably compromise the Church's teaching). It explains phenomena within and without the Church regarding the use of Scripture, and holds promise for enriching the Christian doctrine and practice of Scripture in a lasting way.

Thus systematic bibliology has powerful prescriptive as well as descriptive applications. A theology of Scripture has the power not only to appreciate, defend, and preserve the best of Scripture's uses in the Church (and this would be no small accomplishment), but also to spawn and inform *new* uses for the Bible in the life of the Church. It can guide biblical interpretation in its widest sense, norming and begetting biblical practices that respect Scripture's efficacy in mission, discipleship, worship, prayer, discipline, and divine reve-

---

7. The term is not a neologism: Clark Pinnock, among others, refers to it. See his *The Scripture Principle* (San Francisco: Harper & Row, 1984), p. 86. Its economy and versatility ("bibliological," "bibliologically") compensate for its ugliness.

lation. The occasion of Iconoclasm thus offers a paradigm for developing a kind of second Triumph of Orthodoxy — a *biblical* Triumph of Orthodoxy — in which systematic reflection on the ontology and function of Scripture might further articulate and guide the Bible's role in the life of the Church.

This is not a book about inerrancy, infallibility, authority, inspiration, the principle of *sola Scriptura,* or revelation. Though it features all these themes, it does not concentrate on any one of them as determinative for the Bible's character and purpose. Nor does it propose a set of them, as typologies or models sometimes do. It is neither a survey of biblical hermeneutics nor a program for biblical interpretation, though its conclusions are informed by the history of the Church's use of Scripture and in turn prescribe them in general ways. It is about something more basic and more comprehensive: the Bible's relationship with God and its role in God's plan of salvation. Our bibliology starts where the Bible starts: in the eternal purposes of the Triune God. It goes where the Bible goes: out to the fallen world as God's instrument and medium. And it ends where the Bible ends: in the eternal assembly of the Triune God's worshiping disciples.

Preview: The Structure of Systematic Bibliology

Protestant systematic theology has traditionally placed the topics of revelation and Scripture first in its order of reflection. This arrangement has much to commend it. It solidly grounds the rest of systematic theology, and stresses the sheer divine initiative in any human knowledge and love of God. But it tends to leave the character and work of Scripture behind, undeveloped, as the theology moves on. By contrast, an economic Trinitarian theology of Scripture continually revisits bibliology in light of every other locus of theology. A systematic, Trinitarian doctrine of Scripture is necessarily circular: all the categories that describe it also emerge from it. This circularity liberates the doctrine of Scripture from its prolegomenal ghetto and appreciates the Bible as reaching into the very plan of God and the very heart of the Christian life. Every further uncovering of the mystery of God's economy of salvation — Christology, Trinity, soteriology, eschatology, ecclesiology — is a new warrant and occasion to make another hermeneutical circuit, and develop a fuller account of Scripture, with which the Church can evaluate and shape its biblical practices.

Therefore, this project approaches the doctrine of Scripture as more than simply foundational for the rest of Christian doctrine. Systematic bibliology draws on the developed categories of the rest of systematic theology in order to appreciate the institution of the Christian Bible. It aims to develop a doctrine of Christian Scripture informed by three main convictions. The first is that if Scripture is God's Word, then in some sense it reflects God's character; and if God's character is Triune, then the Bible reflects the triunity of God in some significant way. The second is that if Scripture plays a role in the divine economy of salvation in history, then the work of the Bible in human history and in the lives of its respondents can be seen in terms of that same divine economy of salvation. The third is that if Scripture is written, kept, and performed principally by, for, and to the Church of Jesus Christ, then in some sense its character confers and reflects the character of the Church. In theological language, the three claims are that the Bible's character as the Word of God suggests a Trinitarian ontology of Scripture; that the Bible's role in salvation suggests a historical and personal soteriology of Scripture; and that the Bible's inextricable relationship with the Church in its eschatological setting suggests an ecclesiology of Scripture.

All of these claims are complementary ways of elaborating on the traditional Christian affirmation that the Bible is the inspired Word of God. The first and second perspectives of this project, "bibliology 'from above'" and "bibliology 'from below,'" correspond roughly to others that shed light back on them: ontological and epistemological, theological and anthropological, objective and subjective. Neither makes sense without the other; indeed, the two are kept apart only for heuristic purposes, and only incompletely. They comprise a synthetic, divine-human perspective of *koinonia* between God and humanity in an eternal "descent" and "ascent," the former grounding the latter, the latter never superseding the former, whose center in our present age is the life of the Church.

Chapter 1: The Beginning of Scripture

We will begin with God's "wordliness" and humanity's share in that wordliness, as developed in the patristic East and West by two of each culture's most influential theologians. Athanasius' *On the Incarnation of the Word* provides a grand cosmic narrative of God's self-involvements in creation, beginning with creation itself and its climax in "wordly" humanity, and culminating in the incarnation of the Word himself in human flesh. These two moments locate still another major moment in God's self-intervention in human history: the words of the Law and the Prophets. In this way Athanasius grounds a Christological ontology of both human speech in general, and biblical speech in particular.

Augustine's *On Christian Doctrine* makes many of the same moves, but uses linguistic and rhetorical rather than salvation-historical categories. The homiletical text shows us God's biblical Word not only as rhetorical *logos* effecting God's intended *pathos* and *praxis,* but as a sacramental reflection of God's very *ethos,* self-emptied in human words. Biblical language participates in the *kenosis* of the Son that accomplishes the reconciliation of God and the world.

Two of this century's theological giants, Barth and Balthasar, appropriate this kind of Christological analogy for Scripture, but in very different ways. By drawing on two recent Christological movements, kenotic Christology and Spirit-Christology, this bibliology reaffirms the patristic vision of Scripture over Barth's reformulation of it, draws it out into a truly Trinitarian ontology and economy of Scripture, and looks to Mariology as an analogical guide for exploring the human role in the origin of Scripture. It defines a typological or allegorical "identity-in-contrast" between Jesus and the Bible whose explanation takes the rest of the project. To put it as concisely as possible, in the course of this chapter we find that Christian Scripture reflects and accomplishes the will of the Father, through the ministry of the Son, in the power of the Holy Spirit and the humanity of God's chosen people.

Chapter 2: The Mission of Scripture

This awareness of the Bible's divine-human ontology is not something discoverable apart from the Bible's concrete history. God's involvement in creation invariably takes historical shape — and history invariably witnesses to God's involvement in creation. So Chapter 2 narrates Scripture's role in the human history of salvation, climaxing in the messianic career of Jesus of Nazareth. By both reading Scripture's own narrative and exploring a critical picture of Scripture in its historical context, it seeks to retell both the story and the story's story.

The result is a three-part soteriology of Scripture in which all three parts cohere in Jesus of Nazareth. As son of Israel, God's Anointed, and the head of the Church, Jesus is the center of Christian bibliology. His narrative life is both the ultimate locus of Christian commonality with Israel, and the ultimate point of departure for Christian practice of Scripture.[8] The identity-

---

8. Though less widely recognized, this is equally true of Christian commonality with the Muslim *umma.* Scripture's role in the life of Jesus establishes both the considerable similarities among what the Quran calls "people of the Book," and the unique relationship be-

in-contrast of Jesus and Scripture produces an extremely complex intersection between the two. In uncountable ways, Scripture is Jesus' very language, the human words of the divine Word: it is his heritage, his horizon, his formation, his practice, his authority, his instrument, his medium, his teaching, his witness, his confession, his community, and his glory. We explore each of these relationships in turn.

The first part of this project centers in Israel, which forms and is formed by Israel's Scriptures, becoming a holy people and a messianic community. It relies on the work of Samuel Terrien, John Bright, Paul Nadim Tarazi, Brevard Childs, Michael Fishbane, and others, to tell the story of Israel's Holy Scriptures as, in Athanasius' phrase, "a holy school for all the world." These historical theologians of ancient Israel represent different creative imaginations and confessions, but their findings all portray an Israel fundamentally formed by its own Scripture (here labeled "Tanakh," a traditional abbreviation for "Law, Prophets, and Writings" with firmer theological and historical warrants [Luke 24:44] than "Hebrew Bible," that popular nineteenth-century construction).

The second part focuses on the career of Jesus the Messiah, who is humanly formed by Tanakh, fulfills it in his life, and transforms it in the course of his ministry. The story of Tanakh is important in its own right; yet too often overlooked in Scripture's formative role in Israel's history is its formative role in Jesus' human history. Jewish biblical practice is actually *constitutive* of the human Jesus, and is deeply involved in the human formation of Israel's Messiah (Luke 1:46-52). Scripture is Jesus' authority and practice as a first-century Galilean Jew. It is Jesus' heritage and his horizon, the voice of the Father who sent him (Ps. 2:7). It develops both his worldview and his self-understanding, defines his mission, and predicts its outcome.

With Jesus' baptismal anointing with the Holy Spirit, Scripture's role in Jesus' life undergoes a radical transformation. The one obedient to Scripture is proclaimed Lord *of* Scripture. Without ceasing to be Jesus' horizon or his authority, Tanakh becomes also his pneumatic instrument, his teaching, and a means of his messianic work. Jesus "institutes" the Christian idea of Scripture in the same way that he transforms John's baptism and Moses' Passover. His "dominical obedience" to Scripture frames his messianic offices, atoning work, and divine vindication as Messiah and Son of God. In Jesus' tempta-

---

tween the Christian community and its canonical literature. Accounts of Scripture that are not thoroughly grounded in the concrete relationships between Jesus and Scripture underappreciate both the uniquely Christian shape of the Bible's role in the life of the Christian Church, and the profound points of contact between the Christian tradition and the Jewish and Muslim traditions.

tions, itinerant ministry, and passion, Tanakh is his prophetic text; a criterion defining his work as priest; and an armory of his royal rule. Thus the true work of Scripture is the work of Christ.

Jesus' transformation of the Tanakh transforms it into Old Testament, and authorizes the New Testament writings. Together as the Christian Bible, these form the Church of Jesus Christ and are formed by it. So Scripture is also Jesus' witness, his eschatological teaching, and his kerygmatic confession. The continuing career of the raised and ascended Messiah thus leads to the ecclesial soteriology of Scripture, part three of its soteriology. Its concerns are taken up in Chapter 3.

Chapter 3: The End of Scripture

The Church's setting is the inaugurated eschaton, so eschatology provides the context for the entire chapter's ecclesiology of Scripture. It begins by describing "presence-in-absence," which is the kind of presence an ascended Lord has in a waiting Church, and explores the Bible as a means of both God's presence-in-absence to the gathering and gathered Church, and the worshiping Church's presence-in-absence before God. Here two twentieth-century theologians, Karl Barth and James Barr, radically affirm each of these two features of biblical practice, but in incompatible ways. The chapter returns to Augustine's *On Christian Doctrine* as a way simultaneously to affirm the positive theological significance of both the Bible's prevenient, divine character and its responsive, human characters.

Having affirmed the Bible's full humanity in Chapter 1 and having begun to describe it in Chapter 2, the project goes on in Chapter 3 to delineate the qualities of the Bible in terms of the qualities of its real and ideal human community — the one, holy, catholic, and apostolic Church. To do justice to the Bible's radically human, historical character, it draws on Alasdair MacIntyre's theory of tradition-constituted enquiry. Yet bibliology must soon move beyond MacIntyre's generalized theory, on account of its inability to accommodate the uniqueness of either the Christian Church or its canon.

Unity, holiness, catholicity, and apostolicity are essentially contested concepts among those who claim to belong to the Church. So the question of the Bible's ecclesial qualities leads to the familiar territory of the relationship among Scripture, Tradition, and traditions as the various Christian communities have envisioned it. Recent accounts representative of four major traditions include the work of Dumitru Staniloae (Orthodox), Karl Barth and Ernst Käsemann (Protestant), James McClendon ("baptist"), and Avery

Dulles (Catholic). These represent partly overlapping, partly compatible, partly incompatible appreciations of the eschatological tension between the head and the maturing body of Christ. Our analysis of these visions concludes that both the similarities and the distinctions among the traditions are grounded and reflected in the canon's own broader synoptic vision.

Having described the character of the Church, ecclesiology turns to the work of the Church, which centers on (but is in no way exhausted in) its formal liturgies. This work is appreciated in terms of the *telos* of Scripture, for which the chapter is named: the salvation of the world, and the restoration of the divine-human relationship. The irreducibly personal dimension of this end of Scripture is the Bible's indispensable role in the *ordo salutis,* not only as it is developed in modern soteriology but as Augustine outlines it in *On Christian Doctrine* in terms of the soul's salvific movement into God's direct presence. As the chapter closes, still another sense of *telos* arises: What is Scripture's role *after* the eschaton, if it plays any at all? Is the biblical vision eternally significant, or does the beatific vision supersede it?

To summarize, the three chapters together comprise a systematic bibliology that understands the qualities of Scripture as reflecting the Triune God's character and accomplishing his purpose in the divine economy of salvation. Such a bibliology illustrates the theological indispensability of Scripture to the Christian faith, and constitutes both a preliminary response to imaginary "biblioclasts" and a critique of those who posit the Bible as merely a cognitive, experiential, or linguistic resource (the typology is Lindbeck's). More positively, the insights of a systematic bibliology can ground, norm, and enhance the Church's entire theology and praxis of Scripture, its hermeneutics in the widest sense, and theological education's approach to teaching Scripture — just as Second Nicea's Triumph of Orthodoxy provided the justification and guide for the Church's subsequent incorporation of images more thoroughly into its life than had ever been possible before the rise of Iconoclasm.

A word on the sources: The authorities in this project are chosen for their profound theological or philosophical imagination, the extent of their influence in Christian tradition, their ability to represent their confessional traditions, their ecumenical breadth, their fidelity to the biblical witnesses, their synergy when combined — and, to be frank, the limits of my own horizons and expectations. In these pages they are put to constructive and imaginative uses, rather than merely descriptive uses. Scripture translations are generally based on the tradition of the Revised Standard Version.

A different combination of authorities would inevitably yield a different picture. But as long as such different authorities fairly represented the various theological voices of the Christian tradition, it is hard to believe they would yield a *fundamentally* different picture. If God really is at work when Christians faithfully practice Scripture, then the evidence of that work should be commensurable, wherever its source. This bibliology can of course be substantially enriched by further interaction with Scripture's most perceptive readers. Here we will construct the mere framework of a systematic bibliology, which can then be further refined and enriched in innumerable ways.

Early Indicators: The Bible in the Sensus Fidelium

Before proceeding down these roads, it is prudent to "consult the faithful," lest our theological speculation drift away from the sense of the Church for which it is intended. The rest of this introduction is a brief review of liturgical and theological attitudes towards the relationship between God and Scripture. It is intended to anticipate and guide the fundamental connections that warrant our entire project.

Theologians in all the major Christian traditions have noticed the double meaning of *logos,* and sensed its relevance for the Christian doctrine of Scripture. It is much more than simple lexical correspondence. Just as Jesus bridges human words and the divine Word, so theologians claim that Scripture is "God's Word in human words." Variations on this "Analogy of the Word" occur throughout treatments of Christian Scripture across Christian traditions. A few representative examples show how the relationship is commonly expressed by theologians:

> The Word of God can be expressed precisely and adequately in the language of man. . . . The Word of God is not diminished while it resounds in human language.[9]

> Christians believe that God has spoken His Word not only in the form of a book but also in the form of a person. For Christians, the Word of God is a living man, Jesus Christ, as well as living literature, the Scriptures.[10]

> The Word of God, in providing for our every need, always presents to us what is intangible by clothing it with form. . . .[11]

9. Georges Florovsky, *Creation and Redemption*, Collected Works, vol. 3 (Belmont, Mass.: Nordland, 1976), p. 22.

10. C. George Fry and James R. King, *Islam: A Survey of the Muslim Faith* (Grand Rapids: Baker, 1982), p. 67.

11. John of Damascus, *On the Divine Images* (Crestwood, N.Y.: St. Vladimir's Seminary Press, 1980), 1.11.

A variety of the Christological analogy is even present in Islam.[12] The widespread intuition among theologians of all Christian traditions that there is a connection between the two natures of Christ and the divine and human aspects of the Bible is itself a warrant for a Christological and thus Trinitarian account of Scripture.

But there is a far larger body of Christians whose conclusions on the matter are relevant: the faithful who comprise the worshiping Church. The *sensus fidelium* is an even more powerful warrant for a doctrine of Scripture thoroughly rooted in the doctrine of God.

Given the Protestant Reformation's emphases on both the Scripture principle and hymnody, it is not surprising that Protestant hymnody has a keen sense of the Analogy of the Word. Hymns on Holy Scripture are sometimes entire bibliologies in microcosm. These hymns often feature a close connection between God and the written Word that effects God's saving purpose in the world through the Church. The lyrics below parallel God's creating, incarnate, biblical, evangelistic, and salvific words, fitting them all into God's greater economy of salvation:

> Thanks to God whose Word was spoken in the deed that made the earth.
> His the voice that called a nation; his the fires that tried her worth.
> God has spoken: praise God for his open Word.
>
> Thanks to God whose Word Incarnate heights and depths of life did
>   share.
> Deeds and words and death and rising, grace in human form declare.
> God has spoken: praise God for his open Word.
>
> Thanks to God whose Word was written in the Bible's sacred page,
> Record of the revelation showing God to every age.
> God has spoken: praise God for his open Word.
>
> Thanks to God whose Word is published in the tongues of every race.
> See its glory undiminished by the change of time or place.
> God has spoken: praise God for his open Word.

12. In a fascinating parallel to Christian theology, Islam regards the Quran as "the inlibrate Word," directly comparing it to the Christian "incarnate Word." When pressed by Trinitarians like John of Damascus, orthodox Islam was led to a doctrine of the Quran as the eternal and uncreated Word of God which is nevertheless perfectly represented in the Arabic language. The Islamic parallel is not a direct guide to a Christian doctrine of Scripture, but it demonstrates the power of the Christological analogy of God's Word even outside Christianity. See Seyyed Hossein Nasr, *Ideals and Realities of Islam* (San Francisco: HarperCollins Aquarian, 1994), p. 43.

Thanks to God whose Word is answered by the Spirit's voice within.
Here we drink of joy unmeasured, life redeemed from death and sin.
God has spoken: praise God for his open Word.[13]

In the second stanza of "Book of Books," by Percy Dearmer, the wordplay between the scrolls of Scripture, words from God, and the Johannine Word is repeated. Here the congregation also thanks the human authors of the Bible's poetry, prophecy, scholarship, and hagiography — and finally the evangelists who tell "the story of the Word." The following stanza then extols God for the divine agency of inspiration, incarnation, and illumination. Thus the singers celebrate both the Analogy of the Word, the human and the divine double agency of Scripture, and the eternal knowledge brought to God's people by the uncreated light that shines in the world's epistemological darkness.[14]

A hymn featured in practically every major Protestant hymnal praises the Word incarnate for the word in Scripture, and the Light for the light that Scripture brings:

O Christ, the Word Incarnate, O Wisdom from on high,
O Truth, unchanged, unchanging, O Light of our dark sky;
We praise thee for the radiance that from the scripture's page,
A lantern to our footsteps, shines on from age to age.

The Church from our dear Master received the word divine,
And still that light is lifted o'er all the earth to shine.
It is the chart and compass that o'er life's surging sea,
Mid mists and rocks and quicksands, still guides, O Christ, to thee.[15]

"Break Thou the Bread of Life" treats the Bible as God's veiled yet unveiling agent of self-revelation, in the context of the Word's eucharistic presence:

Thou art the bread of life, O Lord, to me,
Thy holy Word the truth that saveth me;
Give me to eat and live with thee above;
Teach me to love thy truth, for thou art love.

---

13. Words by R. T. Brooks (1918-   ) © 1954, Ren. 1982 by Hope Publishing Co., Carol Stream, IL 60188. All rights reserved. Used by permission.

14. "Book of Books," words by Percy Dearmer (1867-1936). *The Hymnal 1982*, p. 631.

15. "O Word of God Incarnate," words by William Walsham How, 1867. *The Hymnal 1982*, p. 632.

O send thy Spirit, Lord, now unto me,
That he may touch mine eyes, and make me see:
Show me the truth concealed within thy Word,
And in thy Book revealed I see thee, Lord.[16]

Many of these hymns pair their Christological allusions with pneumatological allusions. Several are fully Trinitarian. All strongly connect Scripture
to soteriology, and locate its uses in the worshiping Church. These elements
are the backbone of a comprehensive Trinitarian bibliology.

Eastern Orthodoxy and Roman Catholicism express similar connections, but in their own distinctive ways. Protestantism has tended to focus its
reflections on verbal rather than iconic revelation. But these other traditions
have practiced the faith in ways more respectful of the canons of the Second
Council of Nicea, whose definition portrays a close resemblance among the
divine presence in Scripture, images, and relics.[17] This tendency shows itself
in a more pronounced veneration of the physical books of Scripture themselves. Thus Orthodox and Catholic calligraphic illumination and ornamen-
tation of both the inside and outside of the biblical books testify to God's saving presence in Scripture. The same values pervade their liturgies: The "lesser
entrance" of the book of the Gospels compares only to the "greater entrance"
of the Eucharist itself.[18] (The Protestant practice of offering leather-bound,
gilded, gold-embossed study Bibles as baptismal or confirmation gifts manifests the same sensibility in a way more in tune with Protestant soteriologies
and doctrines of the priesthood of all believers. And the status attached in
evangelical circles to worn out, dog-eared, underlined and annotated study

16. "Break Thou the Bread of Life," words by Alexander Groves, 1913. *Baptist Hymnal,*
1975 ed. (Nashville: Convention Press, 1975), p. 138.

17. "The more frequently [images of Jesus, the saints, and the angels] are seen in rep-
resentational art, the more are those who see them drawn to remember and long for those
who serve as models, and to pay these images the tribute of salutation and respectful veneration. Certainly this is not the full adoration in accordance with our faith, which is properly
paid only to the divine nature, but it resembles that given to the figure of the honored and
life-giving cross, *and also to the holy books of the gospels* and to other sacred cult objects." Norman P. Tanner, ed., *Decrees of the Ecumenical Councils,* vol. 1 (Washington, D.C.: Georgetown
University Press, 1990), p. 136 (emphasis added).

18. Geoffrey Wainwright, *Doxology: The Praise of God in Worship, Doctrine, and Life*
(New York: Oxford University Press, 1980), p. 149. Furthermore, the Catholic liturgy makes
an explicit Christological connection in the Gospel Acclamation during Lent, when the
congregation responds to the Gospel reading with "Glory to you, Word of God, Jesus Christ!"
See Nicholas T. Freund et al., eds., *People's Mass Book* (Schiller Park, Ill.: World Library Publications, 1984), pp. 261, 573-76.

Bibles testifies to the high role Scripture plays there as a physical means of spiritual sustenance and divine mentoring.)

Scripture in its written form also figures prominently in Catholic and Orthodox iconography. One common iconographic convention in particular points vividly to the close relationship between God and God's Word: the books one frequently sees Jesus, the prophets, and the evangelists holding in their left hands. In these icons the figures bear Scripture to the viewer, pointing to the very texts whose messages point back to them. In Eastern iconography, the archangel Michael bears in his left hand his message: *IesouS CHristoS,* Jesus Christ; and even Jesus himself bears the Bible. Just as Michael says, in effect, "I bear the Gospel of Jesus Christ," so Jesus himself says, "I bear *my* Gospel." Indeed, the closed scroll in the hand of the infant Jesus, whose time of exercising the prophetic office is yet to come, graphically represents Scripture's preexistence, inhering from before all time in God's will, and preached before the fullness of time had come to Abraham (Gal. 3:8).

These doxological and devotional uses of Scripture can be multiplied; ever since the ancient Jews took Deuteronomy 6:8 literally and bound God's words to their physical bodies during prayer, God's people have continued to find ingenious new uses for the Bible. All of them witness to the widespread and profound sense that Scripture is a means of divine presence and grace in a fallen world, that the written Word of God is in some sense a participant in the life that God has and offers creation through the Word made flesh.

The Analogy of the Word in Theology Proper

Formal theology joins doxology as a way Christians express their sense of the Analogy of the Word. Among its contemporary uses in theology are explanations for the authority, infallibility, and inerrancy of Scripture that resort to Christological categories. These come from all major Christian traditions, particularly Catholic and evangelical Protestants.

We have seen from the hymns that Karl Barth was not the first to put the Christological analogy to use in developing a doctrine of Scripture. But his treatment of the Word of God in its threefold form, with Scripture occupying the place of the second person of the Trinity, has been so influential that it has set the terms for the twentieth-century discussion of Christology's relevance for bibliology. In a nutshell, for Barth, the writtenness of Holy Writ corresponds to its humanity, its holiness to its divinity. Barth wants this understood as a Christological analogy for Scripture,[19] even criticizing inadequate hermeneutical proposals as "docetic" or "Ebionite."[20] Barth's Christological doctrine of Scripture has received extensive attention in secondary literature.[21] (Rarely mentioned is its *Trinitarian* dimension, which thus warrants a much lengthier treatment below.)

In part because of Barth's influence, theologians in the past century have often appealed to Christological categories when discussing Scripture. Roman Catholic theology is quite amenable to them. The papal encyclical *Divino Afflante Spiritu,* written in 1943, claims an overtly Christological analogy for Scripture:

> "In Scripture divine things are present to us in the manner which is in common use amongst men." For as the substantial Word of God became like to men in all things, "except sin," so the words of God, expressed in human language, are made like to human speech in every respect, except error. In this consists that "condescension" of the God of providence, which St. John Chrysostom extolled with the highest praise and repeatedly declared to be found in the Sacred Books.[22]

The divinity of Jesus is as relevant to biblical exegesis as it is to systematic theology, according to *Pascendi Dominici Gregis,* which in 1907 condemned modernist exegetes like Alfred Loisy. When they write history, it says, "they bring in no mention of the divinity of Christ; when preaching in churches they firmly profess it. . . . Hence they separate theological and pastoral exegesis from scientific and historical."[23] Only in the Church itself is exegesis adequately practiced: *Providentissimus Deus,* whose fiftieth anniversary was the occasion for Pius XII's delivery of *Divino Afflante Spiritu,* claims on strong patristic authority "that the sense of Holy Scripture can nowhere be found incorrupt outside of the Church."[24] Indeed, the Church's entire involvement in the formation of the canon can be described in Nicene catego-

---

19. Karl Barth, *Church Dogmatics* (hereafter *CD*), I.2, trans. G. W. Bromiley and T. F. Torrance (Edinburgh: T. & T Clark, 1956), p. 463.

20. Barth, *CD* I.2, pp. 520, 526.

21. See, for instance, Klaas Runia, *Karl Barth's Doctrine of Holy Scripture* (Grand Rapids: Eerdmans, 1962); James Barr, *The Bible in the Modern World,* 2nd ed. (San Francisco: Harper & Row, 1990); and Paul Ronald Wells, *James Barr and the Bible: Critique of a New Liberalism* (Phillipsburg, N.J.: Presbyterian and Reformed, 1980).

22. *Divino Afflante Spiritu,* §37.

23. Cited in Robert M. Grant, and David Tracy, *A Short History of the Interpretation of the Bible,* 2nd ed. (Philadelphia: Fortress, 1984), p. 123.

24. *Providentissimus Deus,* §15.

ries: "[C]anon-determination . . . was a truly human process as well as being perceived in faith to be a divine one," claims Thomas Hoffman.[25] The Nicene and ecclesiological approach of these strands of Roman Catholic bibliology both predates and survives Vatican II.

Nichols, a Catholic with an abiding interest in Orthodox theology, offers a more deeply developed Christological analogy for Scripture. In a survey of historical theories of biblical inspiration,[26] Nichols criticizes the early hypnotic and the later verbal-dictation theories of inspiration as "Monophysite," then criticizes the theories of subsequent approbation and negative assistance as "Nestorian." Then he searches for a proper "Chalcedonian" account of inspiration, "an account of the Bible which showed how it could be at one and the same time both fully divine and fully human."[27]

What is especially interesting in Nichols's strategy is his warrant for a Chalcedonian account of inspiration. His argument rests on the sheer elegance, coherence, and persuasiveness of such an analogy. The analogy of faith means that "the common faith of the Church is not a set of disparate teachings, each unconnected with the rest, but is a coherent, interconnected unity in which any one part can be illuminated by looking to the rest."[28] To the widespread sense of a connection between Christology and Scripture we see in the treatments of theologians across the traditions, Nichols adds the warrant of coherence. Barth's profound insight that God's self-revelation inevitably and uniquely has a divine shape is such an argument from coherence.

The logic of Eastern Orthodoxy is particularly well suited to the task of developing a Christological analogy for Scripture. John Breck appreciates Paul Evdokimov's Luther-like assertion that "the 'power of the Sacrament' is derived from the 'power of the Word' that it enshrines and celebrates."[29] His reasoning takes us even further along the logic of the Analogy of the Word,

---

25. Thomas A. Hoffman, "Inspiration, Normativeness, Canonicity, and the Unique Sacred Character of the Bible," *Catholic Biblical Quarterly* 44 (1982): 464.

26. Nichols, *The Shape of Catholic Theology*, pp. 114-30.

27. Nichols, *The Shape of Catholic Theology*, p. 122.

28. Nichols, *The Shape of Catholic Theology*, p. 124.

29. As Luke 18:34 and similar passages make clear, though, the scriptural Word is not necessarily self-revealing. Human words can be the very Word of God only through the inspirational and interpretive *dynamis* or power of the Holy Spirit (cf. Luke 24:45-49; Acts 1:4-8). Only the risen Christ, the eternal divine *Logos* operating through the Spirit, can open human minds to understand the Scriptures, bringing to their remembrance the fullness of his teaching and declaring the hidden truths of the eschatological age, to his own glory and to the glory of the Father (John 14:26; 16:13-15). See John Breck, *The Power of the Word in the Worshiping Church* (Crestwood, N.Y.: St. Vladimir's Seminary Press, 1986), p. 14.

opening up its Trinitarian and eschatological dimensions beautifully. For Breck the Word has an "essentially sacramental character." Far from being strictly verbal, as it is often treated in the West, it has a dynamic, "revelatory and saving power as an instrument of the divine will."[30] Indeed, Dumitru Staniloae claims the Bible is a necessary means of the Spirit's work of making the supernatural revelation of God in Jesus Christ "fully concrete," expressed, and effective in his bodily absence.[31] Along with the Church and Holy Tradition, Scripture is a quasi-sacramental agent of God's ongoing actualization of the once-for-all revelation given in Christ.

If Barth is the most famous Protestant to appeal to Christological categories to describe Scripture, he is by no means the only one. Geoffrey Wainwright cites approvingly Vatican II's conclusion that Jesus is present when the Scriptures are read in church, and compares it directly to classical Protestantism's long-standing "strong sense of the presence of God in and through the reading and preaching of the Word."[32] He illustrates this by appealing to the Second Helvetic Confession's affirmation of the real presence of the divine Word.[33] Even the physical book of the Bible that is used in worship is "some kind of sacrament of the Word of God."[34] By virtue of Scripture's inspiration, in Scripture and sermon subsists the saving presence of the Lord Jesus himself through the presence of the Holy Spirit.[35] This last theme foreshadows not only a fuller development of a Christological doctrine of Scripture, but a fully Trinitarian bibliology.

Anders Nygren uses Nicene categories not only to associate Christ, sacraments, and Scripture, but to critique modern attitudes towards all three as "docetic."[36] In the "baptist" camp, James McClendon criticizes the docetism

---

30. Breck, *The Power of the Word*, p. 17, quoting Paul Evdokimov, "Le Mystère de la Parole," in *Le Buisson Ardent* (Paris: 1981), p. 63.

31. Dumitru Staniloae, *The Experience of God* (Brookline, Mass.: Holy Cross, 1994), p. 39.

32. Wainwright, *Doxology*, pp. 180-81.

33. Wainwright, *Doxology*, p. 511 n. 421.

34. Wainwright, *Doxology*, p. 149.

35. Wainwright, *Doxology*, p. 179.

36. "The issue is the same in all these areas. In the Bible, as well as in Christ and in the sacraments, God meets us on our human level. In grace he comes down to our plane. But the natural man objects, retaining his pagan conviction that we can meet God only by rising up to his heavenly level. Such docetism is as objectionable in our view of the Bible as it is in christology or the doctrine of the sacraments. Docetism is Christianity's hereditary foe. Just as Christ did not merely appear to be human . . . but was true man . . . so the Bible does not merely appear to speak in human words, but actually does so." Anders Nygren, *The Significance of the Bible for the Church*, Facet Books Biblical Series (Philadelphia: Fortress, 1963), pp. 41-42.

of modern inerrantist theories, and follows his own narrative Christology to propose a divine-human biblical narrative.[37] Brenda Collin has described the Brethren way of reading Scripture as "Incarnational Hermenetics."[38] And in a recent editorial in *Pro Ecclesia* — commemorating the fiftieth anniversary of *Divino Afflante Spiritu* — Lutheran Carl Braaten calls for a "Chalcedonian hermeneutic" that respects the presence in Scripture of the incarnate Word:

> The relevance of the incarnation to biblical interpretation is spelled out in terms of the Chalcedonian model of explaining the meaning of the "Word made flesh." . . . The Bible is the Word of God completely and irreducibly expressed in human words in all their time-conditionedness. A Chalcedonian hermeneutic of biblical exegesis is on the right track. . . . Just as the Word became flesh — without one being changed into the other or separated from the other, as Chalcedon taught — so we have treasures of divine revelation in vessels of human language and history.[39]

Particular attention to the Analogy of the Word has been paid among evangelicals in their discussions of inerrancy. The Chicago Statement on Biblical Hermeneutics, adopted in 1978, claims in its Article II that

> We affirm that as Christ is God and Man in one Person, so Scripture is, indivisibly, God's Word in human language.
> We deny that the humble, human form of Scripture entails errancy any more than the humanity of Christ, even in His humiliation, entails sin.[40]

---

37. James Wm. McClendon Jr., *Doctrine: Systematic Theology,* vol. 2: *Doctrine* (Nashville: Abingdon, 1994), p. 476: "I would substitute for 'two natures' a narrative model as more appropriate both to the character of Scripture and to Scripture's Christ. *By this model the story the Bible tells is God's own story, told in the way God pleases to tell it.* Scripture is God's book, God's word to us. At the same time, the story the Bible tells is our own story, a fully human story, human in its breadth and depth; human, too, in its foibles and failings. So the wonder, the miracle of Scripture is this: These two stories give us not two interwoven books, one human, one divine, which we can divide at will, but one indivisible Book, one Bible."

38. "Brethren hermeneutics are incarnational hermeneutics because they begin with the Word of God made flesh in the person of Jesus Christ and end with the embodiment of that Word through the Holy Spirit in the faith-life of the believing community. The hermeneutical process begins with a Christocentric focus and ends in discipleship." Brenda Collin, "Incarnational Hermeneutics: The Brethren Approach to Scripture," *Brethren Life and Thought* 36 (Fall 1991): 252.

39. Carl Braaten, "A Chalcedonian Hermeneutic," *Pro Ecclesia* 3, no. 1 (Winter 1994): 20.

40. Chicago Statement on Biblical Hermeneutics, cited in J. I. Packer, *God Has Spoken* (Grand Rapids: Baker, 1979), p. 158. Packer supports this connection wholeheartedly: "As Je-

Many evangelicals (few of whom explicitly endorse Barthian methodology) are attracted to the Analogy of the Word. James Packer adopts this strong Christological analogy for Scripture in order to establish the "dual authorship" of Scripture, affirm the propriety of historical criticism, and argue from the moral perfection of Jesus' humanity to the reliability of Scripture "at all points."[41] Clark Pinnock too finds the Analogy of the Word natural: "As the Logos was enfleshed in the life of Jesus, so God's Word is enlettered in the script of the Bible. In both cases there is some kind of mysterious union of the divine and the human, though of course not the same kind. But in each case both the divine and the human are truly present."[42] Pinnock uses the Christological parallel to call Scripture "sacramental,"[43] to counter bibliological "Docetism" and "Ebionitism," just as Karl Barth does, to describe the veiledness of the Bible's revelation and the accommodation of divine speech to human language in terms akin to *kenosis*,[44] and to go even farther than Barth was willing, using not just Nicene categories but Chalcedonian ones and labeling fundamentalist and liberal bibliologies as "two kinds of Monophysite heresy."[45] Finally, Klaas Runia's exposition on Barth's doctrine of Scripture firmly agrees with the relevance of the Nicene categories to bibliology, taking issue only with the way Barth handles their "indissoluble unity" in opposition to the witness of Scripture itself.[46]

These are but a few examples of instances in which modern theologians recognize the potential in some sort of sacramental or Christological analogy of Scripture. Indeed, the analogy is fruitful enough that each tradition — evangelical Protestant, mainline Protestant, Roman Catholic, and Eastern Orthodox — manages to put Christological moves to characteristically Protestant, Catholic, or Orthodox uses. Evangelicals are generally unwilling to develop the Christological parallels as deeply as Barth does, or as evocatively as their own hymns and liturgies do. For them the payoff is a bare-bones, unadorned apology for biblical authority and inerrancy, where battles are fought over which camp is really Docetist or Monophysite.[47] For mainline Protestants

---

sus of Nazareth was no less truly human than divine, so it is with the Scriptures. The mystery of the Word incarnate is at this point parallel to that of the Word written" (p. 91).

41. Packer, *God Has Spoken*, p. 99.

42. Pinnock, *The Scripture Principle*, p. 97.

43. Pinnock, *The Scripture Principle*, p. 17.

44. Pinnock, *The Scripture Principle*, pp. 97-98.

45. Pinnock, *The Scripture Principle*, p. 105.

46. Runia, *Karl Barth's Doctrine*, pp. 56, 108-9. Runia argues that Barth's principle of the absolute transcendence of God has overdetermined his doctrine of Scripture.

47. Silva calls Origen's doctrine of Scripture docetic and defends the doctrine of iner-

the analogy has more pronounced *soteriological* value, associating Word with sacrament and underlining the importance of the proclaimed Word of Scripture for the salvific work of God in the church. For Catholics it norms the accelerating integration of biblical criticism into Catholic bibliology and practice, serving as a framework for supporting, critiquing, and relating both "human" historical-critical exegesis and "divine" allegorical exegesis. And for the Orthodox, the sacramentality of the Bible further tightens the analogical relationships they love to identify among liturgy and especially Eucharist, incarnation, and Trinity. These denominational tendencies will come back to inform the ecumenical ecclesiology of Scripture offered in Chapter 3. Their existence alone is further evidence that the doctrines of the Trinity and Christ are deeply relevant to formulating a thoroughly Christian account of Scripture.

Another reason for theologians' reluctance to use Christological language for Scripture is the ready availability of other categories for treating the Bible. Among these is the category of inspiration. The biblical language of inspiration (found most famously in 2 Tim. 3:16 and 2 Pet. 1:21) leads many down paths that examine the Bible's origin, proclamation, and reception primarily in terms of the work of the Holy Spirit. These are sufficiently prominent and obvious in Christian tradition not to need a survey of their own.

"Inspiration" accounts of Scripture often remain concentrated on pneumatology, just as "Word" accounts tend to remain concentrated on Christology. It is rarer that bibliologists adequately combine the two sets of categories and reveal the *Trinitarian* character and work of Scripture. But this is not unheard of. Scripture, says Packer, is

> God the Father preaching God the Son in the power of God the Holy Ghost. God the Father is the giver of Holy Scripture; God the Son is the theme of Holy Scripture; and God the Spirit, as the Father's appointed agent in witnessing to the Son, is the author, authenticator, and interpreter, of Holy Scripture.[48]

Packer's is a more than adequate introductory summary for our Trinitarian bibliology. But it can be outdone in several ways: First, other authors,

---

rancy from the same charge, but refuses to use Chalcedonian categories to substantiate or refute either claim: "The analogy between Scripture and the twofold nature of Christ, though very popular in some circles, suffers from some deep ambiguities. Even if it did not, however, one wonders how the charge of [inerrantist] docetism contributes to the discussion, other than by affecting the objectivity of the debate through the 'slur' factor." Moisés Silva, *Has the Church Misread the Bible? The History of Interpretation in Light of Current Issues* (Grand Rapids: Academie, 1987), p. 44.

48. Packer, *God Has Spoken*, p. 97.

Barth notably among them, develop the Trinitarian connection in far greater detail. Second, the human dimension of the biblical economy remains unclear. Third, formal theology is perhaps not the best medium for a rich Trinitarian account of Scripture. The relationship between God and Bible is brought forth more evocatively and fully, as one would expect, in doxological form. An example is this Protestant hymn that frames Scripture firmly in the Trinitarian economy, offering Christological and pneumatic connections but relating inspired Scripture to both the Father and Israel's human authors as well, and above all connecting God's self-revealing speech with God's eternal purpose for the creation:

> God has spoken by his prophets, Spoken his unchanging Word;
> Each from age to age proclaiming God, The one, the righteous Lord.
> In the world's despair and turmoil, One firm anchor holds us fast:
> God is king, his throne eternal; God the first, and God the last.
>
> God has spoken by Christ Jesus, Christ, the everlasting Son,
> Brightness of the Father's glory, With the Father ever one;
> Spoken by the Word Incarnate, God of God, before time was;
> Light of light, to earth descending, He reveals our God to us.
>
> God is speaking by his Spirit, Speaking to the hearts of all,
> In the ageless Word expounding God's own message for us all.
> Through the rise and fall of nations One sure faith yet standing fast;
> God abides, his Word unchanging; God the first, and God the last.[49]

Together these recurring themes point to a widespread sense among the Church's worshipers, theologians, and apologists that God's relationship with his Word is one of far greater intimacy than is often appreciated in theology — even within the traditions that possess "high" doctrines of Scripture. Seen from either God's or the text's perspective, this close relationship can be called a theological ontology of Scripture, a divine quality of Scripture that mediates the presence of the Triune God when the Bible is performed. From the perspective of the hearer or reader whom God addresses, the relationship can be called a theological epistemology, or even a soteriology, of Scripture — understanding God's presence to be a means of saving, gathering grace according to the Trinitarian economy of salvation. From the perspective of the Spirit-indwelt performers who comprise the earthly body of Christ, the rela-

49. "God Has Spoken by His Prophets," words by George W. Briggs (1875-1959). © 1953, Ren. 1981 by The Hymn Society (Admin. Hope Publishing Co., Carol Stream, IL 60188). All rights reserved. Used by permission.

tionship can be called an ecclesial account of biblical inspiration. The first of these perspectives, the Triune ontology of Scripture, is the topic of Chapter 1.

Not So Fast: The Objections of James Barr and Markus Barth

Before we proceed, we should appreciate that the Analogy of the Word has important dissenters. Among these (for different reasons) are the classical Lutherans, John McIntyre, G. C. Berkouwer, Paul R. Wells, and Markus Barth.[50]

The last of these offers a long critique of the Christological tradition in bibliology. After finding traces in the Epistle of Barnabas, Justin Martyr, Clement of Alexandria, and Irenaeus, Barth roots the tradition proper in Origen, who claims that the invisible spoken Word "becomes, as it were, flesh" when written in a book, clothed there by the letter's veil as it was by the veil of Jesus' flesh.[51] This presence, interpreted according to Origen's tripartite anthropology and Neoplatonist cosmology, produced a threefold "sacramental" allegorical hermeneutic that tended to discard the literal sense for the spiritual. (Henri de Lubac vigorously attacks this threefold hermeneutic as heretical, while championing the fourfold allegorical method of Augustine as Christologically warranted and orthodox.[52] Markus Barth does not make that distinction. We will revisit de Lubac's argument near the project's end.) According to Barth, this "sacramental" account of Scripture fared much more poorly than similar accounts of baptism, Eucharist, and the Church itself. The Reformers failed to appeal to a "two-natures" biblical account in championing *sola scriptura*, and only very recently (in Schleiermacher, Brunner, and of course Barth's father Karl) have theologians attempted a recovery.

For the younger Barth, this is a terrible mistake. It licenses fundamentalist and Catholic excesses. It extends the incarnation to impersonal words in an inappropriate way. It ushers in a biblical sacramentalism that turns the Bible into "a magic instrument of worship." It confuses Scripture's own analogies between Christ the master and his disciples, hypostatizing human words. It fails to respect the difference between the two-state career of Jesus' humiliation and exaltation and the single purpose of Scripture to call sinners to repentance. It regards words as images of God, when only *persons* can image the

---

50. Some of these are cited in Wells, *James Barr and the Bible*, pp. 340-49.

51. Markus Barth, *Conversation with the Bible* (New York: Holt, Rinehart and Winston, 1964), pp. 146-47, quoting Origen's *Homily on Leviticus I.* Barth does not accuse Origen of preaching a second incarnation (p. 148).

52. Henri de Lubac, *Medieval Exegesis,* vol. 1: *The Four Senses of Scripture,* trans. Marc Sebanc (Grand Rapids: Eerdmans, 1998).

divine (1 Cor. 11:1; Eph. 5:1). In the end, it takes the step even Origen would not, making the Bible "a second Christ" and driving hermeneutics apart forever into a literal-critical and a spiritual-allegorical exegesis that is Gnostic rather than Christian. Barth recoils in horror at the costs of the Analogy of the Word:

> Should Jesus Christ's twofold ministry be equated with two elements combined in a given piece of matter? Should the justification of sinners be commuted into a transubstantiation of letters? Should a gracious event become a frigid quality? Should all that which has been received by faith, and may be received by faith alone, be delivered into the hands of analogical reasoning?[53]

Who could continue in the face of these dangers? Yet this project anticipates and overcomes just such objections, by drawing more careful distinctions, taking the idea of analogy in a different direction, and making theological moves Barth never makes, even when they are staring him in the face.[54]

James Barr, who enthusiastically endorses Markus Barth's critique,[55] has emerged as a particularly influential opponent of the use of Christological categories in bibliology — indeed, of the general helpfulness of the traditional category, "Word of God." He finds analogies between the Bible's human divinity and Jesus' as problematic as they are widespread. These facile comparisons between Scripture and Christ come from the world of systematic theology, and fail to connect dogmatic categories to concrete scholarly biblical practices. They ignore the cultural distances that preoccupy the practice of hermeneutics. Thus they offer little guidance to (scholarly) exegetes. While their Christological analogies are elegant, there seems no particular reason to accept their validity. Chalcedonian categories were not designed for the Bible; Christ, Bible, and preaching are too different to support Karl Barth's arrangement of them into the threefold form of the Word of God; the resemblances among them are more coincidental than causal.[56] The real motive behind its use is to protect the bibliological convictions of conservatives from serious criticism.

Barr can be rather dismissive about positions to which he objects.[57] Yet

---

53. Markus Barth, *Conversation with the Bible*, pp. 155-70, quoting from 162-63. He goes on to prefer an account of biblical authority that seems exclusively pneumatological, and draws heavily on the category of inspiration (pp. 173-97).

54. See the comments in Chapter 1's "Barthian critique of [Karl] Barth."

55. James Barr, *Biblical Faith and Natural Theology* (Oxford: Clarendon, 1993), p. 197 n. 33.

56. Barr, *Biblical Faith and Natural Theology*, pp. 21-22.

57. In defending the project of biblical theology, Francis Watson takes Barr to task for

here (as throughout his career), his hits do real damage. Bibliologies of revelation have indeed been prone to neglecting the variety and human histories of the Scriptures, and undermining the practice of historical-criticism despite their claims to support it.[58] They often fail to do justice to the deep differences between incarnation and prophetic inspiration (let alone the origin of other biblical genres).[59] This sometimes turns the Bible into something like an incarnation of its own (for instance, T. F. Torrance charges B. B. Warfield's account of verbal inspiration as "incarnating" the Holy Spirit[60]). In a way, paralleling the Bible and Jesus Christ this way keeps their lines from meeting, even though the two in fact intersect intensely over the course of Jesus' life.[61] Finally, Karl Barth's scheme rests on a controlling concept of "revelation." This category (along with the rest of Barth's intellectual framework) has, for Barr, "to a very great extent collapsed in ruins."[62]

The category of inspiration hardly fares any better. Barr finds its prooftexts (2 Tim. 3:16 and 2 Pet. 1:21) biblically marginal, and blown out of all proportion in the subsequent tradition. He also finds inspiration to have been held captive by the categories of inerrancy and infallibility. While he admits that inspiration names "something that seems to be necessary in a Christian account of the status of the Bible,"[63] he still finds the term unhelp-

---

"a tendency to base sweeping criticisms on a very narrow foundation," and a tendency to treat flaws in others' projects as "somehow *foundational* to the whole enterprise." Together these aspects of Barr's style of argument qualify the range over which Barr's criticisms apply. Watson goes on to offer a list of examples of "a casualness and inattention to detail that characterizes so much of his polemic," not only against biblical theology but against fundamentalism, canonical criticism, and Barthianism. See Francis Watson, *Text and Truth: Redefining Biblical Theology* (Grand Rapids: Eerdmans, 1997), pp. 18, 23-24.

58. James Barr, *Old and New in Interpretation: A Study of the Two Testaments* (New York: Harper & Row, 1966), pp. 25, 92-93.

59. Barr, *Old and New in Interpretation*, p. 24. Note below that Athanasius, whose analogy of the Word we will be drawing on, stresses this very point of discontinuity in *Against the Arians*.

60. Wells defends Warfield against this charge, but acknowledges the tendency among those who draw such analogies. See Wells, *James Barr and the Bible*, p. 343.

61. Barr, *Old and New in Interpretation*, pp. 27, 137-38.

62. Barr, *Old and New in Interpretation*, pp. 65-102 and 12. Yet Wells claims that Barr's reason for rejecting the analogy is not a *wholesale* rejection of Barthian thinking, but a "blossoming of seeds already present in Barth's work." Two qualities of the Bible that Barth insists on, the absence of a direct identity between Scripture and the Word of God and the fallibility of the biblical witness, undermine any "two element" Christological parallel and reveal a Bible with one nature only: the human. Barr follows this reasoning to conclude further that the Bible is the *responsive* witness of God's people *to* God (*James Barr and the Bible*, pp. 32-33).

63. Barr, *The Bible in the Modern World*, p. 17.

ful. It remains preoccupied with the moment of Scripture's origin (thus the fundamentalist stress on "original autographs"). It is silent about *in what way* God speaks in human beings; and the verbal dictation theories answering this question have so far proven inadequate to both the humanity of biblical language and the actual history of the Bible.[64]

Barr also examines and rejects "authority" as a helpful category. To its credit, it sidelines the unhelpful categories of inspiration, inerrancy, and revelation. Yet its own problems are insoluble. Barr wonders whether Roman legal categories (what might be called "Constantinianism" today) have been too influential in the Church's practice of authority. He considers older notions of ecclesiastical authority (which appeal to biblical authority) improperly out of step with modern ecumenism and pluralism, and respect for free decision. Trying to adapt the term to this new context only produces confusion.[65]

Finally, Barr proposes "a theologically critical account of the *functions* which [Scripture] exercises." Barr protests that the "theologically critical" quality of his project is not neutral. But he envisions this quality as "encouragement and criticism where appropriate" of what would otherwise remain a neutral account.[66] In other words, Enlightenment objectivity (as practiced in modern biblical scholarship) offers the only promising starting point for a truly adequate account of Scripture. It is with good reason that Barr's project is entitled *The Bible in the Modern World*.

Why continue to pursue the Analogy of the Word in the face of all these problems? First, "the modern world" has hardly been a happy context for the Bible. Today, it is Enlightenment epistemology, not just Barth's intellectual framework, that "has collapsed in ruins." What Barr may find so persuasive in the category of "function" is not its neutrality, but its friendly support for the particular practices of a community ordered around the "Hebrew Bible" — a modern concept if there ever was one — in whose intellectual context the Church's other intellectual contexts are largely unintelligible (and vice versa).[67] The three bibliological categories Barr criticizes (inspiration, revela-

64. Barr, *The Bible in the Modern World*, pp. 15-17.
65. Barr, *The Bible in the Modern World*, pp. 23-30.
66. Barr, *The Bible in the Modern World*, p. 33.
67. To be fair to Barr, in *Old and New in Interpretation* he supports only "relative objectivity," as opposed to the "absolute objectivity" that is the hallmark of the Enlightenment (and that he considers "not particularly important" to the practice of relative objectivity). By this he seems to mean respect for the biblical text itself, rather than for a community's interpretations; and a relegation of communities' interpretations to hypothetical status until they are confirmed, modified, or disconfirmed by the text. He acknowledges that scholarly biblical criticism is a community practice, calling its community "a group formed by coincidence

tion, and authority) happen to characterize three theological traditions with which he as a radical Protestant biblical critic has severe problems — fundamentalism, neo-orthodoxy, and Roman Catholicism.

Our survey has already shown that the depth grammar of the Analogy of the Word is wider than Reformation, neo-orthodox, or Catholic thought. It has been developed differently in different traditions, and can presumably survive the limitations of any one such development. Indeed, Barr has not shown that any of these categories is *necessarily* abusive or unproductive. None stands or falls with the community with which he associates it, and in whose terms he characterizes it. (Nor, we may say, does historical criticism stand or fall with liberal Protestantism, nor with the abuses it has suffered under modernism!)

Furthermore, Barr's practice of separating these categories analytically amounts to a strategy of "divide and conquer." Inspiration naturally fails when it is divorced from Christocentrism. If it is a truly Christian category, it is supposed to. Likewise, authority fails when it is divorced from the ontological categories of inspiration and revelation. It easily becomes the arbitrary authority of an oppressive community (and so it is understood in many modern and postmodern circles). Finally, phenomenology (pursued in Chapter 2), being theory-laden, is never neutral, and shielding it from concerns of community (Chapter 3) or ontology (Chapter 1) only preserves subjectivity in more subtle and distorting forms. Barr is not the first to separate these categories artificially, or to forsake ontological accounts of Scripture in his pursuit of a functional account (see the beginning of Chapter 2). But by buying into the idea that these need to be separated and opposed, Barr reduces his "opponents" to straw men and sabotages his own otherwise worthy project. In contrast, this project seeks to *integrate* Word- and Spirit-Christology, form and function, divine economy and phenomenology, ecclesiology and historiography, so as to honor the complex coherence of the Church's doctrine and practice of Scripture.

This does not allow us to dismiss Barr's insights as might Barr dismiss the insights of his opponents. While his critiques do not *proscribe* the Analogy of the Word's role in bibliology, at times they do *correct* it, and frequently

---

with the meta-languages of a number of disciplines, such as history and linguistics, of which theology is now only one," whose scholarship "uses criteria the status of which does not depend on their place in theology, and about which theology may no longer have any ability to judge" (*Old and New in Interpretation*, pp. 184-85, 180). But these "qualifications" still appeal to the ideas of autonomy among modern biblical scholars and their methods, and their claims of greater objectivity. Barr's qualifications reinforce rather than overthrow his modernism.

they call for clarifications in order that it may not be misunderstood. As we shall see, the category of function and the practice of historical criticism have their place in bibliology. A properly drawn Analogy of the Word neither incarnates nor ignores the Holy Spirit. It identifies and honors the equivocations that distinguish analogy from identity. It respects both human location and divine initiative. It does not gloss over concrete history, nor violate responsible academic (and more importantly, ecclesial) biblical practices, nor turn the practices of one Christian tradition (and surely not the practices of academic theology or biblical scholarship) into a rule for all.

Chapter 1

The Beginning of Scripture:
The God of Word

Entering the Circle

Any truly systematic theology of Scripture that understands the Bible to be a means of God's presence becomes an exercise in disciplined but circular reflection. An important question then becomes where one should enter the circle, and why one point of entry commends itself over the others.

The list of contending entry points is formidable. Here are a few options: (1) It follows from our experience of God through Scripture that God is truly present in Scripture. Thus *the human experience of salvation* is the best place to begin. Or (2) it follows from God's presence in Scripture that that presence is Triune. Thus, *the doctrine of the Trinity* properly frames all other theological considerations. Or (3) it follows from Scripture's inspiration that Scripture is acted upon by the Holy Spirit and in turn does his work. One begins an account of biblical efficacy with the economic Trinity,[1] and we first meet the economic Trinity in *the person of the Holy Spirit.* Thus pneumatology is the point of departure for a bibliology.[2] Or (4) Jesus' normativity as

---

1. See Catherine Mowry LaCugna, *God For Us: The Trinity and Christian Life* (San Francisco: HarperCollins, 1991), p. 223. Of course LaCugna would object to the very term "economic Trinity"; for her there is only *Trinity.*

2. Clark Pinnock explores the various *loci* of systematic theology from a pneumatological perspective in *Flame of Love: A Theology of the Holy Spirit* (Downers Grove,

God's only mediator and revelation means that Scripture must first be understood Christologically. Since the most direct parallel with the written Word of revelation is the divine Word of revelation, *Christology* affords the most appropriate categories for a doctrine of Scripture. Or (5) seeing the Bible's pneumatological and Christological ontologies together implies a fully Trinitarian ontology. Thus one can begin with *either Spirit or Son,* so long as one follows both through to Trinity as the ground of Scripture. Or (6) it follows from the Bible's saving power in the life of the Church and its believers that *soteriology* is the most proper category for beginning the exercise. Since the Bible's primary function is salvific, one best describes what the Bible is and how it works by appealing to its role in the order of salvation. Or (7) it follows from the Church's formation by and obedience to Scripture, as well as its authorship and canonization of Scripture, that *ecclesiology* is the proper starting point. The Bible is the product of churchly witness, and vice versa; thus one must locate one's doctrine of Scripture within the context of the Church.

No one entry point commends itself absolutely, because *all* these aspects of bibliology are relevant. Indeed, Gabriel Fackre's narrative systematics takes the multiplicity of starting points as itself a kind of starting point, endorsing narrative as an ordering principle.[3] A thoroughly Christian account of Scripture must eventually examine all of them. Indeed, they are so intertwined that no one can be examined adequately except in terms of the others. For this reason one must make it clear that Scripture's divine ontology (Chapter 1), mission (Chapter 2), and ecclesiality (Chapter 3) describe not three relationships between God and the world, nor even three discrete stages in the economy of salvation, but one economy seen three ways, three overlapping ranges of the *one* relationship between God and humanity mediated, among other ways, through the Scriptures of the Church of Jesus Christ.

Modern bibliologies generally adopt salvation-historical, phenomenological, or existential points of entry which start "from below," from the human experience of salvation by means of the use of Scripture. This project takes a more traditional, "Alexandrian" entry point in giving ultimate priority to the divine perspective rather than the human. Divine descent precedes and empowers human ascent, and so descent is where this bibliology begins. The

---

Ill.: InterVarsity, 1996). He describes his program on p. 11, and visits the categories of truth, revelation, inspiration, and illumination (biblical and extrabiblical) on pp. 215-45.

3. Gabriel Fackre, *The Christian Story: A Narrative Interpretation of Basic Christian Doctrine,* vol. 1, 3rd ed. (Grand Rapids: Eerdmans, 1996); *The Christian Story: A Pastoral Systematics,* vol. 2: *Authority: Scripture in the Church for the World* (Grand Rapids: Eerdmans, 1987); *The Doctrine of Revelation: A Narrative Interpretation* (Grand Rapids: Eerdmans, 1997).

Alexandrian perspective for speaking about God and creation is firmly grounded in biblical and churchly language, being present at least as early as Colossians 1:15's *prōtotokos pasēs ktiseōs* or (depending on one's reading) Philippians 2:6's *hos en morphe theou huparchon*. This is early indeed. The invisible God can work and even reveal himself through created matter, but only because God is its creator and redeemer. Flesh becomes Word, but only because Word became flesh. Christ's preexistence "is not a question of extending time into eternity, but of founding salvation-history in God's eternity."[4] Of course, we do not know about Scripture's character and work from eternity any more than we know about Christ's; so the theocentric approach taken here is not a denial of the development of doctrines of Scripture over time through human experience. But such experience quickly teaches the Church to reflect from the perspective of eternity. It is from the perspective of preexistence — from the "Alexandrian" perspective of Genesis 1:1 and John 1:1 — that this particular bibliology enters the circle: By appealing to God, creator of heaven and earth. So our point of departure for Christian reflection on the significance of Scripture is the Bible's divine ontology — the relationship between God and God's inspired Word.

We will begin by using several ancient and modern theological authorities critically and constructively as guides and points of departure, men whose works help shape a more accurate understanding of Scripture's Triune ontology. They are Athanasius of Alexandria; Augustine of Hippo; Karl Barth; and Hans Urs von Balthasar. These visionaries have been widely influential (in the case of Athanasius and Augustine, stunningly influential) in helping their fellow Christians appreciate Scripture in terms of God's overall purpose, and put the Bible to use in the life of the Bible's Church. Their Christologies and doctrines of the Trinity are tightly integrated with their doctrines of Scripture and hermeneutical practices. They offer trustworthy leadership, profound distinctives, and ecumenical promise for bibliologians.

The Analogy of the Word will remain central throughout, as it is central to the thought of all four of these authorities. But we will go beyond Alexandrian Word-flesh Christology alone to embrace an Antiochian Spirit-Christology as well, for its categories solve some of the long-standing problems of analogizing between the Word made flesh and the Word made words. Indeed, in the course of the chapter we will move beyond a simple Christological account of Scripture to develop a truly Trinitarian account of the Bible's character and work. To put it as concisely as possible, in the course of this chapter we will find that Christian Scripture participates in

4. Walter Kasper, *Jesus the Christ* (Mahwah, N.J.: Paulist, 1977), p. 172.

the will of the Father, the *kenosis* of the Son, the power of the Holy Spirit, and the humanity of God's chosen people.

I. Athanasius: The Word's Self-Involvement in the World

Athanasius of Alexandria's *On the Incarnation of the Word* frames the discussion from the beginning, for it adopts the broadest possible perspective in narrating God's self-involvement in the world. It marks out succinctly and clearly several pivotal moments in cosmic history when God descends ever more deeply into the created order: creation, fall, inspiration, incarnation, eschaton. Athanasius shows that each of these moments makes sense of the others. It is through all of them that God's eternal plan is made manifest. Athanasius links the moments powerfully, and profoundly biblically, by putting creation, anthropology, fall, law and prophecy, incarnation, messianic ministry, churchly witness, and future return all in terms of the activities of the divine *logos* of the Father, who himself is divine.[5] The result is an ontology of the created order with an anthropology drawn from creation and a Christology drawn from incarnation.

Alongside Athanasius' main project come the rudiments of a bibliology that frames the prophetic and apostolic words of Scripture in terms of creation, fall, incarnation, and the era of the Church. Athanasius' cosmology sees the biblical mediations of God's presence in the fallen order from the perspective of eternity. The Old and New Testaments occupy points along Athanasius' narrative of divine self-involvements in the created order and in the divine economy of salvation. Scripture is not the central character, let alone the only significant character, in his cosmology. His cosmic perspective locates biblical practice within the much broader range of theological *loci:* the character and work of the Triune God, creation and its witness, the many means of grace, the eschaton and its ecclesial gatherings, rival religious traditions, and the like. That perspective guides this bibliology through all three chapters, so it is worth interpreting his argument in detail.

Athanasius' case depends strongly on the multiple associations and cognates of *logos.* But it helps clarify things first to rehearse his argument without resorting to that term at all: The divine agent who created the world and the divine agent who redeems the world are the same being. Creation and re-

---

5. Athanasius, *On the Incarnation of the Word* (Crestwood, N.Y.: St. Vladimir's Seminary Press, 1993), §1.

demption involve the giving and restoring of divine qualities to all creation — and especially to humanity, which in receiving the image of God gains the special ability to know and relate to God. Furthermore, this bestowal and restoration are not divine gifts by simple fiat, but happen only as creator and creation are brought together in the enfleshed Son who creates and redeems. *Jesus* is the perfect analogy — meaning the identity — between God and creation. His speech-acts make God both knowable and known. Humans, who are created in God's image but who have lost their created ability to know and serve the One whose image they bear, have regained that ability in the only way they ever could: redemption by the God-man Jesus Christ. Now they too have become Jesus' means of work in the world, even in his eschatological absence, through *their* speech-acts.

So far this is a relatively straightforward narrative rendition of the entire biblical *kerygma*. But its real power comes from a lexical connection that gives Athanasius' argument a whole further dimension of eloquence: Jesus, the divine creator and savior, is the *logos* who is God, and the divine gift to humanity is that they are made *logikos,* a term often translated "rational," "logical," or "reasonable." Here, to capture Athanasius' pun, let us render it "word-ly" (a neologism that honors language's sense of rationality, logic, and reason, particularly in light of the linguistic turn in modern and postmodern philosophy). God is Word, and God's people are *logikoi,* "wordly ones." The correspondence between God and human speech about God is built right into the relationship between creature and creator. This relationship is nowhere closer than in the incarnate Christ, where the two unite perfectly. But divine-human words prefigure, testify to, and re-present Christ in all holy language, including Holy Scripture.

We read Athanasius too narrowly if we suppose he understands self-involvement merely as self-*revelation.* Though revelation is a crucial aspect of the divine-human relationship, Athanasius understands it in a much wider sense than it often has in the Kantian West (for instance, in Karl Barth). Using J. L. Austin, Nicholas Wolterstorff reminds us that speech is more than propositions, indeed more than words.[6] Likewise, knowledge in the biblical sense is much more than cognition. This wider definition respects the greater scope of Athanasius' project in refusing to restrict either divine or human discourse to revelation.[7]

---

6. Thus Wolterstorff distinguishes between "locutionary acts" and "illocutionary acts." See Nicholas Wolterstorff, *Divine Discourse: Philosophical Reflections on the Claim That God Speaks* (New York: Cambridge University Press, 1995), p. 13.

7. Wolterstorff, *Divine Discourse,* pp. 19-36.

Athanasius develops the Christian affirmation that all things were created through the *logos* (Gen. 1:3; John 1:3; cf. 1 Cor. 8:6; Col. 1:16; Heb. 1:3) in order to show that though the *logos* came to creation in a fundamentally new way in the incarnation, nevertheless "he was not far from it before, for no part of creation had ever been without Him Who, while ever abiding in union with the Father, yet fills all things that are" (§8). By virtue of this participation, the works of creation are a "means by which the Maker might be known" — by "pondering the harmony of creation" (§12). For Athanasius, what we call general revelation and natural theology are grounded Christologically. Creation's power to signify derives from the creative agency of the *logos*. Its splendor exists to glorify and reveal its Maker, not just generally but also specifically in its creatures Israel, Tanakh, Christ, Church, and New Testament. This means it is important to rehearse Athanasius' entire narrative in order to locate God's specific self-manifestations in Scripture.

Nature culminates in the creation of humanity in God's image. Beyond the divine gift of life itself, God gave an extra grace to humanity: the impress of his own image, "a share in the power of the very *logos* Himself." This self-gift gives humanity "shadows of the Word *(skias tou logou)*" and makes human beings *logikoi,* capable of knowing God and existing in relationship (§3).

Maintained by the Edenic garden's produce and its simple law, and joined by grace in union with the Word, humanity was destined to escape the corruption intrinsic to its created nature (§5). So says Wisdom 2:23: "God created man for incorruption and as an image of His own eternity; but by envy of the devil death entered into the world." With sin's entry into the world, the gift begins to vanish into corruption. Knowledge ironically produces not further revelation, but hiddenness and isolation (Gen. 3:8-9). The cosmic intimacy of Eden falls into the secret shame of private selves (Gen. 3:7). Athanasius narrates the accelerating course of sin in the world by drawing on the tenor and text of Romans 1 (§5), while developing it distinctly: "Man, who was created in God's image and in his possession of reason reflected the very Word Himself, was disappearing, and the work of God was being undone" (§6). Sin's consequences distort and destroy the impress of God's image on his human creatures. Cut off from the source of their life, their bodies dissolve into death. One might add to Athanasius' own account that the divine gift of speech, no doubt a product of the human share of the *logos,* becomes distorted, used irrationally for deception and alienation (Gen. 4:8-10) rather than communion. And in response, God's speech to humanity becomes a judging one, cursing and condemning (Gen. 4:11-15). Before long speech itself must be confused at Babel, to check its awesome power for spreading sin (Gen. 11:1-9).

Yet flood and confusion are no real solution to the dilemma facing God, now that sin reigns in his formerly good creation. Athanasius senses a double-bind for God that Anselm too will exploit: On the one hand, were God to revoke his promise of death as the inevitable consequence of disobedience, it would break God's own word and compromise his justice. Such a thing is absolutely unthinkable. On the other hand, letting sin destroy God's *logikoi*, even in punishment, would still be an embarrassing concession to evil. "It would have been improper that what had once been created rational *(logika)* and had partaken of his Word *(tou logou autou metaschonta)*, should perish." This too is "unworthy of the goodness of God. . . . In that case, what was the use of having made them in the beginning?" The Pandora's Box is open, and divine inaction "would argue not goodness in God but limitation" — profounder limitation even than would be ascribed to a God who had not created in the first place (§6).

This no-win situation is God's occasion to overcome the dilemma in an elegant way: his radical, redeeming self-intervention in the fallen order. So into dying creation the creator-*logos* comes to finish what was started: to reassert God's rule over creation *and* to bring the created and corrupted nature of humanity to its intended destination (§7). Thus begins salvation-history as it is usually narrated, with the Word's incarnation, death, and resurrection, in which the Church now participates in hope (§§8-10).

Saving Knowledge: Scripture among the Word's Self-Manifestations

The richness of Athanasius' Analogy of the Word already suggests the basis of a divine ontology of Scripture. But there is still another dimension to this story of creation, fall, and redemption that Athanasius brings out from the perspective of the *logos*.[8] And here his work is directly relevant for bibliology, for Athanasius goes on to develop his soteriology in terms of humanity's *epistemology* of God. The *imago dei* or *eikon theou* has a purpose, a teleology, which is to know its source, for whom it was created in the first place. For Athanasius, humanity is created for the exercise of rationality, which can only happen in relationship with God the *logos*, through whom it apprehends the Father. Human rationality, being derived from its creator the *logos*, can hardly be rational in the ignorance of its Maker. Apart from such knowledge, hu-

---

8. At the end of §10: "This, then, is the first cause of the Savior's becoming Man. There are, however, *other things* which show how *wholly fitting* is His blessed presence in our midst; and these we must now go on to consider."

manity is no better than the irrational beasts, who know nothing but worldly things. Even worse, in the absence of a proper relationship with God, fallen human rationality inevitably fixes itself on a created thing, idolizes it, and begins to decay. Therefore salvation of a fallen humanity that has partaken of a share of the *logos* means, at minimum, a restoration of that rationality. Apart from the knowledge of God there is no salvation; in fact, there is no true rationality at all. Divine *gnosis* is a necessary part of human salvation and of the work of God in the world (§11).

Athanasius affirms the human inability to know God by its own efforts, not just because of the Fall but because of sheer human limitation. Thus, in his grace, God did not leave humanity destitute of such knowledge. Athanasius classifies these media of divine self-revelation into several categories. The first and foremost — logically, not chronologically — is Jesus Christ, in whom humanity gains a share in God's own image. The incarnate Word is the foundation of Athanasius' theological anthropology, just as it is the preoccupation of his entire book (§11).

But Athanasius is generally moving chronologically rather than logically through §§11ff. So having made his point of Christological priority, he returns to salvation-history proper to finish his narrative. The second manifestation of God's gracious gift of self-knowledge is humanity's share of God's image and likeness. Even prior to the Fall, it is by divine grace that wordly humanity perceives the Word, and through the Word apprehends the Father. Athanasius treats this gift not merely as our means to know God, but as powerful evidence of God's nature (§11).

Though this grace is sufficient to reveal the Word and his Father, the pull of sin leads weakened humanity to reject God, forgetting him and fashioning idols in his stead. In the same accelerating terms as those in §5, but now drawn out epistemologically, Athanasius describes the human descent into ignorance through its wounded rationality, the compromised *eikon theou* that once pointed beyond the idols.

The harmony of the created heavens is distorted too, into pantheons of celestial idols (§11). Lower and lower human eyes fall — and so lower and lower the *logos* descends in grace into the created order. He comes secondly as Law and Prophets, delivered by ordinary people, so that "if they were tardy in looking up to heaven, they might still gain knowledge of their Maker from those close at hand." Here Athanasius describes the location of Scripture proper, in the context of his Christological account of God's self-involvement in the fallen world.

In *Against the Arians*, Athanasius has described Scripture Christologically, but only in order to contrast inspiration with incarnation. Making the same point that Barr does in order to undermine the category of "revelation,"[9] Athanasius stresses that in the latter, the *logos* "became human"; in the former, he merely "came into a human."[10] Incarnation is not to be confused with the process by which the *logos* sanctified the saints of old, or by which the prophetic "'Word of the Lord came to' the individual prophets."[11] Therefore Athanasius implies that the *logos* is the common agent in inspiration, sanctification, and incarnation. However, its relationship with human persons is uniquely incarnational in the person of Jesus Christ.

Clearly the effect of the *logos'* inspiring activity does not *remain* in the person of the prophet. This is the distinction Athanasius means to highlight. What then is the nature of the word that a prophet delivers when the *logos kyriou* comes to him or her? In *Against the Arians* Athanasius quickly leaves behind the matter of the *logos'* work in inspiration in order to concentrate on incarnation, so the effect of the *logos'* agency goes undeveloped. However, the topic is taken up again where we left off in *On the Incarnation:* The Law and the Prophets are "a sacred school of the knowledge of God and conduct of the spiritual life for the whole world," presenting an even deeper grace than the earlier signs in creation. In its context of salvation-history, the prophetic and legal Word is the most accessible yet of all the means by which God the Word came into the confusion of his fallen creation in order that humanity would see his signs.

Yet the human gaze remained not only beneath the level of heavens and holy men, but failed even to meet the level of Tanakh (§12). Not only the Scriptures' curses and condemnations went unheeded, but even its blessings and promises, its prefigurations of and preparations for the *logos'* third and deepest involvement with creation.

The Law broken and the Prophets persecuted, God's dilemma is at its sharpest point yet. The stakes have never been so high, God's defeat never so seemingly complete. The rest is familiar to Athanasius' readers: "What else could He possibly do, being God, but renew His Image in mankind, so that through it men might once more come to know Him? And how could this be done save by the coming of the very Image Himself, our Savior Jesus Christ" (§13)? And so because the human *imago dei* has been ruined and the divine

---

9. James Barr, *Old and New in Interpretation: A Study of the Two Testaments* (New York: Harper & Row, 1966), pp. 24-25.

10. The language of adoption Athanasius uses here is entirely appropriate to preserve the distinction between the incarnation of the Word and the inspiration of his believers (see Rom. 8:14, 23). We will see below that not all uses of the language of adoption to describe the process of inspiration are so adequate. The issue is what is adopted, and when.

11. Athanasius, *Against the Arians,* Discourse III, §30. *NPNF* II.4, p. 410.

warnings unheeded, the *logos* condescends even to become human, the perfect analogy between God and creation.

The Role of Scripture in Athanasius' Account

Athanasius' point through these chapters is to develop a Christology and soteriology, not a doctrine of Scripture, so his mention of the Old Testament is confined to several sentences, and the New Testament has not even appeared in his account. Yet locating the divine words within the *logos'* manifold involvement with the world amounts to a Christological, even Trinitarian, basis for Athanasius' theology of Scripture. First, human wordliness, created and redeemed for communication with God himself, provides a basis for a theological account of human language in its widest sense. Second, divine law and prophecy illustrate God's extraordinary initiative in speaking to and against fallen humanity in order to sanctify it. These ground a theology of specifically *scriptural* speech even before the advent of Christ. Third, the *incarnation* of the Word explains how in Jesus human speech can truly be divine speech.

All of these are means of divine teaching, as by a teacher who condescends in kindness to students (§15). Thus, following 1 Corinthians 1:21, Athanasius affirms that it is *God* who "through the foolishness of the *kerygma* saves." Creation of heavens, earth, and humanity, sending of law and prophets, incarnation, and the Church's witness are all means of the *logos'* saving agency. All acquire — or, rather, retain — qualities of the *logos* that abide in their relationship to God and restore it in the face of separation. All have at their deepest nature a divine ontology, though of course none directly, save for the *logos* made flesh. Indeed, as Athanasius affirms, it is the *logos* made flesh that is determinative of God's other gracious means of access, including Scripture.

In no way does Athanasius reduce salvation to human knowledge of God, nor the cross's objective work to revelation or moral influence. But Athanasius never ignores epistemology in his account. In fact, Christ's saving work is appropriated by receiving the *logos'* "teaching" (§20). Knowledge in Athanasius goes hand in hand with salvation, as both a means and a result (§16). Athanasius describes two steps by which God accomplishes his salvation: First, he comes like a king into a city, rendering it safe, reversing the momentum of sin in the world (§9). Second, he restores all that originally belonged to humanity — that is, the *logikos* human nature — by his own teaching and power (§10). Knowledge of God becomes a means of sanctification, as human wordliness is brought back into relationship with its intended object. Athanasius uses the images of teaching and persuasion so often in the final half of *On the Incarnation* that they become synonyms for salvation and sanctification. Christ has filled the whole earth with his teaching (§50), has filled "all things with the knowledge of him" so completely that humanity is surrounded with testimony to the divinity of the *logos*, "shut in from every side" (§45), the entire world "illumined by his teaching" (§55).

The point of this cloud of witnesses is to lead the observer to pass over to the *logos'* teaching (§§27-28) and triumph over death. Athanasius fills his pages with accounts of dramatic changes in the behavior of people "when they hear the teaching of Christ" (§52) and, receiving it, become disciples (§53) — peacefulness, chastity, proclamation, fearlessness, obedience to the point of martyrdom. He calls this pattern of conversion *persuasion* by Christ's preaching: "Christ alone, by ordinary language, and by men not clever with the tongue, has throughout all the world persuaded whole churches full of men" (§47) to become disciples and worship one Lord, and through him the Father (§46). We will see below how congruent with Augustine's *On Christian Doctrine* this Athanasian "rhetoric of conversion" is. The implications of incarnation render all creation without a void of the presence of the *logos*, thus laying the groundwork for a universal, theological semiotics of language such as Augustine's.

Crucial to Athanasius' account of Christ's teaching is its divine as well as human agency. The power of Jesus' teaching does not lie somehow in the words themselves, but has its source in the *living logos*, for the school of a dead teacher could not have such effect (§47). This power brings pagan oracles and Greek "wisdom" to become empty and foolish, fade, and cease (§§46-48, 55), bringing their schools to naught and filling his churches even while "teaching in meaner language" (§50). In sum, the *logos'* teaching is "the Word *of* the Lord Jesus Christ" (§40), conferring "such power in his teaching" (§51) only because the *logos alone* was acting, "by himself" (§53). The connection between the risen Jesus and his teaching is so powerful that it becomes an extension of his earthly presence: Where Athanasius speaks of the incarnation as "the sojourn of our Saviour" (§29), he speaks of the spreading *kerygma* as "the *logos* himself, sojourning here by his teaching" (§49), "sojourning among us" to put a stop to the superstitions of the fallen world (§47). For Athanasius Christ's teaching attains almost a hypostatic status, changing lives and putting away pretenders who lack the source of its power. (We will re-examine the sojourn of the *logos* again under the heading of salvation-history in Chapter 2.)

Yet this divine agency and the power it confers on Christ's teaching do not come unaccompanied by human agents. Even while Athanasius insists on the *logos'* sole agency behind the power of his teaching, he understands that the teaching is mediated ecclesially: Jesus Christ "preached by means of his own disciples, [and] carried persuasion to men's mind . . . to learn to know him, and through him to worship the Father." As a result of the *logos'* saving work of persuasion through the teaching of the Church, "they have come over to the school of Christ" (§51) which is the Church.

While the ecclesial location and salvific effects of Christ's teaching are the subjects of the next two chapters, this account has already had to appeal to them. This is because they are inseparable: The power of Christ's teaching is nothing else than the saving work of the *logos.* There is no independent source of biblical and kerygmatic power but that of God himself, and that power is inevitably seen in the salvation that results from their powerful performance: The Gospel is "the power of God unto salvation" (Rom. 1:16). Remarkably, Athanasius even *transposes* Scripture and Jesus in citing Hebrews 4:12, to affirm that "the Son of God is 'living and active,' and works day by day, and brings about the salvation of all" (§31). If Scripture is living and active, it is so because Jesus is its living *logos.*

As the book closes, Athanasius invites the reader to look for further guidance to where the school of the *logos* looks: the words of Holy Scripture, "spoken and written by God, through men who spoke of God" (§56, cf. John 3:34). There the virtuous reader with eyes to see will find all Athanasius himself has offered, but "more completely and clearly" — so completely and clearly, in fact, that Athanasius compares the intensity of Scripture's truth to the blinding light of the sun (§57). While Athanasius rarely names Scripture to equate it with Christ's teaching, at the book's end he describes it as the source of wisdom of those who teach Christ (§56) and the record of God's revelations to his saints, whose understanding only a pure soul and a Christ-like life of virtue could even hope to attain (§57). Through virtuous lives and dedicated study of Scripture, Athanasius' readers are promised the very fruits of the *logos'* saving work — and in the end a share in the rewards God has prepared for those who love him (1 Cor. 2:9). The relationship between *logos* and Scripture remains ambiguous as *On the Incarnation* closes, but it is strong enough to confer on the biblical Word an epistemological power second only to that of the incarnate Word himself.

Knowledge as a Form of God's Saving Presence

God's manifold self-involvement with the world in the person of the *logos* grounds a Christological account of language, in which to locate a Christological account of Scripture: The divine *fiat* that creates is the divine *logos* who redeems, a word vested not merely with meaning but with living power. The *logos'* culminating creative work in human wordliness is the "natural" basis for the possibility of confident human God-talk in its widest sense. Divine prophecy provides a Christological account of God's initiative in speaking to and against fallen humanity in order to save it, grounding a theology of divine-human speech even before the advent of Christ. And then the *logos* incarnate and redeeming in Jesus makes his teaching — his human speech — identical with divine speech. Thus the restoration of wordly humanity in Jesus divinizes both human rationality and its language, as well as the biblical language that prefigures it. Finally, with the basis for divine-human communion reestablished, the risen Jesus continues to speak to and through "his school," in order that his sojourn may be extended and his saving work brought to fulfillment through the written and proclaimed word of his body the Church. The knowledge of God is made available to the world in the Church's *kerygma*, and in the Scriptures that confer the saving power and wisdom of its preaching. Not only the divine word in Old Testament Scripture, but also that in New Testament Scripture, is a manifestation and continuing work of the *logos*. Scripture, a holy school for all the world, brings the world over to the school of Christ. The Scriptures create and flourish in the restored human rationality that once again partakes in the divine *logos*. The biblical words in the Old and New Testaments first prepare for and prefigure, then witness to and extend, the *logos'* saving presence in the created order.

So knowledge in Athanasius, and of course language, are soteriological goods. They are both means and results of salvation. Knowledge of God is a means of sanctification, bringing wordly humanity back into relationship with the intended object of human wordliness. And sanctification in turn purifies human rationality, magnifying the human appreciation of God revealed in his biblical Word. The entire divine process — creation, rationality, law, prophecy, incarnation, evangelism, sanctification — accomplishes the order of salvation that Athanasius would call *theosis:* "For he was made man that we might be made God; and he manifested himself by a body that we might receive the idea of the unseen Father" (§54).[12]

Athanasius wrote a Christological treatise for Christological purposes, and his account of language and Scripture are thoroughly Christocentric. But the several historical moments he recounts in the *logos'* creating and saving self-involvement with creation are in fact all suggestive of a perichoretic *Trinitarian* relationship among Father, Son, and Spirit in creation, incarnation,

---

12. We re-examine this order of salvation at the end of Chapter 3.

and Scripture. Thus Athanasius' salvation-history of the *logos* implies a fully Trinitarian account: In creation, the Word is the means of the Father's creating work, through the power of the Spirit. In Scripture the Father breathes his prophetic Word-made-words to Israel and to the Church, and through them to the ends of the earth. In incarnation, the Word made flesh, who is the circumscribed image of the infinite Father, is conceived and empowered by the Holy Spirit to do God's messianic work. Below we shall pursue the relationships in these terms.

The alpha-to-omega sweep of the *logos'* relationship with creation shows how a truly Christian epistemology is at its heart an account of Christian salvation-history in its entirety. Thus Athanasius lays the groundwork for this project's next chapter. The scope of Athanasius' narrative brings all of the traditional *loci* of Christian systematic theology to bear on the question of how God speaks in and through the Bible. One cannot separate the question of God's knowability, or of Scripture's character and work, from the categories of Trinity, creation, sin, Christology, pneumatology, soteriology, eschatology, and ecclesiology. Those who look to Christian epistemology to provide a safe foundation for these other disciplines should find sooner or later that they comprise a great web, with the doctrine of Scripture no less intricately dependent upon the others than any other Christian doctrine.

Such circularity has its pitfalls. While strong points strengthen Athanasius' entire project, problems become weak links that leave other points in his theological system vulnerable. As a result, several features of *On the Incarnation* threaten its very usefulness for a Trinitarian bibliology. First, there is the problem that Athanasius is developing a Christology and soteriology rather than an explicit bibliology. While an analogy clearly emerges between God's incarnate *logos* and God's canonical *graphē* — both are sojourns of the *logos* — it is by no means clear on the basis of *On the Incarnation* alone what that analogy actually is. Developing the Analogy of the Word is not Athanasius' concern. Second, as the role of the Holy Spirit is secondary to Athanasius' project, so are issues of ecclesiology. Thus the reader might easily miss the relevance to bibliology of the doctrine of the Church.

Several other features are even more troubling. Third, there is Athanasius' nearly exclusive emphasis on the *redeeming* presence of the *logos*, compared to the fading but still abiding presence of the *logos* in fallen creation. Sin's nearly total corruption of creation makes it hard to find a basis for the *logos'* discernible presence outside the Church proper. This is true even in Israel before the incarnation: In Athanasius' account, God's presence to Israel is practically exhausted in the Law and the Prophets. So the presence in the canon of wisdom that originated outside the community of faith becomes a pressing problem for Athanasius' project, let alone for formal bibliology. With such a radical disproportion between the *logos'* abiding presence in the fallen order and his work in redemption, one is led almost to expect new creation *ex nihilo,* rather than redemption of the original order. (We see an even more radical disproportionality below in Karl Barth.)

Fourth, following the incarnation the pendulum swings to the other extreme. Athanasius' eschatology is so realized and triumphalist that it conveys a nearly postmillennial vision of the kingdom's imminent triumph. Athanasius is so confident of this vision that he stakes his case on the *empirical* results of the *logos'* continuing presence:

> Behold how the Savior's doctrine is everywhere increasing, while all idolatry and everything opposed to the faith of Christ is daily dwindling and losing power and falling . . . while men, turning their eyes to the true God, *logos* of the Father, are deserting their idols, and now coming to know the true God. Now this is a proof that Christ is God the *logos,* and the Power of God. (§55)

Such a vision of accelerating divine presence in the world might have been reasonable in an age when Christianity was the newly licit religion of the Roman Empire. But in the subsequent centuries it so obviously failed to come to pass that it calls into question Athanasius' entire enterprise. Can Athanasius' vision be rescued from its own eschatology?

Since we will encounter many of these same issues even more sharply in the work of other theologians, they are best addressed below. Here it must be enough to note how many questions Athanasius leaves open for bibliology. Their resolution demands attention to all of the systematic and historical *loci* mentioned above.

Toward an Incarnational Ontology of Theological Language

Considering these problems, why not develop a divinity of Scripture by beginning with pneumatological categories instead, and concentrate on the Bible's inspiration? One weakness of such an approach is the threat of verbal docetism: the possibility that the humanity of inspired speech will go underappreciated, as it is in both Greek and Muslim models of inspired speech (and many "Christian" ones as well). Beginning with the analogy of incarnation it offers a more direct account of both the particularity *and* universality of biblical language. The Analogy of the Word anchors human epistemology of God in divine action, without compromising epistemology's true humanity. Furthermore, it recognizes the priority of *Jesus* as God's ultimate speech. Balthasar echoes Athanasius in saying, "God incarnating in a man speaking transforms the man himself into a divine utterance."[13] He notes the correspondence between Christology and saving knowledge of God in terms reminiscent of the Athanasian "idea of the Father": Because God's Word is in himself, God is expressible; and because God's Word has become incarnate, God is humanly understandable.[14]

The incarnation of God's *logos* into a speaking and hearing human being means that history, divine action, and God-talk coinhere. This coinherence "Alexandrianizes" human epistemology, turning conventional ways of knowing upside down. Incarnation transforms the category of inspiration. The marked contrast between Athanasius' approach and the merely historical, phenomenological, or experiential accounts of the relationship between God and God-talk that dominate today shows how deeply Alexandrian Athanasius' bibliology is, and how subversive it is to naturalistic accounts of human knowledge of God.

Yet Athanasius' approach does not entirely discredit these other accounts, as a Nestorian account of language might. By affirming the union between divine *logos* and *logikos* humanity in Christ, and its resemblance in the divine-human words of Israel's and the Church's Scripture, praise, proclamation, and reflection, Athanasius joins the divine and human realms. Naturalistic accounts of Scripture are radically incomplete if they are left on their own; but as parts of a greater picture, they are still entirely warranted. Human rationality and language in their countless forms are media for the divine *logos* to accomplish his saving work in the world.

John Macquarrie's *God-Talk* illustrates this point. Its chapter 6 asks how Christian theologians can convey similar ideas about God using radically different modes of expression. As an example of multifaceted theological discourse Macquarrie picks *On the Incarnation,* because of the way it abruptly shifts among what he calls mythology, symbolism, existential discourse, ontology, analogy, metaphysics, citation of authority, empirical argument, and paradox.[15] Athanasius uses all these literary devices, and at times combines them, to make the same case. What is it about language, Macquarrie asks, that lets Athanasius do this?

13. Hans Urs von Balthasar, *Explorations in Theology I: The Word Made Flesh* (San Francisco: Ignatius, 1989), p. 71.

14. Balthasar, *Explorations in Theology,* p. 19.

15. John Macquarrie, *God-Talk: An Examination of the Language and Logic of Theology* (New York: Seabury, 1979), pp. 126-45.

Macquarrie may or may not have picked a work by Athanasius simply because it is well known and contains widely varying styles of discourse. For Athanasius provides much more than just convenient source material. Christologically rooted analogy, which is not simply one of Athanasius' many modes of discourse but undergirds his entire work, in fact represents not just one of the nine different rhetorical devices Macquarrie identifies, but something crucial to his endeavor — what Macquarrie calls the "'basic logic' of theology" itself: a basis for confidence in the truth of what we say about God. To paraphrase Athanasius in Macquarrie's language, the incarnation rescues human existence from its impending corruption into nothingness by uniting it with God, who is ultimate being. Thus what we *experience* is related to what truly and ultimately *is*. Athanasius' "existential discourse" (and ours) is united with "ontological discourse," and by virtue of the incarnate *logos* the two types of discourse are found to be one.[16] The Kantian distinction between the phenomenal and noumenal realms, whatever its (in)defensibility on other grounds, dissolves forever at the Annunciation.

Furthermore, analogous relationships between the divine *logos* and the various forms of human language not only mediate ultimate reality in human existence, but also make it possible for profoundly different varieties of discourse to express common things. The common truth conveyed in these particulars makes them true *in common*. And this referential commonality unites the various discourses and truth-claims of Christian rationality. Though we are not immediately persuaded by Athanasius' case for the cosmic significance of Jesus' death being in the air, where the demons fly, or for his outstretched arms gathering in Jews with the one and Gentiles with the other (§25), we cannot dismiss them. For they make claims that are consistent with their own rhetorical contexts — contexts determined not merely by imaginative human communities, but by communities in growing fellowship with God their author, savior, and indweller. These claims are true not because of some general interpretive potential in human language, but because of the creating and redeeming work of, and above all the incarnation of, the *logos* who is the divine agent of all creative and redemptive discourse. Or, more accurately, any "general" interpretive potential in human language is itself a result of the presence and work of the *logos* in wordly humanity. Creation's participation in the divine *logos* means that myths, symbols, paradoxes, authorities, prooftexts, physical reality, and human experience of it all cohere. By virtue of their common participation in the one *logos*, they can be transcendently equivalent in what they convey.

16. Macquarrie, *God-Talk*, pp. 138-40.

Thus the incarnation of the *logos* as the only identity of God and creation suggests a Christological and Trinitarian basis for biblical practice. We have access to God because of the *incarnation* of the Word; and we may be confident in God's speech to us and in our speech about God by virtue of the incarnation of the *Word*. If this is true of Athanasius' theology, or of any other form of God-talk, it is certainly true of Scripture itself.

The connection both Athanasius and Macquarrie make between ontology and epistemology ties this chapter to the ones that follow. More immediately, it links Athanasius' account of the divine ontology of human language in Scripture and proclamation, to Augustine's explanation for the efficacy of Christian preaching, which we now explore.

II. Augustine: The Divine Ontology of Biblical Practice

Athanasius promises the diligent reader of Scripture a share in God's rewards. The same kind of promise is made in Augustine's *On Christian Doctrine,* in strikingly complementary terms. Augustine shows how the Athanasian transformation brought about by the incarnation of the Word comes to life in the Church's concrete study and proclamation of its Scriptures.

To be sure, there are differences: Where Athanasius tends to concentrate on the Word, Augustine tends to concentrate on words. Athanasius is more macrocosmic in scope, Augustine more microcosmic. Where the former concentrates more on the ontology of language, the latter concentrates more on its epistemology. The former is distinctively Eastern, the latter distinctively Western. But these are only diverging tendencies of two fundamentally compatible and mutually helpful accounts of the role of the biblical witness in the Christian life. It is easy to overstate the differences; in contrasting Athanasius and Augustine, their substantial continuities are often lost.

These continuities are deeply rooted in a common theological sensibility that draws deeply from the Alexandrian school of Christology. Rowan Greer considers Augustine the most consistent of orthodox "Alexandrian" exegetes,[17] and John Macquarrie calls Athanasius one of the least speculative of the Alexandrian theologians.[18]

The deep relevance of a particular approach to Christology (say, Alexandrian or Antiochian) to one's doctrine of Scripture is not always obvious.

17. Rowan Greer, "The Christian Bible and Its Interpretation," in James L. Kugel and Rowan A. Greer, *Early Biblical Interpretation* (Philadelphia: Westminster, 1986), pp. 183-84.
18. Macquarrie, *God-Talk,* p. 134.

But historical theology has repeatedly shown the connection, which serves as a further warrant for this chapter's Trinitarian bibliology.[19] These two fathers of the Church work together in developing a Christian account of Scripture, and even of all human language, that respects the Alexandrian insistence on the logical priority of divine action to human knowing.

On Christian Doctrine: *Augustine's "Rhetoric of Conversion"*

J. Patout Burns summarizes *On Christian Doctrine:* "Augustine took the opportunity to illustrate divine grace by demonstrating one of the media or instruments through which it operates, the allegories of Scripture."[20] The role of divine grace is so important that John C. Cavadini calls Book 4 of the work "less a theory of rhetoric *per se* than a theory of conversion" that provides the commentary on and hermeneutical key to the rest of the work.[21] Augustine's enormously influential work is famous for its semiotics, its rhetorical account of salvation, its theology of allegory, and its homiletics. All of these are important to constructing our bibliology; but the material on preaching is most appropriate for later chapters. For the purpose of constructing a Trinitarian ontology of Scripture, what immediately concerns us is the ontology that grounds Augustine's account: his theory of signification.

Athanasius outlines his cosmology in terms of the *logos'* relationship with the world. Here Augustine does the same thing. But because his concern is for Christian doctrine, he uses semiotic and rhetorical categories instead. In his opening pages, Augustine offers an epistemological account of Creator, creation, and creatures: "All doctrine concerns either things or signs, but things are learned by signs."[22] "The things which are to be enjoyed are the Fa-

---

19. See, for example, Robert M. Grant and David Tracy, *A Short History of Interpretation of the Bible,* 2nd ed. (Minneapolis: Fortress, 1984), chs. 6 and 7, "The School of Alexandria" and "The School of Antioch"; Manlio Simonetti, *Biblical Interpretation in the Early Church: An Historical Introduction to Patristic Exegesis,* trans. John A. Hughes (Edinburgh: T. & T. Clark, 1994); and Bart Ehrman, *The Orthodox Corruption of Scripture* (New York: Oxford University Press, 1993).

20. J. Patout Burns, "Delighting the Spirit: Augustine's Practice of Figurative Interpretation," in Duane W. H. Arnold and Pamela Bright, eds., *De Doctrina Christiana: A Classic of Western Culture* (Notre Dame: University of Notre Dame Press, 1995), p. 192.

21. John C. Cavadini, "The Sweetness of the Word: Salvation and Rhetoric in Augustine's *De Doctrina Christiana,*" in Arnold and Bright, *De Doctrina Christiana,* pp. 164, 165.

22. Augustine, *On Christian Doctrine,* 1.2.2, trans. D. W. Robertson Jr. (New York: Macmillan, 1958).

ther, the Son, and the Holy Spirit, a single Trinity, a certain supreme thing common to all who enjoy it."[23]

Augustine's Analogy of the Word

The lexical connection between *logos* and *logikos* that marks Athanasius' argument is made remote in Augustine's Latin. But it is still crucial to his argument, for human speech is Augustine's principal analogy for the enfleshment of the Word (1.13.12). When one misses the foundational character of Alexandrian Christology in Augustine's discourse, one easily mistakes *On Christian Doctrine* for a mere assimilation of classical rhetoric into Christian practice.[24]

Mark D. Jordan claims that interpretations that make this mistake miss Augustine's more basic insight that "any method of reading the Scriptures is fundamentally a reflection on words as analogous to Christ the Word." Biblical practices actualize the incarnation in the context of the Church, disclosing its mystery to those chosen to receive it. The point of Augustine's argument "is to construct fundamental analogies between signification and Incarnation."[25]

While Athanasius and Augustine agree that the incarnation of the *logos* is the point of departure for Christian reflection on human knowledge and salvation, they develop this common point in distinctive ways. Augustine is not rehearsing the narrative of God's self-involvement in the world to show the saving power of incarnation. He is not primarily interested in developing an ontology of Scripture. His project is a Christian *epistemology*. So he states in his first sentences: "There are two things necessary to the treatment of the Scriptures: a way of discovering those things which are to be understood, and a way of teaching what we have learned. We shall speak first of discovery and second of teaching" (1.1.1). Books 1-3 are about discovery — about how it is that human beings gain a knowledge of their creator. And so Augustine portrays the world of the Word's immanence in terms of a world of his knowledge.

23. Augustine, *On Christian Doctrine,* 1.5.5.

24. Mark D. Jordan, "Words and Word: Incarnation and Signification in Augustine's *De Doctrina Christiana," Augustinian Studies* 11 (1980): 177-78.

25. Jordan, "Words and Word," pp. 177-78. The point of Jordan's argument is a defense of this fundamental analogy, raising its antinomies and problems and (unsuccessfully) seeking their resolution. A response to his argument might better be made later in this project, when the eschatological context of the Bible's community of readers is in full view.

Augustine also endorses Athanasius' claim that the ultimate divine bestowal in creation was the *imago dei* in "rational" humanity.[26] Augustine makes much less explicit use of the *imago dei* than Athanasius does. But the concept is just as important in his argument, for the rational soul permits the creature to love his or her creator (1.22.21, cf. Deut. 6:5). Furthermore, just as Athanasius affirmed that the *logos* "was not far from us before" the Incarnation (§8), so Augustine sees all the universe in which these divine images live to be overflowing with the knowledge of its Creator.[27] The creation overflows with signs that point back to the image's prototype. Through the proper use of humanity's rational soul, these signs accomplish their intended purpose, linking image and prototype in eternal love.

Augustine's cosmology is controlled by two things: theology — the doctrine of the One who makes and orders the signs, and teleology — the doctrine of the end to which the signs are ordered, which is the love *(caritas)* of the One making and ordering them. Obviously these two can be distinguished but never separated; they are as intimately linked as creation and God. So from the beginning of Book 1, Augustine holds together two qualities belonging to things: first, their ends (expressed in terms of their "use" and "enjoyment," 1.3.3); and second, their signifying properties (expressed in terms of a distinction between a "thing" and a "sign," 1.2.2). Both qualities reveal creation's beginning and end in the love of God.

Everything belongs in its rightful place within the hierarchy of signs and things that culminates in the unqualified enjoyment and love of Holy Spirit, Son, and Father (1.5.5, 1.22.20-22). While a profound qualitative distinction remains between God and all of his creatures, nevertheless love is still due to those created things that "pertain to God . . . or pertain to us and require the favor of God." This love flows upward to the God who alone merits it, surging through the ordered creation like blood through living tissue (1.22.21).

But the significance and hierarchy of things are double-edged swords. In the absence of sin, things may be loved with any of four kinds of love: one directed upward, one directed inwardly, one directed equally and outwardly, and one directed further down the hierarchy (1.23.22). Likewise, things may

26. "A great thing is man, made in the image and likeness of God, not in that he is encased in a mortal body, but in that he excels the beasts in the dignity of a rational soul" (1.22.20).

27. "Although to the healthy and pure internal eye He is everywhere present, He saw fit to appear to those whose eye is weak and impure, and even to fleshly eyes. . . . He came to a place where He was already, for He was in the world, and the world was made by Him" (1.12.11-12).

be used in order to obtain and sustain the enjoyment of God, which is the love of God for his own sake (1.3.3–1.4.4). All these uses and loves mark a person of justice and "ordinate love" (1.27.28). But when subjected to the distorting effects of sin, the hierarchy of signifiers malfunctions, now trapping sinners in a fallen world where signs and means become idols and the God who lies at their end becomes distorted or forgotten altogether. The fallen person still uses and enjoys and loves — but the wrong things, for the wrong reasons. Sin turns desire into lust, prudence into greed, rational soul into darkened mind, love of equals to tyrannical rule over others, and love of God into love of a self that claims to deserve "that which is properly due only to God." Concupiscence produces injustice and war against oneself, and so "such self-love is better called hate" (1.23.23). The signs instituted by humans themselves come to reflect these misplaced priorities, giving rise to arts and sciences that are rarely of real use to disciples of Christ. Signs instituted by humans can even be manipulated by the powers in order to produce society with demons rather than the Triune God (2.39.38).

So Augustine narrates God, creation, and fall along the same lines as Athanasius. His purposes and vocabulary are different, but his cosmology is fundamentally similar, and equally tragic. Athanasius sees a world vanishing into corruption, Augustine a world at war with itself and with its Maker and on the path to self-destruction. The dilemma facing God in Augustine's fallen semiotic cosmos is like the divine double-bind we see in Athanasius and Anselm: It leaves God in the humiliating situation of deciding whether to destroy his once splendid creation, or to leave it to destroy itself.

Into this wretched place comes the Word, to reclaim what is his. In Augustine as in Athanasius, this decisive transformation in the human condition happens in several related ways: first, in the person of Jesus Christ; second, in his prophets and apostles that build his Church; and third, in the divine speech of the writers of Scripture.

The hierarchy of signs has become like a distorted map or a corrupted filing system that no longer points people to their intended goal. So God's Word comes to offer sinners a "voyage home" (1.10.10), breaking into the fallen world to point the way to the Father once again.

If Augustine were simply describing the role of Scripture, his account would resonate deeply with many canonical traditions, especially Islam, whose Quran is a "book of signs" *(ayat)* whose performance does exactly this for its hearers.[28] Seyyed Hossein Nasr describes two basic religious traditions

---

28. We will engage Islamic bibliology below, but note how Augustinian Seyyed Hossein Nasr sounds in his *Ideals and Realities of Islam* (San Francisco: HarperCollins Aquar-

in the world: one of divine descent, into which fall Christianity and Hinduism, and one of divine prophecy, into which he places Judaism and Islam.[29] Nasr's world is one where divine prophecy is sufficient for salvation. But Augustine's is not. Salvation is beyond the power of creation's own instruments, even when they are divinely employed. In such a world a Quran or Bible by itself would be a text of terror rather than hope.

But the Word's inbreaking into the created order is more than just prophecy, even prophecy on an unparalleled level. As in Athanasius and Anselm, here too incarnation is the third way that alone can save: By descending into the hierarchy where God properly does not belong, by allowing to be used the one who alone is properly to be enjoyed, God becomes a sign that points directly to himself, a new use that alone sustains. "'I am the way, and the truth, and the life'; that is, you are to come through me, to arrive at me, and to remain in me.' When we arrive at Him, we arrive also at the Father — since by an equal another equal is known — binding and, as it were, cementing ourselves in the Holy Spirit through whom we may remain in the highest good . . ." (1.34.38).

This way alone can release the futile human grasp on means that pass away rather than ends that never fail, and can even make a place for created human nature at the Father's right hand (1.34.38). It is not just a way out of sin for humanity; it is a way into creation for God himself. "Wisdom himself saw fit to make himself congruous with such infirmity as ours and to set an example of living for us, not otherwise than a man, since we ourselves are men," says Augustine. "Although he is our native country, he made himself

---

ian, 1994): "The most profound reason for the need of revelation is the presence of obstacles before the intelligence which prevent its correct functioning, or more directly the fact that although man is made in the 'image of God' and has a theomorphic being he is always in the process of forgetting it. He has in himself the possibility of being God-like but he is always in the state of neglecting this possibility (p. 23). . . . Man must . . . remember his real nature and always keep before him the real goal of his terrestrial journey. He must know who he is and where he is going. This he can do only by conforming his intelligence to the Truth and his will to the Divine Law *(Sharia)* (p. 27). . . . The Quran is . . . a *furqan* or discrimination in that it is *the* instrument by which man can come to discriminate between Truth and falsehood, to discern between the Real and the unreal, the Absolute and the relative, the good and the evil, the beautiful and the ugly" (p. 49).

29. Nasr, *Ideals and Realities of Islam*, pp. 45-46. Of course, Christians could offer a substantially different portrayal of Judaism: As the prophets realize that the call to prophesy is a death sentence, they see the futility of prophecy alone as a means of salvation, and look beyond their own office to those of the Messiah in their hope for divine deliverance. And so in both Judaism and Christianity, the age of prophecy leads naturally into an age where prophecy is transcended.

also the Way to that country" (1.11.11). Indeed, incarnation does more than merely plot a voyage home; it establishes a home away from home (cf. John 1:14 and 14:6), a dwelling place for God on earth (Eph. 2:22).

From Incarnation to Interpretation: Scripture's Mediating Role

It might seem that in confessing the incarnate Word rather than the prophetic Word as the ultimate signifier, Augustine has foreclosed the kind of Trinitarian ontology of Scripture being proposed here. And he has indeed foreclosed the classical Muslim claim that Scripture is the ultimate divine signifier. But Jesus, the ultimate sign, is not the *only* sign in *On Christian Doctrine*. The book is not Christology as such, but a reflection on biblical hermeneutics that draws formatively on Christology as such. So it is here in the story — and only here — that Augustine places his Analogy of the Word, making explicit the connection between incarnation and discourse that grounds a properly Christological and Trinitarian ontology of Scripture:

> How did he come except that "the Word was made flesh, and dwelt among us"? It is as when we speak. In order that what we are thinking may reach the mind of the listener through the fleshly ears, that which we have in mind is expressed in words and is called speech. But our thought is not transformed into sounds; it remains entire in itself and assumes the form of words by means of which it may reach the ears without suffering any deterioration in itself. In the same way the Word of God was made flesh without change that He might dwell among us. (1.13.12)

One may also compare similar Augustinian statements in *On the Trinity* 15.6.10, Sermon 288, and Sermon 119.7: "Just as my word is offered to your sense, without receding from my heart, so that Word is offered to our sense, without receding from His Father. My word was with me, and proceeded into voice. The Word of God was with the Father, and proceeded into flesh."[30]

One might object that here Augustine is only suggesting another of his many analogies for divine action. This verbal *vestigium incarnationis* would then have no necessarily intrinsic relationship to the Word made flesh. It would just be a useful example. But that is not how Augustinian vestiges operate. The universe is a *signifying* universe, and edifying similitudes and allegories are *always* divinely intended (3.27.38). Furthermore, the speech analogy directly follows references to human knowledge, wisdom, and discourse (1.12.12).

30. Cited in Jordan, "Words and Word," p. 187.

Is Augustine building an ontology of Christian speech in general, or of biblical language in particular? The answer is: both. Augustine's hierarchy of signs is finally exhausted only by creation itself. His cosmology would fall to pieces if some of creation were called insignificant. Yet Scripture is privileged, if only because the use of Scripture is where Augustine intends his analogy to lead. The precise nature of its privilege lies before us, in the doctrines of Christ and Church. But it depends as much on the universality of its language as on the specificity of its divine origin and purpose, so there is no use opposing the two. Besides, what follows Augustine's account of the incarnation of the Word and leads into the rest of his material on biblical interpretation makes the relationship between only-begotten Word and canonical words quite clear already:

> The sum of all we have said since we have begun to speak of things thus comes to this: it is to be understood that the plenitude and the end of the Law and of all the sacred Scriptures is the love of a Being which is to be enjoyed and of a being that can share that enjoyment with us. . . . (1.35.39)

Jordan is right about the importance of the Analogy of the Word in Augustine's theology. It leads from biblical hermeneutics to incarnation and back, both in the logic and in the flow of his argument, because it is the bridge between the two.

The Will of the Father and the Intent of Scripture

The Analogy of the Word connects Augustine's biblical hermeneutics to his Christology and his Trinitarian theology. But the passage above shows that this is not its only use for Augustine. The Analogy of the Word also provides the crucial connection between Augustinian hermeneutics and Augustinian *teleology*. Incarnation tells us as much about the *intent* of Scripture as it tells us about the divine quality of Scripture. And, as the economic Trinity reveals the immanent Trinity, so the intent of Scripture reflects the character of Scripture.

Book 2 of *On Christian Doctrine* concentrates on signs, and right away Augustine distinguishes between "natural" or unintentional signs, and "conventional" or intentional signs (2.1.2–2.2.3). It is the latter variety he pursues, and it is in the latter group that he places all human language, and specifically the words of Scripture, through which the will of God is made known to all the world for its salvation (2.5.6). His claim is that as the flesh of the Son is a divinely intended sign, so the words of Scripture are also divinely intended signs, whose intent is to reveal God's will and to save those who hear and understand.

This "authorial intent" is determinative; "anyone who understands in the Scriptures something other than that intended by them is deceived" (1.36.41). Whether such deception is benign depends on whether it builds up charity; nevertheless, charitable misreadings should be corrected. (Multiple allegorical meanings that accord with "right faith" are a different matter, because they are not misreadings. Augustine says in 3.27.38 that they too are divinely intended, both at the time of inspiration and at the time of appropriation.)

Augustine's affirmation of divine authorial intent should be taken neither as a denial of human authorial intent in the Scriptures, nor as an equation of the human and divine intents. The two overlap but they are not identical, and Augustine is aware (as literary critics are today) that authorial intention can be difficult to prove.[31] This loose relationship removes the apparent contradiction between affirming any charitable (mis-)interpretation, and labeling as deceit any interpretation other than those intended. Scripture arises through human authorial intentions; yet God superintends these in such a way that neither "original" authorial intentions nor later reinterpretations ever limit its meanings.[32] Augustine's proposal is a brilliant way to interpret 2 Peter 1:20-21, which has misled so many bibliologians into endorsing a kind of biblical monotheletism that denies all human intentionality in the inspiration of Scripture.

Why is intention so important? Can the words not stand on their own? Are they not surrendered to their hearers once they are delivered? Ultimately, no: God offers these verbal signs as divinely ordered means of grace, to do God's saving work in a cosmos of confused and manipulated signs. The world's darkness does not overcome their light. Human wills cannot ultimately separate them from their author. After all, the God who orders and maintains them is a Trinity Augustine likens to *memory, intellect, and will,* or to a *lover, beloved, and love* whose intention is to bring creation back into loving relationship with himself.[33]

---

31. See 1.36.40-41: "Whoever finds a lesson [in Scripture] useful to the building of charity, even though he has not said *what the author may be shown to have intended in that place,* has not been deceived, nor is he lying in any way. . . . But anyone who understands in the Scriptures something other than *that intended by them* is deceived, though they do not lie."

32. Compare Stephen E. Fowl's description of biblical interpretation as "underdeterminate," over against modernist "determinate" accounts and postmodernist "anti-determinate" accounts such as Derrida's, in *Engaging Scripture: A Model for Theological Interpretation* (Malden, Mass.: Blackwell, 1998), pp. 32-61.

33. This essay treats Augustine's Trinitarian imagery as fundamentally sound, biblical, and coherent rather than as a betrayal of God as revealed in Scripture. His psychological anal-

Divine intention suffuses the universe and gives its parts their significance. Intention respects the will of the One who sent the Son and Spirit into the world, and thus honors the "Fatherly" aspect of the Bible's Trinitarian shape. The mystery of the Gospel is no less than the newly revealed will of the Father, expressed in the form of words with the power of the Holy Spirit. The alpha and omega of Scripture are simply the love of the Father, Son, and Holy Spirit in their economy of salvation (cf. Eph. 6:23; 1 John 3:1).[34]

Augustine does not leave this divine intention in the abstract. God's intention for Scripture is a saving intention. Scripture mediates nothing less than Christian salvation to its diligent students. So Augustine rehearses a kind of exegetical *ordo salutis* by which the hearer of Scripture is brought into God's presence. The seven steps Augustine outlines in Book 2 by which the hearer of Scripture is brought into the presence of God will be treated explicitly, in terms of soteriology, at the end of Chapter 3.

Scripture as God's Rhetoric

John C. Cavadini claims that *On Christian Doctrine,* and in particular its Book 4, provides "not a treatise on rhetoric per se but on (in effect) the dynamics of conversion," an explication of what it means that God uses the Bible to persuade its hearers unto salvation.[35] So God is the speaker of Scripture, its rhetor; and his rhetorical motive is the saving intent of Scripture. Throughout *On Christian Doctrine,* Augustine finds rhetorical categories fruitful for revealing how Scripture works, precisely because Scripture is God's rhetoric.

The claim that Scripture is God's rhetoric could be used as an alternative structuring principle for this entire project. It comprehends the same fundamental insights of Athanasius' *On the Incarnation,* but with a vocabulary better suited to appreciating both the Trinitarian ontology and the soteriological phenomenology of Christian Scripture. We will briefly tie these rhetorical categories into the concerns of this bibliology, before proceeding to use them to interpret Augustine.

---

ogy of the Trinity and his rendering of the Triune persons in terms of charity in *On the Trinity* are deeply resonant with the roles of divine intention and teleology in *On Christian Doctrine.*

34. This is to affirm with Augustinian tradition that while the external operations of the divine persons are not divided, nevertheless it is possible to appropriate works to specific persons.

35. Cavadini, "The Sweetness of the Word," in Arnold and Bright, *De Doctrina Christiana,* p. 165.

The four basic categories of Aristotle's rhetoric — *logos, ethos, pathos,* and *praxis* — correspond to the central concerns of a systematic bibliology. *Logos* concerns Scripture itself; *ethos,* its relationship with the Triune God who speaks it (corresponding to this chapter); *pathos,* the salvation it confers upon its hearers (Chapter 2); and *praxis,* its saving performance in the context of the gathered and sent Church (Chapter 3).[36] Augustine's insights into the verbal expression of God's saving will give us another perspective on the roles that human language, and especially the human language of Scripture, plays in God's self-involvement with the world.

Here David Cunningham's *Faithful Persuasion: In Aid of a Rhetoric of Christian Theology*[37] is a helpful guide to the structural similarities between theology and classical rhetoric. Cunningham regards all of Christian theology as rhetorical in nature, as a tradition of persuasive argument directed within and without the Church. Even at the level of his chapter titles, what applies to theology in general seems to apply to the Bible in particular:

1. Theoria: Theology and Rhetoric
2. Pathos: The World to Which Theology Speaks
3. Ethos: The Character with Which Theology Speaks
4. Logos: The Word Which Theology Speaks
5. Praxis: Theology as Rhetoric

Despite the similarities, our bibliology in the end follows somewhat different lines. Cunningham enters the hermeneutical circle "from below," with the world to which theology speaks.[38] This project prefers to emphasize the priority of the *divine ethos* that speaks and animates the words of the Bible, for only in the character of God's very being do we stand at the causal and logical foundation of Christian Scripture.[39]

36. See Cunningham (below), p. 18.

37. David Cunningham, *Faithful Persuasion: In Aid of a Rhetoric of Christian Theology* (Notre Dame: University of Notre Dame Press, 1991).

38. Again, this is not to deny the validity of such an approach, or of its other alternatives: One could also begin with *praxis,* using biblical practice as the best (or only) epistemological ground for a doctrine of Scripture. Or one could begin with *ethos,* in the persons of the human writers of Scripture in their original historical contexts (assuming both of these can be historiographically recovered). Beginning with the *logos* itself, with the corpus of revelation contained in Scripture, is perhaps the most popular approach in Protestant systematic theology. All these approaches have strong arguments to commend them.

39. For a moment, Cunningham himself endorses the ultimacy of God's character as an ethical authority: "In the Christian tradition, the ultimate 'character reference' is provided by God. One argument is authorized over another because it is claimed to be God's argument,

Biblical Truth as Divine Ethos

A speaker's character is itself a means of persuasion, mediated by his or her argument but more than the words of the argument itself. Aristotle even claims that "moral character may almost be called the most potent means of persuasion."[40] Fundamentalists express rather the same sentiment when they claim of the Bible, "God said it. I believe it. That settles it." So does Paul when he refuses to accept the finality of Israel's rejection of Jesus the Messiah, against growing empirical evidence, on account of the irrevocability of God's call (Rom. 11:29). The moral authority of the Bible is conveyed not simply by the holiness or power of its human speakers (and at times these are scarce indeed), but by the holiness and power of its divine agent. In Scripture, God gives us his word — in the common sense of "one's word" as one's promise, backed by nothing less than the integrity of one's own character, and putting that integrity in jeopardy until one's word is kept.

The intrinsic connection between the divine *ethos* and the biblical *logos* means two things for a Trinitarian bibliology. First, it means that God is literally invested in the words of Scripture. Second, it means that in speaking, God puts himself at risk.

To say that God is literally invested in Scripture is to say that its character is his character. Such an investment goes far beyond issues of the Bible's propositional inerrancy. God's oracles of promise are as true as God himself (cf. Rom. 3:2-4). The Bible's truthfulness is the very truthfulness of the one who proclaims, "I am the truth" (John 14:6).[41] Its life is God's life. Its blessings and curses are the oaths of the Lord himself (cf. Heb. 7:20-22, on Ps. 110:4).

How this ethical investment transcends categories of propositional truth is vividly illustrated in the story of Jonah, where the word of the Lord comes to Jonah (3:4): "Another forty days, and Nineveh shall be overthrown." The anti-Ninevite prophet pouts when pagan Nineveh's repentance leads *God* to repent of his own threat. God's failure to live up to the criteria of cognitive-propositional truth-claims displeases Jonah exceedingly, and he prays angrily:

---

rather than a human being's. The authorizing character of God's speech is a central feature of the witness of both the Old and New Testaments" (*Faithful Persuasion*, p. 103). But this is a passing reference in a chapter otherwise devoted to the role of the human *ethos* in rhetoric.

40. Aristotle, *Rhetoric*, 1356a4-13, quoted in Cunningham, *Faithful Persuasion*, p. 98.

41. On the personal nature of Christian truth, see Bruce D. Marshall, "'We Shall Bear the Image of the Man of Heaven': Theology and the Concept of Truth," in L. Gregory Jones and Stephen E. Fowl, eds., *Rethinking Metaphysics: Directions in Modern Theology* (Cambridge, Mass.: Blackwell, 1995), pp. 93-117.

"I pray you, Yahweh, isn't this what I said when I was yet in my country? That is why I made haste to flee to Tarshish; for I knew that you are a gracious God and merciful, slow to anger, and abounding in steadfast love, and repent of evil" (4:1-2). In other words, the word of prophecy is tied so closely into God's own character that it shares in his grace, mercy, and steadfast love — even up to the point where it can become propositionally false. Or, as Augustine would put it, because knowledge is the servant of charity (and not vice versa, 1 Cor. 13:8), the interpretation that serves charity is a divinely intended one. Jonah 3:4 is, of course, true — but it is true in the context of God's character and saving purpose, not Jonah's.

Here ethical categories suggest an important nuance to George Lindbeck's famous contention that the crusader's battle cry "Christus est Dominus" is a false statement, even though the same statement in other contexts may be true. Lindbeck is right that statements like these "are false when their use in any given instance is inconsistent with what the pattern as a whole affirms of God's being and will," and that therefore they "are true *only* as parts of a total pattern of speaking, thinking, feeling, and acting."[42] But that pattern is determined by God's self-investment in the words "Christ is Lord." The crusader's "confession of faith" is still true. It will presumably rebound to his eschatological judgment (cf. 1 Cor. 11:29).

Similarly, "forty days and Nineveh shall be overthrown" is the very Word of the Lord, delivered by a prophet and in a context entirely of God's choosing (3:1-2). The statement's *prima facie* falsehood is not caused by the cultural-linguistic context in which it is spoken, but by the dissonance between the *ethos* of its divine speaker and the *ethos* of its human speaker. With respect to God's will to show mercy, Jonah's statement is true and bears rhetorical fruit in Nineveh's repentance. With respect to Jonah's hatred of Nineveh, it is false, failing to come to pass. The result is an ambiguous conventional sign that is open to great variety in interpretation. A theorist of rhetoric would say that it invites a dispute (Is Jonah a false prophet? Is God a liar?) that forces the audience to rely on ethical rather than merely logical judgments to evaluate the truth. Thus Jonah's prophecy needs clarification according to God's character and purpose. For Augustine, this is made clear elsewhere in Scripture: It is the rule of faith, *i.e.*, divine charity. God's *ethos*, not the prophet's, is decisive for interpretation.[43]

---

42. George Lindbeck, *The Nature of Doctrine* (Philadelphia: Westminster, 1984), p. 64: "When thus employed, [the confession] contradicts the Christian understanding of Lordship as embodying, for example, suffering servanthood."

43. The will of the *author* of the *canonical* book of Jonah is another matter, as we shall see below.

The story itself warrants such an account of biblical truth, for both the King of Nineveh and Jonah interpret the prophecy according to the rule of faith. That is why the one is repentant, and the other angry. The fact that Jonah speaks a different "cultural language" than the King, and does so to destroy Nineveh rather than to save it, is immaterial. The truthfulness of Jonah's proclamation, and of all of Scripture, is in the end a function of its relationship with God's character and purpose — with its *divine* ontology and teleology. (This is another reason to ground bibliology first in the doctrine of God rather than anthropology, or salvation-history, or any other theological *locus*.)

Balthasar defines human speech as the "free manifestation of one's inner personality to others in significant sounds." From this definition he concludes that a speaker's word "reveals, if it is true, the very constituents of his being." It shares in its speaker's truth, freedom, and personality, initiating a communion or intercourse between people, a sharing of oneself to others (pp. 80-81). As God's words in human words, the Bible lies at "the center of the divine utterance" (p. 86).

The intrinsic connection between *ethos* and *logos* in the Bible makes it possible to apply divine attributes analogically to the words of Scripture, because they are God at his word, verbal symbols of the Lord who causes them. *Ethos* names the entire range of characteristics that describe how one lives.[44] To confess the Bible's divinity is to understand it in terms of God's character. This means that Scripture reflects God's truth, immutability, mercy, compassion, justice — and ultimately faith, hope, and love. Above all, it means that Scripture reflects these qualities as revealed in Jesus Christ, who as the interpreter and revealer of God in creation, is also the authoritative interpreter of Scripture (Matt. 7:28-29). The question of biblical authority is ultimately a matter of Scripture's participation in God's character, ultimately a question of its divine ontology (though we shall see throughout the rest of this project that its human character is no less important).[45]

Biblical Kenosis: *God's Word Put at Risk*

This ultimacy of divine character and intention is often taken triumphalistically, as a straightforward affirmation of the divine power of Scripture. Such affirmation would deserve a sympathetic response from other canonical

44. Cunningham, *Faithful Persuasion*, p. 99.
45. See also Cunningham, *Faithful Persuasion*, p. 101.

traditions such as Islam. But for Christians, the divine ontology of Scripture implies a Trinitarian ontology in which Scripture does more than simply reflect God's communicable attributes. Athanasius and Augustine have both narrated Scripture as a means of God's *self*-involvement in the world, somehow analogous to his personal involvement in the incarnate Jesus. This leads us to the second implication of God's literal investment in Scripture: In speaking, God puts his *ethos* in jeopardy.[46] The exchange between *ethos* and *logos* runs in both directions. Scripture is God accountable. This takes bibliology beyond a merely revelatory vision of God's economy and into a covenantal, incarnational, and messianic one. It takes us from a "bibliology of glory" to a "bibliology of the cross."

In Book 1, Augustine calls Jesus a voyage home: the beginning point, means, and endpoint of Christian pilgrimage (1.34.38). The Supreme Sign must capture the fleeting attentions of idolaters in their fallen world of semiotic babble, and hold their attention throughout the journey. (We will see a similar focus in Eastern Orthodox iconology, in its view of an image as a means of ascent to the image's prototype.) For Augustine the flesh of the Son captures the attentions of materialistic sinners, and holds them while God is transforming those transfixed by the image. The dreadful implication is that the Son must be delivered into the hands of sinners.

In Book 2, Augustine treats the words of Scripture in the same way: Sacred Scripture was set forth in human languages "that it might be known for the salvation of peoples who desired to find in it *nothing more than* the thoughts and desires of those who wrote it and through these the will of God, according to which we believe those writers spoke" (2.5.6, emphasis mine). The Bible is part of our voyage home, a point of departure for idolaters and a means of sustenance for weary pilgrims. And that must mean that in delivering it to the world, God makes his words vulnerable, for a time, to abuse.

When God gives "his word," when he covenants with his own creatures, he puts his integrity at stake. He pours himself and his reputation into his words. He trusts the treasure of his Gospel to the earthen vessels of human language (2 Cor. 4:7), not unlike the way he trusts his eternally begotten Son to mortal flesh born amid cultural depravity. What Augustine says of the incarnate Word applies, by virtue of his Analogy of the Word (though in a weaker sense, to be distinguished below), to the biblical word:

---

46. "At risk" or "in jeopardy" need not imply indetermination or open-endedness in the outcome of God's acts. God's self-investment in creation plays a part in both visions of providence.

Wisdom himself saw fit to make himself congruous with such infirmity as ours. . . . Since we do wisely when we come to him, he was thought by proud men to do foolishly when he came to us. And since when we come to him we grow strong, he was thought to be weak when he came to us. But "the foolishness of God is wiser than men; and the weakness of God is stronger than men." (1.11.11, quoting 1 Cor. 1:25)

In the same way that the Word was made flesh without change in order to dwell among us, Augustine claims that the thought of a speaker is assumed in the infirm words of human language without suffering change, transformation, or deterioration (1.13.12). His analogy might yield a complete (and heretical) *identity* between the Word made flesh and the Word made words — except that Augustine stops short of describing Scripture as the *point of arrival* in the way that he describes the Son.[47] Instead, he bravely claims that a saint filled unshakingly with faith, hope, and charity "does not need the Scriptures except for the instruction of others" (1.39.43).[48] While Scripture participates somehow in the Word's self-involvement in the world, and particularly in the beginning and middle of the Christian journey, it is not another incarnation of him. Nevertheless, these two sojourns of the Word are similar enough to allow us to adapt Christological categories for bibliological use.

In denying change, transformation, or deterioration, Augustine is clearly affirming what will be the central point of Chalcedon: Incarnation truly unites Creator and creation, without making Creator *contingent upon* creation.[49] The newly incarnate Word is still somehow the same yesterday, today, and forever (Heb. 13:8). The ability of Christ's flesh to save and the biblical word to reveal absolutely depends upon this. If the *logos* were to have changed in any way, God's self-involvement in the course of humanity would simply have replaced the old chasm with a new one.

Nevertheless, the history of the earthly Jesus is the story of the eternal Word brought into the fallen world and put at its mercy (Mark 14:41). In the same way, God's investment in the words of Scripture means that in the shorter term, in their own sojourn into the world, the divine words are sub-

---

47. This points to the eschatological nature and context of Scripture, to be discussed in Chapter 3.

48. We will evaluate Augustine's point at the end of Chapter 3.

49. So Augustine's doctrine of incarnation resists the occasional tendency in modern kenotic thought to blur the lines between necessary Creator and contingent creation. See in particular John Thompson's critiques of kenotic excesses in *Modern Trinitarian Perspectives* (New York: Oxford University Press, 1994), pp. 44-63.

ject to a similar submission to and separation from their heavenly speaker, and a similar surrender to sinful speakers, hearers, and readers.[50] Following Balthasar, we may call the treatment they endure a kind of linguistic *kenosis*.[51]

As soon as God speaks into the world, even before the Fall, he allows his promises to be put to the test and subjected to distortion: "Did God say, 'You shall not eat of any tree of the garden'?" (Gen. 3:1). From the beginning the serpent, the father of exegetical fallacies, is putting God in the double-bind of Athanasius and Anselm: Either punish and be thought a failure, or do nothing and be thought unjust. Early on in the covenantal relationship, God's people too discover the leverage God's linguistic *kenosis* gives them, and take advantage of it. Moses on Mount Sinai sees the double-bind and brings it to God's attention when God threatens to annihilate faithless Israel and start afresh with him (Exod. 32:10-14). He does it again when Israel is intimidated by the spies' report of the Canaanites and prepares to desert the Lord, and a fuming God is ready to extinguish Israel and make Moses the father of his own great nation (Num. 14:1-12). There too, Moses responds,

> If you kill this people as one man, then the nations who have heard of your fame will say, "Because the Lord was not able to bring this people into the land which he swore to give to them, therefore he has slain them in the wilderness." And now, I pray, let the power of the Lord be as great as you have promised. (Num. 14:15-17)

Both of these brave intercessions cause God to repent (enthusiastically, one suspects) of the evil he intends for Israel — because Moses has caught God in his own promises. The divine *ethos* is at stake in Israel's survival. God's reputation will suffer if he destroys his covenant people. What choice has God but to forgive?

In covenantal language we see God binding his character to human words — dwelling in them, in effect, even in the face of human ignorance, misinterpretation, and manipulation. The kenotic character of Scripture is a function of the Analogy of the Word. While we may recognize it as a quality of biblical language already in the Pentateuch, we of course can name it

---

50. "Which of the prophets did not your fathers persecute?" (Acts 7:52). "Rejoice and be glad, for your reward is great in heaven, for so they persecuted the prophets who were before you" (Matt. 5:12).

51. Balthasar, *Explorations in Theology*, p. 80: "God speaks to man from within the world, taking man's own experiences as a starting point, entering so intimately into his creature that the divine *kenosis*, to be fulfilled later in the incarnation, already has its beginning in the word of the Old Testament."

"kenotic" only after having seen *kenosis* in its hypostatic form, in the person of Jesus Christ.

The common *kenosis* of inspired Word and incarnate Word offers an answer to one of the sharpest questions facing any bibliology that draws on the Analogy of the Word: Where are the limits of a Christological or Trinitarian bibliology? Where does it break down? Or, as Karl Barth framed the question, can there be a real relationship between the infallible Word of God and the human words of Scripture? Our answer will involve a long detour into the most influential bibliology of the twentieth century.

III. Barth: The Threefold God and the Threefold Word

Barth is the most famous (and infamous) modern theologian for developing a Christological and Trinitarian bibliology that asks such questions. He treats these issues in the aborted *Göttingen Dogmatics,* then again at great length at the beginning of his *Church Dogmatics,* and continues to face them throughout his theological career. His answers have set the terms of twentieth-century doctrines of Scripture. So *CD* Volume I is the next source for our bibliology.[52] There we will explore the shape of Barth's Analogy of the Word. Ironically, Barth's greatest usefulness for this project is not as a resource for developing a Christological doctrine of Scripture — Athanasius and Augustine have already done this — but as a resource for expanding it into a properly Trinitarian account of the Bible. We will present Barth's Trinitarian bibliology in detail, then evaluate it from the "patristic" perspective of Athanasius and Augustine.

Barth devotes an entire volume of *Church Dogmatics* to the doctrine of the Word of God, and at least four sections (4 and 19-21) explicitly to the question of the relationship between God and Scripture. This material is a deeply detailed discussion of the interrelationship among God, Scripture, and Church. Barth's doctrine of Scripture in terms of the threefold Word of God in §§4 and 19-21 poses both promise and pitfalls for a bibliology that associates the doctrines of God, salvation, Church, and Scripture in a way that each sheds light on and strengthens the others.

Barth recognizes the danger of linking the doctrines of God and Scripture so closely: Just as the necessary task of exegesis runs the risk that the church will imprison the Bible and silence the witness that confronts it

---

52. This analysis does not feature material from the *Göttingen Dogmatics,* in order to respect the development of Barth's thought between the two projects.

(I.1.106), so the use of a theology of Scripture might smother the biblical witness under a defective theology. Nevertheless there is nothing to do but see the danger for what it is, and move on in spite of it.

Barth treats Scripture in terms of two strongly guiding features. The first is its existence as the second of three forms of the Word of God (who is the second person of the Trinity, I.2.675). This conviction, brought out in §4, structures the rest of *CD* I, and becomes the umbrella under which is brought all the material of §§19-21. Under this umbrella Barth treats three aspects of Scripture, each of which roughly corresponds to a person of the Trinity. The second feature is the uniqueness of Scripture as the second form of the Word, and the consequent uniqueness of its own Trinitarian qualities. These two features of Scripture cannot be separated, however much the patristic, medieval, Catholic, and Neo-Protestant "heresies" want to do so.[53]

Scripture as the Second Form of the Word of God

The threefold form of the Word of God is the logical extension, developed in §4, of a phenomenology of Scripture. Barth characteristically begins with the data of the Church's own experience, in this case the canon that has time and again confronted the Church. Though the idea that the Church would stand on itself rather than some other foundation is "reasonable" (I.1.100), we in fact know that the Church is *not* self-constituted, because Scripture exists in the first place; that it is the *canon* — the standard — indicates that it is the Church's primary access to revelation.[54] The Bible is the only foundation on which it stands ("built upon the foundation of the apostles and prophets," Eph. 2:20a; cf. I.2, 520).[55] If the *proclaimed* Word of God were canonical, then

53. Unfortunately, Barth's own polemic against Catholic and neo-Protestant ecclesiology unavoidably brings issues of ecclesiology into the discussion that would better be left until Chapter 3's ecclesiology of Scripture. Treating them here must draw us into the argument to some extent.

54. Here Barth adopts the characteristic, Western vision of canon as epistemic norm to which William J. Abraham objects in his *Canon and Criterion in Christian Theology* (Oxford: Clarendon, 1998), pp. 363-90. This characteristic of Western theology is treated at greater length in Chapter 3.

55. Barth, of course, does not consider apostolicity to be an inherent attribute of the Magisterium: Apostolic succession "must mean that [the Church] is guided by the Canon" in its proclamation; see I.1.104. He is true to form, and right, in insisting that the very existence of Scripture as canon indicates its nature. But it is legitimate to criticize Barth for making one possible interpretation of "canon" normative for his entire treatment. That one thing exists as a standard for others does not indicate that the other things derive their similarities from

it would be the canon. But in fact it was the Bible that "imposed [impressed] itself upon the Church as such, and continually does so," and so it is the Bible that is the canon.[56] Any question seeking to extract a more central source of authority within the Bible, such as the historical data underlying it or the existential responses to God's action on its writers, is an inappropriate search for another canon beyond the canon.

Yet after this faith claim has been made unqualifiedly, the legitimate question arises of *what impresses itself through the canon*. Barth finds this to be the *content* of Scripture, which is the witness of God's self-revelation in Jesus Christ, the Word of God in its first form (I.1.107, 119). This witness so confronts the Church that the Church *must* in turn proclaim what it has heard. Thus proclamation — the Word of God in its third form — arises as an activity distinct from Scripture but dependent upon it (I.1.108). Scripture itself, then, is the Word's second form, through which the Church is made able to recollect in its third form that first form to which Scripture points (I.1.109, 112). The first form causes the second (I.1.115) and third (I.1.117). Only only knows any one of these through the others. Thus there is no bypassing the witness of Scripture, nor are there alternative forms of witness to God's revelation that do not derive from the Bible itself. The three are neither separable nor supplementable (I.1.120-21).

Having begun with the three forms of Jesus the Word of God, Barth quickly ties them together by making clear that they are not three words of God but one. This triunity of divine revelation is a true *vestigium trinitatis*. In fact, it is the only true vestige of the Trinity available. The only analogy Barth can offer for the threefold Word is the Trinity itself (I.1.121), and vice versa.[57] The exclusivity of this analogy is reasonable according to Barthian suppositions, for the existence of a worldly vestige of the Trinity must be a possibility in order for humans to conceive of the Trinity. And when God is *wholly other,* the only truly possible worldly vestige would have to come from the definitive form God's revelation takes in the world: Jesus, his biblical witnesses, and the Church's proclamation of those witnesses (I.1.339).

Therefore the importance of this analogy for Barth cannot be taken too lightly, for the threefold form of the Word of God can be the only available analogy to the doctrine of the Trinity. There are simply no *vestigia trinitatis* to be found in the world other than the threefold form of Jesus, Scripture, and

---

the standard, only that it is that to which they are compared and normed. Scripture need not be the Church's only access to God's saving presence in order to be its normative form.

56. I.1.107. A better translation of *imponieren* would be "to impress" rather than "to impose," since there is no compulsion involved.

57. See §8.3, Vestigium Trinitatis (I.1.333ff.).

proclamation in which God has revealed himself (I.1.347). Any analogue to God must be a direct result of God's revealing act; it cannot be a coincidental correspondence, like a spring-stream-lake or sun-rays-heat. This is a profound observation that strongly supports some form of Trinitarian ontology for Scripture.

Barth understands the idea of the *analogia entis* to vest an essential Trinitarian disposition immanently in created objects "quite apart from their possible conscription by God's revelation." Any such immanence would undermine the grounding of theology in revelation alone, and suggest that the Christian doctrine of the Trinity does not in fact describe a wholly other God, but a purely human construction, even "a mere cosmology or anthropology" (I.1.334-335). Thus the uniqueness of the threefold Word of God and Barth's rejection of the *analogia entis* go hand in hand. The aptness of this lone analogy is all Barth will offer as support for his exposition of the Word of God in its threefold form, and given Barth's methodology, the threefold form of the Word of God becomes the central evidence for his doctrine of the Trinity.[58]

If this is so, then it is rather surprising that when Barth treats the question of Scripture in *Church Dogmatics* I.2, he does so in *three* sections rather than one, each of which subtly but explicitly corresponds to one divine person's presence through the Word of God in Scripture: §19 to the Father, §20 to the Son, and §21 to the Holy Spirit. How can *one* form of the Word of God warrant three such treatments? Yet the arrangement makes sense if one treats these three aspects as descriptions of the *relationships* among the forms of the Word, analogous to the relationships among the divine persons. Together these sections comprise an intricate Trinitarian bibliology: "The doctrine of the triune God had to divide into the doctrine of the incarnation of the Word and that of the outpouring of the Holy Spirit. The same division will be necessary to understand the reality of its certification and transmission by Holy Scripture" (I.2.539). Hence the Trinitarian structure of §§19-21: God is revealed for the Church (§19) through the work of the triune God: objectively through the incarnation of the divine Word in Jesus, which effects the authority of Scripture in the Church (§20), and subjectively by the outpouring of the Holy Spirit, which effects the freedom of Scripture in the Church (§21) (I.2.538). Section 19 concerns the divine action that causes the Bible as revelation; §20 concerns the authority of the Bible for the

---

58. Here Barth puts himself firmly in the theological tradition that considers the immanent Trinity to be knowable only as the economic Trinity. God is known in the act of savingly revealing himself; the understanding of the forms of God's self-revelation is the understanding of God *in se*.

Church, which is Jesus' own Lordship mediated solely through it; and §21 concerns the life, power, and freedom of the Bible in the Church, all features of the presence of the Spirit in Scripture. Thus Holy Scripture, though only one form of the Word of God, mediates God's presence according to Barth's doctrine of the Trinity, in the Trinitarian correspondence he finds between God and God's Word.[59]

These three Trinitarian dimensions to §§19-21 are subtle and overlapping. And one should expect as much, in order for Barth's theology of Scripture to be truly Trinitarian, rather than just a superficial and defective facsimile, whether crudely dispensationalist or monarchian or reflective of any other defective conceptions of God.[60] For instance, one of the inevitable complications of the overlapping trinitarian patterns that Barth treats throughout *CD* I concerns the inspiration of Scripture. This is a matter of the relation between the Bible and the Holy Spirit, as Barth himself states (I.2.514). Thus it is somewhat misleading for Barth to treat it formally in a long digression under §19 (I.2.514-526). Yet under no section would the topic neatly fit, for it is through inspiration that God reveals, prophesies, rules, and rebukes (see, *e.g.,* Joel 2:28/Acts 2:17-18; 2 Tim. 3:16; 2 Pet. 1:21), and these dominical functions are more properly acts of the Son or even the Father. To draw absolute boundaries around the functions of Scripture and assign them exclusively to one or another person of the Trinity would yield a modalist bibliology, not a truly Trinitarian one.

Only here and there does Barth hint that Scripture's source, authority, and freedom are analogues to the Father, the Son, and the Holy Spirit; and only rarely does he explicitly compare them. Yet under the surface, the analogy bears enormous weight, not only in supplying the only available vestige of the Trinity, but also, in structuring §§19-21, in framing and guiding Barth's

---

59. Barth's Trinitarian reasoning runs as follows: "The truth and force of Holy Scripture in its self-attesting credibility is itself . . . a single and simultaneous act of lordship by the triune God, who in His revelation is the object and as such the source of Holy Scripture. But if we ask how this truth confirms itself to us . . . then without denying the unity of the divine Word we have to distinguish between that which enlightens and those who are enlightened, between something objective and something subjective. . . . Only by making this distinction can we see them together as is needed, and therefore understand the reality of the witness to revelation in Holy Scripture, i.e., grasp it in the possibilities actualized in it. By attempting to grasp these possibilities as such, *we repeat, as it were, on a lower level the division into the doctrine of the incarnation of the Word and that of the outpouring of the Holy Spirit.* The possibilities are — objectively the authority of Holy Scripture instituted in the Church . . . and subjectively the overruling freedom of Holy Scripture in the Church . . ." (I.2.539, emphasis added).

60. On this point Barth shows indirectly how other triadic theologies of Scripture or hermeneutics may be less trinitarian than they seem.

doctrine of Scripture. This usually implicit relationship becomes both the central strength and the central weakness of his thought for our efforts to understand Scripture and God in each other's terms.

Barth's methodology is a great strength in that his phenomenology of the threefold Word (developed in §§4-6), phenomenology of Scripture (developed in §§19-21), and exegetically derived doctrine of God (developed in §§8-12) become mutually supporting. Close correspondence between them is exactly what one should require of a valid trinitarian bibliology. Even more profound is simply Barth's deep appreciation that the Bible participates strongly in the work of God in the Church and in the wider world. If only in this one way, Barth would be valuable in pointing the way toward a renewed understanding of the close relationship between the Triune God and God's written Word.

Barth's Analogy of the Word

These are the strengths and weaknesses of Barth's theology of Scripture at their broadest. An adequate treatment of it demands detailed examinations of all three sections of Barth's bibliology, comparing it to the more patristic (here meaning "Athanasian and Augustinian") conception of the relationship among God, Bible, and preaching examined above. At various points Barth's bibliology is congruent with, superior to, and inferior to the patristic bibliology. The main difference between the two is that the patristic alternative is less averse to the *analogia entis* because of its stronger sense of the lingering, once fading, now resurgent presence of the *logos* in fallen and restored creation. All sacramental modes of divine presence — Bible, baptism and communion, the Church itself, and doctrine, to name a few — mediate the real, saving presence of the Triune God. These are not *signa* of *signa*, or *signa* of *signa* of *signa*, but simply *signa*, for wherever God is present, he is present "absolutely."[61] Thus the patristic vision agrees that the Bible truly mediates the Triune God, but differs in how it sees the Bible as a unique means of God's presence in the present Church and in the wider world.

In §19, "The Word of God for the Church," Barth concentrates on the Bible's relationship to the form of the Word of God that "precedes" both proclamation and Scripture: God's revelation (I.2.457). Barth takes over Augustine's language of God as *res* and Bible as *signum*, reading "sign" in a

61. Cf. Barth on I.2.583: Even Scripture is "only a sign. Indeed, it is the sign of a sign, i.e., of the prophetic-apostolic witness of revelation as the primary sign of Jesus Christ."

strong, sacramental (I.1.88-189) sense.[62] The Bible's sign-ificance makes God's Lordship a present *fact*, which becomes the basis — for Barth, the sole basis — of obedience. There is no questioning this fact or looking for its grounds; by definition God's revelation may only be grounded in God himself (I.2.458). Any justification of biblical authority jeopardizes that obedience (I.2.461-462). Christians simply respond in faith, hearing in the Word of God the voice of their shepherd. Those believers whose words are preserved in Scripture were the privileged respondents to that revelation, which happened in the past and will happen in the future, but does not happen in the present.[63] Thus their obedient responses are the church's (only) extant "witnesses of revelation," which means that (only) Scripture is "in the power of the revelation of the Word of God attested by it" (I.2.459), the sole foundation for authority (§20) and freedom (§21) in the Church (I.2.462).

Barth's analogy — incarnate Son as sign of the Father, Bible as sign of divine revelation — leads him to speak immediately to the question of the Bible in its written form. For Barth, the writtenness of Holy Writ corresponds to its humanity, its holiness to its divinity. Barth clearly understands this as a Christological analogy for Scripture.[64] Thus the Bible is not half-human, half-divine; it is fully both. Its words are human words just as Jesus' flesh is human flesh; but the words are *made* holy. That holiness points them towards their *res*, revealing, albeit only "in some degree," their object (I.2.464-465). Because of that holiness this accommodation and limitation do not problematize the Bible's claim to reveal; "what we hear is revelation, and therefore the very Word of God" (I.2.473). So it is not open to scrutiny based on the foreign anthropological assumptions of "scientific" historical-critical readers (I.2.467). Nevertheless it is inclusive of all humanity, just as Jesus' humanity is representative of all humanity. And so, because of the *analogia fidei*, the revelation of God in its verbal forms draws all human speech "into the darkness and light of its mystery," interpreting all human words by its own, self-derived hermeneutic (I.2.471, 468). Just as Jesus is the paradigm for humanity, so the Bible becomes paradigmatic for written words (and presum-

---

62. "In contrast to Roman Catholicism and Protestant modernism, we felt that we ought to take this sign seriously" (I.2.457). The priority of the Word leads Barth to consider it sacramental (along the lines of the Eucharist) even after abandoning the idea of the sacramentality of baptism.

63. In this respect the early Barth might be called a cessationist. One wonders how he might have appraised the rise of Pentecostalism and the wider Church's charismatic revival.

64. "There is no point in ignoring the writtenness of Holy Writ for the sake of its holiness, its humanity for the sake of its divinity. We must not ignore it any more than we do the humanity of Jesus Christ Himself" (I.2.463).

ably, proclamation becomes paradigmatic for spoken words), in the end bestowing upon them their only hope for true meaning. Here Barth's insight is
profound: Hermeneutics is not the science of reading the Bible the way we
read texts in general, but of reading the Bible and then other texts along the
terms set by the Bible itself in its mediation of God's revealing, saving presence. Anthropocentric hermeneutics produce no end of innovative readings;
but they would point the biblical sign away from the object to which it is
pointing during the event of revelation.

The Word's divine claim on humanity means that wherever God's Word
is truly heard, it compels its hearers to repeat it. Crucially for Barth, this repetition is nothing other than the Word of God itself, though in a different
form. The Gospel preached is the Gospel heard, which is the authentic Gospel
of Jesus (I.2.491). Only insofar as the Gospel's hearers repeated it in writing
— not in their brilliance or personality or rhetorical facility — are they also
holy (I.2.491). The Gospel is simply the Word of God, in "indirect identity"
(I.2.492), and thus it demands that it be interpreted on the terms of its own
witness, not in anthropological or purely literary or purely historical terms.
One could hardly state the divine ontology of Scripture more basically: The
Word of God is not to be found encrypted within the biblical text nor recovered from the historical events beneath it; it is the witness to Jesus Christ of
the text itself (I.2.494). Interpreted in any other way than this, the Bible is
simply human words, "a historical document for the history of ancient Israel
and its religion, in so far as it is also a document for one aspect of the religious
history of Hellenism and can therefore be used as a collection of historical
sources" (I.2.495-496).

The Divine Transcendence of "Indirect Identity"

Yet this indirect identity is never to be confused with a *direct identity*. For
Barth, such a confusion would be equivalent to confusing the natures of
Christ.[65] This makes the Bible's character as the Word of God one of genu-

---

65. "It is quite impossible that there should be a direct identity between the human
word of Holy Scripture and the Word of God, and therefore between the creaturely reality in
itself and as such and the reality of God the Creator. It is impossible that there should have
been a transmutation of the one into the other or an admixture of the one with the other.
This is not the case even in the person of Christ where the identity between God and man . . .
is an assumed identity . . . and to that extent indirect. . . . When we necessarily allow for inherent differences, it is exactly the same with the unity of the divine and human word in Holy
Scripture" (I.2.499).

ine witness. To Barth, this implies indirectness, distance, limitation, and perspective, even error and fallibility. (It also introduces a Christological inconsistency in Barth's Analogy of the Word, which we will explore below.) Yet along with these comes the joyful awareness that something greater is available: "the best, the one real thing, which God intends to tell and give us and which we ourselves need" (I.2.507).

The Bible's mediation of the Word of God makes the Bible truly alive, and thus not subject to the decisions of even the Church: "It is not for us or for any man to constitute this or that writing as Holy Writ," even for the men who originally declared the individual Scriptures canonical. Their decisions were merely acknowledgments of what already was the case (I.2.473). Throughout *Church Dogmatics* Barth stridently opposes any claim for the Church's power or authority that does not derive from Scripture and subordinate itself to it. The authority is so asymmetrical that the Church's decisions on the canon must forever remain open, as Barth claims they effectively have throughout its history.[66] Here Luther's famous subjection of *all* the biblical books (not just those at the margins) to Christological testing meets with Barth's tacit approval, and the canon is even open to the Church's extension of it beyond its present borders (though only to include further genuine prophetic or apostolic witness, such as some Pauline letter to the Laodicians) (I.2.478).

Thus neither the diachronic nor the synchronic variety of the Church's canons is a problem for Barth. Nor is either one an indicator of the Church's control of Scripture, but an indication of the very opposite. The "fluidity of the basic text," the existence of multiple textual traditions even across languages rather than our possession of original autographs, "belongs to the human and therefore the divinely authoritative being and character of Holy Scripture, to the freedom of the Word of God in relation to its readers and expositors"[67] (I.2.602). These ecclesial qualities of the Scriptures are all simply manifestations of indirectness and no more. Their value is purely negative, in that they preserve the utter transcendence of the One the Scriptures reveal. For the early Barth the Bible's humanity is deeply relevant to its divinity — but only for the infinite qualitative difference it offers between its revelation and the Revelation himself.

---

66. See I.2.475-479. "The insight that the concrete form of the Canon is not closed absolutely, but only very relatively, cannot be denied even with a view to the future" (I.2.476).

67. Presumably this renders much textual criticism inappropriate, for it judges the biblical text according to external grounds. The Septuagint, the Vulgate, even the Majority Text are expressions of the freedom of the Word of God. It is conformation and standard-setting, not diversity, that is the enemy of divine sovereignty.

The Church is in right relationship to Scripture not when it plays the role of judge but when it plays the role of witness (I.2.481). By analogical extension, the same is true of the competing theories of the Trinity: Cappadocian, Augustinian, and social trinitarian theology show not that God is a construction of theologians, but that theologians are imperfect witnesses to the true Triune God who forever eludes their categories. Theology's limits are themselves signs of God's sovereignty, not humanity's.

Section 19 is a lengthy unpacking of the primary strength of Barth's doctrine of Scripture: his acceptance of the Bible's Christological character and thus its ability, though only in the event of revelation, truly to mediate Jesus' presence and, through him, the presence of the Father, in spite of whatever problems might be involved in the veiled unveiling of this divine Word in purely human words.

Obedience and Freedom: The Two Hands of the Word of God

Section 20, "Authority in the Church," is at its heart an extended discussion of Christ's Lordship through the Bible. "To say that Jesus Christ rules the Church is equivalent to saying that Holy Scripture rules the Church" (I.2.693). According to Barth, authority in the Church is the objective, dominical aspect of the revelation of God's Word in the Church. Scripture, which is the Christological expression of the Word of God, is the normative authority for the Church, because while the revelation of God is the "original" form of the Word of God, Scripture itself is the most "primitive" form present to the contemporary Church, the oldest extant record of the Church's witness. Therefore the Bible's authority is unique and singular (I.2.540). But because of the lack of total unity between the humanity and divinity of Scripture, because of the indirectness of its identity with the Word, the Bible's authority is only "mediate, relative, and formal." Scripture remains subject to the higher authority which is the true and original Word of God, and which is known by the Church on the grounds of faith. "The real obedience of the Church is to an authority which has to be distinguished from Holy Scripture, to something immediate, absolute and material, which has to be sought or has already been found side by side with or even beyond Holy Scripture" (I.2.540-541). As we shall see, the distinction between divine Word and human words leads to different answers among the Church's various traditions on where that immediate authority is to be found, and how to understand its relationship with Scripture. We will return to the topic in Chapter 3. In the meantime, Barth's affirmation of the Bible's supreme authority in the Church is powerful testimony to the Lord's saving presence in and through Scripture. For Barth, as for Athanasius and Augustine, Scripture's saving work could only be rooted in its divine character and purpose.

The freedom of Scripture (§21) as its subjective counterpart to obedience (I.2.662) should not be considered *the Church's* power of subjective appropriation of the Bible. The Spirit makes the biblical Word of God alive and free, its own subject (I.2.684-685). For Barth, the Bible's objectivity is the Christological aspect of Scripture, which commands obedience, while its subjectivity is its pneumatic aspect.[68] Barth's treatment of the third divine person's involvement in Scripture completes his bibliology and proves its truly Trinitarian structure: not just in featuring fatherlike, sonlike, and spiritlike qualities, but in showing in detail how the Triune God accomplishes his divine economy of salvation through the Bible (I.2.673).

The Spirit is the Spirit of Jesus, and so the Spirit's role in Scripture is never to be taken as independent of the Son's. The Spirit is not a divine freelancer; and so the relationship between freedom and obedience is every bit as close as the relationship among the divine persons (I.2.666). Neither undermines the other. Barth, writing ten years before Orwell in an increasingly fascist Europe, can still say that through the Word, and only through it, "obedience is freedom" (I.2.670).

God's gifts of obedience and freedom manifest themselves, in §20 as the authority of the Church, in §21 as the true freedom of the Church. In order for this to be true freedom, it must be a freedom entirely contingent upon and under the Word of God (I.2.669), and thus (for Barth) entirely contingent upon and truly under Scripture. This subordinate freedom means that while the Church is compelled to appreciate (I.2.666) and repeat (I.2.671) its freedom, it may never try to hold onto or duplicate it. The prophets and apostles are "copies attesting the freedom of Jesus Christ Himself, but at the same time they are prototypes attesting the freedom of all human faith and witness in the Church founded by their Word." Nevertheless — or therefore — the Church may not appoint "successors" to the apostles or prophets any more than it may continue to write Scripture, for the relationship of the prophets and apostles to their Lord was a unique one (I.2.671).

Thus Barth's vision of Scripture's role in the Trinitarian economy of God's redemption becomes apparent: Scripture, though strongly analogous

---

68. "Just as God in His revelation is the Holy Spirit no less than the Son, so God's Word in Scripture is Spirit no less than Word. . . . As the Son can be revealed only by the Spirit, and in the Spirit only the Son is revealed, so authority must necessarily be interpreted by freedom, and freedom by authority" (I.2.666).

only to the second person of the Trinity, in fact bears a fully Trinitarian image, having a form of revelation, a form of authority, and a form of freedom, all of which truly reflect the revelation, authority, and freedom of the Triune God himself. And Scripture in turn conforms the Church to its image, lending the Church its own revelation, authority, and freedom. In their respective forms of witness, Scripture and Church are made signs that participate in and reflect that to which they witness (I.2.669).

This signifying relationship in turn means, for Barth, that only Scripture can bestow the image of the Triune God upon the Church. And such bestowal is never permanent. It never becomes autonomous. The fact that the Church's freedom can exist only under the Word (I.2.671) means it does so only and entirely under Scripture (I.2.673). This is perhaps where §4's Trinitarian correspondence between revelation, Scripture, and proclamation comes in, for that correspondence is unique. The Bible cannot be substituted, paralleled, or copied any more than there can be more than one Son. Both Jesus and Scripture are *monogenēs*. No one stands alongside the Son, and so nothing stands alongside the Bible.

Evaluating Barth's Proposal

Barth's explicitly Trinitarian structure complements the patristic bibliological vision, drawing out points in which Athanasius and Augustine could be further developed very fruitfully. (Indeed, Balthasar does exactly this, as we shall see.) And a major feature of Barth's proposal is startlingly like a feature in both Athanasius and Augustine: the prominence of the Analogy of the Word.

But Barth's vision remains quite different, most notably in two respects: first, his stress on revelation as necessarily an "event" of limited duration in time and space; and second, his rejection of any kind of redeeming presence of the *logos* mediated otherwise than by Scripture. In combination, these features of Barth's theology beget several bibliological problems that call for correction by other theologians.

A Vestige of Which Trinity?

The first and foremost problem in Barth's proposal is that classical Trinitarian categories do not suggest quite the vestige of the Trinity that Barth proposes. In the Bible's own witness Jesus Christ is not one *form* of the *logos*, but the *logos* himself. The Word of God is not analogous to an *ousia* subsisting in three *hypostases.* He is himself a *hypostasis.* By making the Son the Word in its first form, and positing two derivative forms according to a "trinitarian" pattern, Barth has given the Word his own Father-like relations of begetting and breathing. Furthermore, the Bible usually discusses Scripture not in terms of the Son, but in terms of the Holy Spirit. The most direct texts on the nature of Scripture, 2 Timothy 3:16 and 2 Peter 1:20-21, treat Scripture not as *logikos* but as *theopneustos.* The Spirit is associated equally with Bible and proclamation. Finally, if we apply the analogy to the Trinitarian relations (as the Trinity's only true vestige should) and not just to the general concept of threeness, then saying that the Church's proclamation is "(only) a sign of (only) a sign," is, in Trinitarian terms, like saying that the Holy Spirit proceeds *only* from the Son, as if the Nicene claim that the Spirit proceeds from the Father could be formally dropped without material effect. In other words, Barth's rather artificial distinction between "Scripture" and "proclamation" demands Trinitarian analogies that are too forced. In each of these ways, what Barth calls the "close correspondence" between the threefold God and the threefold Word has severe limits. It neither reflects the relations among the divine persons, nor respects the Bible's stress on the Holy Spirit in Scripture's economy.

These are fundamental criticisms of Barth's entire doctrine of Scripture. Do they defeat Barth's general insight that Scripture is a vestige of the Trinity? Fortunately, they do not, because what is truly vestigial in Scripture need not be what Barth takes it to be. The patristic alternative refuses to draw the correspondence among the persons and the "threefold form of the Word of God" as linearly as Barth does. One need not claim that the Spirit proceeds only from the Son (or from the Son at all) in order to confess that the Spirit is truly the Spirit of Jesus. Athanasius and Augustine can honor the involvement of all the Trinitarian persons in all divine actions in the world, without making the earthly Jesus (and by extension the written Bible) the universal channel through which all other grace must proceed, and the Holy Spirit (and by extension the Church's oral proclamation) a necessary but entirely secondary channel.

If Revelation Is an Event, Why Does Scripture Cite Scripture?

According to Barth, as preserved witness Scripture incompletely but truly testifies to God's *future* and *past* revelation in Jesus Christ. Its witness is primary and necessary to the life of the present-day Church only because of the absence of direct revelation in the present. Barth's scheme respects God's transcendence and the Bible's primacy in ages lacking prophets and apostles, but it has trouble accounting for the prophets' and apostles' own reliance on the second form of the Word of God. It fails to explain the roles Scripture played when direct revelation *was* in the present. Those birthing the New Testament writings (whether as writers, shapers, or redactors), presumably acting under the direct influence of divine revelation, still find it important to interact deeply with the preserved witness of the Jewish Scriptures. Why? Why would Paul, a witness to God's very presence (1 Cor. 15:8), care so deeply about interpreting Scripture in his letters? Above all, why would Jesus himself bother to practice Scripture? Why should the Church have found its preserved witness so formative in helping it understand Jesus even when he was right there with them?

As we shall see in the next chapter, the problem is even more acute when one considers the formative role Israel's Scriptures played in the life of the maturing Jesus (Luke 2:41-52). During the Galilean's childhood, the roles are radically reversed, and past revelation tutors present Revelation! How can this be?

The patristic vision has its own explanation for the phenomenon of New Testament exegesis of the Old. Both mediate the same God; they depend upon each other; and neither conflicts with the other. "Present presence" does not bypass preserved presence nor render it redundant. In fact, because both are presences, preserved presence is no less normative. "New spirits," even the Holy Spirit himself (1 John 4:2-3), even the Son (John 5:39), can thus be tested. Scripture thus has functional, but not ontological, primacy over present and future revelation.

The Union between Divine Word and Biblical Words

The "eventness" of Barthian revelation has a further consequence of much greater import to our Trinitarian ontology of Scripture, for it controls the relationship Barth sees between the Word of God and the human words of Scripture. Barth entertains two inconsistent conceptions of the indirectness of the identity between the two. On the one hand, it rehearses the difference between the two united natures of Christ (I.2.499). On the other hand, it rehearses the distinction between Jesus' united natures and the single human nature of the apostles and prophets (I.2.500). Since Barth has already compared the relationship between the first and second forms of the Word to the relationship between the *Father* and the Son, both of these are odd characterizations. Yet even beyond that, the two are not equivalent.

When the first way is taken, the result is indirect *identity,* the noun receiving the greater weight. The witness's two natures are united after the way Jesus' divinity and humanity are united: "In the relationship between Jesus Christ and the apostles there is therefore repeated or reflected in some degree the economy of the incarnation of the Word" (I.2.487). The analogy with incarnation extends (though with qualification) even to the unity of natures as Chalcedon describes it.[69] Thus the Bible, "the Word of God in the sign of the word of man," can properly be called the Word of God (I.2.500).

Barth takes the Analogy of the Word in the second direction, which stresses the *indirectness* of the identity. This other direction is more problematic. Barth develops indirectness so that it explicitly allows for the existence of fallibility and error on the part of the witnesses (I.2.529). Exegetes who look for errors and inconsistencies even in the realm of faith and practice can find them. For according to Barth it is not in its own substance that the Bible is free from these, but only in the *miraculous event* that bypasses them through faith (I.2.507). The Bible's humanity is imperfection, its divinity perfection; we believe when miraculously God chooses that we hear the divine Word *in spite of* the vulnerability and capacity for error that are a part of the Bible's humanity (I.2.508-509). This has the advantage of countering some of what Barth calls the "docetic" doctrines of Scripture that characterized the patristic, medieval, and Protestant Orthodox eras without resorting to the opposite Christological error of "Ebionitism" to which liberal Protestantism fell prey (I.2.520, 526).

In treating the relationship between the Bible's humanity and its inspiration in terms of docetism and Ebionitism, Barth has appealed to Nicene categories for understanding the Bible. He has fallen back on the Analogy of the Word. Yet his commitment to revelation as always and necessarily an event soon takes away the power of the Nicene analogy. In the face of the text's humanity, Barth makes the miracle of Scripture's truth an event in the present, in the continual "removing of an offense which is always and everywhere present" (I.2.529). Such a miracle makes the presence of God's Word in the Bible not "an attribute inhering once for all in this book as such," nor identical to it, but a divine *use* of the Bible here and now, "as an instrument in the hand of God . . . like the water in the Pool of Bethesda" (I.1.111). This happens — and here Barth follows Nestorius rather than Cyril — when he claims that the inaccurate, contradictory, uncertain, (particularly) Jewish words of the Bible are

---

69. "[Confusion of natures] is not the case even in the person of Christ where the identity between God and man . . . is an assumed identity . . . and to that extent indirect. . . . When we necessarily allow for inherent differences, it is exactly the same with the unity of the divine and human word in Holy Scripture" (I.2.499).

"*adopted* and made use of . . . in all their fallibility" (I.2.531). Each time the exegetical waters stir, the relationship between the Word of God and the words of men becomes another temporary adopting of the latter by the former. Only in this way is the relative, mediated witness made absolute and immediate (I.2.694). Only for the duration of the event do the signs of the words of men truly point to the Word of God (cf. I.2.500). Outside of that special presence, the Bible's words merely signify the historical figures and objects of an ancient Near Eastern religion. They are signs of things, but not signs of the Word.

It jeopardizes Barth's entire Christological analogy to the Bible, and therefore his entire Trinitarian doctrine of Scripture, to posit a Christological Analogy of the Word, then drop the hypostatic union from that analogy. If the Bible has Christological qualities, then there must be some verbal analogue to the hypostatic union. If there is, then there is no reason to appeal to the single nature of its apostles and prophets. If there is not, then one wonders why Barth, the "most relentlessly Chalcedonian of all Christian theologians,"[70] would resort to Christological categories at all. Replacing verbal union with verbal adoption replaces repeated or reflected incarnation with inspiration, which as Athanasius insists, is something else entirely. If the Word is not in some respect circumscribed in the words, if Chalcedonian categories do not apply analogically to the Bible, it is disingenuous to criticize competing doctrines of Scripture as being docetic or Ebionite.

This discontinuity raises the problem of how inspiration then figures into Barth's Trinitarian analogy. Does this continual adopting mean the Bible is only inspired in the miraculous event? Yes and no, depending on one's eschatological perspective. Yes, because inspiration simply means the faulty text "is as such used by God and has to be received and heard," and "in relation to the concrete text and no less concretely to ourselves, it is a matter of the event or the events of the presence of the Word of God in our own present" (I.2.533). No, because the Bible's inspiration happened "once and for all in the resurrection of Jesus Christ and in the outpouring of the Holy Spirit, as the establishment of the Church" (I.2.535). The texts were inspired not in the writing, but in the new creation itself. So on the one hand inspiration involves *only* illumination, only the concrete text used by God in the present; and on the other hand it happened long after the Tanakh was a concrete text yet before the New Testament texts existed at all. How these two perspectives are to be understood together, or even separately, Barth leaves unclear.

This divine adopting of the human texts produces what one could call a Calvinist doctrine of Scripture — but named after the cartoon character

---

70. Wolterstorff, *Divine Discourse*, p. 64.

rather than the French Reformer. Calvin's little pet tiger Hobbes speaks, walks, acts, and guides him; but all the while the rest of the world mistakes him for just a stuffed animal. Of course, Hobbes *is* a stuffed animal; he is never transformed into something other than a stuffed animal. He is fully stuffed and fully alive — not all the time, but only when he is miraculously made present to Calvin. Yet it is always Hobbes, and not some other stuffed animal, that animates, because the continuity between episodes of Hobbes's animation lies in the stuffed animal's election once and for all. The jaded world around him might call Hobbes's consciousness merely a figment of Calvin's imagination, but Calvin himself does not have it in his power to animate Hobbes, let alone anything else. An adult might take the tiger from his owner, subject him to various tests — even open him up and show Calvin the stuffing — to prove to the little boy who Hobbes "really is." But Calvin knows better. Hobbes might look for all the world exactly like a construction of his imagination — no one has any reason to think otherwise — but Hobbes's presence compels Calvin to know differently. He is "not allowed to doubt in face of the forces of human subjectivity" (I.2.534). Nor can he even point to any other datum to support the reality of Hobbes's life (I.2.535), for any such datum must itself derive from the presupposition that Hobbes really is alive (I.2.536).

There can be no falsifying Barth's doctrine of Scripture any more than there can be a falsification of Calvin's doctrine of Hobbes. This section of *Church Dogmatics* is a perfect example of Lindbeck's contention that "theoretical frameworks shape perceptions of problems and their possible solutions in such a way that each framework is in itself irrefutable."[71] The only way to evaluate this kind of claim is to ask whether Barth's circular reasoning is so tight, his circle so small, that it has indeed excluded "other grounds for the authority of Scripture" (I.2.536) that he cannot accommodate. Barth will be content to answer, in the same way that he ends §19 by answering D. F. Strauss's similar criticism,[72] that (true) Protestantism's refusal to enlarge the circle makes this "its weakest point, where it can only acknowledge and confess, it has all its indestructible strength" (I.2.537).

Barth's system is a consequence of his insistence that the Analogy of the Word breaks down at the point of union between the divine Word and human words, because the hypostatic union of divine Word and the human

---

71. Lindbeck, *The Nature of Doctrine*, p. 10.

72. "Who can now attest the divinity of this witness? Either itself again, which is nobody: or a something, perhaps a feeling or thought in the human spirit — this is the Achilles' Heel of the Protestant system."

flesh of Jesus is outside the analogy. That conviction honors above all God's overriding transcendence, a hallmark of Barth's dialectical thought, his Kantian philosophical heritage, and his Calvinist tradition.

If we respect the intentional nonfalsifiability of Barth's bibliology, we can still evaluate it according to its logical consequences. When we do so, the problems that surface in Barth's account are grave. In fact, they seem to threaten the very idea of a Trinitarian bibliology, because no other major theologian's doctrine of revelation ties the doctrine of Scripture so thoroughly to the doctrine of God.

The Word of God and the Word of Jesus: A "Barthian" Critique of Barth

One feature of Barth's account (and many others' accounts as well) both casts it into doubt and suggests a fruitful alternative: Barth's (in)attention to Jesus as Scripture's historical source. Because prophets and apostles have only a human nature, Barth claims that revelation occurs when their human words are temporarily adopted as the Word of God. What then are the words of *Jesus?* They are the words of someone whose humanity *is* one with God, whose humanity *is* taken up into the glory of God (cf. I.2.500). "Heaven and earth will pass away, but my words will not pass away" (Mark 13:31). If Jesus' words were *not* truly the Word of God, then all that he would have been and done would not be truly revelatory. Indeed, he would not truly have been the Word made flesh except for the fact that "because he is Word, and, as Word, took flesh, he took on . . . a body consisting of syllables, scripture, ideas, images, verbal utterance and preaching."[73] Since Jesus is truly Word made flesh, his words (whether preserved in writing or not) *are* truly the Word of God in human words, without qualifiers. Dominical sayings are authoritative for Jesus' disciples simply because Jesus said them, no questions asked (cf. 1 Cor. 7:25).

The speech of Christ is the logical point of departure for a truly Christocentric exploration of the second and third forms of the Word of God. Astonishingly, Barth pages over this one certain instance of fundamental, direct identity between the Word of God and the words of human beings, and begins instead with the concept of Scripture as a secondary, extrinsic, derivative apostolic witness to Jesus Christ.[74]

73. Balthasar, *Explorations in Theology,* p. 149.
74. So does Barth's son Markus, in spite of the fact that he grasps precisely this point! In

Can one really build an account of all Scripture on the foundation of Jesus' own words? Are not his Old and New Testament witnesses still *mere* witnesses to the one, unique manifestation of divine-human speech in the created order? They are not. When identifying God's Word and human words, one must center on the actual words that come from Jesus' lips. But one cannot stop there. For conceding the point that Jesus' words *are* truly the Word of God in human words begins a chain of reasoning that leads in a totally different direction than Barth's own thinking in *CD* I. We will follow it in greater detail in Chapter 2, but we must preview it briefly here.

First, consider *what* Jesus speaks so often in his career: Holy Scripture. Jesus commonly speaks biblical language as his own words. Where he reinterprets these words, he does so to intensify rather than dilute them. Their indirectness of revelation may be said to become directness in Jesus' own mouth. So as the direct speech of God we find the *citations* of Jesus alongside the *sayings* of Jesus.

Nicholas Wolterstorff, in a brief review of Barth's doctrine of the Word of God, grasps the heart of the issue. For Barth, Jesus is unqualifiedly the Word of God. He is intrinsically God's revelation. By contrast, human words, Scripture or otherwise, are at best extrinsic to divine revelation. They must be taken up in the moment of revelation.[75] Thus "the Bible is not God's book; God did not speak by way of the authoring of these books nor by way of the assembling of them into a canon. God speaks by way of a human being only if God *is* that human being — Jesus Christ."[76] But when Jesus opens his mouth and speaks Scripture (whether Old Testament or New), Barth's distinction evaporates. The boundary between intrinsic and extrinsic revelation dissolves.

---

the same book in which he denies a Christological analogy in Scripture and pursues a pneumatological account of authority, he later reads Hebrews as claiming that "what God the Son says to God the Father, or to a congregation, is as much the word of God as what the Father says to the Son, or the Spirit to Israel. It is because of Jesus Christ that the whole of the Old Testament, including the human voices of God's chosen people, may be called 'Word of God.' . . . The interpreter who seeks faith in Jesus Christ will also seek to understand the words of men as Word of God the Son" (*Conversation with the Bible* [New York: Holt, Rinehart and Winston, 1964], p. 216). Again, summing up: "Through Jesus Christ the highest word was brought down to earth and said in a human voice; the most desperate human cries were placed (!) in the mouth of the Son of God" (p. 296). This insight, the germ of a thoroughly Trinitarian account of Scripture, helps Barth formulate his entirely proper account of Bible as "dialogue" among God and humanity, but it never causes him to question the single-nature ontology he has already developed.

75. Wolterstorff, *Divine Discourse*, pp. 64-66.
76. Wolterstorff, *Divine Discourse*, p. 70.

Furthermore, when Jesus quotes Scripture, he does it as *canon.*[77] Jesus does not quote as if appropriating sources on sinful human hopes and aspirations that eventually match his own message (indeed, this is just what the devil tempts him to do in the wilderness). Instead, he re-lives Israel's divinely ordained life (Deut. 6–10) with perfect integrity. He shows no indication of favoring some of the divine words over others. As a faithful Jew, his tacit endorsement of Tanakh is complete (Matt. 4:4; 5:18). *All* of its words are his.

Then how can the biblical passages he does not quote be any more *indirect, extrinsic,* or *derivative* forms of true revelation than those he does? Anyone who affirms that only Jesus' spoken words are truly the Word of God, or even affirms it only of the words of Scripture repeated in Jesus' own mouth, "red-letterizes" the Bible, subjecting it to the very "separation" and "gradations" that Barth rightly abhors (I.2.496) — and with full dominical precedent: "You have heard it said . . . but I say to you" (Matt. 5:21-22, etc.).[78] Such an account ironically yields a doctrine of revelation that is more Muslim than Christian.[79]

77. William Abraham's exploration of the canonicity of Scripture has the same point of departure as Barth. He spends only several sentences in his entire project on the Jewishness of the particular Christian understanding of canon (p. 28). Substantively, he begins his exploration of canonicity with the process of the *New Testament's* canonization, rather than with Israel's canonical institutions or Jesus' concrete treatment of them. He treats the concept of Old Testament as emerging only after Marcion, rather than from a dynamic in Jesus' career that unfolds in the apostles' appropriation of Israel's Scriptures.

By beginning with the Church rather than its Lord or his nation Israel, Abraham can distinguish between canon and criterion, and claim that "before there was any epistemology, any canon, and any community, there was Pentecost, and before Pentecost there was the work and ministry of Jesus Christ" (p. 466). But whether or not there was such a thing as epistemology in first-century Judaism or its predecessors, there emphatically was *a* canon, and *a* community. Without them, the work of Jesus and the event of Pentecost are not only unintelligible, they are impossible. Chapter 2 details this point theologically and historically.

78. Then there is the problem of the authenticity of Jesus' words as recorded in Scripture. In order for them to enjoy direct identity with the Word of God, must they be quoted directly, or paraphrased, or translated, or is inference itself enough? At what point does directness become indirectness?

79. Consider a question a modernist Muslim poses to Christians: "Would Christian theology be willing to say that the discourse of Jesus Christ in Aramaic (and not Greek; *the distinction is important*) at a precise time and in a precise place on Earth is related to God the Father as the Qur'anic discourse in Arabic transmitted by Muhammad is related to the Archetype [or "Mother"] of the Book retained in the presence of God transcendent?" Mohammed Arkoun, *Rethinking Islam* (Boulder, Colo.: Westview, 1994), p. 32, emphasis added. To Muslims, Jesus' words are the Word of God because he is a Messenger of God. The relationships between the Word of God and the words of Paul, or the Gospel writers, or of Jesus' words in translation are fundamentally different.

This is to miss the interplay in which Jesus and Tanakh authorize each other. The one life that is truly divine and human is the one life that fulfills Israel's Scriptures. And the one life that conquered through faithfulness to Tanakh is the one life authorized to proclaim the end of history (Rev. 5). The canonical shape of Jesus' life means the Christian canon is not simply a matter of a community creating a text, or a text creating a community, or even each creating the other. All these affirmations are true — true of Christians, Muslims, Mormons, university departments of literature, Star Trek fan clubs, and U.S. Senate committees. But these affirmations are only theologically *defensible* and *coherent* for Christians because, above all, the Christian canon is the canon *of Jesus.* When Gerard Loughlin claims that "the Scripture makes the Church and the Church makes the Scripture; they are mutually constitutive," he leaves out the one ultimate creator of both, who alone keeps bibliology after modernity from drifting into fideism.[80]

Jesus' career does more than endorse the Tanakh. He transforms it. As Jesus takes John's baptism and makes it his own, new baptism, and as Jesus takes the Passover and makes it the Lord's Supper, so Jesus takes Tanakh and creates the Old Testament (and not the "Hebrew Bible," nor the "First Testament," nor the "Jewish Scriptures"). In the central events of his ministry — at Jerusalem's east gate, at the Temple, and in the Upper Room — Jesus reads the texts of Scripture as referring to himself.[81] Chapter 2 explores in greater detail what we may call Christ's "institution" of Scripture. Here we need only notice that just as Jesus' institution of baptism and Lord's Supper opened up room for the Church's further transformation of these rites in Jesus' remembrance, so Jesus' institution of the Old Testament creates room for a transformed hermeneutic of Israel's Scriptures, and for inclusion into the canon of inspired texts that remember him. In instituting the Old Testament, Jesus also authorizes a New Testament.[82]

---

80. Gerard Loughlin, *Telling God's Story* (New York: Cambridge University Press, 1996), p. 36, adapting Paul McPartlan's similar language about Church and Eucharist. The matter is treated again in Chapter 3.

81. The canonical recollection of each of these events survives rigorous historiographical scrutiny (for instance, in the work of E. P. Sanders). Though historical criticism is not constitutive of Christian Scripture, it does witness to Christian Scripture's dominical constitution.

82. As we will see in Chapters 2, 3, and 4, Jesus' use of Scripture also authorizes a new hermeneutics towards Old and New Testaments alike. This is well captured in David Dawson's *Allegorical Readers and Cultural Revision in Ancient Alexandria* (Berkeley: University of California Press, 1992), where Dawson compares the allegorical reading strategies of Philo, Valentinus, and Clement of Alexandria. Where the ultimate authority for Philo is the preexistent text of Tanakh (what Muslims call "the Mother of the Book"), and the ultimate

Jesus' own words preserved in those New Testament texts (whichever they are, whatever one regards as authentic preservation in the precanonical tradition-history of the New Testament) are truly God's speech, truly the Word of God in human words. So the actions of the earliest Church indicate (1 Cor. 11:23-25). This is not simply because Jesus is divine in an abstract sense, but because he is the Spirit-anointed Son: "For he whom God has sent utters the words of God, for it is not by measure that he gives the Spirit" (John 3:34). And the earliest Church was also apparently confident that in the Holy Spirit, in its role mediating Jesus' speech to itself, its own speech was also, truly, Jesus' speech (John 16:12-15; 20:22-23; Matt. 10:19-20; 18:18-20). And why should they not have been? The same Spirit who brought the Word of God to the apostles and prophets brought it to Jesus' own lips: "The Spirit of the Lord is upon me, because he has anointed me to preach good news to the poor" (Isa. 61:1, in Luke 4:18). Jesus' prophethood is a spiritual gift he shares with his community. Thus, despite Jesus' uniqueness, his inspired words are no more divine than those of the apostles and prophets. Not only Word-Christology, but also Spirit-Christology, bears upon the divine humanity of New Testament Scripture — as we shall see below.

Barth's central equivocation in his Analogy of the Word is an "infinite qualitative distinction" between the infallible Word of God and fallible human words. Both the Son's incarnation and his baptismal anointing with the Holy Spirit annihilate that distinction. The investment of God the Father, the humanity of God the Son, and the indwelling of God the Holy Spirit revolutionize the transcendence of the God who speaks.

The Later Barth and His Implications

In the years following the publication of *CD* I, the revolutionary implications of incarnation continued to unfold in Barth's theological vision. There is reason to believe that the changes in Barth's own thinking about the nature of

---

authority for Valentinus is a *gnōsis* that transcends all texts and personalities, the ultimate authority of Scripture and pagan literature alike for Clement is the personal *logos* of John 1 and Justin Martyr's Middle Platonist Christology. Philo's "revisionary appeal to a 'first text'" is thus distinguished Christologically from Clement's "appeal to a 'first voice'" (p. 206). The authority of Jesus Christ warrants Clement's "final domestication of radical Christian *gnōsis*" under the Church in Alexandria (pp. 218, 222). His Christocentric transformation of both Scripture and Tradition warrants the transformation of Hellenistic Alexandrian allegory into the truly Christological, ecclesiological fourfold allegory of later orthodox Christianity, which we will briefly examine in the Afterword.

revelation since *CD* I have fundamental implications for his doctrine of the threefold form of the Word and his trinitarian analogy for divine revelation, particularly with respect to the Bible.

In *CD* IV.3 Barth explicitly affirms the existence of true words outside the Church. The implications of Christ's work outside the Church are two: "parables of the kingdom," which arise as miracles from "the strange interruption of the secularism of life in the world," meaning the reconciling activity outside the Church of Jesus, the light of life (IV.3.117, 118, 135), and "lesser lights," nature's own words that arise from the theater of Jesus' life and work which is creation itself (IV.3.139, 137).

When Barth alludes to the threefold form of the Word of God in §69's "The Glory of the Mediator," without any special flourish he adds a subtle but revolutionary qualifier to his old schema:

> By a lengthy detour we are thus brought back to the theme of the Prolegomena to the *Church Dogmatics*, to the doctrine of the threefold form of the Word of God as revealed, written and proclaimed. In this context, we cannot establish, develop and present it again as is done in detail in *C.D.*, I,1 and 1,2. In explication of the present question [of the "other true words" outside the Church] it is enough to say that, recalling our earlier conclusions, we should simply maintain that alongside the first and primary Word of God, and in relation to it, there are *at least* two other true words which are distinct yet inter-related in the above-mentioned sequence. (IV.3.114, emphasis added)

Recall that the two strongly guiding features for Barth's treatment of Scripture in *CD* I are its existence as the second of three forms of the Word of God, whose effects manifest a Trinitarian pattern of revelation, obedience, and freedom; and the uniqueness of Scripture as the second form of the Word, along with its own Trinitarian qualities. The new assertion of "at least" three forms of the Word destroys the one all-important analogy between the forms of the Word and the divine persons — unless there are "at least" three persons of the Trinity. What has happened?

Apparently Barth has spent the years between Vol. I and Vol. IV reflecting more deeply on the nature of the Word's role in creation and redemption.[83] Along the way Barth has come to realize a ramification of the incarna-

---

83. This shift is still evident even if we accept Bruce McCormack's criticism of Balthasar's *Theology of Karl Barth: Exposition and Interpretation* (San Francisco: Ignatius, 1992). McCormack claims that Barth's theological trajectory is not characterized by a shift from a dialectical to an analogical approach to theology, but that a "critically realistic dialec-

tion that had not been as obvious to him in the heat of his battle against anthropocentric nineteenth-century liberal theology: that "[in God's] deity there is enough room for communion with man. . . . God requires no exclusion of humanity, non-humanity, not to speak of inhumanity, in order to be truly God. . . . His deity *encloses humanity in itself.*"[84] This follows from the significance of the eternal hypostatic union of Jesus' two natures.[85] So *The Humanity of God* seems to return to Barth's first, Chalcedonian, way of conceiving indirect identity between human and divine: "there is only *one* analogy to the humanity of God in this respect, namely, the message of the great joy — which comforts but in so doing really judges — which is prepared for man by God and which he in turn may have in God."[86] The Gospel itself reflects the unity of human and divine in Jesus Christ. This has far-reaching implications for all human God-talk, for Christology brings up "the *correspondence* — here the concept of analogy may come into its right — of our thinking and speaking with the humanity of God."[87] In III.2 Barth begins speaking of the problem of God's unknownness rather than the problem of his knownness, explaining it in terms of sin rather than human limitation. This new perspective marks the rest of *Church Dogmatics* to an extent that would be shocking in the context of the discussion in I.2: "The world in which [the community] has to work has not been abandoned by Him even apart from the action or assistance of the community," says Barth; "it is not wholly destitute of the Word which the community has been set among it to proclaim" (IV.3.115).

Athanasius could not agree more: "The incorporeal and incorruptible and immaterial Word of God comes to our realm, howbeit he was not far from us before. For no part of Creation is left void of him: he has filled all things everywhere, remaining present with his own Father." Likewise, Athanasius believes the *logos'* redemptive activity not only restores whatever

---

tical theology" marks Barth's career from *The Epistle to the Romans* through the end of the *Church Dogmatics*. For McCormack, Barth's major shift is from a time-eternity dialectic to an anhypostatic-enhypostatic dialectic, which occurs in 1924, long before the shift in emphasis between the volumes of *Church Dogmatics*. If this is so, then the shift we sense from *CD* I to *CD* IV (and which Barth admits in *The Humanity of God*) is a deepening appreciation for the enormous implications of the anhypostatic-enhypostatic dialectic. See Bruce L. McCormack, *Karl Barth's Critically Realistic Dialectical Theology: Its Genesis and Development* (Oxford: Clarendon, 1995), pp. 366-67.

84. Karl Barth, *The Humanity of God* (Richmond, Va.: John Knox, 1960), p. 50.
85. Barth, *Humanity*, p. 46.
86. Barth, *Humanity*, p. 61.
87. Barth, *Humanity*, p. 52.

is lost from sin, but transforms creation so that the Christian capacity to know and speak of God surpasses that even of humanity before the Fall.[88] While Barth continues to reject the term *theosis,* or divinization, for this process of restoration and reconciliation, preferring to speak of "conformity to God, i.e., an adapting of man to the Word of God" (III.2.238), with respect to the knowability of God through the divine revelation the two doctrines are virtually identical.[89]

That God *is* really revealed even outside the Churchly sphere of his redeemed creation is another reason that Barth's strict threefold typology for the forms of the Word of God breaks down, and its analogy to the doctrine of the Trinity goes with it.[90]

However, the qualification of his earlier trinitarian scheme is not fatal to our own Trinitarian ontology of Scripture, for our bibliology's Trinitarian structure does not follow the early Barth in reflecting a unique analogy between Father-Son-Spirit and Jesus-Bible-Proclamation.[91]

Lessons from Barth

Then what is the lesson of I.1 and I.2's long exercise in developing the doctrine of the Word of God in its threefold form? There are several major lessons, all of which discipline and enrich our alternative account of God's saving Triune presence in Scripture.

First, it demonstrates an instantiation of the trinitarian structural principle that George Hunsinger finds in Barth's doctrine of God, in which "the 'whole' is understood to be included in the 'part' without rendering the other 'parts' superfluous."[92] Barth's argument in §§19-21 may be "trinitarian" only in this sense, but this remains an important and valid sense: The different forms of God's Word are still God's Word, and none of them is redundant.

---

88. Athanasius, *On the Incarnation* 8.1, 16.3, 18.4, 45, and 54.3.

89. "The idea that in Jesus Christ human beings are brought into an 'ontological kinship' with God is an idea that comes within a hair of the traditional Eastern Orthodox understanding of salvation as 'divinization' *(theosis)."* George Hunsinger, *How to Read Karl Barth* (Ann Arbor, Mich.: University Microfilms International, 1989), p. 202. It should be noted that the hair's breadth remains significant to Barth!

90. This of course calls into question the early Barth's doctrine of the Trinity; but that critique is beyond this project's scope.

91. Wolterstorff shows at any rate that the phenomenon of Scripture is not intrinsically important to Barth's doctrine of revelation (*Divine Discourse,* p. 64).

92. Hunsinger, *How to Read Karl Barth,* p. 103.

Any of God's signifiers truly signifies, and as a signifier it need not be subordinated or privileged relative to others (though it may be *tested* according to previously acknowledged signifiers, such as canonical Scripture). This takes the Protestant principle of *sola Scriptura* in a patristic direction, though without betraying its spirit.

Second, §§19-21 develop Barth's profound point that all God's acts of revealing himself are triune activities (if they are truly self-revelatory) and thus take triune forms, in fact being the necessary causes of any true *vestigiae trinitatis* that Christian theologians for ages have sought and found. This is Barth's way of affirming the intentionality and divine ontology of signs that Augustine is so concerned about, and the necessary self-involvement of the *logos* in any of his interventions as described by Athanasius (creation, sending the prophets and apostles, and the Word's own incarnation). Barth's intuition that Scripture repeats and reflects — *participates* in — the work of the Trinity is fundamentally correct, even if we must develop it in a different way. And his insight that the phenomena of any true vestige will necessarily correspond to one's doctrine of the Trinity is a powerful methodological check for any examination of one in terms of the other.

Third, Barth's practice of locating Scripture in the divine economy of salvation, in the life of the Church and the world, profoundly respects the fact that a theology of Scripture refers to the *economic* Trinity, God-for-us rather than simply God-*in-se*. Barth's return to this Christian conviction after centuries of modern neglect makes him a modern pioneer of narrative bibliology.[93] Categories of creation, atonement, ecclesiology, and eschatology are deeply relevant to theological reflection on the work and nature of Scripture. This relevance carries our bibliology from the intransitive quality of revelation in Chapter 1 to its transitive and reflexive qualities in Chapters 2 and 3. It also means that an alternative trinitarian bibliology can accommodate many of the particulars of Barth's own treatment without being committed to the whole. Because their underlying metaphors are grounded in the trinitarian economy, Barth's "trinitarian," "Chalcedonian," and "Hegelian" formal patterns (whose underlying metaphors are incarnation, crucifixion, and resurrection)[94] make much of the material in *CD* I compatible with alternative trinitarian ontologies and soteriologies of Scripture.

Fourth, while Barth is weak where evangelical bibliology is strong — in the attention he pays to the original *inspiration* of prophets and apostles — he is strong where evangelical theology is traditionally weak: in his focus on the

---

93. Fackre, *The Doctrine of Revelation*, pp. 133-34.
94. Hunsinger, *How to Read Karl Barth* p. 103.

Holy Spirit's role in *illumination.*[95] Biblical authority is more than historical events, original autographs, and humanly intended meanings "behind" the texts in their present form. Barth's inattention to original inspiration leaves him open to critique by the very people who need most to hear what he does affirm: that the text as it stands is still an indispensable product and medium of the Holy Spirit's work of new creation. This is so even when it is not critically appreciated, even when it is not particularly well translated, even when it is interpreted without its Magisterium and preached in weakness. What *finally* matters is the gift of faith that allows it to be heard as God's Word.

Fifth, Barth helps focus attention on precisely where the Analogy of the Word equivocates. Christological analogies for Scripture often leave this crucial question unanswered. Either God the Son and Scripture are identical, or at some level there is a difference between the Word of God and the words of Scripture. Either there is an Identity of the Word, or (at most) an Analogy of the Word that *must* break down somewhere. And where it breaks is determinative for Scripture's divine character.

The Personification of Biblical Narrative: Does the Analogy Equivocate?

For indirect proof of this we can look to a theological project that refuses to equivocate. Gerard Loughlin's *Telling God's Story* treats Jesus' narrative as itself a hypostatic manifestation of the incarnate Word.[96] For Loughlin, Jesus *is* his own story, and the Church's relationship to Jesus is exhausted in its relationships with his story.[97] He makes the strongest Christological connection

---

95. So Fackre concurs with Carl Henry that critical scholarship reduced inspiration into experiential and existential categories. He claims that Karl Barth's "actualism," which was rooted thoroughly in earlier Calvinism's doctrines of divine sovereignty and the internal testimony of the Holy Spirit, left him without the equipment to recover it (*The Doctrine of Revelation*, p. 137). Fackre calls inspiration a "lost chord in the doctrine of revelation," and uses Henry to play it anew (p. 155).

96. Loughlin calls the story of Jesus "his personhood or *persona*" (*Telling God's Story*, p. 216).

97. According to Loughlin, "The unity of a human life is *no more than* the unity of the narrative enacted in that life" (*Telling God's Story*, p. 213, emphasis added). Thus Loughlin calls *the story of* Jesus the alpha and omega (p. 215, cf. Rev. 22:13); he calls baptism immersion into Jesus' *story* (p. 215, cf. Rom. 6:3); he calls the eucharist an absorption of and into the story (p. 223); and the biblical narrative is a text to be consumed like the eucharist, since the body of Christ "is a kind of book" (pp. 244-45, following Pierre Bersuire). Revelation's image of John the Seer eating the scroll of God's future plans (which in the context of Revelation's

possible — full identity — between the biblical narrative and the *logos*. Jesus is "the Christ-phrase" (p. 189).

Loughlin's appreciation of the significance of biblical narrative is laudable, and this project reaches many conclusions similar to his. But his refusal to equivocate between Jesus and Jesus' story causes serious theological problems. First, in hypostatizing Jesus' narrative, Loughlin effectively dissolves Jesus *into* his narrative. The immanent Trinity becomes a Lindbeckian rule governing the community's performance — meaning that apart from the Church's narrative performance, God is impersonal (p. 196). Second, God is Triune in that God and the Church tell *three* stories — "the stories of Father, Son, and Spirit," which constitute each other without ceasing to be distinct stories. Thus there is no longer *a* Gospel, but three: "the threefold story of God" (p. 194). The Church no longer simply tells *one* Gospel (cf. Eph. 4:4-6). Its integrity is fractured, and the Church is left with three "mutually constitutive" stories of, say, the Annunciation, or Christ's baptism. Third, having reduced the persons to their stories, Loughlin can make the extraordinary statement that because the Church prays Jesus' narrative back to God the Father, "one can say that the Spirit narrates Father and Son, and thus that Father and Son proceed as much from the Spirit as that the Spirit proceeds from one or both of them. . . . One can speak of a processional indeterminacy" (p. 192). Furthermore, because a story told is a story processed from speaker to audience, and because all three stories or "persons" tell the others' stories (meaning that all three Trinitarian relationships are codeterminative), all of the divine persons' relationships can be reduced to procession (p. 195). Father is no longer unbegotten, Son is no longer begotten, Holy Spirit is no longer distinct from the others, and the Filioque is no longer meaningful (p. 194).[98] Both the Eastern and Western Trinitarian visions are turned on their head, and the Church is left worshiping its own story.[99]

---

use of the Old Testament makes John a prophet like Ezekiel, after Ezek. 2:1–3:10) is for Loughlin "both Christ's risen body in the bread of the Eucharist and the divine logos in the word of Scripture" (p. 245). This implies that its experience of God is complete, its eschatology entirely realized, in its verbal and sacramental remembrance.

98. Contrast Pannenberg's *reciprocity* of Father-Son and Father-Holy Spirit relations (Wolfhart Pannenberg, *Systematic Theology*, vol. 1 [Grand Rapids: Eerdmans, 1991], pp. 308-27). Pannenberg's move is unproblematic since the relationships are neither identical nor indeterminate.

99. It is here that Loughlin's respect for premodern theological tradition, so deep elsewhere in his book, evaporates: "Thus it is not necessary to speak of an ordering below or subordination in the stories or persons of the Trinity. Nor is it necessary to hold to or not hold to the *Filioque*. What is necessary is that we learn to move more freely, more adventurously, in the stories of God" (*Telling God's Story*, p. 194).

When the analogous nature of the Analogy of the Word is lost, Frei's "consuming text" consumes more than the world; it consumes God himself.[100] Loughlin is right to resist modernist and postmodernist biblioclasm, but the logical consequence of his answer is bibliolatry.

If we reject Barth's argument, are we left with the alternatives of biblioclasm and bibliolatry? Fortunately, we are not, because there are alternative ways of conceiving the Analogy of the Word, which save us from the false choice between identity and unqualified difference. As we have seen, Augustine places the equivocality elsewhere. His Analogy of the Word respects the sacramental nature of the Word's verbal signs, but clearly distinguishes between the Word and his human words: He claims that Scripture participates in the beginning and middle of the Christian journey into God's presence, but not in its endpoint. While this argument has considerable strengths, Chapter 3 will reject it for other reasons.

A different approach, resonant with Athanasius' reasoning in *Against the Arians* III.30 and with the insights of Spirit-Christology, finds the equivocation elsewhere. This approach draws out the connections between Jesus' Spirit-anointed speech and the rest of the Bible's Spirit-anointed speech to find the clearest equivocation simply in the fleshlessness of spoken and written words. Barth is right that the uniqueness of the hypostatic union is where the Analogy of the Word equivocates. But the uniqueness of incarnation is *hypostatic* union, not hypostatic *union*. Verbal union is not hypostatic union in that language is not full personhood. Inlibration is not incarnation because words are not flesh. The *hypostasis* of a human person is not one with the divine *hypostasis* of the Son in one, human-divine person.[101] This means that God's presence in the human words of apostles, prophets, lawgivers, sages, priests, royals, and the like is real presence, but not full personal presence. It resembles Paul's presence in his words to the Corinthians: "Though absent in body I am present in spirit, and as if present, I have already pronounced judg-

---

100. See Loughlin, *Telling God's Story,* pp. 97-103.

101. This treatment accepts John McIntyre's criticisms of interpretations of Chalcedon that affirm Jesus' preexistent divine *hypostasis* but not the concrete *hypostasis* of his human nature. Rather than abandoning Jesus' human *hypostasis* in fear of the Nestorianism it seems to imply, McIntyre endorses the Christology of Ephraim of Antioch. According to Ephraim, "while the two natures as such are not confused or compounded one with the other, the two *hypostaseis* are. Accordingly the *hypostasis* of Jesus Christ is a fusion of the human and the divine *hypostasis*: it is *synthetos hē hypostasis*." See *The Shape of Christology: Studies in the Doctrine of the Person of Christ,* 2nd ed. (Edinburgh: T. & T. Clark, 1998), p. 101. The applicability for bibliology is that the human words of Scripture are fully particular, concrete, and contingent. Their relationship to Jesus is one between human words and a human person. Their divinity is *in no way* a compromise of their humanity.

ment" (1 Cor. 5:3). In the sense that Paul's "spiritual" words remain *Paul's*, they are truly "personal" in mediating his presence — but they are not Paul's *personhood*. By analogy, the double-agency of biblical language respects that biblical language is the speech of God and the speech of human beings, mediating personalities but not constituting personhood. In Barth's words, because "God's deity in Jesus Christ consists in the fact that God Himself in Him is the *subject* who speaks and acts with sovereignty," the *logos* "is not only different from" Jesus' human words, "but also one" with them.[102]

The patristic Trinitarian bibliology of Athanasius and Augustine locates the divine presence in Scripture in relation to *this* Christological correspondence, not the one Barth lays out in I.1 and I.2 (though similarities persist), and not in the extremes of either radical historical-criticism or radical narrativism. Thus the patristic Analogy of the Word can accommodate God's other true words in creation without qualifying either the functional normativity of the Bible or the absolute normativity of Jesus Christ among the multiple modes of God's revealing, saving, Triune presence. It can respect the lasting divine quality of biblical words without compromising God's transcendence.

Augustine puts it bluntly in *On the Trinity*'s commentary on John 12:47-50 (1.12.26): "The commandment of the Father is not one thing, and the word of the Father another; for he has called it both a word and a commandment. Let us see, therefore, whether perchance, when [Jesus] says, 'I have not spoken of myself,' he meant to be understood thus — I am not born of myself. For if he speaks the Word of the Father, then he speaks himself, because he is himself the Word of the Father." Similarly, on John 7:16, Augustine claims identity between the words and Word of Jesus (1.12.27): "For when he says, '[My teaching] is not mine, but his who sent me,' he makes us recur to the Word itself. For the teaching of the Father is the Word of the Father, who is the only Son."[103]

This is the direction our bibliology will explore and endorse. Much remains to be said about this equivocation, for there are still many ways it might be misunderstood.

---

102. Cf. *Humanity*, p. 48, referring not to Jesus' words in particular but to Jesus in his entire humanity.

103. Though here the equivocation rests in the distinction between the *logos'* form of God and his form of a servant, a kenotic relationship that bears much weight in *On the Trinity* 1.

Kenosis *as the Answer to Barth's Project*

We have finally begun to answer the question that brought Barth into the discussion: How does one construe the relationship between the character of God and the vulnerability of his human words? Barth has been wrestling with its awesome dialectic from at least as far back as the preface to the first edition of *The Epistle to the Romans*.[104] If one does not follow Barth, how does one proceed?

The question arose under the heading of God's "covenantal speech," where God puts his *ethos* at stake in committing to human speech. This ethical investment was likened to linguistic *kenosis*.

Such a term would make Barth worry that God's sovereignty and transcendence are being compromised. His own sensibility of the biblical words' sojourn into the world has a distinctly un-kenotic ring to it. What he calls the continual suffering of the Word in Scripture — its being neglected, distorted, rejected, and simply missed in previously inconceivable ways — is according to him the Word's withdrawing from its would-be readers on its own initiative (I.2.684), as the Bible in God's agency spreads darkness as well as light (I.2.635). God is never truly invested in his human words, for apart from the event of revelation they point aimlessly. When sinners abuse them, God remains untouched and impassible. Indeed, such abuse is divinely intended as a withdrawal out of the world, not a self-emptying into it. It is on this point that Wolterstorff offers his principal criticism of Barth, and distinguishes his own account of how Scripture gives us God's speech.[105] Against the tradition that God cannot be obliged, Wolterstorff affirms that God *can indeed* speak — really speak, as people do, investing themselves in words spoken "in character," taking on obligations for which they can be held liable, performing acts for which they are morally culpable, and taking the risks of being manipulated, misunderstood, and contradicted.[106]

Barth's reluctance to affirm the real vulnerability of God's scriptural Word has continued to influence the Barthian tradition. In *Narratives of a Vulnerable God*, William Placher draws on Barth to explore the vulnerability of the self-emptying Son and to trace the recent desertion of the old patristic doctrine of divine impassibility, then turns his attention to "The Vulnerabil-

---

104. The opening sentences of that preface are still a classic juxtaposition of the Bible's humanity and divinity. See Karl Barth, *The Epistle to the Romans* (New York: Oxford University Press, 1968), p. 1.

105. Wolterstorff, *Divine Discourse*, pp. 73-74.

106. See "Could God have and acquire the rights and duties of a speaker?" in Wolterstorff, *Divine Discourse*, pp. 95-113.

ity of Biblical Narratives," in which he explores the theological lessons of the multiplicity of canonical Gospels.[107] Yet only in the chapter titles is there any kind of implied correspondence between the vulnerability of the human Jesus and the vulnerability of the human Bible. In the text of neither chapter does Placher make any kind of connection between the two. What he so strongly affirms with respect to Jesus, he passes over in silence with respect to Scripture. And we have already seen that one of Markus Barth's criticisms of the Christological analogy for Scripture is that two-stage Christology is incompatible with its single purpose "to call sinners through the word of his witnesses to repentance, life, and joy."[108] In reducing the function of Scripture to witness, the younger Barth blinds himself to the Bible's own range of human linguistic activity.

If we reaffirm the patristic Analogy of the Word over Barth's and adopt a stronger correspondence between hypostatic union and verbal union, we are led to entertain a truly kenotic notion of God's ethical investment in the human words of his people and their Scripture. And this offers an alternative account of biblical contingency, fallibility, and error.

In Jesus, the immortal second person of the Trinity makes himself mortal. In a similar way, the divine Word utterly commits himself to his human words. When Jesus sows the seed of his Word, he entrusts it to the contingencies of fallen systems of human discourse, and then he lets the fragile seed fall where Satan himself can steal it away (Mark 4:15). Only thus is he truly a prophet, willing to live and die by the character of the one for whom he speaks *(ethos)* and both the form *(logos)* and reception *(pathos)* of his message. When Christians claim that Jesus is the ultimate prophet, the "prophet like Moses" (Acts 3:22-23), the successor of Moses and Elijah (Matt. 17:3, 8) and John the Baptist (Mark 1:7), they are not confessing a Word who can make himself aloof from the biblical message at will. They are confessing a Word made vulnerable in his own biblical narrative, obedient even unto death on a cross (Phil. 2:8). The two are inextricable.

Linguistic *kenosis* means that God blesses, curses, promises, and reveals in the frailty of human language, taking on and overcoming all of its limitations and risks. His statements no less than his Nazarene flesh "circumscribe the uncircumscribeable God," in the language of the Eastern Fathers. "God himself," says Balthasar, "has bound himself by his word."[109] The two live and

---

107. See William C. Placher, *Narratives of a Vulnerable God: Christ, Theology, and Scripture* (Louisville: Westminster/John Knox, 1994).

108. Markus Barth, *Conversation with the Bible,* pp. 161-62.

109. Balthasar, *Explorations in Theology,* p. 83.

die together. Barth has given us the indelible image of John the Baptist's index finger as an analogy for biblical witness. But for a more accurate metaphor for the divine ontology of the Bible's human language, one should look not at the Baptist's finger on the right margin of the Isenheim altarpiece, but to the cross at its center. There one finds not just the dead body of the incarnate One, but the dead words that proclaim him King.[110]

Linguistic *kenosis* understands the "failure" of Scripture not to be through a fault of its own, but due to God's condescension to speak in human language, and thus a dimension of the Bible's very power to save. Its kenotic soteriology depends on its kenotic ontology. C. S. Lewis, analogizing from Christ's divine humanity, says the literary opaqueness of Paul, the Psalms, and the rest of Scripture "finally let through what matters more than ideas . . . Christ Himself operating in a man's life."[111]

Therefore, linguistic *kenosis* solves an earlier problem in the way Athanasius handles his Analogy of the Word. The Word's victory is so complete in Athanasius' present day that it has begun to sweep darkness out of the world inexorably. If Athanasius is writing in 318, only five years after the Constantinian revolution, such an optimistic reading of the signs of the times is understandable. Nearly eighteen centuries later, the picture looks considerably different. Though the Church is far larger and comprises a far greater share of humanity, Athanasius' own hometown is a cultural and intellectual center of a tradition that adamantly *rejects* the incarnation of the *logos*. Constantine's legacy has proven to be a mixed blessing, and we speak now of Christianity after Christendom. So much for Athanasius' contention that the growing visibility of the Word's victory in the world is "proof that Christ is God the Word" (§55).

Macquarrie dismisses this problem in Athanasius' empirical argument and goes on to examine the next mode of his discourse.[112] But the failure of the empirical aspect of Athanasius' case seriously calls into question both his triumphalist soteriology and the theory of Christian knowledge that rests on it. In fact, it even calls into question his account of incarnation, in the same way that the failure of Barth's *vestigium trinitatis* calls into question his doctrine of the Trinity. If the incarnation of the Word is as he believes it to be, then why have its effects not matched the ones he expects? Where is the *Analogy* of the Word?

---

110. Balthasar, *Explorations in Theology*, p. 51: "Something of the logic of the object testified to, above all the cross and resurrection of Christ, colors the logic of the expression."

111. C. S. Lewis, *Reflections on the Psalms* (London: Geoffrey Bles, 1958), p. 114.

112. Macquarrie, *God-Talk*, pp. 143-45.

One way to correct Athanasius (taken in Chapter 3) is by qualifying his triumphalist eschatology by placing it alongside a more sober, apocalyptic vision of the *logos'* presence in the time between the times. Another is kenotic: In their current eschatological context, the various presences of the *logos* in the world in the wake of his incarnation and ascension continue to share in his suffering. They "complete what is lacking in Christ's afflictions for the sake of his body" (Col. 1:24). The triumph of God's Word is final — yet God's creatures continue to groan as they await God's redemption (Rom. 8:23). Biblical language is a language of charity, but it is still a language of faith in and hope for what remains unseen. The impotence of Scripture's message in the world, and the world's rejection of it, are not contrary to the Triune ontology of Scripture. They are further demonstrations of it (1 Cor. 2:1-5). They are not evidence of God's aloofness from his own words, nor of biblical "error" or "fallibility" in itself, but of the powerful weakness of God's radical self-involvement in the Bible.

IV. Balthasar: The Word of the Holy Spirit

We find a deep appreciation of linguistic *kenosis* in Balthasar's *Explorations in Theology: The Word Made Flesh*.[113] Balthasar describes the trajectory of the Word in creation and redemption in a way that closely resembles the patristic vision: The Word becomes invested in creation at creation, through the *analogia entis* but especially in the gift of the *imago dei*, then in the Law and the Prophets, then penultimately in the incarnate Word that grounds and fulfills all other types of presence, then in the pneumatic speech of the Church of the incarnate Word.[114] One even finds in Balthasar's account of human history traces of Athanasius' triumphalism as one might expect it to appear 1,600 years later.

Whereas Barth rejects a quasi-sacramental ontology for Scripture, Balthasar embraces it.[115] So it is surprising that Balthasar is still so committed to

---

113. See especially "God Speaks as Man," pp. 69-93.

114. Balthasar, *Explorations in Theology*, pp. 87-93. And on p. 23 he compares his version to Maximus the Confessor's account, similar to the patristic accounts detailed above, of the *logos'* progressive self-involvement in nature, Scripture, and Christ.

115. Balthasar never calls Scripture a *proper* sacrament. Indeed, "scripture does not contain the word in the manner of a sacrament" (*Explorations in Theology*, p. 17). But the differences between Word and sacrament should not obscure their similarities. He analogizes from the sacraments, particularly the eucharist, to describe ways the Word "delivers himself over to the Church" and "places himself in her hands in . . . corporeal forms" (p. 19). "Scrip-

Amazon Marketplace Item: Living and Active: Scripture in the Economy of Salvation
(Sacra Doctrina...
Listing ID: 0819B800499
SKU: PW-39468-U11
Quantity: 1

Purchased on: 29-Aug-2006
Shipped by: wrightbooks@comcast.net
Shipping address:

Ship to: Kristin Wilson
Address Line 1: 8224 Key Royal Cir Apt 211
Address Line 2:
City: Naples
State/Province/Region: FL
Zip/Postal Code: 34119-6797
Country: United States

Buyer Name: Kristin Wilson

Here are the details of your completed Amazon Marketplace sale:

the overriding category of *witness* as an all-purpose descriptor of Scripture. His reflection on "The Word, Scripture, and Tradition" opens with the Barthian statement that the testifying word of Scripture is distinguished from the testified-to Word as a reflection is to its image. "Although it is truly God's Word it is so only in the mode of testifying to his revelation." It is even "only the mode of God's self-witness in words, while there are besides other modes of his self-witness."

The dialectic Balthasar negotiates between describing Scripture as "only a witness" and as a quasi-sacramental participation in what it witnesses to is the same dialectic of *CD* I, or rather a Catholic appropriation of it — right down to "indirect identity" (in Balthasar's "incomplete distinction between the two forms of the Word of God," 51), the parallel with Eucharist (see *CD* I.1.88), and the intentional imprecision of calling the relationship between incarnate and biblical Word "a fluid one, varying from *clear contrast* to *actual identity*."[116] Clearly Balthasar is indebted to Barth's bibliology in many ways, even while taking issue with its incompatibilities with Catholic tradition. Balthasar's summary of his own trinitarian bibliology could have come from Barth: "Scripture participates in God's self-revelation in Jesus Christ through the Spirit." The two theologians develop their common thesis in very different ways, but from the same starting point.

Balthasar's bibliology takes a more explicitly pneumatological route. Scripture is the witness of the Spirit, whose very language is pneumatically "authorized": The Holy Spirit's word that refers to the Father's Word (50-51).

One could take the claim that Scripture is the word of the Holy Spirit to mean either that the Spirit has a word of his own, or that his word is also the Word of the Father. The terms "reference" and "witness" are ambiguous about which meaning is intended. If Balthasar were to speak only of witness and reference, his characterization might make Scripture a parallel "incarnation" of the Holy Spirit, a "second Christ." The Speaker's Breath could be a second Speaker of a second Word. And then the two divine persons would seem to go their own way — one to decrease and one to increase, one the way of the Baptist and one the way of the cross, one to point and one to be pointed to. When people think in terms of analogy between Christ and Scripture, they often imagine just such terms: the divinity of Christ is to the

---

ture makes the incarnate Lord present in a way analogous to that in which the eucharistic body makes present his historical body" (p. 16). The Bible's inspiration is a "permanent, vital quality" of Scripture (p. 14).

116. Balthasar, *Explorations in Theology*, p. 13, emphasis mine.

humanity of Christ as the divinity of Scripture is to the humanity of Scripture.[117]

This is why Balthasar's language of "witness" and "reference" depends upon his language of "participation." A major point of his essay is the nature of the *unity* of the two forms of the Word of God. Thus his language shifts from that of "witness" to that of "participation": to a unity of Word and words ultimately grounded in the mutual participation of Jesus and Scripture.

This is a crucial move to an adequate Analogy of the Word. It suggests where the analogy univocates and where it equivocates. "Participation" specifies both the basis of the Analogy of the Word, and its concrete shape. We have already claimed, against many other forms of the analogy, that the unity of human and divine is not where the analogy breaks down. Instead, it breaks down in the distinction between humanity's fleshly personhood and language's fleshless impersonality.

The question then arises: Are these two modes of the Son's presence mutually dependent, or independent? Balthasar's participation language answers: The Word's verbal humanity anticipates, causes, reflects, and helps consummate the Word's fleshly humanity. They are so mutually dependent that, for all their contrasts, they finally are one. God does not do one thing in Scripture and another in Jesus; God does one thing in Scripture-*and*-Jesus. The Bible and the Messiah are two aspects of the one grand sojourn of the *logos* in the one economy of salvation that centers on him (Matt. 21:33-41). Thus the narrative framework of Athanasius: Creation, verbal inspiration, and inscripturation all prepare for incarnation, participate in it, and reflect it.

We could paraphrase Balthasar to say that the Analogy of the Word describes both the literal investment of God's own *ethos* in the canonical words of the prophets and apostles, and the bodily investment of God's being in the personal flesh of Jesus. Each of these investments depends upon the other, so that the Analogy of the Word is an *intersection* of words and flesh, rather than a *parallel*. Balthasar deftly sums up his argument in saying that "the word of Scripture is primarily the work of the Holy Spirit who as Spirit of the Father effects, accompanies, illumines and clarifies the Son's incarnation (before and after the event), and who as Spirit of the Son, embodies his self-manifestation in permanent, timeless forms" (11-12). When Balthasar claims "the two

---

117. This is Paul Ronald Wells's illustration of the analogy, in *James Barr and the Bible: Critique of a New Liberalism* (Phillipsburg, N.J.: Presbyterian and Reformed, 1980). Following John McIntyre, Wells concludes: "The relation of the elements in Christ in an analogy of proportion tells us nothing about how the elements are related in the Bible" (p. 346).

forms of the Word are ultimately the one Word of God testifying to itself in the one revelation" (11-12), that the divine presence in Scripture anticipates and remembers rather than rivals incarnation (22-23), his warrant is the quasi-sacramental participation of God in God's human words, "covered with a warranty sealed in blood" (53).

"Participation" language (and Balthasar's endorsement of the Filioque, 32) suggests an identity-in-contrast between the Word of the Father and the word of the Spirit. Augustine has already anticipated him, in his appeal to the Holy Spirit's shared essence with Father and Son in *On the Trinity* (II.15.26), where he comments on the Spirit's agency in delivering the commandment of God (which is the *logos* himself) at Sinai: "Why do we not . . . understand the Holy Spirit to be spoken of, since the Law itself also, which was given there, is said to have been written upon tables of stone with the finger of God, by which name we know the Holy Spirit to be signified in the Gospel?"

Understanding both the contrasts and the identity is necessary for a proper appreciation of the divine economy and its various instruments.

Contrasts

We have already seen dangers in identifying God's presence in Scripture with God's presence in Jesus. It is the contrast between the two (along with their underlying identity) that makes the intersection of Tanakh, Jesus, and New Testament so interesting — and it is only the concrete intersection of the three that makes their identity-in-contrast clear.

Apart from incarnation, God's biblical words lie unfulfilled. They are sovereign, but not triumphant (Acts 15:10). They are powerful, but not victorious. They are holy and just and good (Ps. 119; Rom. 7:12), but not powerful unto salvation (Acts 13:39; Rom. 1:16). They cannot be broken (John 10:35), but they also cannot but *be* broken (Rom. 3:9-20). They promise deliverance but do not yet deliver (Isa. 61; Acts 8:30-31; Heb. 10:4-10, 15-18). Incarnation, then, is not simply "more of the same." It is the qualitative difference in God's humanity that makes the previous (and following) interventions of the Word truly effective, that finally writes the divine words upon human hearts (Jer. 31:33).

These affirmations, unqualified, can appear to negate the very real salvation available in Israel, and authorize supersessionist readings of the Old Testament. But they do not. God's saving presence in Tanakh was and is real (Gal. 3:8). Yet the Word's *personal* arrival in Jesus is such a fulfillment as to make the earlier light, though real and true, a shadow by comparison (Heb. 8:13, on Jer. 31:31-34; Heb. 10:1). And (lest this contrast sound like simple supersessionism) the promise of his final coming in the age of the Church is enough to make even the day of Easter's new creation and the light of the Church's Gospel like dark before the dawn (Rom. 13:12; Heb. 13:14).

The distinction between verbal and personal presence is not Luther's Law/Gospel distinction, because both Law and Gospel are words. It is not Old/New, because the New Testament is just as verbal (and just as subject to abuse) as the Old. It is not time/eternity, because both words and flesh are temporal (which is not the same as mortal). It is not even promise/fulfillment, because (like Israel) the Church lives in an age ultimately of both, making do with the Bible while longing for the face-to-face reunion. It is not letter/Spirit, for that would render Paul's flesh/Spirit dialectic unintelligible. The distinction is one of absence/presence — or more accurately, *impersonal* (i.e., verbal)/*personal* presence. Scripture's mode of the Son's presence is anhypostatic, mediating (like all inspired speech) the Father's *logos* in the Spirit's power, but in less than his full personal presence; Jesus himself is the Word not just *really,* but *fully* present. It is incarnation that gives inspiration its participatory power (and vice versa). It is the flesh that gives saving significance to the words (and vice versa). The flesh is both the *fulfillment* of earlier promise and the *basis* of later proclamation (and vice versa).

To say that Jesus is the fulfillment and basis of Scripture is, in a way, to say everything. Jesus' endorsement of Tanakh in word and deed, according to Balthasar, assimilates all of Scripture into Jesus' life. Jesus brings together biblical word and flesh in an unprecedented way, not simply repeating Scripture but fulfilling it.[118] That Jesus fulfilled Tanakh proves that the content of both Tanakh and New Testament is Jesus himself, that Yahweh's *logoi* to Israel and the world are the Father's *logos* and not something else, and that these manifestations of the *logos* are not parallel incarnations.

Identity

The mutual participation among these contrasting forms of God's sojourn into the world means that the Tanakh, Jesus, and the New Testament are mutually constitutive, though the modes of the Word's presence are asymmetrical. In one long act of divine self-involvement, the Spirit speaks, then conceives, then speaks again, the Word of the Father who sends them both. In the

118. Balthasar, *Explorations in Theology,* p. 13.

economy of salvation, Scripture forms Jesus, *and vice versa,* in a relationship so complex it will take half a chapter to describe.[119]

Jesus is the content of Scripture, both Old and New. Therefore he does not merely *repeat* Scripture, as if it were a "second Christ" alongside him which either superseded him or rendered him redundant. He does not merely *mirror* it, as he images the Father. He does not *overthrow* it, as he overthrows sinful and oppressive powers and principalities. He does not *ignore* it, as he ignores the nations who are outside the scope of his present mission. He does not *redeem* it, as he redeems good Israelite institutions that nonetheless fall short of God's glory. He does not *supersede* or *abolish* it, as he supersedes institutions like temple sacrifice whose purpose is solely anticipatory. He grounds and *fulfills* it, which is to say something else altogether. Jesus is no enemy of the Law — he *is* the Law (Matt. 5:21-48), and the Law's best friend (Matt. 5:17-20). The Law, Prophets, and Writings bend before him, but do not break. Jesus' arrival fulfills Scripture, each one shaping the other around its divine form. Like the Israelite priests who took scrolls into the Temple, Jesus takes the Tanakh into the temple (of his body, John 2:21) as *his* canon. And when from his glory at the Father's right hand he pours his Spirit onto his Church, what comes is *new* canon — new Scripture that testifies to him from the other side of his climactic life. He shapes the two testaments, and they him, like the back and front halves of a mold.[120]

What can we call this relationship of basis and fulfillment? The patristic ideas of typology and allegory (which are analogies of participatory relation) come as close as anything in describing the mutually signifying identity-in-contrast of Jesus and Scripture. One is a *type* or *allegory* of the other. The Analogy of the Word is one of typology or allegory. Though the two categories overlap considerably, typology is perhaps more appropriate in the context of Chapter 2's history of Scripture, and allegory in Chapter 3's ecclesiology of Scripture.

119. Cf. Barr, *Old and New in Interpretation,* pp. 137-38: "May we not suggest that the humanity of Jesus means that he, like other men, learned of his mission and calling through scripture studied with the help of the Holy Spirit? . . . His understanding of himself, and his planning of work, is formed upon biblical patterns. . . ."

120. While the Tanakh's shaping of Jesus might be relatively uncontroversial, the claim that the New Testament shapes him as well seems patently anachronistic. Yet the Gospels testify that words of contemporaries, whether parents, John the Baptist, disciples, interlocutors, disciples, or strangers, shaped Jesus' career and even self-understanding as profoundly as those of Tanakh. And the inspired words of evangelists, apostles, prophets, and redactors too shape the Messiah as heard in his Church. He reigns at the Father's right hand, still human even in glorification, hearing the prayers of his people and interceding for them. Barr is right to emphasize Scripture as human response, and Markus Barth to stress the Bible as conversation. Why would the Gospels and Epistles have left Jesus unchanged?

Every strand of the New Testament witness testifies to one or another aspect of this identity-in-contrast: the synoptic fulfillment quotations and sermons, most pronounced in Matthew and in Acts' apostolic sermons; John's incarnational language; Paul's Christological transformation of the Tanakh; Hebrews' (and Matthew's) sharp typologies, presumably directed at forgetful Jewish believers; James's royal law of the Lord Jesus Christ (1:22; 2:1; cf. 2:8); 1 Peter's eschatological reorientation of the prophets (1:10-12), 2 Peter's scriptural witness to Jesus in prophets and apostles (3:2; 3:14-18); the old and new commandments of the Johannine epistles (1 John 2:1-8; 3:11; 2 John 4-11); and Revelation's Christological transformation of apocalyptic.

Let us then embrace Balthasar's category of "participatory witness" as truly helpful to describing the Analogy of the Word. Our next task is to thicken it historically and theologically. The typological analogy between Christ and Scripture, though intact, still needs concrete treatment to be truly illuminating. The interaction between the two has not yet been explored in detail. Nor has the distinction between the inspired discourse of canonical Scripture and other inspired discourses. We will call on three theological resources for this examination, which constitutes the rest of our bibliology: first, the Eastern Orthodox ontology of images, which draws upon Christology and pneumatology to warrant the use of icons in Christian worship, in ways that apply to Scripture at least as well as they do to images; second, an explicit link between biblical language and the Trinitarian relations, which draws out the Analogy of the Word according to the insights of Spirit-Christology; third, a phenomenology of the Bible's trajectory in human history that centers on its relationships with Jesus Christ, beginning in Chapter 2.

Biblical Word as Icon: Applying the Iconodules' Case to Scripture

We introduced this project with a thought-experiment: What if the practice attacked in the Iconoclastic era were not the Church's uses of images, but of the Bible itself? Certainly, the problems being thought through so exhaustively in the eighth century would pertain directly to Scripture rather than to icons. But the course of the Iconoclastic controversy suggests much deeper parallels than that. Given the theological resources of the Eastern Church at the time, we might expect the Church to have arrived at a "thick description" of Scripture that is similar to its account of images. Thus Iconoclasm is more than a parallel for this project's occasion. It is a methodological guide for bibliology.

As we have already claimed, the Iconoclastic challenge called for nothing less than a thoroughly Christian ontology and phenomenology of images. On Christological grounds, Iconoclasts stipulated that images were one in essence with their prototypes; for God the Son was the image of God the Father (2 Cor. 4:4; Col. 1:15) only because of their *homoousion*. So they accused Iconodules of associating God with wood and paint in such a way that confused the natures of Christ. By grounding their objections theologically, the Iconoclasts demanded no less than a superior theological and Christological answer from Iconodules.

Working from the metaphysical and theological groundwork laid by Church Fathers like Athanasius, the Iconodules built their defense of images from the doctrines of Trinity and Christ, pneumatology and eschatology, salvation and Church. The linchpin of their argument was a repudiation of the Iconoclast assertion that images and prototypes shared a common essence. While conceding that the Son is the "living, essential, and precisely similar image of the invisible God," John of Damascus held that only this one "natural image" shares in both God's essence and likeness. Other images, whether "material signs" or "verbal signs," share only in God's likeness, and then only because in incarnation, God gave the created world himself in creaturely form.[121] Thus an image of Jesus shares only the material essence of his humanity. Paying respect *(proskunēsis)* to his image does not confuse the natures; it honors God's saving work in becoming incarnate for humanity's salvation. God's condescension in Jesus calls for a revolutionary reappraisal of the significance of the material world, because God the Son entered into it personally.[122]

In the next few decades of the controversy, the Iconoclasts refused to surrender the Christological high ground, and elevated their argument from the Nicene level to the Chalcedonian. They posed a Christological dilemma: Since divinity cannot be portrayed, an icon of Christ must either separate his human nature from his divine nature in a Nestorian fashion, or confuse the two in Eutychian fashion.[123] So writing fifty years after John of Damascus, Theodore of Studium crafted a Chalcedonian response. Because in Jesus the divine and human natures are united in one person, an image of Jesus' humanity is truly an image of his person. It is not just Jesus' humanity, but his hypostatic union or personal unity, that is represented in the image. The Iconoclasts' dilemma was a false one, formulated according to a defective understanding of the hypostatic union. In Jesus, the uncircumscribeable God is

---

121. John of Damascus, *On the Divine Images* (Crestwood, N.Y.: St. Vladimir's Seminary Press, 1980), 1.9, p. 19; 1.4, p. 15; 1.13, p. 21. Theodore of Studium later develops this distinction formally, calling the former a "natural image" and the latter an "artificial image." See *On the Holy Icons* (Crestwood, N.Y.: St. Vladimir's Seminary Press, 1981), 3.B.2, p. 100.

122. John of Damascus, 1.16, pp. 23-25.

123. See Catharine Roth's introduction to her translation of *On the Holy Icons*, pp. 10-11.

circumscribed. If he were only uncircumscribeable, the hypostatic union would be a docetic illusion. Likewise, if he were only circumscribed, the so-called incarnation would only have produced an Arian Christ.[124]

Equally important to Theodore's argument, however, is an answer to the problem of how an image participates in Jesus Christ:

> If one says that divinity is in the icon, he would not be wrong, since it is also in the representation of the cross and in the other sacred objects; but divinity is not present in them by a union of natures, for they are not the deified flesh, but by a relative participation, because they share in the grace and the honor.[125]

Portraying Jesus does not extend the incarnation, but it does communicate the glory of the incarnate one. Image and prototype are related economically. What takes shape in Theodore's defense of images is a graphical rhetoric of the divine economy according to Aristotle's categories: The image takes on the qualities of its prototype, and communicates God's saving energies to the perceiver, eliciting a response of faith and worship. Because the image shares in the prototype's grace, honor, power, and glory,[126] "the unity in veneration is not divided."[127]

These answers, elegant as they are, leave open the question of whether images of anyone else are appropriate. Can one appeal to the hypostatic union to justify images of the saints? The Iconodules constructed a second argument from somewhat different premises: Saints are members of Christ's body, indwelt by the Holy Spirit. They share in Jesus' glory, being conformed to his image (Rom. 8:29) and partaking in his divine nature (2 Pet. 1:4).[128] Their images and relics remember and participate in God's living earthly Temple, the Church. The respect due them is proportional to their relative participation in God's grace and honor, according to a kind of sacramental hierarchy descending from the divine matter of Jesus Christ through the mediating work of the Holy Spirit.

It is crucial that the pneumatological dimension of the Iconodules' argument is tied to the Christological dimension. The argument stands or falls on the integrity of both. We will seek only to strengthen this connection in the rest of the chapter.

---

124. Theodore the Studite, 1.4, p. 23.
125. Theodore the Studite, 1.12, p. 33.
126. Theodore the Studite, 2.27, p. 60.
127. Theodore the Studite, 1.14, pp. 34-35.
128. John of Damascus, 1.19, pp. 26-27.

Are Words Like Images?

Theodore's account has such obvious applicability to the character and use of Scripture that the parallels hardly need to be worked out. One could build an impressive bibliology simply by substituting "Scripture" for "icon." Indeed, since John of Damascus considers words a subclass of images, leaving the two undistinguished in his typology of images, such a substitution would be entirely in keeping with the Iconodules' reasoning.[129]

But the fundamental distinction between verbal signs and material signs — only material signs are material — poses a threat to this approach. Since God's materiality is what the incarnation changes, John of Damascus' argument from incarnation and its divinizing effect seems not to establish Scripture's ability to mediate God's saving presence in the way it establishes that quality in images. If it did, those who preserved God's name and words in the Tanakh would have been guilty of idolatry. If Christology grounds bibliology at all, it must do it in a different way.

Or must it? Too much can be made of the difference between verbal and material signs. The immateriality of language is no longer a defensible assertion. Human language in any form (mental, oral, and written) must be mediated materially. Whenever God acts sacramentally in creation, even in the minds, words, and acts of prophets, he authors material self-revelation. So the materiality of God's presence is not new in the event of the Word becoming flesh. What *is* new following incarnation is God's *full*, fleshly presence in creation. The Christological ontology of Scripture is grounded in the incarnate Word's *humanity*, not just his materiality.

Just as Christ's personal unity anchored the Iconodules' argument, so it anchors our Trinitarian ontology of Scripture in a way different from the early Barth. Hypostasis, not union, is the real equivocation in our Analogy of the Word — but it is also the ultimate ground for the analogy itself. Since personhood fully subsists neither in words nor on images, one can appreciate God's real material presence in both word and image, even in ancient Israel (for example, in the Book of the Law and the bronze serpent, as the Iconodules were fond of pointing out), while upholding Jesus' uniqueness. Yet since in Jesus' face and lips the image and words of God are then revealed as truly personal and truly human, one can still appreciate the unique fullness of God's presence in Jesus that gives all other words of Scripture their sacramental power to mediate his personal presence and work.

Then why is it acceptable to portray God in verbal imagery and name

---

129. John of Damascus, 1.13, p. 21; 3.18-23, pp. 74-78.

him with human sounds and written letters even before he comes to use them himself, yet forbidden to make graven images? The answer may simply be chronological: God delivers his name and message to Israel before he delivers his image. He can announce "I am *Yahweh* your God. . . . You will have no other gods besides me. You will not make for yourself any carved idol, or any likeness of any thing that is in heaven above, or that is in the earth beneath, or that is in the water under the earth" (Exod. 20:2-4), because God is not yet incarnate. There is already much to speak of, but literally nothing to picture. The eschatologies of the two media, while connected, are inaugurated at different times and places (Heb. 1:1-2).

So iconology provides a very helpful guide indeed for outlining a Trinitarian ontology of Scripture. God's Word takes human words, and so transforms our appreciation of human language. God's words are mediated pneumatically through the words of his disciples who receive the Son's gift of the Spirit. All these words participate in each other, through the Spirit's mediating work. The logic of iconology honors both Balthasar's sacramental participation language and his Barthian witness language, without making God-talk a parallel "incarnation of the Holy Spirit." In spite of the valid distinctions between pictorial signs and verbal signs, and fundamental distinctions between the Church's imagery and the Church's canon (to be brought out below), Iconodulia shows that Christology, pneumatology, and eschatology inform a Christian account of language in general and of Scripture especially. The gift of the Holy Spirit is the personal power of Scripture written and preached; the Son is its message; and the Father is its source. As the Holy Spirit mediates the ascended Son, so the biblical word shares in the roles the divine Word plays in God's saving economy, both as a semiotic means of his presence-in-absence, and as a medium for his worship. This leads to our second strategy of clarifying the relationship between the Spirit's word and the Father's Word: by clarifying the relationships between the Holy Spirit and the incarnate Son.

Unsubordinating the Spirit:
The Role of Spirit-Christology in Scripture

The bibliologies of Athanasius, Augustine, Barth, and Balthasar, and the iconologies of John of Damascus and Theodore of Studium, are all deeply informed by the particulars of their doctrines of the Trinity. All are shaped by their authors' close attention to the relations of begetting and proceeding among the divine persons. Their broad similarities derive at least in part from the influence of Alexandrian Word-flesh Christology on their economies of biblical language. All center their arguments on the incarnation of the Word, and proceed from this center to explore others' roles in God's economy by appealing to pneumatology and ecclesiology.

But Alexandria was not the only source of fruitful Christological thought in the early Church. The "Word-man" Christology of Antioch, and its modern counterpart in Spirit-Christology, must also contribute to a full account of Scripture's divine ontology and economy. Antioch's strengths are its focus on several events in Jesus' earthly ministry and its conclusions about what these events reveal of the roles of Spirit, Son, and Father in God's personal entry into the created order. We will explore these events in detail in Chapter 2, but several highlights demand attention here.

For instance, Antioch rightly sensed a profound importance in the Spirit's descent upon Jesus at his baptism. When too much was made of this event, Christological adoptionism resulted: The Son's sonship was mistakenly perceived to have begun at some point in his earthly life through the coming of the Holy Spirit. Catholic reaction against all forms of adoptionism subsequently led to a stress on the Son's sonship being determined by his eternal relationship with the Father; and this at times subordinated the Spirit to the Son. The Spirit's role in the economy was understood to proceed from the Father and (or through) the Son, and to point back to the Son — and not much more. The stage was set for the reduction of the Spirit's work, including his work through Scripture, to one of witness.

Lately the spirit of Antioch has been reviving. The rise of Spirit-Christology has helped recover the relevance of the Holy Spirit as the One who conceives, anoints, and empowers Jesus' work in the created order, not just the One who points to it and carries it on in Jesus' absence.

The missions of the Son and Spirit in the economy of salvation are intimately intertwined, but they are distinct. This is as true at Jesus' annunciation as it is at his baptism, resurrection, and the Spirit's Pentecostal outpouring. Each person is sent in his own way to accomplish the Father's will. And although there is a relative shift in emphasis at the end of Jesus' earthly ministry from his own presence to that of the Spirit, the two missions are always simultaneous. Finally, at all times their intercourse in the economy reflects the inner relationships among Father, Son, and Spirit in the life of the Trinity *in se*.[130] This reflection appears in every divine involvement in the world: creation, Law and prophecy, incarnation, Church, the Spirit's witness in Church

130. See Ralph Del Colle, *Christ and the Spirit: Spirit-Christology in Trinitarian Perspective* (New York: Oxford University Press, 1994), pp. 27-29.

and Church's Scripture, and the divine meeting of Church and Lord when the Bible is performed in worship.

Spirit-Christology points us to several events in particular that stress the Spirit's radical involvement in the mission of Jesus before Pentecost: his conception (Luke 1:35), his baptism (all four Gospels, and Acts 10:38), his earthly ministry, and his death and resurrection (Heb. 9:14; 1 Cor. 15:4). Each of these is relevant to the Trinitarian shape of our bibliology.

Annunciation and the Double Agency of Biblical Speech

Jesus is "conceived by the Holy Spirit." The very lips and breath with which he speaks God's words depend upon the Spirit's prior action. This one fact has gone grossly underappreciated in the history of Christological reflection. When it is recovered, a whole new dimension of bibliology takes shape.

Consider how it deepens Augustine's parallel between incarnation and speech. Let us gloss Augustine's Analogy of the Word accordingly, first for a fuller account of incarnation, second for a fuller account of biblical inspiration:

In order that what we are thinking	In order that the Word of the Father	In order that the Word of the LORD
may reach the mind of the listener	may reach the world	may reach the mind of the audience
through the fleshly ears,	through fleshly humanity,	through human reason,
that which we have in mind	he	the Word which the Father has in mind
is expressed	*is conceived by the Holy Spirit*	*comes through the Holy Spirit's inspiration,*
in words	in flesh	in spoken and written words,
and is called speech.	and is called Immanuel.	and is called Scripture.
But our thought is not transformed into sounds;	But the Word is not transformed into flesh;	But *ha dabar-yhwh* is not transformed into sounds;

112

it remains entire in itself and assumes the form of words	he remains entire in himself and assumes the form of flesh	it remains entire in itself and assumes the form of biblical language
by means of which it may reach the ears	by means of which he may reach humanity	by means of which it may reach human minds
without suffering any deterioration in itself.	without suffering any deterioration in himself.	without suffering any deterioration in itself.

(Augustine, *On Christian Doctrine*, 1.13.12)

Explicitly mentioning the Holy Spirit gives more Trinitarian depth to the account, without compromising its Christocentricity. It brings out parallels between incarnation and inspiration that do not appear otherwise. In both, one sees the Father's causation and the Spirit's agency. One sees the presence of divine Word fully and personally in Jesus, and verbally in the inspired words of prophets and apostles. Yet an explicitly Trinitarian Analogy of the Word still respects the uniqueness of the in*carn*ation, in that the inspired human words of the prophets and apostles never *become flesh*. The limit of the analogy between incarnation and inspiration is finally the uniqueness of Jesus' flesh and its unity with the eternal Word in one fully human, fully divine person. It is not that biblical language is ultimately only truly divine or truly human, or that the divine and human are not truly one word. Jesus is present wherever and whenever the biblical message is delivered in the power of the Spirit (cf. 1 Thess. 1:4; 1 Cor. 5:4). He was proleptically present in ancient Israel, even in the predictions of his own arrival. He (not "it") is manifested, vindicated, *preached*, believed on, and taken up (1 Tim. 3:16). Wherever the Spirit mediates, he mediates the *logos*. Wherever the *logos* is present, he is present through the Spirit's agency. So "both forms of the Word are ultimately the one Word of God testifying to itself in the one revelation."[131] Thus the Word of God is truly living and active (Heb. 4:12). It is in this conviction that Christians find Jesus fulfilling the Old Testament's near hypostatization of Israel's biblical wisdom (Matt. 11:19; 1 Cor. 1:24; cf. Prov. 8:22, 30; Wis. 7:25-26; 9:4, 10; Sir. 24:3-7; Baruch 3:35).

But Spirit, Word, and Father were not the only actors on the day the Word became flesh. In order to bequeath humanity to the Son, God used a human mother. As pneumatology explains the divine agency of biblical language, so Mariology explains by analogy the human agency of biblical language. The

---

131. Balthasar, *Explorations in Theology*, p. 12.

double agency of prophetic and apostolic speech[132] is a verbal type (i.e., *tupos*) of the virginal conception, birth, and rearing of Jesus.

Attending to Mariology saves bibliology from a host of errors. It respects the role of prophets and apostles as *logotokoi*, "Word-bearers" whose human bodies introduce God's eternal Word into the world in human language. By highlighting this real unity of divine Word and human words in the prophets' Spirit-conceived speech-acts, it explains how they can truly be *prophets and apostles*. Mariology's emphasis on God's prior initiative highlights God's sovereign election and sanctification of the speaker as well as the speech, accounting for the privilege of those who speak on God's behalf (Jer. 1:4-10; Isa. 6:5-10; Acts 2:17-18; and again, cf. John 16:12-15; 20:22-23; Matt. 10:19-20; 18:18-20). The Bible is only God's true story if God is its ultimate author.[133]

Yet at the same time, Mariology deeply honors the full humanity of biblical speech on account of the full humanity of all who bear it. Later we will explore the modern (and modernistic) battle between Barth and Barr over whether Scripture is the Word of God *to* humanity, *or* humanity's faithful response *to* God. Mary shows us that any opposing of the two has already ruined both. "Behold, I am the slave girl of the Lord," she tells the angel, "let it be to me according to your word" (Luke 1:38). Her agency in the Son's arrival is both an event that could not have come from her initiative alone, and one that needs and receives her cooperation. James Barr insists that the Bible is the human words of the covenant people offered to their covenanting God in praise and petition.[134] Indeed it is — as Jesus of Nazareth is the human son of the covenant people, offered to God as an eternal high priest. Every word of Scripture is a human "let it be" to God's initiative.

Mariology recognizes the ethical investment of the Bible's human shapers and the relevance of their characters in the origin and inspiration of Scripture, not merely the later reception of their texts by reading communities.[135] Humanity's maternal role in the birth of Scripture shows why it is incorrect to claim, as canonical critics often do, that the actual author(s) and

---

132. Wolterstorff, *Divine Discourse*, p. 38.

133. James Wm. McClendon Jr., *Systematic Theology*, vol. 2: *Doctrine* (Nashville: Abingdon, 1994), pp. 40-41: "We can make *full sense* of biblical narrative only when we see its implied narrator not as the human author (who, to be sure, is fully involved at his or her own level), but as the very God of whom Scripture speaks."

134. In Wells, *James Barr and the Bible*, p. 29.

135. What about Jonah, the pouting prophet? If his character is compromised — it is certainly not redeemed at the book's close — where does the moral authority of his book lie? One should remember in responding that the book of Jonah is not autobiographical. Its anonymous *narrator* is its human *ethos*.

originating community or communities of biblical texts are entirely irrelevant to their canonicity.[136] The early Church's criteria for canonicity rightfully went beyond the contemporary reception of texts, not least because both the Scriptures' divine and human authors continue to be remembered and associated with their texts (1 Cor. 5:3-5; cf. Luke 1:48-49). (For instance, while some of Judas Iscariot's words may have become canonical in Gospels narrated by others, his own diary could not, for he forfeited his apostleship [Acts 1:25].) Mariology draws attention to the maternal formation of divine messages during their times of gestation and childhood, as they are brought into being either through one human author, or through the *paradosis* of an entire community, then brought to maturity during the formative tradition-historical periods when they are further shaped and canonized. (It did, after all, take a village to raise the young Jesus.) Barr grants that this kind of account of the Bible's humanity is still compatible with a Christological analogy (while still denying the necessity or advantage of drawing it!).[137]

In this way a truly Marian analogy for inspiration leads the reader of 2 Peter 1:20-21 away from the textual docetism (cf. Luke 2:52, "and Jesus increased in wisdom and in stature") and monotheletism (again, cf. Luke 1:38) of crude verbal-dictation theories (what Fackre calls "oracular" accounts of inspiration).[138] Barr fears that the Marian analogy underwrites a fundamentalist attitude of biblical superhumanity and perfection that fences off the Scriptures from critical enquiry. In fact, properly understood, it does the exact opposite.[139] Jesus is not merely God's Son "dictated" through Mary. He is truly *her* firstborn son, she truly his *mother* (Luke 1:43; 2:7).

Furthermore (and in tension with the Catholic dogma of Mary's im-

---

136. "For example, a Christian who feels that the well-established scholarly views that Moses did not write the Pentateuch and that Paul did not write the Pastorals undermines the authority of scripture, has not properly understood that, for Christians, the text of scripture is canonical, not the authors of particular biblical books" (Fowl, *Engaging Scripture*, p. 180).

137. James Barr, *Biblical Faith and Natural Theology* (Oxford: Clarendon, 1993), pp. 196-97.

138. Fackre, *The Christian Story*, pp. 62-63.

139. Barr, *Old and New in Interpretation*, p. 204: "Like the Virgin, [for fundamentalism] the Bible is the human visible symbol involved in salvation; and like her freedom from all contagion of human imperfection, it has a kind of perfection and sublimity which makes it sacrilegious for us to analyse and criticize its seamless fabric." But for Barr, Mary is like *the fundamentalist Bible*, whereas for us Mary is like its human authors. Barr's analogy is misplaced. The fundamentalist Bible is (in caricature anyway) more like an Apollinarian Christ than an immaculate Mary. Evangelicalism's low appreciation for Jesus' humanity translates not into a higher doctrine of Mary, but a lower one; in the same way, its low appreciation for the Bible's humanity translates into a weaker emphasis on the human character of its authors.

maculate conception), a Marian analogy respects the roles sinful people and communities play in authoring holy texts. Mary, no stranger to sin, does not compromise the holiness of her son either biologically or socially (Luke 1:35). Likewise, a checkered past (and even a checkered present) is no impediment to speaking God's opinions. Paul is "unfit to be called an apostle," but God's grace to him was not in vain (1 Cor. 15:9-11). Another persecutor, Pilate, authors the prophetic epitaph that eternally frames both Jesus' death and his resurrection. From this perspective, the Church's authorship of its own Scriptures is one long exercise in irony.

Does this affirmation of biblical holiness sanctify the "texts of terror" that work across God's saving purposes? It does indeed — but not in the way in which many have grown accustomed to thinking. Our treatment of the holiness of the words of sinners will come at the conclusion of Chapter 2.

Many Christian hands have been wrung over the progressive nature of revelation and the developmental history of Christian doctrine. What did Israel know, and when did it know it? Antiochian extremism refused to admit Christological content in the Tanakh unless its prophets had foreseen the whole Christological fulfillment of their words, and Alexandrian extremism sometimes divorced divine and human intent completely. Mariology offers a middle-ground soft and solid enough to reject both interpretive determinacy and indeterminacy: "Mary kept all these things, pondering them in her heart" (Luke 2:19). She need not have known the full story of her son in advance to recognize it as a fulfillment of the old patriarchal promises (Luke 1:54-55). Mariology honors the human limitations of biblical writers, and even their ignorance of the full import of their messages, without making human authorship arbitrary. The significance of each moment in Jesus' life, and each verse in the Christian Bible, is real; but it is fully available only in the context of the whole.

In all these ways, Mariology defines the acceptable range of how we may understand several aspects of what Wolterstorff calls double-agency discourse: God's *superintendence, authorization,* and *representation* of human speech. Some accounts of superintendence[140] and authorization[141] respect

---

140. Wolterstorff, *Divine Discourse,* p. 41: "On one end of the degree-of-superintendence continuum are . . . cases in which the discourser herself produces the text. Right next to those are the cases . . . in which the discourser 'dictates' to a scribe or secretary the words to be inscribed. Further along the continuum are those cases in which the discourser merely indicates to the secretary the substance of what she wishes to say. Yet further along are those cases in which the secretary knows what the executive wants to say without the executive explicitly telling him or her even the substance of that. . . ."

141. Wolterstorff, *Divine Discourse,* p. 41: "In one or another way the discourser *authorizes* the text — that is, does one thing or another to the text such that her doing that

the divine-human double agency of biblical speech, while others do not (for instance, Barthian "adoptionism" and fundamentalist verbal-dictation theory). These are unacceptable not because God did not really appropriate Egyptian wisdom into Israel's canon of Proverbs, or because prophets were not really deputized by the Holy Spirit to speak from God, but because the theological accounts themselves respectively underappreciate the sheer divine initiative and the full human trajectory that is common to both these phenomena of divine discourse. God's favor both deputizes Mary, and appropriates her humanity. Indeed, in the light of Christology, Wolterstorff's distinctions between the two should not be understood as hard classifications in the case of biblical language. By the time the words of apostles, prophets, lawgivers, worshipers, sages, narrators, and editors come together in the rich institution of canonical Scripture, they are both deputized *and* appropriated discourse.

Finally, in the Presentation at the Temple, others can see themselves as biblical discourse's new audiences and presenters,[142] and not merely its spectators and repeaters. Having received the promise of a son in faith, this daughter of Israel proceeds to present her boy *to* God at Jerusalem as holy to the Lord (Luke 2:22-23). Simeon, a righteous elder who awaits the *paraklēsis* of Israel, sees the Lord's Christ before he tastes death, as he was promised. But more importantly, in the Spirit he shares in the blessing (2:27-35). Anna the prophetess gives God thanks, and proclaims to *her* audience the coming redemption of Jerusalem (2:36-38). The sight of human beings (parents, elder,

---

counts as her performing some illocutionary acts, with the consequence that that text becomes the *medium* of those illocutionary acts." Wolterstorff offers several examples of authorization. The first is "deputized" discourse, a "speaking in the name of" another, such as an ambassador's authorized proclamation on behalf of a head-of-state, or a prophetic or apostolic commissioning to deliver God's good news (pp. 42-51). The second is "appropriated" discourse, a "speaking the speech of someone else," such as a speaker quoting the words of another, or God canonizing the work of narrators, sages, psalmists, and editors (pp. 51-54). Canonization is then a divine endorsement, and canonicity a divine act of metanarration.

Wolterstorff's appropriating is not the same as Barth's adopting, because appropriating does not *overcome* the necessary limitations of human discourse, nor does it necessarily *rescue* what is appropriated from sinful origins. The appropriated speech is no different in its humanity, and may not even be different in its divinity (Jesus' words are appropriated along with Pilate's in the Gospels).

142. Wolterstorff, *Divine Discourse*, pp. 55-56, on presentational vs. authorial discourse: "By way of a single locutionary act one may say different things to different addressees." Furthermore, regardless of a given text's authorship, one may use it "*on different occasions* to say different things to the same or different addressees — or indeed, to re-say the same thing to the same or different addressees. . . . It may be that God *now speaks to us* by way of our now being *presented* in some fashion with that text."

and prophetess) presenting the Lord to the Lord is a guide to understanding the mystery by which the Church hears the words of others as God's, and presents them back to God and to the world as its own inspired discourse. To Wolterstorff's category of double agency, we can add the category of (divine-human) *double audience*. Here Mariology offers us resources for Chapter 3's account of biblical practice in the Church. We learn how it is that, in the axiom of the Reformation, the Word of God preached is the Word of God,[143] how it is that the others come to share in Jesus' work of prophethood and apostleship, how it is that in Scripture, both God and humanity address each other, and address themselves.

Mariology shows us that while the Virgin Birth is an absolutely unique event (in that incarnation is hypostatic union, while inspiration is merely verbal union), it is still entirely consistent with the way God involved and involves himself in the world through those who speak on his behalf. God does not act one way in the Old Testament and another way in the New. He sends his apocalyptic message into the world with servant after servant; and when these are all turned away, he sends still one other, a beloved son (Mark 12:6). All are servants, and all are sent; only one is the heir, but the others bear a common message and authority. The others do not merely act as the heir's witnesses, bringing news that he is coming, but as his viceroys. They are not actors in some parallel economy of salvation, but characters in one common story. If Aidan Nichols is right that elegance, coherence, and persuasiveness validate the Analogy of the Word, then the birth narratives offer a validation that is unsurpassed.

Jesus' Baptism: The Word in Spirit and Power

Annunciation is only one of Spirit-Christology's important bibliological resources. Indeed, in both the Gospels and Epistles, Jesus' *baptism* is far more prominent than his conception. It is understandable that the event is less important to subsequent Christology, not only because of the adoptionism its overstatement precipitated, but also because his anointing with Holy Spirit is missing from the Apostles' and Nicene creeds. But it is a pity nonetheless. It often seems that the theologian must choose between Alexandria and Antioch, between Word-Christology and Spirit-Christology.

Yet not all see incompatibility. James D. G. Dunn's study of New Testa-

---

143. Second Helvetic Confession, I.4. See Philip Schaff, ed., *The Creeds of Christendom* (Grand Rapids: Baker, 1990), 3.237.

ment Christologies concludes that the Bible's diverse conceptualizations of Jesus Christ simply cannot be squeezed into one shape; therefore he refuses to confine orthodox Christology to one particular type or to play one off the other.[144] Bruno Forte sees "reciprocity and complementarity" between the Only Begotten and the Paraclete in their one economy. "The Christology of the Word — which sees the Paraclete accomplishing the work of Christ, and that of the Spirit — which sees Christ as the Anointed of the Spirit, are . . . both present and working in the New Testament witness."[145]

Once the two are no longer seen as antithetical, the possibility emerges of allowing each to inform the other, and to preserve the other from its characteristic heresy. Word-Christology safeguards the Gospel from adoptionism. Likewise, Spirit-Christology safeguards God's triunity by refusing to treat divinity simply as an abstract substance. It safeguards both the humanity of Jesus and the utter profundity of the Son's incarnate *kenosis,* in two ways: First, it refuses to abstract humanity from its hypostatic reality.[146] Second, it distinguishes between the quiet, pre-baptismal Jesus and the charismatically anointed worker of signs and wonders who emerges from the Jordan.

The early Church sermon preserved in Acts 10:34-43 describes the profound change in Jesus' activity following his baptism:

> You know the word which he sent to the sons of Israel . . . the word proclaimed throughout all Judea, beginning from Galilee after the baptism which John preached: how God anointed *(echrisen)* Jesus of Nazareth with the Holy Spirit and with power; how he went about doing good and healing all that were oppressed by the devil, for God was with him.[147]

If from birth the Matthean Jesus is God with *us,* from baptism the Holy Spirit is God with *Jesus.* John's baptism (which is really the Father's baptism) is a divine empowering of the one divinely conceived. Jesus' words before his baptism were truly the human words of God; but Jesus' words in the wake of his anointing are the powerful, pneumatically efficacious, human words of God. Jesus' own appropriation of Isaiah's words in the synagogue suggests the

---

144. James D. G. Dunn, *Christology in the Making: A New Testament Enquiry into the Origins of the Doctrine of the Incarnation* (Philadelphia: Westminster, 1980), pp. 266-67.

145. Bruno Forte, *The Trinity as History* (New York: Alba House, 1989), p. 125.

146. McIntyre, *The Shape of Christology,* p. 101.

147. There is no note of embarrassment in this preaching, as is so commonly alleged to be felt by the Gospel writers about Jesus' baptism. They seem to me not embarrassed by Jesus' offering himself in John's baptism of repentance, but emphatic that his offer was enthusiastically accepted and empowered by God, after the manner of Yahweh's fire from heaven in 1 Kings 18:16-39.

change: "The Spirit of the Lord is upon me, because he has anointed *(echrisen)* me to preach good news to the poor" (Isa. 61:1; Luke 4:18).

The effects of Isaiah's anointing and Jesus' anointing are distinguished only in that in Jesus, Isaiah 61 is *fulfilled* (Luke 4:21). Prophetic anointing and messianic anointing are typologically related. To be sure, the earlier anointing witnesses to the later one. But the reverse is true too. Isaiah's ministry is a foretaste and *arrabon* of Jesus', a proleptic anticipation of it. The prophets point to Jesus, and Jesus points back, as if to say, "These are my words too, which will never pass away."

With Pentecost (both the Lukan and Johannine), the essential similarity between Jesus' anointing and the pneumatic anointing of his forerunners is extended also to his disciples. This is our ultimate ground for the pneumatic, Christological, Trinitarian ontology of the New Testament witness. As Mary was overshadowed by the power of the Most High (Luke 1:35), so the disciples are clothed with power from on high (Luke 24:49). The crucified Son gives the Spirit who descended and remained upon him (John 1:32) over to the beloved disciple and his mother (John 19:30), and when risen (and ascended?) to all the disciples (John 20:22).[148]

The distinctions between Jesus' speech and the Church's *kerygma* are actually participatory relationships. The power of Jesus' divine-human speech is, through the grace of his Spirit, the power of the Church's biblical proclamation. The beloved, now inspired, disciple writes a true witness to these things (John 21:20-24) in order that readers may believe and have life (John 20:30-31). Peter's preaching is equally powerful: "While Peter was still speaking these words, the Holy Spirit fell on all hearing the word" (Acts 10:44).

Kenosis *and Power Reconciled*

Spirit-Christology informs bibliology in a third way, by nuancing the kenotic quality of divine speech. When the divine *kenosis* is treated solely according to the categories of Alexandrian Word-Christology, insoluble antinomies emerge. If Jesus is divine, did he manifest all divine attributes, or simply refuse to exercise them, or relinquish them entirely? And if God appears without God's attributes, how can he be said to reveal God? (Can a duck that doesn't waddle or quack or swim really show us what ducks are like?)

These kinds of problems have their force only in an environment where

---

148. I owe this insight to an ecclesiological point made by David Yeago.

incarnational Christology is artificially separated from Spirit-Christology. When Jesus' divinity is treated in the abstract, one worries that the knowledge Jesus exercised in his prophetic office, or the power he exercised in working signs and wonders, might have compromised the limits of his true humanity. Humanity begins to pull apart from divinity; the two come to be seen in tension rather than perfect unity. But Spirit-Christology's attention to the Holy Spirit as God's agent of power in Jesus' ministry resolves the problems. If Jesus' power to preach and to work miracles is the same as others', then signs and wonders compromise his humanity no more than they do Moses'. Analogically, Scripture's power to save is appreciated as a quality of divine anointing that subsists in the biblical words (cf. John 1:32: *emeinen ep' auton,* "it remained on him"), like the reserved sacrament of Catholic eucharistic practice.[149] But the Spirit of Scripture is wholly united with the letter, neither superseding it nor elevating biblical language to the superhuman level.

Furthermore, when the power of Jesus' ministry is recognized as a manifestation of his Spirit, and not just the straightforward power of Jesus' incarnate divinity, the subtlety of incarnation is brought into its own. While Jesus before his baptism is fully divine, his divinity is so veiled that his own brothers, sisters, and neighbors can miss it (Luke 4:22), and can later mistake his *charismata* for the signs of insanity (Mark 3:21).[150] In the same way, linguistic *kenosis* sends the divine Word into the world *sub contrario,* under a contrary form, without suffering change, transformation, or deterioration.[151] Scripture participates in both the powerful power of the sovereign Spirit, and the powerful weakness of the obedient Son (1 Cor. 1:25). Spirit-Christology and

---

149. Note that the anointing remains on the *words,* but not necessarily on the *speakers.* Athanasius insists that the Word "became man, he did not come into a man. It is essential to grasp this point, in case the impious should fall into thinking . . . that it was just like the former occasions on which the Word 'came' into the various saints, and that now too he had come to reside in a man in the same way, sanctifying him and manifesting himself in him just as he had in the others. If this had been the case — if he had just appeared in a man — there would have been nothing extraordinary about him at all." *Against the Arians,* Discourse III, §30, *NPNF* II.4, p. 410.

150. To be veiled is to be *not quite* covered; to be subtle is to be *not quite* invisible. To see God's "backside" (Luther, *Heidelberg Disputation* 20, after Exod. 33:23) through his suffering servant is still to see God. The Son *has* exegeted the Father and made him known (John 1:18), not simply hidden him in a new way.

151. Balthasar is right to hold up Luther's theology of the cross as a profound insight into the mystery of God's work in the world, yet also right to point out the problems caused by Luther drawing out God *sub contrario* in terms of unresolved paradoxes. The point of incarnation is that in Christ, the simultaneous opposites *(simul . . . et . . .)* that characterize Lutheran theology are *resolved.* See *Mysterium Paschale* (Grand Rapids: Eerdmans, 1993), pp. 61-62, quoting E. Seeberg, *Luthers Theologie* (Stuttgart, 1937), vol. 2, pp. 8ff.

Word-Christology together offer a bibliology of "cruciform glory" that re-fuses to place "glory" and "cross" in contradiction. The two are not in tension: They are simply the two hands of the Father working his will.

Conclusion: A Bibliology of Word and Spirit

It is no wonder the Analogy of the Word has had its critics. By itself, a Word-Christological ontology of Scripture is liable to subordinate the Spirit to the Son, and thus subordinate the rest of Scripture to the words of Jesus. The words in black become little more than pointers to the words in red. Further-more, it is liable to neglect the significance of the Bible's concrete humanity and historicity. Finally, in practice it can easily become an apologetic for a biblical Apollinarianism in which human language is significant only as a car-rier of divine language, and the Bible's historical particularities are neglected.

Conversely, a pneumatological, or Spirit-Christological, ontology of Scripture by itself is prone to neglect the uniqueness of Jesus' messianic career and the words most directly relevant to it, flattening out the Bible's peaks and valleys into one homogeneous inspired corpus, or even raising the Montanist prospect of new words on a par with the dominical and canonical (and even incarnate) words. At its extreme, it sees Jesus as simply another *rasul Allah,* an adopted Messenger of God succeeding Moses, David, and Jonah in the same way that Muhammad succeeds Jesus. It is liable to reduce historical criticism to phenomenology, making humanity the righteous initiator and God the well-pleased recipient of the Bible's words.

But when combined properly, mirroring the Son's and Spirit's relation-ships in the biblical narrative of Jesus' life, Word-Christology and Spirit-Christology keep bibliology in orthodox Trinitarian perspective. The two ap-proaches hold together both Jesus' uniqueness and his universality as God with us. By analogy, they hold together Jesus' uniqueness in revealing God in the created order, and the commonality between his charismatic speech and the charismatic speech of Israel's lawgivers, prophets, apostles, and grafted-in Gentiles. Together they simultaneously draw and blur the lines between the incarnate Creator and the creatures whom he adopts as brothers and sisters, and allows to act in his name. They portray a Christocentricity that elevates the biblical Word even as it firmly subordinates it to Father, Son, and Spirit, by locating its power in the power of the Triune God. They demand close at-tention to the actual course of Scripture in *human* history, while never forget-ting that human history is a *salvation-history* moving towards the realization of *God's* will.

The two ontologies together provide the proper contours of the Analogy of the Word. Without their blurry lines, the rest of our project — an orthodox exploration of God's sojourn into the world in Scripture and the response it precipitates in Christ's earthly body, the Church — would be impoverished.

Chapter 2

The Mission of Scripture:
A School for All the World

Form* versus *Function?
The False Dilemma of Postmodern Bibliology

David Kelsey's *The Uses of Scripture in Recent Theology*[1] portrays a theological landscape largely divided into three visions of biblical authority: one rooted in Scripture's divine ontology and cast in positivist terms, another rooted merely in Scripture's function and cast in narrative terms, and a third rooted in Scripture's expression of saving events and cast in symbolic terms.[2] Kelsey's clusters of visions fit nicely into George Lindbeck's cognitive-propositional, cultural-linguistic, and experiential-expressive accounts of truth. Gerard Loughlin offers a similar typology of "three accounts of meaning: literal, historical, and religious," or story, history, and religious truth.[3] This is not surprising, since Loughlin so closely follows Frei and Lindbeck. These Yale theologians present sophisticated bibliologists with several options for appreciating Christian Scripture and Christian doctrine: as a means of preservation of the content of revelation, as a narrative that remembers saving agents, and a collection of expressions of the experience of salvation. For the first group, Kelsey says, the

---

1. David Kelsey, *The Uses of Scripture in Recent Theology* (Philadelphia: Fortress, 1975), pp. 30-31.
2. See Kelsey, *Uses,* pp. 15, 23, and 50.
3. Gerard Loughlin, *Telling God's Story* (New York: Cambridge University Press, 1966), p. 130.

value of Scripture is in its concepts. For the second group, the Bible's authority lies in "its narrative *and not* its didactic aspect." For the third, "Scripture is not theologically important because it tells a story. Instead, by 'expressing' the occurrence of the revealing and saving event, scripture somehow links us with that event."[4]

In the first part of this bibliology, we found that as God's Word, the Christian Bible proceeds from and reflects God's Triune character and embodies it in the created order. Kelsey would presumably call this conclusion a "biblical concept theology" and locate it within the first group, since it finds Scripture authoritative "because of some intrinsic *property* of the text." In doing so, he would say, it resembles Protestant orthodoxy, twentieth-century evangelicalism, and pre–Vatican II Roman Catholicism. Kelsey contrasts this vision of Scripture with the others, which "understand 'authority' *functionally, i.e.,* as a function of the role played by biblical writings in the life of the church when it serves as the means by which we are related to revelation."[5]

Kelsey claims that the Church need not face a radical choice between these two visions of Scripture. In fact, a single theologian's bibliology may feature aspects of every one of his seven models of biblical authority. And he realizes that "biblical concept theologies" usually share an intense appreciation for the function of Scripture in and out of the Church. Their distinguishing feature is in locating the source of Scripture's power in its own divine character. Yet Kelsey's typology differentiates each of his bibliological clusters so sharply that he effectively offers the biblical interpreter a choice: Scripture as propositional, *or* narrative, *or* symbolic. Kelsey's dilemma-by-typology does subtly what Barr's divide-and-conquer-by-typology strategy in *The Bible in the Modern World* does explicitly: It presses the reader to find and choose the one stalk of wheat among the tares. Given the alternatives of a text with intrinsic properties and a text with a life in the Church, the choice is hardly an agonizing one; and so the "biblical concept" vision of Scripture has been increasingly abandoned by theologians of postmodernity.

But is a choice between biblical form and biblical function inevitable? Is the opposite not true, that biblical form and biblical function depend on each other? And then why must a bibliology ontologically rooted in the divine nature be merely a "biblical concept theology"? If we grant that bibliologies of content in the nineteenth and twentieth centuries are by and large concept-driven, does it follow that ontological bibliologies *must be* narrowly cognitive-propositionalist? Or, rather, is Francis Watson not right to claim that the

4. Kelsey, *Uses*, pp. 32 and 56, emphasis added.
5. Kelsey, *Uses*, pp. 30-31.

common dichotomy between historical or cognitive hermeneutics and narra-tive hermeneutics inevitably has disastrous effects?[6]

The sacramental and narrative quality of God's presence in Scripture offers itself as readily to an ontological analysis as a functional analysis.[7] Ellen Charry's analysis of the character-forming intentions of Christian theology rejects Locke's and Hume's overly narrow construal of truth, not in order to deflect the issue of truthfulness, but in order to replace Enlightenment empir-icism with a therapeutic account of truth whose rules and standards are anal-ogous to those of clinical medicine. Christian knowledge is a rigorous but "soft" knowledge of both *scientia* and *sapientia,* both science and wisdom, that requires trust in God's truthfulness while testing it through practices of discernment.[8] For Charry, theology is a practical exercise in healthy thinking that negotiates ontology according to its own purposes, rather than either dodging the question or subordinating itself to the Enlightenment's demands for what authentic "knowledge" must be.[9]

Charry is right to resist the polarization between form and function that emerged in the Enlightenment and persists in some anti-Enlightenment traditions. There is no such rigid distinction in premodern theological tradi-tion, let alone in the biblical traditions themselves, and there need be no such distinction today. So our own functional bibliology *follows from* our ontolog-ical one: If Scripture's character participates in the Father's will, the Son's *kenosis,* the Spirit's power, and the humanity of God's elect, then its use must participate in the divine economy of salvation. And this means that the work

---

6. Francis Watson, *Text and Truth: Redefining BIblical Theology* (Grand Rapids: Eerd-mans, 1997), p. 9. Again, Watson finds this dichotomy influential in the work of James Barr (pp. 18-28).

7. Likewise, Rahner's axiom that the economic Trinity is the immanent Trinity, and vice versa, should indicate the deficiency of any reduction of Scripture to either its divine character or its role in divine action.

8. Ellen Charry, *By the Renewing of Your Minds: The Pastoral Function of Christian Doctrine* (New York: Oxford University Press, 1997), pp. 5-16. She appeals to Janet Soskice's "cautious critical theological realism" as a similar construal of truth, in which theological terms "putatively refer to possibly real entities, relations, and states of affairs." Nevertheless, Charry does not make too much of Kantian categories of objectivity or reference in her own proposal (p. 11).

9. "Perhaps it would clarify matters to take a cue from St. Augustine and recognize that for theology, science is a necessary preliminary to sapience. . . . What science calls truth is only part of what theology calls truth, for theology insists that truth is salutary — that God is good for us. Rather than render sapience dependent on science, however, a truly liberated understanding of the truth of God must be bold enough to say that the wisdom of God made known in the story of Israel and in Jesus Christ stands as a norm of truth and goodness on its own terms, as Karl Barth pointed out" (Charry, *Renewing,* pp. 238-39).

of the Bible in human history and in the lives of those it encounters can be appreciated and even informed in terms of both the categories of Christian soteriology, and the historical phenomena of Israel, Jesus, and the Church. Accordingly, this chapter offers a soteriology of Scripture grounded in and proceeding from Chapter 1's Trinitarian ontology of Scripture.[10]

Why develop yet another functional bibliology, on top of all the others? On the Bible's power to save, much reflection has already taken place, especially in Protestantism, whose appreciation for the saving power of God's biblical Word is unparalleled. We revisit the issue here only to locate Christian appreciation of God's work through Scripture firmly in terms of God's character (Chapter 1) and God's community (Chapter 3). Many recent accounts of Scripture proceed phenomenologically and anthropologically, starting from the human history and human experience of Jewish and Christian Scripture and their real and imagined reading communities. Because God truly works through the biblical Word, such accounts are not invalid. Indeed, they supply needed epistemological grounds for the present project. But in the interests of strengthening the connections between Scripture's divine character and its divine work, this bibliology prefers to continue speaking of Scripture theocentrically, in terms of its mediation of the Trinity and its role in God's mission of cosmic deliverance.[11] Therefore the shift in emphasis between chapters is not from God to humanity, but from immanence to economy. And because the initiative in salvation belongs to God alone, the full treatment of the human location and agency of Scripture will be put off even further, until Chapter 3's ecclesiology of Scripture, in order to highlight the sheer priority of God's agency in its formation and use.

---

10. Again, this does not mean that our appreciation of Scripture's character is *epistemologically* prior to our appreciation of its work. God's work, including God's work in Scripture, causes human knowledge of God; but God's being is logically prior to his action.

11. Says Karl Rahner: "Throughout the Old Testament there runs the basic theme that God is the absolute mystery, whom nobody can see without dying, and that it is nevertheless this God *himself* who conversed with the Fathers through his actions in history. This revealing self-manifestation is, in the Old Testament, mediated mostly (not to mention Yahweh's angel, etc.) by the 'Word,' which, while causing God to be present in power, also represents him; and by the 'Spirit,' who helps men to understand and to announce the Word. When these two are not active, Yahweh has retreated from his people. When he bestows upon the 'holy remnant' his renewed and forever victorious mercy, he sends *the* prophet with his Word in the fullness of the Spirit. (The Torah and Wisdom doctrine of sapiential literature is only a more individualistic version of the same basic conception. It pays less attention to historical development.) God is present in the unity of Word and Spirit." *The Trinity* (New York: Crossroad, 1997), p. 41.

Scripture as Divine Missionary

This priority is well captured by the common prophetic construction, "The Word of Yahweh [came] to me," *dbar-yhwh 'elai*. But Scripture's mission is enunciated in other powerful ways. Athanasius provides a particularly arresting image that frames the mission of Scripture when he speaks of the spreading *kerygma* as "the *logos* himself, sojourning here *by his teaching*,"[12] "sojourning among us" in the "meaner language" of humanity (§50) to quench the superstitions of the fallen world (§47). If the Bible is a means of the sojourn of the *logos*, then the Bible's work is a dimension of his saving work.

Nicholas Wolterstorff provides a less poetic but no less accurate term for the Bible's mission as the "transitivity" of revelation, its revelation *to someone*, which follows from its "intransitivity," its quality as revelation *per se*.[13] In the mission of Scripture we see God's biblical Word in transitive mode, in the act of accomplishing the Father's will by the power of the Holy Spirit.

One can also name Scripture's mission in the classical rhetorical categories mentioned in Chapter 1. We used *ethos* to describe the divine character of the biblical *logos*. The work of Scripture brings up Scripture's *pathos*, the movement it effects in its hearers and readers. Wolterstorff, correcting Hans Frei, would call this the *point* of the biblical narrative.[14] Chapters 2 and 3 now unpack the *pathos* of Scripture in the history of Israel, its Messiah, and his Church.

In each of these images the Bible's work is distinct from its character. Yet everywhere the two are so intimately related that one could adapt Karl Rahner's axiom and say that "the economic Bible is the immanent Bible, and the immanent Bible is the economic Bible."[15] In Scripture, Israel and the Church experience God's powerful, saving presence. Because God's spoken-and-written Word is not inert, but acts and is acted upon, it leaves its own wake in the rest of human and divine history, and they in it. Each sheds light back on the other, revealing Scripture's divine and human authors and their authorial intentions. And because the Bible acts in ways consistent with God's

---

12. Athanasius, *On the Incarnation*, §49.

13. Nicholas Wolterstorff, *Divine Discourse: Philosophical Reflections on the Claim That God Speaks* (New York: Cambridge University Press, 1995), p. 65.

14. See Wolterstorff, *Divine Discourse*, pp. 232-34. Against Frei's anti-referentialism, Wolterstorff asks, "What else could the point of a narrative be but the point of someone's offering us the narrative — or the point of our putting the narrative to one and another use?" (p. 234).

15. Cf. Rahner, *The Trinity*, p. 22.

overall plan of salvation — mediating, demonstrating, and accomplishing it — the Bible's work can be understood according to soteriological categories. Indeed, once the relationship between Christian soteriology and the Bible's work has been established, one can reverse direction, informing and enriching one's bibliology according to the insights of Christian soteriology. Thus our soteriology of Scripture operates dialogically, alternating among historical-critical, salvation-historical, and soteriological perspectives.

The Bible operates both macrocosmically, altering the trajectory of human history, and microcosmically, altering the person who receives its message. These two ranges meet fully in the person of Jesus Christ. Thus the soteriology of Scripture divides into three sections: the Bible's role in God's history of salvation, its role in the career of Israel's Messiah, and its role in the social and personal salvation of its hearers. We will explore each aspect in turn: the first two in the two parts of this chapter, and the third in Chapter 3.

I. My Hope Is in Your Word:
Scripture's Cosmic Mission to Israel

The first question that meets anyone today presenting a history of God's mission to Israel through its Scriptures is: Which history? The canonical history, or the historical-critical? Which "canonical history," among the countless reappropriations of the Jewish and Christian canons? Which "critical history," among the multitudes of historiographical worlds already available? It is no longer possible, even in fundamentalist circles, to re-narrate the stories of Scripture without describing or at least defending their critical historicity, and it is no longer persuasive, even in historicist circles, to treat texts as dispensable vessels from which to recover underlying events. In what sense is God's mission to Israel "event," and in what sense is it "text"?

Johann Philipp Gabler would have us use Israel's texts merely as means to the original events, while Loughlin would reduce events to texts.[16] But nei-

---

16. Actually, when following Austin Farrer, Loughlin mentions a dialectic between event and text, but refuses to place ultimate causality in one or the other (Loughlin, *Telling God's Story*, pp. 111-12), even with respect to Jesus Christ (p. 113). More typical is Loughlin's treatment of the Annunciation and other events of Jesus' narrative, which juxtaposes John Shelby Spong and Hans Frei as representatives of the "event" and "text" camps (pp. 120-32), in order to endorse the latter. Stephen Fowl adopts a somewhat more nuanced dichotomy, arguing that "Christians can and should make use of [professional] biblical scholarship when and as they need to" (*Engaging Scripture: A Model for Theological Interpretation* [Malden, Mass.: Blackwell, 1998], p. 186). Yet he still treats the "profession" as something fundamentally for-

ther the complex interrelationships between "speech" and "acts," nor the biblical writings themselves, offer us an opportunity to choose between the two:

> To the saints God chose to make known how great among the Gentiles are the riches of the glory of this mystery, which is Christ in you, the hope of glory. Him we proclaim, warning everyone and teaching everyone in all wisdom, that we may present everyone mature in Christ. For this I toil, striving with all the energy which he mightily inspires within me. (Col. 1:27-29)

Throughout the course of the biblical story, God's saving work on behalf of his people Israel shades into God's further work of revelation through prophets and apostles. What is finished at the Passover, or Sinai, or the Jordan, or Golgotha, continues to unfold through those who remember and proclaim it. The event preached becomes effective again in the event of its preaching. This dialectic of biblical remembrance *(anamnēsis)* is particularly well appreciated in the Pauline corpus. While it has been respected throughout the Christian tradition, it influenced Protestant theology enormously, through Luther's and Calvin's insights and later through Wesley's, through both the eras of Protestant Orthodoxy and of Protestant liberalism, and enjoyed a powerful recovery in the rise of evangelicalism and the kerygmatic theology movement in the twentieth century.

The dialectic between the event preached and the preaching event has always been fragile. Emphasis has tended to fall toward one or another pole. But the already uneasy tension between event and text in premodern biblical interpretation was pure serenity compared to the situation following the rise of modern historical criticism. Both the practice of historical-critical exegesis and its rejection have tended to crush the dialectic altogether. The Church has found neither radical historicism (personified by Adolf von Harnack), nor radical subjectivism (personified by Rudolf Bultmann), nor even radical narrativism (personified by Hans Frei) a truly satisfying way to read canonical sources. Even Barth, so celebrated for radicalizing the dialectic in his introduction to *The Epistle to the Romans*,[17] has been criticized for paying little

---

eign to the "church" (p. 187). Yet the Catholic tradition of biblical studies in particular has recently been quite successful at integrating rigorous practices of critical scholarship into the Bible's ecclesial life, precisely *because* they are warranted by Christ's and the Church's humanity and historicity. (For an example of the theological warranting of historical criticism of Scripture, see Walter Kasper, *Jesus the Christ* [Mahwah, N.J.: Paulist, 1977], pp. 26-40.) N. T. Wright's Christological project is a similar attempt within evangelical Protestantism. This argues that the common estrangement between biblical critics and theological readers of Scripture is unnecessary.

17. New York: Oxford University Press, 1968, pp. 1-2.

more than lip service to historical-critical insights in his actual exegesis. Furthermore, many recent moderate attempts to relate past events and present biblical texts have borne surprisingly tasteless fruit.[18]

So Church and academy remain mired in a seemingly interminable debate about the relationship between the event preached and the preaching event. This debate is conducted largely in European Protestant, Enlightenment, and post-Enlightenment categories, but it is not nearly as new as it seems. The debate is actually an ancient (and theologically profound) one: How does the *biblical* Word share in the work of the *incarnate* and *anointed* Word?

Athanasius' Soteriology of Scripture

The ancient debate over event and text took one famous form in the tensions between the schools of Alexandria and Antioch. Their distinct Christological methods informed distinct approaches to appreciating and performing biblical texts. Still preferring to begin with Alexandria's wider scope (while appreciating Antioch's attention to historical particulars), we return to Athanasius' *On the Incarnation of the Word.* His cosmology is just as relevant to the Bible's divine work as it was to the Bible's divine character. It narrates no less than a cosmic "salvation-history" of the sojourn of the *logos* into the world. His perspective is broad enough to encompass both the biblical events preached and the events of biblical preaching. Within Athanasius' narrative we can locate both event and text, in the hope of honoring their elusive dialectic. Indeed, this chapter's entire soteriology could be conceived as an extended commentary on this section of *On the Incarnation,* or on the comparable passages of Augustine's *On Christian Doctrine,* with which it shares so many affinities.

To repeat: Chronicling the self-involvements of the *logos* in the cosmos, Athanasius begins with his role in creation, which culminates in the creation of *logikos* humanity. Sin rapidly brings God's good creation to irreligion and lawlessness, and the knowledge of his *logos* to utter ignorance. But, Athanasius pleads, it is not as if the *logos* has hidden himself from their eyes! On the contrary, he has unfolded his self-revelation "in many forms and by many ways" (§11), making graceful provision for human carelessness. The works of

18. See, for example, technically sophisticated monographs and collections of essays on critical issues in the "Hebrew Bible" such as Steven L. McKenzie and M. Patrick Graham, eds., *The Hebrew Bible Today: An Introduction to Critical Issues* (Louisville: Westminster/John Knox, 1998), which offers no theological judgment whatsoever, Jewish or Christian, on the texts of the Old Testament.

creation in general are some of these; but they are not enough to catch the downcast eyes of sinners. So God condescends even lower into the created order, sending his knowledge in a law and in prophets in order to provide divine instruction in an even more effective way, "for men are able to learn from men more directly about higher things." In these holy messengers God builds "for all the world a holy school of the knowledge of God and the conduct of the soul" (§12).

Israel is that holy school. The Tanakh is its required text.

Athanasius' commentary on these events is a soteriology of the Tanakh that brings us to the threshold of the New Testament era. For the remainder of this chapter we trace the story of Scripture through its shadowy origins in Israel's primordial memory and its later literary trajectories in settled, exiled, restored, and occupied Israel. This story climaxes in the career of Jesus of Nazareth as the one who sets Israel's Scriptures along their new course as Old Testament, and authorizes a New Testament for inclusion with the Old Testament in the Bible of the Christian Church.

Along the way we will be negotiating the treacherous dialectic between the canonical shapes of Israel's and Jesus' story and the various historical-critical pictures. No exercise in "salvation-history" can escape either pole of this dialectic, for each offers resources the other lacks for appreciating the nature of God's self-involvements in the created order. Our object is to retell the story, without forgetting the story's own story, or letting one telling crowd out the other.

To achieve this aim, first, our retelling relies on mainstream accounts of ancient Israel's history and scriptural traditions, from John Bright, Samuel Terrien, and Paul Nadim Tarazi. It does not attempt the thankless task of developing a comprehensive Old Testament theology, but merely offers a theological narration of Scripture's and Israel's history of shaping each other. Second, it sticks to cautious and moderate accounts, in order not to get sidetracked into arguments about particular historical points, and that its overall argument not be overturned when scholarly consensus changes or when a particular point is contested. Third, it seeks support for Scripture's importance in Israel from *both* the responsible confessional and the responsible historical-critical pictures. Both the chronological depth of God's words in the Old Testament and their changes over time in Israel's tradition inform our soteriology of Scripture — so there is no reason to neglect either responsible Old Testament historical criticism, or the canonical text as it now stands. Accordingly, Terrien and Tarazi represent more of a historical-critical perspective, Bright a more canonical perspective, but all of them appreciate Scripture and Israel in ways that are sensitive to both poles of the dialectic of event and text.

There is no surer way than this to call down the wrath of scholars who disagree over the use and conclusions of historical criticism. Objectors should note that this section is an experimental appropriation of confessional and historical-critical pictures of Scripture's story, held together in creative tension. It is meant to show the compatibility of the two pictures more than it is meant to endorse a particular vision of both, to the exclusion of all rivals. A similar study conducted under either more canonical or more critical lines (Israel Finkelstein and Neil Asher Silberman are the latest headline grabbers)[19] would yield a qualitatively similar account. However, an approach that radically subsumes criticism under canonicity might erase the tension between the historical-critical and confessional pictures, and one that radically subsumes canonicity under criticism might read the tension as uninformative or even destructive, rather than constructive, at least during the most remote ages of Israel's past. The common ground of the historical-critical and canonical schools is both the middle ground of biblical-theological scholarship, and the most appropriate context for this aspect of our project.

A Conversation Cut Short and Restored: The Saving Work of God's First Words

We begin with an account of beginnings that has no precise historical-critical equivalent at all: the creation story.

A modern-day Athanasius would use the creation story to stress that God's relationship with creation has been linguistic from the beginning: "God said, 'Let there be light'" (Gen. 1:3). Augustine's meditations on time and eternity reveal the linguistic nature of God's creative work to be rooted in the eternity of the Word himself (*Confessions* 10.7.9). As God creates, God speaks (*vahomer*, Gen. 1:6, 9, 11, 14, 20, 22, 24, 26).

Nevertheless, something changes profoundly once God has created humanity in his image, for now and only now does he speak *to them (vahomer lahem,* 1:28; cf. 2:16's *al-ha'adam*). Only now does his temporal word take a transitive form. Only now is it received as well as sent. The man who hears is moreover a man who speaks, who has a share of God's own linguistic power. He can even take dominion over God's other creatures by naming them. Of all God's creatures, only woman shares his name *(ish/ishah)*, rule, and verbal powers (Gen. 2:18-23).

19. See Israel Finkelstein and Neil Asher Silberman, *The Bible Unearthed: Archaeology's New Vision of Ancient Israel and the Origin of Its Sacred Texts* (New York: Free Press, 2001).

But the powers soon subvert the divine intent of language (Gen. 3:1-5), and its abuse evokes God's powerful curses rather than blessings (3:14-19; cf. 1:28). The relationship is ruined. And for all the seeds of hope in God's subsequent words and deeds (3:15, 21; 6:18; 8:21-22, etc.), the relationship is still estranged, human language hopelessly corrupt (Gen. 11:6-7), as the patriarchal age dawns.

It is then that God begins to speak to particular people in a new way, and language slowly begins to reflect more than human sinfulness and divine retribution. God's words create the nuclei of new communities of interpretation, in the families of Abraham, Isaac, and Jacob. Words of promise (Gen. 12:1-3 etc.) begin to be remembered and transmitted across lost numbers of generations, and these words of promise regather the communities who remember them.

In terms of anthropology, the origins of Israel are lost in antiquity. But however it happens, from Egypt and Canaan arises a "People of the Book"[20] whose stories, laws, and promises remember God's electing, liberating mercy, and whose peculiarity offers a channel for all the world to gain the saving knowledge of its Creator and Redeemer God.

Athanasius' account respects the biblical and historical picture of a people gathered by and around a message that comes repeatedly and insistently from beyond it. The story of Israel reflects the saving power of God's words in a variety of ways: in the *antiquity* of its confession, in the *continuity* of its confession, and in the *evolution* of its confession.

It is easy (and not entirely improper) for Christians, Muslims, and Jews to retroject a fully developed idea of Scripture upon ancient Israel, imagining that the *full* Gospel really was preached beforehand to Abraham (cf. Gal. 3:8) and that on the eve of the Jordan's crossing Moses handed Joshua five finished scrolls, as Charleton Heston does in *The Ten Commandments*. Source criticism offers very different (and usually conflicting) pictures. But they are still pictures of a people formed by words they understand to originate in and belong to Yahweh, God of the Hebrews. Samuel Terrien characterizes most of the content of Jewish Scripture as reflecting "Mosaic and prophetic Yahwism" far more closely than it reflects the Judaism of the Second Temple period. For all the shaping and formalizing that went on later in Judaism, the oral traditions later Jews focused on were more Hebraic than Jewish, more the faith that created Judaism than Judaism's product.[21] John Bright similarly affirms

---

20. The term is Qur'anic: *ahl al-kitab*, and reflects a meaning Muslims too would endorse.

21. Samuel Terrien, *The Elusive Presence* (San Francisco: Harper & Row, 1978), p. 7.

that all the books of the Pentateuch and the Former Prophets contain material of greater antiquity than the books themselves.[22] Athanasius' precritical vision respects the Old Testament's most primitive traditions: The Tanakh stands in great continuity with its own past.

Yet if the antiquity and continuity between the Hebrews' oral traditions and Israel's later fixed written forms constitute proof of the importance of the divine words in these communities, the change wrought by later Judaism on its own traditions does too. Source, form, and redaction criticism backwardly attest to the subsequent influence of the divine words on the nation that received and would later inscribe them. That Israel spent such enormous energy shaping them and passing them along to others shows that even before being written down, let alone canonized, God's words were living and active. The "problem" biblical dynamism introduces for the historian who seeks to uncover the pre-biblical events is no problem for orthodox bibliology. As long as the tradition's trajectory of interpretation respects the object of the tradition's interpretive effort, both reveal the saving power of Scripture.

Scripture as Presence

It is even easier to retroject *logocentricity* upon ancient Israel. For ancient Israel, the role played by Scripture *qua* Scripture was less central than it came to be in later exilic and rabbinic Judaism. Protestants in particular have often been prone to Protestantizing ancient Israel (as well as Catholicizing first-century Judaism). Samuel Terrien offers a more balanced account of Israel's experience of God as one of "elusive presence." Even as it is today, this ancient presence was mediated in human words, but it was also mediated through worship, epiphanies, theophanies, holy objects, holy people, dreams, and natural and supernatural phenomena. Words were only one mode God used to convey salvation to Israel. This rich variety can drop out of view easily in a project concentrating so intensely on Scripture. Its importance is nothing less than the event-text dialectic that makes the text significant in the first place.

Even so, a fundamental part of God's mercy to Israel certainly took the form of words, which proved themselves extraordinarily flexible in communicating many different aspects of divine presence. Indeed, Israel's constitutive practices were preserved mainly — even entirely, in times of great cultural disruption — by their careful preservation in the ongoing practices of Scripture. The sheer variety of the texts of the Tanakh attests to their power

22. John Bright, *A History of Israel*, 3rd ed. (Philadelphia: Westminster, 1981), p. 145.

and versatility in maintaining the traditions of Israel that remembered, mediated, and anticipated God's presence. Consider the volume of material given over to the physical dimensions of God's various tabernacles and Temples, to civil law, to the title deeds of the various tribes, to genealogies, to directions for how to observe sacred festivals, to war histories, to common-sense wisdom borrowed from other nations, and to other dimensions of Israelite and Jewish life. Modern Christians may be puzzled to find such things in "Scripture," which they now regard as merely a manual for personal holiness or success, or a series of pointers leading directly to and from Jesus Christ.[23] But ancient Israel (like modern Judaism) apparently had a far more versatile account of the work of God's written Word.

While the divine words were only one mode of God's saving presence, they accompanied and interpenetrated all of the others (Deut. 6:6-9). Yet the center of the biblical traditions was not merely the recitation and preservation of words. It was corporate worship, whose concerns deeply shaped the Pentateuch, the Former Prophets, Latter Prophets, Psalms, and Writings such as Chronicles and perhaps even Job.[24]

The interrelationships between biblical Word and every other aspect of Old Testament life, particularly gathering in worship, make all the more uneasy the distinction between mission and Church that divides this chapter from the next. Yet the distinction still respects something invaluable: the fact that the Word *sojourns,* coming freely to an unprepared humanity, not brought down into creation by human whim and magic or brought into being purely by human creativity. This priority and sovereignty of God's action in revealing himself is, according to Terrien, the fundamental distinction between Israel's theology of presence and those of its neighbors:

> Divine intervention in human affairs is generally, if not exclusively, represented as sudden, unexpected, unwanted, unsettling, and often devastating. The feature of divine disruption is typical of all literary genres in all periods of biblical history. . . . Biblical man is always "surprised by God."[25]

---

23. Are these Christians simply following Paul's vision that the Old Testament was written not to the ancients but to the present community (1 Cor. 10:11; Rom. 10:5-10), but being less perceptive than Paul and his predecessors in seeing *how* the Old Testament is written for the present community? Cf. Richard Hays, *Echoes of Scripture in the Letters of Paul* (New Haven: Yale University Press, 1989), pp. 154ff.

24. Terrien, *The Elusive Presence,* p. 13. See also Hughes Oliphant Old, "The Roots of the Christian Ministry of the Word in the Worship of Israel," ch. 1 in *The Reading and Preaching of the Scriptures in the Worship of the Christian Church,* vol. 1: *The Biblical Period* (Grand Rapids: Eerdmans, 1998).

25. Terrien, *The Elusive Presence,* p. 28.

In those rare occasions when God becomes immediately, blindingly present to his chosen mediators, a trajectory of revelation is begun. Around these elect witnesses grow communities of interpretation where the theophany lives on in oral and written, cultic and sacramental — that is, ecclesial — form. The fleeting divine disruptions are mediated through prophets and apostles, who are pivotal figures in the biblical history. Their participation makes the difference between disruptions that cease and presence that lingers. They simultaneously demonstrate the rarity of God's direct theophanic presence and the commonality of its continuation. Their stories describe the relationship between Scripture's first cause in God's saving initiative, and the human agency always involved in Scripture's mission.[26]

God's chosen messengers are the schoolmasters of Athanasius' school of the *logos*. Their words are determinative for the communities who gather around them. This rhetorical power manifests itself long before anything like scriptural canonization, and even before their words take standard written forms. So Terrien rightly draws influences radiating outward from God's theophanic presence towards prophethood, community, cultic practice, then canon.[27] We will retrace these steps by returning to where we left Athanasius' narrative — in the primordial Israel God's words were putting together — and examine the major moments of God's scriptural speech that radiate outward from those words.

From the Patriarchs to the Conquest: The Word as Gatherer and Deliverer

The Patriarchs

While later steps in this chain of influence — those dating from the Exile and Return — are more accessible to modern historiography, it is impossible to

---

26. Cf. Terrien, *The Elusive Presence*, p. 29.

27. "*Canon* was originally not a dogmatic structure imposed from without by institutionalized collectivities but an unspoken force which grew from within the nature of Hebrew-Christian religion. The obligations of the Sinai covenant were remembered as the 'torah' of Yahweh, a growing collection of instructions which were inserted within the context of the narratives of the Sinai theophany. Thus, the cultic *anamnesis* of the event during which the divine presence disclosed itself to the people through the mediation of Moses prepared and promoted the development of the canon." Canonicity was a "*fait accompli*" when Josiah's servants found the Book of the Law and Huldah the prophetess confirmed its conformity to God's living, prophetic Word (Terrien, *The Elusive Presence*, p. 32).

recover the exact original shape of the patriarchs' promises that are preserved in Israel's Scriptures. But the names of the figures involved, the covenantal style, and the names of God all attest to the age and authenticity of the patriarchal material. Genesis 12ff. is no "mere retrojection of the Sinaitic covenant" upon Israel's formative age, but a verbal relationship with God carried forward into later ages by the covenant community's remembrance.[28] "The Genesis picture of a personal relationship between the individual and his God, supported by promise and sealed by covenant, is most authentic. Belief in the divine promise seems, in fact, to represent an original element in the faith of Israel's seminomadic ancestors."[29]

Yet it is not just the original epiphanic events that illustrate the saving work of God's words. Equally compelling is the *anamnesis* that makes historiographical recovery of the original events both possible and difficult. Both the remembering and what is remembered are crucial to the power of Scripture. The promises are retold because of their power in shaping the people Israel; and the retelling of the promises unleashes and multiplies their power anew. Israel and Church owe their very existence to the powerful arrival and the powerful residence of God's words in their histories.

The Exodus

Yet Israel's relationship with God is much more than a covenantal or verbal one. As the Word made flesh who alone brings Christian salvation is no mere word, so "Israel's" divine liberation from Egyptian captivity[30] was no mere text. Israel's single most remembered divine mercy is one in which words play a comparatively minor original part.[31] Passover, exodus, and God's presence to Israel in the wilderness are of course recorded and practiced scripturally, and their continuing practice has played an extensive part in God's saving work in and through Israel. But here the divine words are working more in their classically Barthian role as witness. They point first of all to saving events. Indeed, were they not remembered at all, were the

28. Bright, *A History of Israel*, pp. 98-99.
29. Bright, *A History of Israel*, p. 101.
30. "Israel" here may well be anachronistic, if only some fraction (possibly the tribe of Ephraim) of those who entered Canaan were actually residents of Egypt. Even so, in becoming adopted into the greater confederation of tribes that is Israel, these latecomers would have learned to see the exodus as the definitive moment of their own liberation.
31. In this respect, as in so many others, the exodus typologically resembles Jesus' passion and resurrection.

exodus completely forgotten, the original captives would have been no less delivered.

Sinai

Yet were the exodus completely forgotten, the captives' descendants would not have known the One who saved them! They would not have become *Israel*. The remembrance of the saving event and the incorporation of those saved into the people of God are vitally important dimensions of God's grace to Jacob. Furthermore, right after the exodus comes a quintessentially verbal saving work on God's part: Sinai, where Israel receives the resources necessary to become and remain Israel.

Here too the dialectic of event and text is too complex to be described solely in terms of witness. At Sinai, the text *is* the event. This is true not only of its reception, but also of its transmission. It may be that at Sinai the Israelite tradition of publicly reading Scripture in worship is born.[32] Because the covenant is between a gracious God and a people obedient to God's Word, it is through the public reading of Scripture in worship that Israel enters into and maintains its covenant relationship with God.[33] The Law's role as means of grace and Moses' role as liturgist and preacher in representing and leading Israel make Israel's worship of Yahweh at Sinai "the prototype of Christian worship."[34]

The form of the Law undoubtedly changed over time. But the evidence of Israel's experience there in receiving its law and covenant is ancient, authentic, and anamnetic: "In some of the earliest poems that we have, Yahweh is referred to as 'The One of Sinai' (Judg. 5:4f.; Ps. 68:8; cf. Deut. 33:2). A tradition so unanimous and so ancient must be presumed to rest on historical events."[35]

---

32. Old, "Roots of the Christian Ministry," p. 22, following W. Beyerlin, *Origins and History of the Oldest Semitic Traditions* (Oxford: Blackwell, 1965).

33. Old, "Roots of the Christian Ministry," p. 24: "The reading of God's Word in the book of the covenant and the vow to live by that Word are the basis of the covenant fellowship sealed in the sprinkling of blood and experienced in the covenant meal. Obviously the reading of the Law in the worship of Israel is understood as essential to establishing and maintaining the covenant relationship."

34. Old, "Roots of the Christian Ministry," p. 27. If this is not true of all Christian worship, it is certainly true in Old's Reformed tradition.

35. Bright, *A History of Israel*, p. 126. Bright also reads the Song of Miriam (Exod. 15:1-8), perhaps the oldest text preserved in Scripture, as probably referring to Sinai.

At Sinai, "Mosaic Yahwism" is born as the classic embodiment of our elusive dialectic between saving event and saving text. This faith brings together the verbal and nonverbal aspects of God's genesis and deliverance of Israel into one grand saving work. This synthesis is symbolized both by the remarkably diverse Torah that remembers it all — creation, alienation, promises, exodus, and covenantal law — and by the central figure at both exodus and Sinai: Moses. Israel's Torah is the five "books of Moses," and Moses is at once Israel's archetypal wonder-worker, deliverer, leader, lawgiver, intercessor, prophet, rabbi, and scribe (Deut. 34:10-12).

None of these roles is dispensable to Israel's formation. The story insists that if not for Sinai, God's saving work in Egypt would have been for nought (Exod. 32:12). Sinai inspires the overwhelming majority of Pentateuchal material, the name "Torah" that comes to describe the whole, and the institutions that put it to use.[36] The story of the golden calf vividly illustrates Israel's conviction that it owes its very existence to God's Law and to the priesthood the Law inaugurates. Israel's ability to worship God justly and experience God's elusive presence depends upon obedience to his commandments. The Mosaic Law, a tradition both "in its origins exceedingly ancient"[37] and in its course through Israel's history truly evolutionary, is from early on an essential aspect of Yahweh's salvation, actualized through worshipful reading and obedience.[38]

The Ark

As the Virgin Mary is the most fitting symbol for Chapter 1's exploration of the divine ontology behind the human authors and words of Scripture, so this chapter's favorite image of the salvation inhering in God's written words is the Ark of the Covenant. The stone tablets hewn from Sinai illustrate the sacramental nature of God's words. God's *dabar*, which connotes both a "word" and a "thing," is fully both: a material object, here a stone tablet, that

36. The suzerain-vassal treaties of Moses' era call for their own ceremonial reading in solemn assembly. Old finds in the similarity between Deuteronomy's sermons and suzerain-vassal treaties further confirmation that Scripture reading and interpretation in worship is built into Israel's covenant relationship with God ("Roots of the Christian Ministry," p. 29). Deuteronomic practice, which principally reflects the activities of the Levites, thus establishes the Jewish and Christian traditions of expository preaching (pp. 29-30).

37. Bright, *A History of Israel*, p. 172.

38. Old, "Roots of the Christian Ministry," p. 33: "The Law is the basis of the worship; quite naturally, then, it is read at worship."

mediates God's very address to his people.[39] It is *in* the Ark of God and *in* the words said to reside there that ancient Israel sees God savingly present.

The Ark symbolizes the entire process Terrien outlines whereby divine presence authors human prophethood, community formation and preservation, cultic remembrance, and canonical authority. The Ark originates in the desert and becomes the focal point of priestly Yahwism after the Conquest. As the focus of God's presence, it is God's instrument of the Conquest. It is not only for particular military campaigns, but symbolizes the Conquest in its entirety: Like the "strong east wind" *(ruah qakim 'azah)* of Exodus 14:21 that divides the Sea of Reeds, it parts the waters of the Jordan and allows Israel to enter into the fulfillment of God's promises (Josh. 3–4).[40] It centers and unites the league of diverse Canaanite tribes that conquers and holds (however tenuously) God's promised land.[41] It acts as the first icon of Israelite worship. King David's relocation of it in his new capital of Jerusalem "must have done more to bind the feelings of the tribes to Jerusalem than we can possibly imagine."[42]

Israel's fortunes rise and fall according to Israel's fidelity to the Ark and what it represents. In the canonical picture, this is no more and no less than Israel's fidelity to God through the Law of Moses. Whether the Ark originally contained the tablets or this tradition is the creative *anamnesis* of the Deuteronomist,[43] the symbol of Israel's inheritance, unity, and access to God was associated with the divine *dabar* that formed Israel and alone could preserve it from extinction. The Ark symbolizes God's deliverance of Israel from Egypt, through the wilderness, to Sinai, across the Jordan, and into the promised

39. Muslim theologians were quick to notice that the Quran is material in its written, proclaimed, *and* memorized forms, not just in its written form. Their insight is equally applicable to Jewish and Christian doctrines of Scripture. Not only the proclaimed *kerygma* but the inspired *graphē* and the remembered *rhēma* are sacramental: Instituted by Christ, used by God, practiced in Church, they are material signs that mediate the deep reality of God's saving presence.

40. The "strong wind of the covenant" is a splendid picture of biblical inspiration, especially in view of Sinai's renewal at Pentecost.

41. "The league had its focal point at the shrine which housed the Ark of the Covenant, at least by the end of the period located at Shiloh. There the tribesmen would gather on stated occasions to seek the presence of Yahweh and renew their allegiance to him, and also to adjust matters of controversy and mutual interest among the tribes" (Bright, *A History of Israel,* p. 166).

42. Bright, *A History of Israel,* p. 201.

43. Terrien prefers to call the Ark "the Ark of Yahweh," attributing the biblical view that it housed the tables of the law to later Deuteronomistic retrojection (*The Elusive Presence,* p. 163). But the covenant's presence in such an object would be both precedented (Terrien, p. 214 n. 5) and fitting, given Israel's experience at Sinai. The traditional image of the Hexateuch and 1 Kings 8:9 is a better symbol of Israel's faith at any rate.

land. If Israel is a collection of Semitic refugees from Egypt and the desert, joined together with Canaanite tribes absorbed on the basis of their acceptance of Yahweh, as today's historical picture suggests,[44] then the Ark of the Covenant is the very sacrament of the gathering of Israel. It is fitting that John the Seer would find it the most appropriate symbol for God's regathering of Israel on the Day of the Lord, in Revelation's central text, the heavenly hymn of 11:15-19:

> Then God's temple in heaven was opened, and the ark of his covenant was seen within his temple; and there were flashes of lightning, voices, peals of thunder, an earthquake, and heavy hail.[45]

Yet it should also be remembered that the Ark was, in the end, dispensable.[46] Just as the Virgin Mary is a necessary but secondary medium of Jesus Christ, so the Ark is a necessary but secondary medium of God's written Word. Augustine expresses a similar view of Scripture's dispensability in the life of a saint, as we shall see below.[47] On earth, the covenant would outlast the Ark, and come into its own under the influence of Jerusalem's priesthood as the normative shaper of exiled and restored Israel.

The State and Its Critics: Holy Words of Kings and Prophets

The Ark alone was not sufficient to bind together the tribes and cultures of Israel during the Conquest. Under pressure for greater centralization than a tribal federation could offer against Philistine threats, Israel opted to follow its neighbors and proclaim a king. The Deuteronomistic editor of Joshua-Kings has forever stamped God's disapproval on this move. Yet it is to the

---

44. Bright, *A History of Israel*, pp. 133-37.

45. Elizabeth Schüssler-Fiorenza locates Rev. 11:15-19 in the center of Revelation's grand chiasm. "The main theme of Rev.," she says, "is shortly but precisely expressed in the hymn in 11:15-19 which is composed in the center of the book." *Revelation: Justice and Judgment* (Philadelphia: Fortress, 1985), p. 56.

46. "I will give you shepherds according to my heart, who shall feed you with knowledge and understanding. And it shall come to pass, when you multiply and increase in the land, in those days, says Yahweh, they shall say no more, 'The ark of the covenant of Yahweh!' Nor shall it come to mind; nor shall they remember it; nor shall they miss it; nor shall that be done any more. At that time they shall call Jerusalem the throne of Yahweh; and all the nations shall be gathered to it, to the name of Yahweh, to Jerusalem; nor shall they walk any more after the stubbornness of their evil heart" (Jer. 3:15-17).

47. Augustine, *On Christian Doctrine*, 1.39.43.

monarchy that Israel's Scriptures (including Joshua-Kings!) owe their existence as Scripture.

Paul Nadim Tarazi rightly stresses that the literary output of ancient Israel was a state-sponsored enterprise. The literary shaping of earlier traditions in the hands of the Pentateuch's authors had motives both cultic and political. Indeed, the two were inseparable. Tribes were written into and out of histories, and political and meteorological fortunes were read in terms of God's purposes, in order to tell the state's story, or to subvert one state's story in favor of another's.[48] This is equally true of liturgical writing: From David's reign on, the Psalter was "strictly under the control of the royal sanctuaries."[49] The Psalms are, by and large, the royal family at prayer.[50]

And so a new tradition of divine words comes alongside the older one, as Israel changes from a charismatically led tribal league into a monarchy, and then an empire.[51] In the categories of Israel's anointed offices, God's *royal* words join the priestly and prophetic words preserved in the Mosaic traditions. The unconditional Davidic covenant emerges to warrant and explain the innovation of a king over a "united" Israel and narrate the golden age of the Davidic Kingdom.[52]

---

48. Paul Nadim Tarazi, *The Old Testament: An Introduction,* 3 vols. (Crestwood, N.Y.: St. Vladimir's Seminary Press, 1991-1996), vol. 1, pp. 49-139.

49. Tarazi, *The Old Testament,* vol. 3, p. 77.

50. Of course, this does not mean that every psalm is a royal psalm, or that the Psalter as it now stands is an entirely royal production. In *The Psalms Through Three Thousand Years* (Minneapolis: Fortress, 1993), William Holladay chronicles the shaping of the Psalter from Ugaritic sources, Egyptian borrowings and echoes, and Davidic, Solomonic, northern, and Second Temple eras, to widely ranging Palestinian and Diaspora forces that move it towards its canonical form.

51. Terrien (*The Elusive Presence,* p. 189) sees this source-critically: "The original nucleus of Nathan's oracle which opposed David's plan to erect a temple — Yahweh walks but does not sit down (2 Sam. 7:6) — was absorbed within a dynastic oracle on David's election and his posterity forever in Jerusalem (2 Sam. 7:8-29). The choice of Zion as the permanent residence of Yahweh on earth, as well as the divine election of David and of his dynasty in Jerusalem, became indissolubly linked in ritual and narrative alike."

52. Bright claims an early date for the development of Israel's royal ideology, finding it in early texts like 1 Sam. 25:30, 2 Sam. 5:2, Ps. 78:67-72, 2 Sam. 9, 2 Sam. 20, and 1 Kings 1–2. "The dogma was soon developed that Yahweh had chosen Zion as his eternal dwelling place and had made covenant with David that his line would rule forever. This dogma was probably already well established in the reigns of David and Solomon, and helps to explain the loyalty of Judah to the Davidic house. Charisma and divine designation had, in theory, been transferred in perpetuity from the individual to the dynasty" (*A History of Israel,* p. 224). Others posit a much later date, retrojecting decades of lost glory on a more provincial kingdom. At any rate, it is here not in Rome, that Constantinianism is born.

The royal tradition soon develops a trajectory of its own, coming to interpret, displace, and co-opt the conditional Mosaic covenant. This in turn fosters the later development of a rich biblical resource — the Writings, at the center of which are the royal psalms and proverbs traditionally attributed to David and Solomon.[53]

The Psalter is an amazingly diverse literature, almost a miniature Bible in doxological form.[54] It contains not only thanksgiving, praise, petition, and intercession, but also contains historical narrative, prophecy and eschatological discourse, wisdom, and divine command. In later tradition King David comes to be the Psalms' speaker of choice, appropriating for himself the functions of the priest as Israel's worship-leader and advocate, the functions of the prophet as its truth-teller and critic, and the functions of the sage as its elder. Thus the Davidic figure assimilates to himself the qualities of Moses the Deliverer before him, and of the Anointed One to follow him.

Royal sponsorship comes at a steep price. The monarchy's conviction of its own eternal divine election and its willingness to syncretize for political ends blind it to the caveats of the Mosaic tradition, and create a smugness on the part of the royal tradition of interpretation that is eventually its downfall. Even the stimulus to reform brought by the Book of the Law under Josiah, so important to reviving the flagging prophetic and priestly traditions, is unable to overcome the royal momentum. Indeed, under Josiah "the Mosaic covenant, its demands supposedly met, became the handmaid of the Davidic covenant, guaranteeing the permanence of Temple, dynasty, and state."[55]

Collapse and Exile

Prophethood in its later form emerges in reaction to the royal tradition's excesses. The classical prophets, beginning with Elijah, deliver divine words that

53. See Bright, *A History of Israel*, p. 225. Tarazi goes so far as to claim that most of the canonical psalms are royal, not only because of their content and shared vocabulary but because of the decisive importance an official pedigree in the Jerusalem temple liturgy must have had for a psalm to be included in the canonical collection of 150 psalms later preserved in the Tanakh. See Tarazi, *The Old Testament*, vol. 1, p. 77.

54. The final Psalter's fivefold structure (1–41, 42–72, 73–89, 90, 106, 107–150), probably after the Pentateuch, indicates how profoundly later Judaism appreciated this quality of the psalms. See Tarazi, *The Old Testament*, vol. 3, pp. 99-104. We will return to this below.

55. Bright, *A History of Israel*, p. 323.

critique Israel's new institutions by the standards of its ancestral, tribal, covenantal institutions.[56]

Joshua-Kings (shaped of course from the prophetic perspective) presents the prophets as the real players in royal and priestly Israel (Samuel the kingmaker raised in the temple at Shiloh, Nathan the savior of David's career). Like Mosaic Yahwism, Israelite prophecy mediates an "aggressive" word that reaches out to those "who are not" in order to form them into those who are. Unlike the priestly form of God's words, the prophetic will not be confined to liturgical space or time. Unlike their royal form, the prophetic words require no state sponsorship and have no vested interests. Whereas "the Lord was present in his instruction *(torah)* at the altars and in his wisdom at the city gates . . . even accessible in an immediate way through the 'men of God' (the seers) for special requests," with the prophets "God took the initiative," both in the timing of the message and in the place of its delivery — in streets and homes as well as sacred spaces.[57] Reformers and charismatics have found this picture of the priority of God's prophetic Word to both sacramental and political practice compelling ever since.[58]

The prophets' speech-acts reveal the sovereignty and initiative of Scripture's ultimate speaker. The Spirit of Yahweh will not be tamed. When earlier media of divine presence are domesticated, God breaks out beyond their old boundaries to create an urgent new conversation. Through interventions like these, the former prophets preserve early monarchical Israel through the failings of the first kings, and the latter prophets mediate the resources that will see Israel through her own political death.[59]

It is tempting to draw from these episodes of Israel's history a very qualified soteriology of Scripture: that traditions such as the Davidic covenant were anything but redemptive in Israel's history, that they were a kind of "early early catholicism" that smothered the authentic *kerygma* of primitive Israel's Mosaic Yahwism. A struggle between the prophetic schools of Jeremiah and Hananiah may reflect precisely this kind of conclusion among some of Israel's canonical interpreters.[60]

---

56. Says Bright: "Elijah embodied the strictest tradition of Yahwism. . . . His was the God of Sinai, who brooked no rival and would exact blood vengeance for crimes against covenant law such as Ahab had committed. Elijah therefore declared Holy War on the pagan state and its pagan god" (*A History of Israel*, pp. 246-47). And so it is here, not in Donatism or in the radical Reformation, that anti-Constantinianism is born.

57. Tarazi, *The Old Testament*, vol. 2, pp. 4-5.

58. Bright, *A History of Israel*, p. 249.

59. Bright, *A History of Israel*, p. 266.

60. See Tarazi, *The Old Testament*, vol. 1, pp. 124-25, citing Jer. 28:1-17. Old cites Jer. 2:8,

Yet the Davidic covenant was a check on royal power as well as a source of it. The divine right of kings comes with divine strings attached, and as long as Israel's throne was justified theologically, the prophetic and priestly schools retained powerful footholds.[61] Furthermore, these schools themselves found things of value in God's royal words. The classical prophets do much more than simply repudiate the royal prophets and priests and reassert old-fashioned Yahwism. Instead, like today's "evangelical catholics," they give the royal theology a new lease on life by subjecting it to a massive reinterpretation, synthesizing the Davidic and Mosaic covenants into a divine promise of restoration both assured and contingent upon repentance. Israel's classical prophetic tradition reasserts prophetic Yahwism in a society that has forgotten it; but it does so without repudiating the very real blessings to Israel of David's and Solomon's era.[62] The curses of the Mosaic law are revealed to be divine chastisements, and the blessings of the Davidic covenant eschatological promises.[63]

Indeed, in the end, the prophetic transformation of the royal traditions confers unprecedented power upon them. The exilic prophetic tradition brings new life to the hints of Israel's cosmic significance to humanity that have been present ever since the patriarchal promises. The universal scope of Israel, which in the face of Israel's national failure seems as ludicrous as the promise of an eternal Davidic throne, instead gains more power than ever.[64]

The Beginnings of Tanakh

We have intentionally characterized Israel's various prebiblical traditions in terms of the categories of Israel's anointed offices of prophet, priest, and

---

Micah 3:11, and later 2 Chron. 15:3, as examples of Israel's history of prophetic indictments of the priesthood ("Roots of the Christian Ministry," pp. 31-32).

61. "If David's dynasty was to be firmly established, it was because God had decided to make a 'covenant' that would ensure the steadfastness of His love for David and his descendants. In other words, kingship would ultimately survive in Israel as long as God acted to ensure that the king's will fully reflected His own. It was as if, through this covenant, God had taken into His own hands the reins of the kingdom in Judah and Israel" (Tarazi, *The Old Testament,* vol. 1, pp. 114-15).

62. Bright, *A History of Israel,* p. 295.

63. Bright, *A History of Israel,* p. 297.

64. See Bright, *A History of Israel,* pp. 357ff. The vision is worked out with particular clarity in Isaiah 40-66, which becomes a guide for the first Christians' mission to the Gentiles. See of course its use in the writings of Paul (particularly in Rom. 15), along with the echo of Isaiah 45 in James's speech in Acts 15:18 and others. It may be here that an adequate alternative to both Constantinianism and anti-Constantinianism can be grounded.

king. A Christian will recognize here the *munus triplex* of Christ.[65] The significance of the correspondence between Israel's literary traditions and Christ's anointed offices will become clear below. But already one sees a parallel: As these various charismatic institutions achieve an unprecedented and final unity in Jesus' messianic career, so by the time of the Babylonian Exile, these diverse traditions of God's remembered words are on their way to achieving an unprecedented and permanent coherence in the mind of Israel and in the canon of Scripture that has begun to coalesce. The priestly language of purity and intercession, the royal language of wisdom and promise, and the prophetic words of judgment and hope have come to make sense of each other as one body of holy literature. Never again will one dominate or crowd out the others. Each of these linguistic traditions plays its own part in forming, re-forming, and sustaining Israel over its turbulent history, "making ready for the Lord a people prepared" (Luke 1:17).

Remarkably, this coherence and power arrive at a time when throne and Temple are only memories, and true prophets few and far between. Following the monarchy's collapse, Scripture's mission takes it to a new and central stage in Israel's formation. First, the psalmist appropriates the roles of prophet, priest, king, and sage; then the written Word itself and its readers appropriate the roles of the psalmist. Each strand of Israel's literary tradition enters into a greater biblical tradition, overcoming the limitations of its originators and bestowing immortality upon them. Royal words of promise eclipse failed dynasties; a Law of purity judges impotent and even corrupt priesthoods; promises of blessings and curses outlive the prophets who deliver them. These institutions all live on, but now in the textual life of Israel's oral and written traditions. Indeed, in their textual forms they finally achieve a state of holiness. Moses' words cross the Jordan forbidden to him and announce the coming of one even greater. The royal words promise (and eventually herald) an eternal dynasty rather than the Davidic soap opera. The wisdom of a foolish world becomes a type of the Wisdom to come. In all of these cases, the texts escape the sin and corruption of their originating communities. They can be trusted to yield life in the present, and in the coming Savior who will fulfill rather than correct them. It is in its captivity that Israel begins to appreciate the saving power of God's words with an intensity it will never forget, and Judaism is born.

> During the exile, though we cannot say precisely how or where, the records and traditions of the past were jealously preserved. In these, which both

---

65. Appreciation of Christ's Threefold Office is by no means restricted to the Calvinist tradition. For an ecumenical treatment, see Geoffrey Wainwright, *For Our Salvation: Two Approaches to the Work of Christ* (Grand Rapids: Eerdmans, 1997), pp. 103-9.

awakened recollection of Yahweh's past deeds toward his people and held an earnest of hope for the future, the community *lived*. The Deuteronomic historical corpus . . . was reedited, added to, and adapted to the situation of the exiles. The sayings of the prophets, now vindicated by events, were likewise preserved, orally and in writing. . . . The cultic laws that comprise the bulk of the so-called Priestly Code, and that reflect the practice of the Jerusalem Temple, were likewise collected and codified in definitive form at about this time. . . . As the community thus clung to its past it prepared itself for the future.[66]

Inner-Biblical Exegesis: The Work of Scripture on Scripture

In this massive project of biblical preparation, in the evolution of Scripture, we see the saving power of God's words amply demonstrated. The Tanakh's development does more than ready texts for their subsequent uses in Judaism. It enshrines a tradition of biblical interpretation in Scripture itself. The Jewish practice of what Michael Fishbane calls "inner-biblical exegesis" creates trajectories of interpretation that not only reveal early Jewish hermeneutical dynamics, but set precedents for how God's people may interpret and even change God's words. In both these ways, evidence of inner-biblical exegesis sheds bright light on Israel's deepening appreciation of the living work of God's words. Fishbane's thorough study of inner-biblical exegesis in the Tanakh concludes with this assessment:

> The texts and traditions, the received *traditum* of ancient Israel, were not simply copied, studied, transmitted, or recited. They were also, and by these means, subject to redaction, elucidation, reformulation, and outright transformation. Accordingly, our received traditions are complex blends of *traditum* and *traditio* in dynamic interaction, dynamic interpenetration, and dynamic interdependence. They are, in sum, the exegetical voices of many teachers and tradents, from different circles and times, responding to real and theoretical considerations as perceived and as anticipated.[67]

In other words, the Tanakh is more than just the object and genesis of Israel's tradition of biblical interpretation. It is, in a sense, the tradition itself. Tanakh

---

66. Bright, *A History of Israel*, p. 350.

67. Michael Fishbane, *Biblical Interpretation in Ancient Israel* (Oxford: Clarendon, 1985), p. 543.

is Israel's origin, its nucleus, its history, its product, its eschaton — the written means of its salvation.

How can the "outright transformation" of one scripture in another be evidence for the *authority* of Scripture? Is it not the opposite? The answer to this question lies in some of Fishbane's examples of the transformation of earlier texts in light of later convictions. Fishbane reads Deuteronomy 7:9-10 as a revision of Exodus 34:6-7, and calls it "an outright contradiction and rejection of a divinely proclaimed *traditum*. . . . With one stroke, later tradition thoroughly controverted an earlier revelation, and *authenticated its novel viewpoint by means of a presumptive misquote*."[68] Texts like Joel 2:12-14 and Jonah 3:8-10, already mentioned in the previous chapter, follow even more radical trajectories from Exodus 34:6-7. In both these cases, the *traditum* is reworked thoroughly in the conviction that God repents of his own evil plans.[69]

Fishbane's examples are striking, and even troubling. But it is unfair to call these texts contradictions and rejections of the letter and spirit of Exodus 34. They seem instead to be sensitive reworkings of the text, wholly consistent with God's extraordinary repentance in the face of Moses' interceding for idolatrous Israel in Exodus 32. The transformative *traditio* of inner-biblical exegesis need not betray the transformed *traditum*. (Indeed, it *cannot*, if both are legitimate.) Fishbane's examples of inner-biblical exegesis in the Tanakh, like the examples of the New Testament's use of the Old Testament that come below, point to something far beyond simple revision, refinement, or contradiction: The *traditio* develops along with Israel's deepening appreciation of God's character and the purpose of his textual presence. Israel's "doctrine of Scripture" develops in accordance with Israel's doctrine of God. Because God's words take on God's character and do God's work, Israel's growing intimacy with God inevitably transforms its category of "divine word." We will see the climax of this process in the apostolic Church's reexamination of Israel's Scriptures in light of Jesus Christ.

Fishbane offers several other examples that illustrate this faithful amending of earlier traditions, as time and experience deepen Israel's appreciation of God's words. In 2 Chronicles 14:1-4, the Chronicler glosses 1 Kings 15:11-13 to stress that Asa's obedience was not simply to Yahweh, but also to *Torah and commandments*.[70] An even more striking substitution is "go *in my Torah* as you went before me" (2 Chron. 6:16) for "go *before me* as you went

---

68. Fishbane, *Biblical Interpretation*, p. 343, emphasis in original.
69. Fishbane, *Biblical Interpretation*, pp. 341-47.
70. Fishbane, *Biblical Interpretation*, pp. 385-86.

before me" (1 Kings 8:25).[71] A third example is more speculative: The redactor of Joshua-Kings takes an ancient exhortation to "be strong" or "not to fear" in the face of a difficult (often military) task (see Deut. 31:4-6), and associates it with obedience to the Torah (Josh. 1:6-9).[72] These recontextualizations have the same effect on the patriarchal promises as the later prophets' reintroduction of the Mosaic covenant had on the Davidic covenant. They juxtapose conditionality and unconditionality, transforming both. And given the jeopardy in which human sins continually put the divine promises in the ancient narrative itself, the resulting synthesis betrays neither tradition.

In these texts Torah is portrayed as "filling in" for God: It acts sacramentally, as a material means by which God makes himself savingly present to Israel. Forever preserved in the canon is evidence of the capacity of God's words to mediate God's presence even apart from God's other presences to Israel: Ark, Temple, throne, and living prophets. Its power will allow rabbinical Judaism to form in exile, prosper in dispersion, regather and regroup under Nehemiah and Ezra, and eventually continue for centuries in the total absence of these other means of God's presence.

Indeed, Isaiah envisions a day when through Israel's Scriptures, God's presence will someday be mediated *beyond* Israel: "Out of Zion shall go forth Torah, and the word of Yahweh from Jerusalem" (Isa. 2:1-4). Scripture has become a means of fulfilling God's universal promises to Abraham. The sojourning *logos* has truly been creating a wordly community, as a holy school for all the world.

A Very Present Help: Scripture's Pneumatic Mediation of Salvation

Scripture's power to function as a substitute for Ark, Temple, throne, sage, and prophet brings us back to the question of the correspondence between the Tanakh's prophetic, priestly, and royal traditions, and the Threefold Office of Christ. Such a correspondence is not an artificial projection of late Christian soteriology onto the "Hebrew Bible." Israel's discrete literary traditions remember and continue God's redeeming presence in the absence of their originating agents. In fact, it is in the absence of the original agents that the writings gain their greatest power, as the bedrock texts of Judaism.

God's absence is crucial to the founding of Judaism. "Hebraism had

---

71. Fishbane, *Biblical Interpretation*, p. 386.

72. Fishbane, *Biblical Interpretation*, p. 384. He finds a parallel in the Deuteronomist's reworking of 2 Sam. 7:12-16 in 1 Kings 2:1-9 (p. 385).

been founded on divine presence," says Terrien. "Judaism arose from divine absence. The fathers had seen the *Magnalia Dei*. The sons knew only national dereliction."[73] Moses and his revivalists, the Levitical priesthood, and David's dynasty all give rise to bodies of literature to assist them in their divinely ordained work. All of these institutions come to a tragic end in the course of Israel's history. Yet every time, their bodies of literature survive them to continue their work. The prophets' protests against syncretization and abuse of wealth and power continue to shake principalities and powers to the ground, long after the original evils have been annihilated. The Priestly Code and Deuteronomic Law survive and transcend the societies to which they were delivered and in which they made the most literal sense, to become the very fabric of exilic, ancient, medieval, and modern Judaisms that have no priesthoods to carry out their requirements. The Psalter lives long after the fragile political structure on which it is built crumbles, to become the devotional and liturgical canon of God's faithful, whether Jew or Gentile, Constantinian or anti-Constantinian. In every case, God's anointed servants continue to do their old work, but in strikingly new contexts.

This can happen because the sacramental quality of God's words enables them to mediate divine presence in places of divine absence. Conceived in the full light of God's presence, they continue to shine as light in the darkness. Holy writ is such an effective means of God's "presence-in-absence"[74] that for centuries, biblical Israel can look forward to a prophet like Moses, a new Temple, and a restored throne, without anything but Scripture to sustain it — because in Scripture it has all three. Tanakh mediates the past and proleptically anticipates the future involvement of God in creation to redeem his people Israel.

God's absence changes biblical Israel as profoundly as it changes Israel's Bible. The settled monarchies become exiled refugee communities. Scripture preserves Israel-in-exile from cultural annihilation by re-forming it as a *remembering community*.

> Whereas the simple appellation "God" or "Lord" was self-explanatory and thus sufficient in pre-exilic Jerusalem, where the deity was enthroned in the visible temple of a tangible nation, the anti-historical God of nascent Judaism had to be constructed time and again as a reality in the mind of the gathered congregation. . . . [I]n such recollection lay the definition and ultimately the very presence of both Israel's God and God's Israel.[75]

73. Terrien, *The Elusive Presence*, p. 390.

74. See Chapter 3 for a discussion of "presence-in-absence" as describing dialectical Christian eschatology.

75. Tarazi, *The Old Testament*, vol. 3, p. 91.

Christians confess that these three anointed offices come together not ultimately in Scripture, but in the person of Jesus the Anointed. The Spirit-filled Messiah assumes and transcends the roles of Israel's old charismatic deliverers. He literally redefines prophethood, priesthood, and kingship. Yet, paradoxically, the old figures do not fade into insignificance beside him. Instead, in Jesus' messianic career, their work is revealed as part of God's own personal work, and thereby magnified. Moses, Aaron, and David, and their various literary traditions, are parts of God's one economy of salvation.

Accordingly, Christians did not and do not abandon Israel's or their own Scriptures — if not even in Jesus' full presence, surely never in his absence! Tarazi directly links the Tanakh's anamnetic function in exilic, Second Temple, and Diaspora Judaism to the Bible's anamnetic function in the gathered and expectant Church of Christ.[76] As the original figures lived on in remembrance and grew in power in their literary traditions, so the Messiah's powerful saving work is made even more powerful after his ascension, in the continuing work of the Paraclete (cf. John 14:12). Sent back to earth by the seated and ruling Christ, the Holy Spirit continues and mediates the work of the Son whom he empowered in the Jordan, not least in the work of inspired Scripture.

The dialectical relationships between Israel's anointed officers and their inspired literary traditions anticipate the dialectical relationship between Son and Spirit. Actually, it is more accurate to say that they are *established* there, in the economy of the Triune God. To the extent that the words of Israel's Scriptures assist and accomplish the work of these offices, they participate in Christ's own salvific prophethood, priesthood, and kingship.[77] They too are God's anointed agents. Already, in the earliest recoverable stages of the Bible's history as Bible, we can speak of biblical inspiration using the terms of the divine economy of salvation.

---

76. Tarazi, *The Old Testament*, vol. 3, pp. 91-95.

77. It is in this sense that we can see the rise of rabbinical Judaism as a natural, positive response to the loss of throne, Temple, and prophetic community on the part of late first-century Judaism. Synagogue-centered Judaism brilliantly preserved the power of Israel's anointed offices and institutions in their physical absence. A Christian should charitably ask: Does it also continue to mediate in some way the presence of the anointed Messiah for which much of "Israel according to the flesh" still hopes?

Restoration: Israel Regathers around the Tanakh

If it is in defeat and exile that Israel's Scriptures become a template for life apart from Temple and throne, it is under Ezra and Nehemiah that they become a template for renewed life in Palestine. The reconstruction probably began with a public reading of Torah at the Feast of Tabernacles, and accelerated as the demands of the Law were brought to bear on the compromised marital, cultic, and economic lives of Judah's inhabitants. The nation of Israel was literally reorganized around the Torah. Scripture played so profound a role in Israel's restoration that Ezra would be called a second Moses.[78] Ezra oversaw the process by which the Torah reconstituted the nation of Israel in the form by which it would survive down to the present day. Torah had become the defining mark of Judaism, over political, genealogical, or linguistic identity — even over participation in the Temple cult.[79] With Torah, the worship of Yahweh finally began to gain the upper hand in its eternal battle against syncretism.

In a word, under Ezra, Israel's Scriptures were *canonized*. The literary creation of a community of faith was now its creator and sustainer.[80] Through the canon of Scripture the *logos* was doing his work of gathering and regathering his covenantal and messianic people — and through it, preparing for his own coming.

The main streams of this congealing canon — law, prophets, psalms — have already been described. At their margins arose two literatures that deserve further attention: wisdom literature and apocalyptic. Both of these had roots deep in Israel's earlier traditions, but developed trajectories of their own in Second Temple and Diaspora Judaism. And despite their "marginal" nature, both played pivotal roles in the mission of Scripture, particularly in the rise of Christianity.

Human Wisdom and Its Lord

Wisdom, one might say, is the adequation of one's mind and life to the world. It is presented as both a divine gift and a product of personal experience; both a social good and a personal good; both an inheritance from one's ancestors

78. Bright, *A History of Israel*, pp. 387-89.

79. Bright, *A History of Israel*, pp. 389-90. While there is disagreement over how proper it is to call Ezra's scriptures "Torah," the term is fitting in spirit, if not also in letter.

80. Bright, *A History of Israel*, p. 431: "The law no longer merely regulated the affairs of an already constituted community; it had created the community!"

and a life lived within God's will. That later Jews and Christians take the dialectics of these very different aspects of wisdom for granted is canonical wisdom literature's greatest theological achievement.

We have already called Jewish wisdom a "royal" literary tradition.[81] But the roots of wisdom lie behind the monarchy itself, in the folk wisdom of earliest Israel, delivered at the gates of Israelite cities by judges, elders, rulers, and sages. This means that ancient wisdom was a good dispensed by the ruling elite of Near Eastern societies. So it was only natural that as the tradition grew in size and sophistication, it was assimilated to the figure of the Jewish king, and particularly to the figure of Solomon.[82] Wisdom influenced the priestly and prophetic streams of Israel's precanonical traditions (Gen. 2; 2 Sam. 6, etc.; Amos, Isaiah, Esther, Psalms).[83] But wisdom's royal connotations were always the strongest, and these only strengthened over time.

To speak of Jewish wisdom is to speak of Solomon. His tragic figure is an appropriate personification of the tradition. He is famous (and infamous) for his Davidic heritage, his education, his cosmopolitanism, his syncretism, his piety as builder of the Temple, his life experiences (both as God's disciple and as an apostate), and his unrivaled status as leader of the Near Eastern world during its brief Golden Age. Solomon, like no other Israelite, lived both sides of Israel's "prosperity gospel," and wisdom offers a theological account of both his stunning prosperity and his ultimate failure. The tradition attaching to his legend embodies his life's theological significance.

On first glance it is rather surprising that wisdom should be personified so specifically, for wisdom more than any other literature carries the aura of universality. Tarazi bluntly states that

> wisdom is basically universal. A given saying cannot be wisdom here and folly there. . . . If, then, we place an adjective of locality before wisdom — such as Chinese wisdom, Indian wisdom, Greek wisdom — we cannot mean by that a kind of wisdom valid solely in that place. It simply means that those specific wisdom sayings were developed in that area; their value, however, is universal.[84]

81. Tarazi too analyzes the psalms and wisdom as royal traditions, personified in David and Solomon, respectively (*The Old Testament*, vol. 3, pp. 127-28).

82. See, for instance, 1 Kings 3:16-28.

83. See Brevard Childs, *Biblical Theology of the Old and New Testaments* (Minneapolis: Fortress, 1992), p. 188. On the other hand, Childs notes that Israel's other traditions had very little influence upon wisdom itself.

84. Tarazi, *The Old Testament*, vol. 3, pp. 113-14. He claims this is why kings from throughout the world sought Solomon's wisdom (1 Kings 4:29-34, 10:1-9) and why Aesop's fables continue to be handed down in America today.

Israel's wisdom was borrowed in part from other cultures (Prov. 22:17–24:22, cf. the Egyptian "Instruction of Amenemope") and transmitted throughout the world in subsequent Judaism, Christianity, and Islam. So why did a literature that purportedly bestows universally valid truth need to be made concrete in a historical figure? What is the added value of a king's name, and particularly of Solomon's name? Would it not have been just as powerful coming from the Queen of Sheba, or even King Saul?

Of course not — and here lies the danger in simply labeling Jewish wisdom "universal." To rob wisdom literature of its adjectives is to detach it from both its historical and rhetorical context, from its uses and "forms of life," and from its particular role in Scripture's mission. First, as we have seen, wisdom is more than a sage's words; it is the sage's own character. No oriental royals would flock to Israel to gain the wisdom of Saul! Solomon's name is powerful in a way that Saul's is not. The positive and negative lessons of Solomon's own life are the sayings' original fruits-test. Second, Solomon is more than a convenient figure with which to measure the validity of Semitic and Egyptian folk wisdom. He is a pivotal figure in salvation-history. Wisdom's affiliation with Solomon reveals its role in Scripture's mission to Israel and to the world. Wisdom is indeed universal, but not in the abstract, disembodied way that many imagine. It is much more than chicken soup for the soul or principles of worldly success.

Under Solomon, the Israelite kingdom was said to have gained unsurpassed status in its world. Israel's Golden Age presented an opportunity for it to be Yahweh's light to the world (and a corresponding risk of becoming indistinguishable from the world in the process, reducing Yahweh to just another regional deity). The tradition-history of canonical wisdom literature represents an aggressive response to this risky opportunity, and a profound theological vision of Israel's role in world history. Like Solomon's Temple, the wisdom tradition selectively appropriated and re-created the resources of the nations, towards an end that only Israel saw.[85]

In adopting other wisdom traditions in its own corpus, Israel did not endorse other traditions of rationality without qualification. Rather, it "circumcised" them by recontextualizing the knowledge of the nations under the overarching authority of the God of Israel. As Israelites accepted the name "El" for the Lord of Sinai, so over time Israel came to see in other traditions the presence and providence of Yahweh. Wisdom's message is not so much

---

85. So Childs (*Biblical Theology*, p. 187) rightly stresses the authentically Jewish roots and character of the wisdom tradition, a quality often lost in all the attention paid to its synthetic qualities.

that *all* truth is God's truth, but that all truth is *God's* truth. As the tradition evolves, this message is made increasingly clear in two ways: First, redactors stress the wisdom of Torah along with and above the wisdom of experience (Prov. 1:7; 28:4-9; 29:18; prologue to Sirach, Wisdom 7:22-27a).[86] The wisdom of the nations is only complete, only *truly* wisdom, when it is brought under the penumbra of Israel's special knowledge. Second, the personification[87] of wisdom makes Wisdom a quasi-divine subject: She is God's agent in creating the world and leading it to the saving knowledge of God (Prov. 8). As in Solomon we see Israel's king as emperor, so in wisdom we see God's knowledge as imperial. Its vestiges have already spread throughout the world, with the mission of bringing the world back to its source.

This gives the nations' wisdom an intentionality that goes unappreciated when wisdom's universality is mistaken for disembodied truthfulness. Because the wisdom tradition can incorporate the best of the nations' knowledge into Israel's specific rationality, it can achieve a degree of commensurability with other traditions of enquiry.[88] This commensurability is *preparatio evangelica,* a basis for the translation and spread of Torah into the languages of the nations.[89] Wisdom's incorporation of foreign materials is a prelude to mission. "In the Wisdom of Solomon the law is the salvation of the world," says Brevard Childs, "and without it wisdom cannot be understood (6:1ff.; 9:9ff.)."[90] Tarazi finds the same concerns in his reading of Song of Songs and Ruth, both of which invite Gentiles to be "married" to Israel and accept the Law as the ultimate expression of God's wisdom.[91] Into this mode of Jewish evangelism one can place both the exegesis of Philo and the rhetorical strategy of Paul in Athens (see Acts 17). The two stand firmly within the broad tradition of Hellenistic Judaism, which was strengthened immeasurably by early Israelite and later Jewish wisdom.

86. Cf. Tarazi, *The Old Testament,* vol. 3, pp. 131-32, 145-46, 153-54. Tarazi finds the same message in Ecclesiastes, where "Qohelet" is Torah, the assembler of Israel and its ruler in the new Jerusalem (vol. 3, p. 134).

87. Whether this personification amounts to "hypostatization" is another matter. Childs follows von Rad in avoiding the term (*Biblical Theology,* p. 189). On the other hand, feminist Christology is far more likely to favor the hypostatization of Wisdom. For an example, see Elizabeth A. Johnson, *She Who Is: The Mystery of God in Feminist Theological Discourse* (New York: Crossroad, 1992), pp. 86-100.

88. For an examination of the limited commensurability between traditions of enquiry, see "Tradition and Translation," in Alasdair MacIntyre, *Whose Justice? Which Rationality?* (Notre Dame: University of Notre Dame Press, 1988), pp. 370-88.

89. See Tarazi, *The Old Testament,* vol. 3, pp. 126-27.

90. Childs, *Biblical Theology,* p. 189.

91. Tarazi, *The Old Testament,* vol. 3, pp. 140-41.

Appropriating across traditions is always a risky enterprise. Its opposite risks are overtranslation and undertranslation — that is, acculturation to foreign traditions and acculturation to the home tradition. So it is no surprise that four of the "five disputed books" in early rabbinical Judaism are wisdom literature: Proverbs, Ecclesiastes, the Song of Songs, and Esther. Acculturation, both Jewish and Gentile, probably fueled the disputes over the canonicity of these books, as well as apocryphal wisdom literature's failure to achieve canonicity in Palestinian and in later rabbinic Judaism. Hellenistic Jews may have been fond of Sirach and Wisdom, but there is no evidence of even a *debate* over their canonical status (whether they "defile the hands") in rabbinic tradition. They and the other apocryphal books were never considered canonical by even a vocal minority of Palestinians.

These mixed results notwithstanding, the wisdom tradition embodies an influential Jewish vision of cosmic salvation. This is why wisdom's assimilation and transformation of Israel's and the nations' rationalities into the texts of Tanakh is as much a theological as a literary achievement: It critically appropriates, adopts, and remakes fallen creation in the confidence that God's presence can be found there and restored in its original fullness. It privileges Israel and Israel's Law, but without excluding the nations from its blessings. It too describes Athanasius' vision of the Law and Prophets as schoolmasters for all the world.

The Rise of Apocalyptic: The Word as Judge

On the other side of the coin of Israel's awakening sense of universal cosmic significance stands apocalyptic literature. In exile a new style of prophecy arose in Isaiah and Ezekiel, which flourished in Second Temple Judaism as the literary genre of apocalyptic. Apocalyptic shares wisdom's mixed record on the matter of canonicity — many apocalyptic writings failed to find acceptance in the Jewish and Christian canons, and Ezekiel is the fifth of the "five disputed books." Yet the genre's vivid picture of God as eschatological judge is powerfully present in both testaments, enormously influential in subsequent Judaism and Christianity, and integral to the salvific mission of Scripture.

Apocalyptic shares wisdom's cosmic perspective on Israel's significance, but sees that significance from a vastly different perspective. It sees in Israel's destruction and exile God's coming victory, in its desolation the universal scope of salvation, and in God's imminent, final judgment a promise of eternal hope for the world.

Wisdom literature portrays a world where the righteous prosper and the wicked suffer. The wise are blessed and saved, the wicked judged and condemned. God's mercy is then a kind of converse of God's justice. The apocalyptic vision turns this conception of salvation on its head. In a world where the wicked prosper and the righteous suffer, one is not saved *from* God's eschatological judgment. Rather, one is saved *from* injustice and wrath, *through* God's eschatological judgment. God's justice is itself a dimension of God's mercy.

This complementarity between salvation and judgment is hardly an apocalyptic innovation. God's judgments against Adam and Eve, Cain, Noah's neighbors, Babel's builders, and on throughout the entire biblical saga never conclude God's involvements in the world. Instead, they always create new beginnings. They save by temporarily restoring the conditions of justice that allow the divine-human relationship to see another day. Apocalyptic's innovation, and its greatest strength, are the qualities of *universality, finality, inevitability, imminence, urgency, hope,* and *unity* it brings to God's words of judgment and mercy. Unpacking these qualities reveals apocalyptic's special role in the mission of Scripture.

The judgment apocalyptic foresees is *universal.* It is not just Israel that is judged, and not just after some particularly onerous sin. Rather, the entire world and even the heavens are judged on the Day of the Lord, a time entirely of God's choosing, for all they have ever done. God's decisive intervention into the fallen creation can thus open up a final new age of peace between God and creation. Judgment Day's *finality* secures the new age's eternity. This necessary connection between final judgment and eternal justice is what makes the Last Day's arrival *inevitable,* only a matter of time.

How much time? In wisdom literature, human existence is fleeting but the days multiply on indefinitely. In contrast, apocalyptic shouts that history itself is fleeting. Only a few more events remain before history will be closed forever. One of the most powerful devices of apocalyptic is its *immediacy.* As Daniel closes, someone asks the inevitable question: "How long shall it be to the end of the wonders?" (Dan. 12:6). The answer is so frustratingly vague that even Daniel the seer, the one with unrivaled insight into the semiotics of heaven, cannot understand it. Daniel reopens the matter and is rebuffed: "Go your way, Daniel; for the words are closed up and sealed until the time of the end" (12:9). Daniel is left in a "between-times" — sent back out of God's presence into the world of his absence, with no more than the assurance that the presence will return in "a time, times, and a half."

How to interpret such a message? Millenarians and literalists have their own hermeneutical proposals. These continue to enjoy great persuasive power, particularly in evangelicalism worldwide, despite their utter failure as historical predictors. The rest of the Church has tended to view these schools of exegesis with a mixture of fear, embarrassment, and scorn. Partisans of "realized eschatology" dismiss apocalypticism as a "blind alley . . . into the barren sands of millenarianism."[92] Others (Augustine notably among them) read apocalyptic narratives allegorically, yielding interpretations generally rich in symbolic power but poor in their faithfulness to the promised nearness of God's return, and to the Jewish character of the genre.

McClendon offers a different answer by asking a different question: not "What do these texts *mean?*" but "What do they *do?*" Bracketing questions of the propositional content of apocalyptic discourse, he finds two devices at work: first, a "foreshortened sense of future time" that misleads when taken literally, but comforts when recognized as the literary device that it is; and second, a "prophetic (or baptist) vision" that teaches the reader to see "the present under the form of the biblical past," that narrates the present and future in canonical categories in order to reveal their true significance.[93]

McClendon is right to conceive of apocalyptic texts as speech-acts that work rhetorically rather than simply communicate propositionally. Daniel is better understood in terms of the soteriology of Scripture than in terms of past and future geopolitics. It aims to change its readers, not simply inform them. But does recognizing foreshortening *as* foreshortening not rob the device of its literary power? Does McClendon's hermeneutic honor apocalyptic rhetoric, or merely unmask it? How can one gain a "second naïvete"[94] about such texts, once one knows how they work?

A more thoroughly soteriological account of apocalyptic can better interpret McClendon. Apocalyptic's gospel that the end is near does more than raise awareness about God's final judgment; it actually *participates* in it. Apocalyptic always brings together the warning of final judgment and the delivery of present judgments upon present human sins. Contemporary empires are judged and marked out for eternal destruction, cities are condemned, and ruling figures are cursed. Apocalyptic is not an external account of these judgments, as if the judgments happen apart from it, but is itself their medium. God judges *through* the prophecies themselves: "*Mene,* God has numbered the days of your kingdom, and brought it to an end; *Tekel,* you have been weighed in the balances, and found wanting; *Peres,* your kingdom is divided, and given to the Medes and Persians" (Dan. 5:26-28).

---

92. See C. H. Dodd, *The Apostolic Preaching and Its Developments,* 2nd ed. (New York: Harper & Brothers, 1944), pp. 40-41, on the eschatology of Revelation, which he calls a "relapse into a pre-Christian eschatology."

93. James Wm. McClendon Jr., *Systematic Theology,* vol. 2: *Doctrine* (Nashville: Abingdon, 1994), p. 92.

94. Paul Ricoeur, *The Symbolism of Evil* (Boston: Beacon Press, 1969), p. 351.

Insofar as the present judgments participate typologically in God's final judgment, God's final judgment is made imminent in them. Foreshortening is indeed a literary device, for judgment is delivered in the words of judgment themselves. But the foreshortening is real. The feeling of *urgency* it evokes is equally real, and not merely the result of rhetorical manipulation. God's little judgments against empires and peoples are foretastes of the one great judgment to come. The scriptural words mediate God's imminence through their sacramental power to bring God's future judgment proleptically into the present. This power, not literary skill alone, gives apocalyptic its power to offer comfort and *hope* in the present to people who suffer in the present, no matter how many ages have yet to pass before the Day of the Lord arrives in fullness. In disparaging the apocalyptic perspective, C. H. Dodd and other proponents of realized eschatology ironically miss the realized aspect of apocalyptic literature itself. It too presents an inaugurated eschatology, as irreducibly present as it is irreducibly future.

Apocalyptic sees an eschatological singularity in all of God's saving and judging actions. There is one salvation, one mercy, one judgment, one condemnation, manifested in innumerable ways on innumerable occasions. When God judges through apocalyptic discourse, the full force of his eschatological wrath is brought to bear on every instance of his condemnation — and the full force of his eschatological mercy is likewise brought to bear on every instance of his liberation. Apocalyptic prophecy's mediation of eschatological judgment in the present explains its power to induce immediate ethical change in its contemporary audiences. They truly experience God's imminent, final judgment — and sometimes the experience causes them to embrace God's imminent, final salvation.

Apocalyptic practice has a further mission: to tie together the various strands of Scripture into one temporal and spatial *unity*. By typologically collapsing the distance between God's acts of saving judgment, apocalyptic portrays salvation-history in crushing coherence. The apocalyptic vision overcomes the dilemma moderns and postmoderns think they face between endorsing the historical-critical and the canonical stories of Israel. In associating discrete past, present, and future events with God's one definitive act of deliverance, apocalyptic shows it would be perfectly proper for the biblical writers and redactors to retroject the exodus, the wilderness wanderings, and Jordan's crossing into the histories of Canaanite and desert Semitic tribes, or for the Yahwist to call the one appearing to Abraham at Mamre "Yahweh," or for the Deuteronomist and Priestly Writer to portray all 613 canonical commandments as originating at Sinai. Whether or not these are historical events in the modern sense, the typological connections among them are already grounded eschatologically in the unity of God's saving work. The primordial curses, the patriarchal promises, the Law's blessings and curses, the prophets' warnings, ancient history's triumphs and tragedies, Wisdom's everyday judgments, the theodical anguish of Job and the imprecatory psalms — the apocalyptic vision appropriates the symbolic discourses of all of these and focuses them on one eschatological moment. While apocalyptic literature makes up only a tiny space at the margins of Tanakh, it gives the rest of Israel's Scriptures a decisive eschatological perspective. It pulls the other writings into what can truly be called a "biblical" frame, one in which the past and future bear upon the present, and Jerusalem occupies the center of the world.

The result is the familiar consciousness of the many different currents of first-century Judaism in which Jesus and his followers traveled. Like the other strands of the Tanakh, apocalyptic too helps create the conditions in which Israel's Messiah does his work of cosmic judgment and redemption.

Torah from Temple to Synagogue

As Israel's canon took shape, it took on an ever larger role in Israel's worship practice. As important as the Temple was in Israel's memory, especially at pivotal moments in its interaction with the outside world, Temple worship proved not to be of ultimate importance to Judaism. Some might infer from this a necessary competition or trade-off between word and cult.[95] Not so; the two were mutually dependent.

The Second Temple was the very center of Jewish biblical practice. The Temple housed and defined the canon of Israel's Scriptures: The canonicity of a particular scroll was affirmed when it was taken into the Temple to reside there in Israel's normative library, where it would no longer defile the hands.[96] It is out of the Temple and its priesthood that the Jewish office of scribe appears.[97]

The commission of God's words to writing implied their reading, and ancient reading was public reading. From the Temple God's words were read seasonally, at the high points of Israel's sacred year.[98] Teaching went on regu-

---

95. See Bright, *A History of Israel*, p. 435.

96. See Roger T. Beckwith, "Formation of the Hebrew Bible," in Martin Jan Mulder, ed., *Mikra: Text, Translation, Reading and Interpretation of the Hebrew Bible in Ancient Judaism and Early Christianity* (Minneapolis: Fortress, 1990), pp. 39-45, 62-63.

97. M. Bar-Ilan, "Scribes and Books in the Late Second Commonwealth and Rabbinic Period," in Mulder, ed., *Mikra*, p. 22.

98. See Charles Perrot, "The Reading of the Bible in the Ancient Synagogue," in Mulder, ed., *Mikra*, pp. 145-49.

larly in the Temple's forecourts, so that the center of Israel's corporate worship was "the site of the Word and hence of teaching," as well as the locus of covenant renewal.[99] The physical subsistence of God's words in writing necessarily located them in a particular place; and their natural home was God's dwelling place in the Temple. Thus the Torah scrolls replaced the Ark as the verbal sacrament of God's presence. On the Day of Atonement, the high priest read out the Law in the Temple courts — another powerful image of Scripture's sacramental power to save.[100]

The era of the Temple's and Jerusalem's rebuilding also ushered in a new, Torah-centered form of Jewish worship that both respected and transcended the Holy City and its Temple. The public reading and exposition of Torah (or some form of it) recorded in Nehemiah 8:1-18 prefigured and inspired the Torah practice that came to stand at the center of Sabbath worship in the synagogue.[101]

As a means of filling in for the worship, fellowship, and teaching that went on at the Temple, the institution of the synagogue and the figure of its doctor of the Law arose. Pharisaic scribes were planting synagogues throughout Palestine in the second century B.C. as local centers of gathered worship and instruction. As Sabbath practices focused on the reading and teaching of the Torah, the relationship between word and cult was further redefined and enriched.[102]

Synagogue and scribe thus shaped the biblical canon and its reading practices into the forms in which we recognize them in Jesus' world. By the first century, according to Philo, Josephus, and Acts, "the reading of the Tora on the morning of the sabbath was a universally accepted custom . . . both in Israel and the Diaspora."[103]

It is notoriously difficult to reconstruct with much chronological precision the liturgy of the synagogue during the last centuries before Jesus' birth. But one can reasonably posit that what emerged in talmudic Judaism was present in various rudimentary forms before the destruction of the Temple.[104] The

---

99. Perrot, "The Reading of the Bible," p. 150. Scripture and Temple are still functioning this way in John 7:14 and Acts 3:11-12.

100. Perrot, "The Reading of the Bible," p. 149.

101. Perrot, "The Reading of the Bible," p. 150. Old suggests that preaching may have been the central act of Sabbath worship long before, since the Fourth Commandment connects Sabbath practice to Israel's experience at Sinai ("Roots of the Christian Ministry," p. 27).

102. Bright, *A History of Israel*, p. 437.

103. Perrot, "The Reading of the Bible," p. 137.

104. Perrot, "The Reading of the Bible," p. 138.

institution of Sabbath Scripture-reading in local assemblies was already well enough established in the first century A.D. to be attributed to Moses.[105] Acts 13:15 suggests that one common pattern was a reading of the Law and Prophets, followed by "a word of exhortation for the people." Fourth Maccabees 18:10-18 offers a pattern of Law, then reflections on the Prophets, Psalms, and Hagiographa.[106]

Further literary clues are to be found in the Tanakh itself, notably the Psalter's fivefold structure, a structure predating the creation of the Septuagint. Tarazi sees the books of psalms as referring respectively to (I) the beginning of David's reign, (II) David's latter reign through Jerusalem's destruction, (III) Israel in exile, (IV) the end of the exilic period, and (V) the promise of restoration to the New Jerusalem.[107] Tarazi calls the collection as it stands "a book of eschatological prophecy," "an attempt to reprise, in a liturgical manner, the Law and the Prophets in order to present the 'story of the biblical God' which can only end by pointing to the future."[108] These books of psalms are also well suited to allegorizing the books of the Pentateuch. Synagogues' various lectionary cycles must have reflected these different structures at least to the extent that "the law and the prophets and the psalms" would be a recognizable expression to first-century Jews (Luke 24:44). In the synagogue as in the Temple, Tanakh was finding new ways to form and re-form Israel around the remembrance of its past salvation, the experience of its present sustenance, and the promise of its eschatological future.

God Speaks in Greek Too: The Septuagint's Development

Scripture not only restored and maintained Judaism's geographical center at Jerusalem, but served as a center-away-from-the-center for the huge populations of Jews that by now lived outside Palestine. The performance of Scripture outside Palestine became the primary means of extending God's saving presence far beyond the Temple to the entire world.[109] And this provided an

---

105. Perrot, "The Reading of the Bible," p. 150.

106. See Perrot, "The Reading of the Bible," pp. 151-52.

107. Holladay offers a more tentative but basically complementary description (*The Psalms*, pp. 76-80).

108. Tarazi, *The Old Testament*, vol. 3, p. 104.

109. That the Temple and throne were not up to this task is abundantly demonstrated in the political and cultic fortunes of the divided kingdom, which before Ezra's day had developed into the polarized nations of Judah and Samaria. The one substantial institution these groups still had more or less in common was the Pentateuch.

impetus to another transforming moment in the mission of Scripture: its translation into Greek.

Hellenization produced a world Jewry more familiar with Greek than Hebrew. Scripture provided a center for the Jewish tradition that could bridge (though imperfectly) this cultural as well as geographic distance. The Septuagint brought the Law into the Greek-speaking world (where it would become the first Bible of the Greek Church).[110] This move both intensified and widened Israel's vision. Judaism achieved a theological breakthrough as it realized that God's words were sovereign over and translatable into even the languages of the nations.[111] Just as the covenant had once assimilated desert and Canaanite tribes into the family of Israel, so the multilingual Tanakh helped assimilate Gentiles into practicing Jewish communities across the world.[112] Over the time of its development (which may have spanned 400 years and any number of earlier versions),[113] the LXX helped begin the fulfillment of the vision of Isaiah 2:1-4.

The LXX preserved both the content of Hebrew Scripture and the inner-biblical exegetical techniques it took to render the Tanakh in a foreign tongue. Some books and passages relied on free hermeneutics, others on literal hermeneutics. Translators often resorted to Hebrew exegetical traditions for guidance on difficult passages. Their efforts cannot be called wholly successful.[114] But a powerful tradition of biblical translation was begun that spread God's words from the original Hebrew to the common and imperial languages of the ever-multiplying worlds of Diaspora Judaism. In each of these linguistic families the Tanakh performed the same creative feat it had performed in Israel under Ezra: It went from being the product of a community of interpretation to a creator of a subsequent community of interpreta-

---

110. Bright, *A History of Israel*, p. 415.

111. However, the privileged status of Hebrew as God's chosen language was not abrogated. The LXX's embrace by Christians would lead later rabbis to repudiate their fathers' project. Says *Massekhet Soferim* 1:7, "It happened that five elders translated the Pentateuch into Greek for King Ptolemy. That day was as hard for Israel as the day the calf was made, because the Pentateuch could not be translated properly" (quoted in Emanuel Tov, "The Septuagint," in Mulder, ed., *Mikra*, p. 163). The later Church, particularly during the Reformation, would experience the same tensions. We will treat them in Chapter 3 as matters of the Bible's apostolicity and catholicity.

112. Bright, *A History of Israel*, pp. 443-46.

113. Tov, "The Septuagint," pp. 161, 163.

114. Tov, "The Septuagint," pp. 170-73. The LXX's exegetical triumphs and failures (see Tov, pp. 170-71 for examples) go some way to explaining the Church's equivocations over the relative status of the LXX, MT, and other authoritative translations. But deeper issues are at stake, which will come to the fore mainly in the next chapter.

tion — or, more accurately, several partially overlapping communities of interpretation. At the same time the Tanakh was being translated into Aramaic, Hebrew's successor language in its own homeland. It was Scripture in these forms, acting as Judaism's source of conservation, renewal, and mission, that Jesus and his disciples inherited. And it was in these forms that Scripture became a springboard for Christianity's rapid spread to the nations.

Second Temple Judaism's Biblical Practices: Scripture Made Personal

The Tanakh played a pivotal part in the Temple practice that lay at the center of Judaism, and an even more pivotal part in the synagogue life that was each community's local center. But God's words were working at even more intimate levels than these. Daily corporate prayers involved the use of *tefillin*, which began not as permanently closed receptacles for bits of Scripture, but as containers of crucial Scripture passages meant to be opened and used during prayers. Similarly, inscriptions known as *mezuzot* preserved Scripture passages as talismans on the lintels and doorposts of Jewish homes — precisely the places where the Passover blood was sprinkled in Exodus 12:21-25.[115] These practices acknowledged the sacramental power of God's words, and their determinative influence on Jewish life and its memories of once and future liberation. They also had the effects of supporting Israel's scribes and widening literacy among its population — a social development that ultimately seems to have displaced the priestly scribes from their oligarchical role in Jewish society and given rise to the widespread biblical literacy of Pharisaic Judaism.[116]

Second Temple Judaism's appreciation of the Torah's nourishment of Israel and the knowledge it offers the world is most clearly and powerfully expressed in Scripture's language of adoration, for instance in the praise of Psalms 1, 19, and 119. The first psalm uses stark contrasts to compare the life-giving way of Torah to the fruitlessness of sinful wandering. The nineteenth juxtaposes the natural revelation of God's glory that is shouted everywhere but never heard (19:1-7) to the special revelation of Torah that restores souls, produces wisdom, lightens hearts, enlightens eyes, discloses sins — in sum, that makes righteous those who practice it (19:8-15). God speaks through all creation, but God *saves* through Torah. Psalm 119 offers a similar account that is more powerful only in its repetition. Hymns like these offer apt summaries of

115. Bar-Ilan, "Scribes and Books," p. 25.
116. Bar-Ilan, "Scribes and Books," p. 22.

a life given over to God and filled with his blessings. Their doxologies describe the salvation Israel associated with hearing and keeping the Torah.

In every way we have examined, through every epoch in Israel's mythical and critical history, God's written words became a means of grace through and to the little nation. They created, gathered, liberated, commanded, promised, blessed, cursed, and dispersed. They warned and judged and delivered. They revealed and they concealed. They stood in for God in his own absence, mediating his saving presence. They assisted God's anointed servants as literary creations, then carried on the servants' work when the servants were no more. Tanakh was the linguistic center of God's wordly community.

II. The Language of the *Logos*: Scripture and Jesus

With the coming of the Word made flesh, Scripture's salvific role in Israel's history takes a radical new turn. Jesus' relationship with Scripture is the climax of the Tanakh's salvation-history, and the focus of the rest of the chapter. Furthermore, because Jesus' disciples share in his relationship with Scripture, it is also the basis for the Bible's ecclesial character and role in personal salvation that will be explored in the next chapter. We next examine several dimensions of Scripture's work in Jesus' context and career, in an order that roughly follows the narrative of Jesus' life. What we will see is a series of roles the God-breathed words of Scripture play in the incarnation, ministry, and legacy of God the Son. These reflect the presence and work of the Father, the Son, and the Spirit in the Triune economy of salvation. Let us examine each in turn.

The first dimension of Scripture's role in Jesus' career is straightforward and uncontroversial: It makes Jesus *intelligible*. Without a cultural and historical context for the events of Jesus' life, they would be indecipherable, if not altogether meaningless. The recovery of this insight has been indispensable for the modern practice of Christology. Wolfhart Pannenberg, Walter Kasper, Raymond Brown, N. T. Wright, Gerald O'Collins, and countless others — not to mention life-of-Jesus scholars like E. P. Sanders who would not describe themselves as Christologians — have repeatedly demonstrated both the dangers of interpreting Jesus out of context and the benefits of paying careful attention to Jesus' Jewishness. Messianic expectation (and messianic apathy), Jesus' social world, its theological interpretations of Rome's occupation of Palestine, competing schools of Torah practice, attitudes towards outsiders, and above all the biblical picture of God all set the stage for Jesus' ministry and make sense of it. This insight is now so commonplace in biblical scholarship and theology that it hardly needs mentioning.

Jesus' setting is more than Scripture; it is the entire Greco-Roman world of the first century. But both Jesus and his setting are deeply scriptural — fundamentally shaped by the texts of the Tanakh and by contemporary biblical practices. As the Bible is the indispensable backdrop of a seventeenth-century Puritan, so Israel's Scriptures are the indispensable backdrop of Jesus the first-century Jew. It is against the horizon of Jewish tradition, built upon the Tanakh, that Jesus becomes intelligible to his disciples, to his enemies, and to himself. If Jesus the Word made flesh is the text who exegetes the invisible God (John 1:18), then Scripture the Word made words is the context that grounds his exegesis.

Creation Becomes Creator: The Canon's Formation of Jesus

To be sure, the New Testament writers see Scripture as far more than just an indispensable context for understanding Jesus as a first-century Palestinian Jew, even an extraordinary one. They mean something more ambitious in claiming that Scripture makes sense of Jesus. For them Jesus is the One to whom Scripture's characters, images, and promises point. He is no less than their fulfillment — the missing unity of the Tanakh, Gerhard von Rad would say.[117] *He* makes *Scripture* intelligible. With Jesus' arrival, the tables are turned, and the man becomes the new context for the biblical text.

But this anticipates Jesus' new creation of Tanakh as the Old Testament. First comes the Tanakh's creative role in the new creation who is Jesus Christ. The next dimension of Jesus' relationship with Scripture is that the biblical Word is instrumental to the incarnation of the *logos*. Canonical Scripture plays an indispensable part in Jesus' *human formation*.

We can explore this by recalling the meaning of canon and applying it to the Son's incarnate life. Canonicity implies that a people's literary creation is also its creator. This dialectical relationship of canon and community is by no means restricted to Christian Scripture. It is shared by all communities and their canons — for instance, America and its founding Constitution.[118]

---

117. See Gerhard von Rad, *Old Testament Theology* (San Francisco: Harper & Row, 1965), vol. 2, pp. 410-29.

118. The parallel is intentional on the part of America's Ezras and Nehemiahs, the Founding Fathers. Says Sebastian Mallaby, Washington bureau chief for *The Economist*, "The Founders . . . infused their precious ideas with the aura of scripture, hoping this would protect them from the wear and tear of everyday debate. George Washington pleaded that 'the Constitution be sacredly maintained,' while James Madison described the founding documents as 'political scriptures,' hoping that they would acquire 'that veneration, which time

Yet Israel's canon, its mission, and its created community share an even more striking relationship. For here Scripture the product and producer of Israel has its ultimate origin in God the creator of heaven and earth. Explaining how this works brings us back to the verbal *kenosis* whose ontological dimension is treated in Chapter 1. It is God who creates and rules Judaism as a biblical community. However, God's creating and ruling words always operate through the human agency of those through whom they come. God allows his words to be spoken and repeated and even his name invoked by his creatures. The words' power and holiness are mediated through weak and fallen human beings. The salvation they bring comes through the very people who need it. In investing his own character in the words, God allows his sinful audience to speak in his name; God's sovereign speech undergoes a kind of humiliation. The worldly mission of kenotic Scripture is analogous to the humiliation of Christ.

The outcome of this verbal *kenosis* into the canon of God's people resembles the climax of the hymn of Philippians 2:5-11: Even the worst human failures and manipulations cannot finally subdue God's words. God's word goes out in humility, but it returns vindicated (Isa. 55:10-11). As the message triumphs over the powers that would silence it, it receives an authority which is above every authority. The human words of canonical Scripture carry unqualified divine authority among all "peoples of the book." They rule and reform those who speak and hear them. So the fruits of Scripture's victory are analogous to the glory of the exalted Christ.[119] This two-stage trajectory is how the canon of inspired Scripture creates its own community.

The relationship between canon and community is even more striking (and convoluted) where Jesus is concerned. For at the point where Scripture and Jesus meet, God's biblical words are not just a participation in Christ's

---

bestows on every thing, and without which perhaps the wisest and freest governments would not possess the requisite stability.' And so Americans established a civil religion in place of a spiritual one. Their Protestant reverence for the Bible was transferred to the founding texts.

"The Founders' civil religion has been preached enthusiastically by their successors. In 1837, on the fiftieth anniversary of the Constitution's drafting, John Quincy Adams, paraphrasing from the instruction to the Israelites in Deuteronomy [6:7-9], urged his countrymen to 'Teach the [Constitution's] principles, teach them to your children, speak of them when sitting in your home, speak of them when walking by the way, when lying down and when rising up, write them upon the doorplate of your home and upon your gates.'" "Stop the Celebration," *The New Republic* 219, no. 3-4 (7/20-27/1998): 19.

119. While this is obviously a quality of Christian Scripture, it is no less a quality of the Jewish and Muslim canons. Both respect (but not always thoroughly) the humanity and contingency of God's words.

humiliation, but also a *means* of his humiliation. In becoming human, the God who brings a community into being through its own canon is made a creature of that particular community, and is subjected to his own words of blessing and cursing. Jesus' human sensibility is formed according to the Scriptures — the same Scriptures by which he brought the community into being through itself. He is a Jew: His worldview is a biblical worldview; his worship is biblical worship; his categories are biblical categories; his hopes are biblical hopes.

Incarnation, as the entire process through which God the Son becomes a particular ancient Jew, from conception through gestation, birth, child-hood, and adolescence, deeply incorporates the Tanakh into the human life of God. God's word now returns to God in a new way. It is no longer simply a word addressed to the world; now its author is also its audience. God lives on both sides of the divine covenants, laws, promises, praises, and wisdom. Scripture becomes not only a medium for exchange from God to creation and from creation back to God, but also a medium among Father, Son, and Holy Spirit in their interactions. Both Israel and its God speak Scripture, and Scripture addresses both God and Israel.

It is thus that we can theologically appreciate Jesus' remarkable attitude towards holy writ. This brings us to the next dimension of Jesus' relationship to Scripture: dominical obedience.

The Work of the Son as the Will of the Father

We already described the Bible as participating in the will of the Father, in the *kenosis* of the Son, and the power of the Holy Spirit. Through the Scriptures God's saving will is revealed, God's character put at risk, and God's power made manifest. These functions of Scripture gain a whole new measure of complexity and dialectical power once it is appreciated that Jesus is not only the divine-human subject of the Bible's address, but its divine-human object as well. In both modes Scripture functions as Jesus' *authority*. Jesus does the will of the One who sent him, taking the form of a servant, suffering and be-ing raised according to the Scriptures; and the sovereign power of God rests upon him. Each of these aspects of Jesus' incarnate ministry reveals a dimen-sion of his relationship to Scripture.

Obedience names Jesus' respect for the will of the Father (John 6:38-40). Jesus' obedience takes concrete shape as obedience to Scripture. As a child of the covenant, he humbly accepts God's total claim on his life. As the creator of Israel becomes a son of Israel, so the creator and content of Israel's

Scripture grows up obedient to Scripture (Luke 2:41-52; John 6:38). In Jesus' life Scripture acts as the revealer of God's will for humanity and for the Son of Man. It commands Jesus' obedience and so defines his mission. The Tanakh reveals the Father's will for Jesus' career like no other institution in Jesus' world.

This is why the life lived according to the Father's will is the same life lived according to the Scriptures, why not just isolated or mythologized events in Jesus' life, but his life itself, "fulfills Scripture." Scripture textually embodies Christ's Gospel in prospect, in retrospect, and in process. Jesus is not only the antitype of the Old Testament's predictions and pointers. It does not simply map out a course that leads others to him. The Tanakh discloses Jesus' significance to others because it first discloses Christ to himself. In the Tanakh, the written Word encounters the incarnate Word. Jesus listens to the voice of the Father, and hears — himself.

Did Jesus know at some point in his itinerant ministry that he was Israel's Messiah? It is notoriously difficult to distinguish Jesus' own view of himself and of Scripture from the views of the early Church (and it should be, if he succeeded as a teacher). Our exercise here does not depend on one answer or another.[120] But if Jesus' self-awareness was an effect of his anointed prophethood (as the earliest New Testament witnesses suggest) and not merely of his status as incarnate Word, then it was also in large part a function of Jesus' relationship with Scripture. N. T. Wright traces likely indications of Jesus' messianic self-awareness in the Gospels, and concludes that Jesus' baptism is as likely an inauguration of messianic consciousness as any. And at the center of Wright's speculations is the fact that if Jesus became aware of his own messiahship, he did so on the basis of the Tanakh's descriptions of messianic anointing. If the earthly Jesus knew he was Messiah, he knew it from his own exposure to Scripture.[121]

120. James D. G. Dunn's review of critical attitudes towards Jesus' self-awareness of both divinity and messiahship (*Christology in the Making: A New Testament Enquiry into the Origins of the Doctrine of the Incarnation* [Philadelphia: Westminster, 1980], pp. 22-33) concludes that it is irresponsible to attribute self-awareness of divinity to the earthly Jesus, but important to respect Jesus' "high christology" of himself, a sense of messiahship extending possibly even beyond the idea of a Davidic messiah (p. 33).

121. N. T. Wright, *Jesus and the Victory of God* (Minneapolis: Fortress, 1996), pp. 536-37: "Psalm 2.7 and Isaiah 42.1, commonly regarded as standing behind the voice heard at Jesus' baptism, point at least in the first instance towards Messiahship as the meaning of the whole incident. Jesus' anointing with the divine spirit can be read as a deliberate allusion to such passages as Isaiah 11.2 (the Messiah's anointing with YHWH's spirit) and 1 Samuel 16.13 (where YHWH's spirit comes powerfully upon David after Samuel has anointed him). However much the text may have been influenced by post-Easter reflection, there is no rea-

At its best, the tradition of typological interpretation begun by Jesus himself and carried on enthusiastically by his disciples captures the richness and subtlety of the fulfillment that Jesus' obedience to Scripture brings about. Several of the episodes that survive rigorous and fair historiographical scrutiny illustrate his typological imagination at work.[122] When Jesus chose twelve men to represent the regathered tribes of Israel, he was setting himself up as Israel's eschatological King. When he chose to enter Jerusalem upon a colt, he was acting prophetically, making himself the fulfillment of Zechariah 9:9-10.[123] His disturbance at the Temple is harder to interpret, but given the Triumphal Entry, it is not implausible to see his actions as the intentional fulfillment of Zechariah 14:21 (as the Johannine tradition does). Most of all, in choosing the Passover as the backdrop for his final meal with the disciples, in which the bread and cup became his broken body and liberating blood, he narrated his own impending death as the typological fulfillment of Israel's central soteriological ritual, offering a sign that comprehended all his earlier signs. "Temple and Torah dominate the landscape" of symbols Jesus chooses to enact and explain his own career.[124] In all of his symbolic speech-acts, and especially in the upper room, he acts as a son whose obedience to God's will simultaneously determines his significance, seals his fate, and fulfills the Scriptures.

Jesus' life of obedient fulfillment opens a new dimension of his relationship to Scripture. In obeying and fulfilling Scripture, he is revealed to be more than its servant. He is the very Lord *of* Scripture. As through being a faithful son of Israel Jesus is Israel's King of Kings, so through perfect obedience to Tanakh Jesus is Scripture's ultimate authority (Phil. 2:5-11). It is both *in* and *through* God's words that Christ is humiliated and exalted. So we can speak of Jesus' "dominical obedience" to Scripture's authority.

This is forcefully demonstrated throughout the Gospels in Jesus' use of Scripture. We could see it in Jesus' reformulation of the Law on the Mount, his exegetical battles with scribes and Pharisees, his own parabolic wisdom

---

son historically to deny that at John's baptism Jesus became aware in a new way of a messianic vocation."

122. See E. P. Sanders, *The Historical Figure of Jesus* (New York: Penguin, 1993), pp. 120, 252.

123. Wright, *Jesus and the Victory of God*, p. 490: "Jesus . . . was as capable as any of his contemporaries of deliberately performing actions which had rich symbolic value. Within his own time and culture, his riding on a donkey over the Mount of Olives, across Kidron, and up to the Temple mount spoke more powerfully than words could have done of a royal claim."

124. Wright, *Jesus and the Victory of God*, p. 437.

sayings, or his chilling words from the Psalter on the cross. Here instead we will consider the temptation narratives, which both illustrate the current point and lead us to Scripture's next role in the divine economy.[125]

In Jesus' wilderness experience, his anointed offices, having been formally conferred at his baptism (through the descent of the Holy Spirit), are tested for the first time. The exchange between the devil and Jesus (Matt. 4:1-11; Luke 4:1-13) is a battle of interpretation over the meaning of Messiah. And the weapons are the texts of Tanakh: Deuteronomy 8:3; Deuteronomy 6:13; Psalm 91:11-12; and Deuteronomy 6:16 (to follow the Lukan order). With Torah, Jesus refutes the twisted interpretations of Messiah that the devil (perhaps here reflecting popular messianic expectation) offers him. At once he both places himself in subjection to its commands, and shows himself its authoritative speaker and interpreter. The pupil (cf. Luke 2:46-47) emerges as the master. According to Luke, the exchange ends when Jesus turns the tables on his adversary, now *saying* Scripture, not merely as one to whom it is written (Luke 4:12; cf. 4:4 and 4:8) but now dominically, Jesus the speaker and the devil the audience: "It is said, 'You shall not tempt the Lord your God.'"

In this exchange, Deuteronomy 6:16-19 has undergone an extraordinary transformation. Jesus has not only applied the original story of Massah and Meribah (Exod. 17:2-7) to his own exchange with the devil, but has recapitulated it. His own messianic obedience has reversed its tragic outcome and honored the commandment that followed it, gaining the blessings (Deut. 6:18) that eluded Israel in the wilderness. Most strikingly, he has arguably re-

---

125. One might object that in the temptation narratives we are manifestly not hearing the words of the historical Jesus (cf. Mark 1:12-13). Yet the critical picture of the temptation narratives still reveals a Jesus who fasts and prays and faces temptation in obedience to God (Sanders, *The Historical Figure*, p. 117). And beyond that critical picture, the canonical accounts brilliantly illustrate a pattern that can be securely established from other parts of the Gospels. Sanders summarizes their lesson: Jesus "worked within the general framework of the ideas about God and Israel provided by the Jewish scripture, and accordingly he pointed not to himself but rather to God. It is noteworthy that, in answering the tempter, he did not speak in the first person. He did not say, 'That is not the way I do things,' but rather, in effect, '*That is not according to God's will as revealed in Scripture*'" (Sanders, p. 116, emphasis added). Even if these are the words of the early Church, they are written in the true Spirit of Jesus.

N. T. Wright's critical history of Jesus goes as far as to portray the temptations as Jesus' "initial victory" over the devil, who represents doomed Israel's triumphalist expectations for the Messiah (*Jesus and the Victory of God*, pp. 457-59). His reading is fundamentally compatible with the one given here. We will characterize the work of Christ in similar terms, as an exegetical battle over the meaning of Messiah.

ferred its "the Lord your God" to *himself*.[126] The *coup de grâce* is delivered, the Scripture is fulfilled (Deut. 6:19: "thrusting out all your enemies from before you, as the Lord has promised"), and the devil flees.

Sword of the Spirit: The Word of God in Jesus' Hands

The exchange demonstrates more than just Jesus' double relationship with the Law. It shows us the next dimension of Christ's relationship with Scripture, as his *instrument*. Jesus' dominical use of the Tanakh inaugurates a revolution in biblical interpretation. What happens in the wilderness continues to happen throughout Jesus' career: The Holy Spirit's presence turns Israel's Scriptures from merely (!) media of the Father's will into means of messianic power.

James McClendon, with intentional modesty, calls the Christian transformation of Israel's canonical images "catachresis" — the creative, innovative naming of the new in Christ in terms of Israel's canonical stock of categories. Christian categories like justification, sanctification, healing and salvation, adoption and rebirth, redemption and reconciliation, even faith itself are all rooted in (but *only* rooted in) the soil of ancient Israel. With Jesus' arrival they all take a decisive new turn.[127] The original Christian catachresis is not unlike the new uses Christians find today for the stock of their own cultural vocabularies to describe the kingdom of God to which they belong ("God is my co-pilot"). Ancient and modern Christians re-create their languages according to the demands of the *kerygma*. They baptize their own inherited categories and transform languages — whether biblical Hebrew, Aramaic, and Greek, or Latin and English — into media of the Holy Spirit.

Yet Jesus' and the disciples' use of Scripture goes far beyond the common senses of catachresis and metaphor. On their lips, the biblical practices of Israel undergo a kind of *epiclēsis*. The dominical transformation that turns John's baptism of repentance and the Passover seder into the sacraments of the Church turns Israel's biblical practices into messianic biblical practices.

The immediate danger of the language of *epiclēsis* is the way it suggests biblical adoptionism. If Jesus' messianic use of Scripture lends it its authority, if it is "instituted" by Christ as the sacraments are, then has it any special sta-

---

126. This is neither the sense of the Matthean parallel, nor the only possible sense of the Lukan version. But at least two factors favor the more dominical interpretation: First, Luke 4:13's *panta peirasmon* (cf. Matt. 4:11) reinforces 4:2's stress that the devil is doing the tempting, not Jesus. Second, verse 13's *kairou* emphasizes the temptations yet to come (such as Luke 23:39?), which are temptations of Jesus, not Jesus' temptations of God.

127. McClendon, *Doctrine,* pp. 107-13.

tus in earlier Israel? Does speaking about Jesus' pneumatic fulfillment of the Old Testament's types not bring back the worst rather than the best of ancient typological practice?

The trouble stems from a failure to appreciate the Trinitarian dialectic between Jesus' obedience to Scripture and his sovereignty over it. He is not only obedient, as an Ebionite would affirm. He is not only sovereign, as a Marcionite would affirm. When Jesus interacts with any of God's media, he does so from both sides of his relationship. Jesus, and then Jesus' disciples, are at once obedient to Israel's biblical practices and sovereign over them (cf. Phil. 2:8-11) — at once their servants and their new masters.

Consider the Jewish institutions of John's baptism and Israel's *pesah*, which begin and end Jesus' journey to the cross. Even before they meet the incarnate Son, they are already more than mere water or food. In participating in them and redefining them, in no way do Jesus and his disciples dispense with their meaning. Rather, their appropriation and Christological transformation *intensify* their meaning. They gain a new dimension of coherence in God's history of salvation, and a new pneumatic power to mediate the salvation Jesus has won.

Likewise, Jesus' intensification of Scripture's power in no way annuls its mission beforehand. He is obedient to it precisely because of its divine character and purpose, and he gains his messianic authority over it as its fulfiller, not its conqueror. Its subsequent transformation in his hands and in the hands of his disciples amounts to a vindication and intensification of its former power.

So it would seem proper to find the beginnings of the Christian revolution in biblical interpretation in Jesus' own use of Scripture. But how much of the Christian hermeneutical revolution really comes from Jesus, and how much is merely the catachretical innovation of the later Church? The examples used above to illustrate Jesus' use of Scripture have undergone embellishment by those who preserved them and put them to use in the lives of their churches. There is undeniably a new hermeneutic at work in the New Testament Church. To what extent is Jesus behind it?

There is no consensus among scholars about the answer, but neither is there a shortage of solid conclusions from which to choose. C. H. Dodd's examination of the early Church's use of biblical "testimonies" concludes with the suggestion that the early Church's innovative readings of Scripture must come from one "originating mind," and that mind is most likely that of Jesus himself.[128] E. P. Sanders's sober assessment finds a historical figure of Jesus

---

128. "Among Christian thinkers of the first age known to us there are three of genuinely creative power: Paul, the author to the Hebrews, and the Fourth Evangelist. We are pre-

who regards himself as a divine "viceroy" who represents God and enjoys unparalleled divine intimacy.[129] Jesus radically reinterprets the claims of Scripture when he presumes for himself the power to forgive sinners apart from their conformance to the requirements of the Law.[130] And R. T. France's apologetic for the reliability of the Gospels' account of Jesus' attitude towards Scripture persuasively appeals to the cumulative effect of the New Testament's many reports of Jesus' biblical practice. Taken individually, these reports might be explained as the early Church's own innovations. But taken together, they amount to what John Wenham calls "a great avalanche" of innovative exegesis, whose most plausible originator is the one to whom it is attributed.[131]

Donald Juel offers a countervailing Lutheran view that traces Christianity's hermeneutical revolution back through a logical chain of kerygmatic leaps the early Church has made between formerly unconnected texts, originating *necessarily* and *totally* in its *kerygma* of Jesus' crucifixion and resurrection.[132] The trouble with Juel's intricate chain of reasoning is that it has no chronological shape or support, and it leaves the Church with a mute rabbi whose own teachings and uses of Scripture bear no relationship to his disciples'. His "imaginative exercise" in defense of Nils Dahl's *The Crucified Mes-*

---

cluded from proposing any one of them for the honour of having originated the process, since even Paul, greatly as he contributed to its development, demonstrably did not originate it. What forgotten geniuses may lurk in the shadows of those first twenty years of Church history about which we are so scantily informed, it is impossible for us to say. But the New Testament itself avers that it was Jesus Christ Himself who first directed the minds of His followers to certain parts of the scriptures as those in which they might find illumination upon the meaning of His mission and destiny. . . . To account for the beginning of this most original and fruitful process of rethinking the Old Testament we found need to postulate a creative mind. The Gospels offer us one. Are we compelled to reject the offer?" C. H. Dodd, *According to the Scriptures: The Substructure of New Testament Theology* (London: Nisbet, 1952), pp. 109-10.

129. Sanders, *The Historical Figure*, p. 248.

130. Sanders, *The Historical Figure*, pp. 234-35: "There is no instance in which Jesus requires the wicked to do what the law stipulates in order to become righteous. . . . He seems to have thought that those who followed him belonged to God's elect, even though they did not do what the Bible itself requires. . . . Jesus' self-assertion was not, strictly speaking, against the law. He did not tell people *not* to sacrifice; on the contrary, in [Mark 1:40-45 and Matt. 5:23f.] he approved of sacrifice. Although he did not oppose the law, he did indicate that what was most important was accepting him and following him."

131. See R. T. France, *Jesus and the Old Testament* (London: Tyndale, 1971), and John Wenham, *Christ and the Bible* (London: Tyndale, 1972), pp. 36-40.

132. Donald Juel, *Messianic Exegesis: Christological Interpretation of the Old Testament in Early Christianity* (Philadelphia: Fortress, 1988).

siah mainly shows the extraordinary lengths to which an account of Christian exegesis must go in order to leave Jesus' own practice out of the picture.[133] Juel's argument is an indirect proof of Jesus' hermeneutical influence within the tradition that claims him as its Lord.[134] (Nevertheless Juel's insights on the development of the Church's *kerygma* will find an important place below.)[135]

133. Here see also Paul M. van Buren, *According to the Scriptures: The Origins of the Gospel and of the Church's Old Testament* (Grand Rapids: Eerdmans, 1998). Following Juel and Dahl, van Buren argues that it was *Pilate* who first made the connection between Jesus and the messianic king-figure of Israel's expectation (p. 17), and the post-Easter Church that discovered or invented the Gospel from its own search of the Tanakh, apparently without any input from its Master (pp. 7-8). Peter's confession of Jesus as Christ (Mark 8:29) is read as Peter's refusal to accept Jesus' refusal of the name Messiah, and his subsequent rebuke as a satan not because of the title's connotations to Peter, but his use of the title itself. No reference to the Triumphal Entry appears in the book.

134. Cf. Joachim Jeremias: "The Gospel that Jesus proclaimed precedes the Kerygma of the primitive community. [Jesus refuses to be simply absorbed into an anonymous primitive community.] The Kerygma . . . refers us back from itself at every turn. . . . Whatever utterance of the Kerygma presents itself to us, its origins are always to be found in the preaching of Jesus." See "The Present Position in the Controversy Concerning the Problem of the Historical Jesus," in *Expository Times* 69 (1958): 335, quoted in Ernst Käsemann, "Blind Alleys in the 'Jesus of History' Controversy," in *New Testament Questions of Today* (Philadelphia: Fortress, 1979), p. 25. Käsemann disagrees with him because Jeremias radically distinguishes between the preaching of Jesus and the *kerygma* (see pp. 26ff.).

Wright also explicitly endorses Dodd's view over the view represented by Juel that Jesus' itinerant ministry is not the beginning of the theological and hermeneutical revolution that takes his name. Wright looks forward "to a new day, in which Jesus himself is acknowledged, in his own right, as a thinking, reflecting, creative and original theologian" (*Jesus and the Victory of God*, p. 479).

135. Juel summarizes his argument: "The confession of Jesus as the crucified and risen King of the Jews stands *at the beginning* of christological reflection and interpretation of the Scriptures — at least the reflection and interpretation that form the substructure of NT Christianity" (*Messianic Exegesis*, p. 171, emphasis added).

Juel is right to stress the fundamental shift in the Church's view of Scripture occasioned by Jesus' death and especially his resurrection appearances (cf. 1 Cor. 15:3-4 and Luke 24:25-27, 44-46). We will examine that shift as the next dimension of Jesus' relationship to Scripture. Furthermore, there is no reason to deny that many of the connections he examines between Old Testament texts and Jesus' death and resurrection were first made by Jesus' disciples. But *many* is one thing, *all* quite another. To establish such a case he must posit a development of Christological exegetical tradition without appealing to any kind of sequential causality, thus "the development of traditions for which I have argued has been analyzed more in terms of logic than chronological sequence" (*Messianic Exegesis*, p. 177). The effective denial of Jesus' own agency in the birth of Christian biblical practice finally makes Juel's task unsustainable. And the crucial details of Jesus' use of Jewish tradition and Scripture that survive historiographical scrutiny are more than enough to show the profound influence he had on his disciples' practices.

Let us then assume that while the earthly Jesus' use of Scripture is not documented with modern journalistic precision in the Gospels, at the very least his own biblical practice provides a fundamental warrant for subsequent biblical practice in the New Testament Church. The shaping of oral and written traditions between the time of Jesus' earthly career and the times of the New Testament writings makes it impossible to draw confident distinctions between Jesus' and the disciples' uses of the Tanakh. But the Gospels still give us a defensible picture of a Jesus who hears in Scripture his Father's speech to him and who regards himself as its referent (cf. Luke 4:18-21; Mark 11:2 and parallels), whose messianic authority relativizes the Law without abolishing it (Mark 2:27-28 and parallels; John 5:39-40), who assumes unprecedented authority to reinterpret it radically and even to add to it (Mark 1:22-27 and Luke 4:31-37; Matt. 5–7 and Luke 6:20-49), and who uses it against his adversaries (Mark 12:28-37 and parallels, Matt. 4:3-11 and Luke 4:3-13). At the foundation of the Christian exegetical tradition lies Jesus' own use of Scripture. To return to the categories of the Messianic Offices: Tanakh is Jesus' prophetic text; a criterion defining the work of his priesthood; and an armory of his royal rule. In all these roles it is a medium of the saving work of the Spirit of Jesus.

Sin, Grace, and the Hermeneutics of Salvation

We began and ended the previous section with conflict narratives from the Gospels. They repeatedly depict Jesus in contests with Jewish authorities where Israel's Scriptures are arsenals for both sides. "Have you not read this Scripture?" Jesus asks his opponents,[136] or "Go and learn what [the Scripture] means."[137] These conflicts set the stage for the course of Jesus' messianic career, and for the crucifixion that stands at its climax. The next dimension of Jesus' relationship to Scripture is the *crisis of interpretation* his use of it brings.

The interminability of conflicting readings of Scripture has always presented a problem for any who would describe biblical practice in terms of God's saving purpose. If God spoke through the prophets, why is the message so often misunderstood? Why is supposedly perspicuous Scripture so opaque? Can we even describe Scripture's purposes when people disagree

---

136. See Mark 12:10; Matt. 12:3-5; 19:4; 21:16; 21:42; 22:31; and Luke 10:26, cited in E. Earle Ellis, "Biblical Interpretation in the New Testament Church," in Mulder, ed., *Mikra*, p. 693.

137. See Matt. 9:13; also Matt. 11:27-29, cited in Ellis, "Biblical Interpretation," p. 698.

about its use? Or are Scripture's "purposes" simply the competing wills of its readers?

Crises of biblical interpretation are as old as the biblical texts themselves. Just as the royal and prophetic theologies struggled during the decline and fall of Israel and Judah, so the restoration saw competing schools of biblical interpretation arise, each with its own vision of the nature and work of Tanakh. First-century Judaism was just as divided — into parties of Sadducees, Zealots, Essenes, Hellenists such as Philo, Samaritans, and of course Pharisees (themselves hardly a monolithic tradition, whose differences are canonized in rabbinic Judaism). Proliferating traditions of biblical translation only increased the diversity of these hermeneutical factions. By no means could all this variety be accommodated under a common theological or practical umbrella (particularly in the case of Essenes, Hellenists, and Samaritans). Each group staked out its own position on the role of Israel; each had its own christology; and each read Scripture in a different way.

Every hermeneutical battle in Israel's history was a battle over Israel's future. And Israel's future was as unclear in the first century as it was in the age of the prophets. Which party was right? Which would prevail over the others? Which could survive Roman occupation and the coming destruction of the Temple? Israel's life-or-death hermeneutical struggle frames Jesus' ministry as both historical criticism and the New Testament remember it. Indeed, one might say that one of Scripture's most important soteriological functions is in constructing the competing thought-worlds that together send Jesus to the cross.[138]

The Gospels' conflict narratives offer a *christological* answer for the struggle between Judaism's factions and their incompatible readings of the Bible: They are rooted in Scripture's own character and mission. Conflicts

138. Says James Barr, "The conflict between scripture and the existing Jewish interpretations of it, and the dialectic between it and Jesus' own religious ideas and ideas of himself, brought about the deep and tragic conflicts between Jesus and the leaders of his people, which in turn brought him to rejection and death, and brought mankind to salvation. Thus the Old Testament is not only intellectually essential in providing categories and imagery for the understanding of Jesus Christ, it is also functional in salvation through the chain of events within his ministry and up to his passion." *Holy Scripture: Canon, Authority, Criticism* (Philadelphia: Westminster, 1983), p. 11.

Citing Sanders, Josephus, 1 and 2 Maccabees, and Philo, Wright concurs in his description of Shammaite Pharisees: "Their proverbial strictness in regard to Torah was not simply a matter of religious observances. It was a matter of guarding Israel from paganization and, more positively, attempting . . . to throw off the pagan yoke altogether. It was this agenda which, I suggest, brought Jesus into head-on collision with the dominant Pharisaic movement of his day" (*Jesus and the Victory of God*, p. 384).

over Scripture happen at crucial points in Jesus' ministry. The Matthean and Lukan temptation narratives cast the life of Jesus in images of an eschatological war between competing Jewish traditions of biblical interpretation. Jesus' encounters with scribes and Pharisees during his ministry flare into bitter hermeneutical battles over the meaning and purpose of the Tanakh. In all four Gospels' trial scenes, the Jewish authorities contest Jesus' interpretation of Scripture and of himself. Moreover, at each point Jesus' teaching utterly fails to persuade his adversaries.

This, the Gospels proclaim, is part of God's plan. Their predominant explanation for the friction between the disciples' hermeneutical practices and those of Judaism's other biblical authorities is that incomprehension, division, abuse, and rejection are fundamental parts of Scripture's mission:

> And he said, "Go and say to this people: 'Keep listening, but do not comprehend; keep looking, but do not understand. Make the mind of this people dull, and stop their ears, and shut their eyes; so that they may not look with their eyes, and listen with their ears, and comprehend with their minds, and turn and be healed.'" Then I said, "How long, O Yahweh?" And he said, "Until cities lie waste without inhabitant, and houses without people, and the land is utterly desolate; until Yahweh sends everyone far away, and vast is the emptiness in the midst of the land." (Isa. 6:9-12, NRSV; cf. LXX)

Jesus apparently endorses this view. Isaiah 6:9-10 is widely given as a reason for his two-level discourses and for Jewish rejection of the early Church's preaching (Matt. 13:10-15; Mark 4:12; Luke 8:10; John 12:39-41; Acts 28:26-27). Jesus' opponents are predestined as opponents.

The first Church formulates and canonically preserves polemics against competing readings of Scripture and of Jesus that see detractors as simply lacking the ears to hear the voice of their own shepherd. In effect, these passages claim that one cannot adequately understand how the Bible functions and "malfunctions" apart from the categories of sin and grace. Scripture plays a role in divine election: God's oral and written words purposefully create communities of *misinterpretation* within and without its communities of interpretation. And these conflicting communities become the context for God's saving work through Israel, Jesus, and Church. At least some of the Bible's opacity must be seen not to frustrate but to further God's saving purposes.

The Election of Scripture

This dimension of Scripture's relationship to Jesus' mission calls for several remarks on the doctrine of election as it has developed in Christian tradition, lest this bibliology become a captive to the doctrine's abuses and endless controversies.[139] Each centers upon a different stage in Jesus' messianic career.

The Asymmetry of God's Decrees, and Their Overriding Purpose of Blessing

The first consideration concerns God's purpose in creating communities of biblical misinterpretation as part of "salvation." Are we really to understand the mission of Scripture in terms of the twin decrees of double-predestinarian Calvinism?

Not exactly. Isaiah 6:9-10 does look quite like a decree unto damnation. But the treatment it has received in Calvinism has often fallen short in several respects. First, God's decrees unto damnation are anything but equal opposites to his decrees unto salvation. The two are not symmetrical. Second, the divine decrees do not arbitrarily divide humanity into two groups for an arbitrary and eternally mysterious reason. Third, election in the biblical witness is a thoroughly Jewish doctrine, inextricable from its context. The forms the doctrine takes when it is treated apart from that primary context are monstrous departures from the doctrine in its proper biblical perspective.

Romans is of course a crucial text for the doctrine of election. When the letter is read as an account of how individuals are saved by their faith in Jesus Christ apart from their own works-righteousness, chapters 9–11 appear to support the classical Calvinistic form of double-predestination. They describe how individuals are predestined to salvation or perdition according to God's inscrutable purpose. But when Romans is read (as it increasingly is) as an account of how Jews and Gentiles are saved by the faith of Jesus Christ, apart from works of the Torah such as circumcision, these chapters gain a whole new meaning. They are not about how God directs decrees towards individuals as individuals, but about whether God has abandoned his elect, the nation of Israel, in the wake of their rejection of Messiah. In Romans 9–11 Paul is writing the next chapter of Israel's salvation history. And the figures he

---

139. The fuller treatment each observation deserves must remain out of the scope of this project. However, some are more fully developed in Telford Work, "Annunciation as Election," *Scottish Journal of Theology* 54, no. 2 (2001): 177-99.

uses as examples of God's predestination are key figures from its earlier chapters. Jacob and Esau (9:10-13; cf. Mal. 1:2-5) are rivals for Isaac's and Abraham's blessings, and for God's redemptive purpose for humanity through Isaac (9:7). Moses and Pharaoh (9:15-18) are rival interpreters of God's promises to save Israel, in accordance with his promises to Abraham, Isaac, and Jacob.

The symmetry is illusory. Election is ordered toward inclusion, but not exclusion. Jacob and Moses are elect not because God intends to *restrict* his blessings to them, as much of Calvinism would claim, but because it is through them — and their rivals! — that God wants to bless *others* — even the rivals themselves (cf. Gen. 27:29; Isa. 19:19-25; Rom. 11:30-32). God's softening and hardening is done with the purpose of fulfilling God's blessings to Abraham, elected so that through him all the families of the world would be blessed (Gen. 12:1-3). In both testaments God's electing decrees are the means by which God's saving purpose is extended to others. Grace is not made immediately available to all the world, but neither is it restricted to those expressly elected. "Just as you were once disobedient to God but now have received mercy because of their disobedience, so they have now been disobedient in order that by the mercy shown to you they also may receive mercy. God has consigned all to disobedience, that he may have mercy on all" (Rom. 11:30-32). In other words, just as Israel is hardened so that *Israel* may be saved in Isaiah 6, so Jesus' opponents are hardened so they may subsequently be offered (Acts 3:17-21) and accept (Acts 4:4; 6:7) Jesus' salvation.

Finally, the figures Paul cites are representative of their competing nations: Israel versus Edom, and Israel versus Egypt. The elect personify their peoples. Election has an irreducibly personal dimension (cf. Acts 13:48), but it is by no means merely a matter of individual response. This is as true in the Church as it is in Israel. As the prophets symbolize Israel and Judah in their sometimes bizarre speech-acts, so the Twelve symbolize regathered, unified Israel under the headship of Jesus, who is himself the Elect One (Luke 9:34) and Israel's ultimate embodiment. As God's elect, the disciples are meant to understand Jesus' two-level discourse and participate in Jesus' tradition of biblical interpretation because they have received the secret of God's kingdom (Mark 4:11-12 and parallels). The scribes, Pharisees, and Sadducees whose opposition they meet are representatives of the schools who have not yet received the secret, and so they cannot yet understand the Scriptures' true meaning.

But again, the boundaries between insiders and outsiders are permeable. The secret is meant to be revealed once the Son of Man is raised from the dead (Mark 9:9). Jesus mentors the Church to become a community of scribes trained for the kingdom of heaven, able to bring out of Tanakh treasures new and old (Matt. 13:51-52) with which to wage its spiritual warfare. But these scribes are being trained to go and spread Jesus' tradition to all nations (Matt. 28:19-20). Jesus' insiders are a school for outsiders.

Biblical Misinterpretation as Divine Judgment

A second consideration when treating Scripture's mission of election concerns the *cause* of its misunderstanding. While divine intent is a factor, it is by no means the only one. The misunderstanding it accomplishes must also be understood in terms of divine judgment on sin.[140] This is a logical consequence of the Church's repudiation of Pelagianism. Prevenient, pneumatic grace is a prerequisite for both receiving (1 Thess. 1:5) and speaking (1 Cor. 12:3) God's words in power. To attribute hermeneutical failures simply to the humanity of biblical language (as many do) is to fail to appreciate the distinction between humanity and sin. Ignorance of the biblical message is a consequence of the darkening of human minds brought on by sin (Rom. 1:21). Even one's inability to understand God's words in a foreign tongue is a consequence of God's intervention at Babel (Gen. 11:6-7). Both Athanasius' and Augustine's hamartiological accounts of biblical misinterpretation respect this point (as we have seen in the previous chapter).[141]

God's triumph over humanity's epistemological depravity involves taking on and defeating the linguistic powers that darken human minds. The biblical message represents God's extraordinary initiative to overcome the obstacles to his own knowledge and glory. Isaiah's salvific ministry (which continues whenever his words are repeated in the New Testament and in the Church's confession) entails a hardening of his audience, not in order to oppose the salvation God intends for Israel, but to accomplish it. Isaiah 6 is not God's last word to Isaiah, nor Isaiah's last word to Israel. It is a beachhead, a violent introduction of truth into a tradition not yet able or willing to appreciate it. Israel's salvation is prepared and inaugurated through Israel's judgment.

Jesus' prophetic ministry functions in the same way. The Word and Wisdom of God empties himself of language and wisdom, in order to reclaim both as a human being in a fallen world. God overcomes Isaiah 6's curse of

---

140. This is so in the same way that, in John 9, the man born blind is born this way because of sin, but not because of sin on his own part or his parents'.

141. See Athanasius, *On the Incarnation* §§5-6, and Augustine, *On Christian Doctrine* I.35.39 and I.36.41.

biblical misinterpretation, by personally entering Israel's tradition of interpretation and interpreting truly from within it (Luke 24:25-27, 44-48).[142]

Of course, hermeneutical disputes continue even after the victory is won. Jesus and his disciples suffer the rejection of prophets, and Jesus leaves the scene having extinguished neither sin nor biblical misinterpretation — not in the world, not in his nation, not even in his own community. Isaiah 6's curse is not annulled by Jesus' school of interpretation. Instead it is carried over into the eschatological age (Acts 28:23-28), where we will revisit it under the heading of ecclesiology.

Scripture's Reliance on External Authorities

Jesus' failure to persuade either his opponents or his disciples during his time of humiliation brings up a third consideration of Scripture's role in election: the fact that incompatible traditions of interpretation often fight each other to stalemates. Though Jews and Christians confess the ultimate authority of Scripture, their many warring hermeneutical factions reveal how frequently Scripture fails to function as its own ultimate interpreter. Often in the course of the Bible's history, exegetical disagreements have proven to be interminable. Neither the texts nor the gifts of interpreters seem to have the sufficient resources for definitive interpretation.

Interpreters thus resort to external authorities to settle hermeneutical disputes. Jews appeal to the Talmud for assistance in interpreting Tanakh, Christians to the New Testament. Calvinists appeal to the internal witness of the Holy Spirit, Catholics to the Magisterium and its *regula fidei*, Eastern Orthodox to the Seven Holy Ecumenical Councils, Lutherans to the criterion of justification by grace through faith. Enlightenment interpreters (including some fundamentalists) appeal to universally accessible standards of rationality, and many postmodernists to the authority of the reading community or the wills of individual readers, who exercise power over texts of infinite elasticity in order to impose meaning on them. In sum, however helpful the Augustinian principle is that one interpret Scripture with Scripture,[143] in the history of biblical interpretation the *final* endorsement or repudiation of a community's reading of Scripture has often come from outside Scripture.

142. Wright, *Jesus and the Victory of God*, p. 437: "Jesus assumed the god-givenness of the institutions [of Temple and Torah]. He stood firmly within one of Judaism's oldest traditions, that of offering prophetic critique from within."

143. Augustine, *On Christian Doctrine* 3.27.38, 101-2.

This is no less true of Jesus' practice of biblical interpretation and the signs and wonders of his ministry. They do not stand on their own. Jesus' claim to be an authoritative interpreter of Tanakh through his own teachings and actions is hardly accepted at face value. Different observers interpret the signs of his ministry in radically different ways. Crowds think Jesus to be a John the Baptist, or an Elijah, or one of the prophets (Mark 8:28). His own family thinks him a lunatic (Mark 3:21). Jewish authorities consider him demonically empowered (Mark 3:22), a false prophet and blasphemer come to lead Israel astray (Mark 14:61-64; Matt. 26:63; 27:63). Roman authorities consider him a rebel with royal pretensions (Mark 15:26). And his disciples consider him the Messiah — though their perceptions turn out to be no less distorted than the others (Mark 8:29-33; 14:10)! Juel is right to emphasize the fact that "though there is surely an 'implicit Christology' in Jesus' ministry of teaching and healing, revealing perhaps some unique sense of relatedness to God, the confession of Jesus as Messiah is not its predictable outcome."[144]

Jesus' reaction to these responses is puzzling. He seems both frustrated by people's inability to understand, and intent on creating further misunderstanding — especially in Mark's narrative. Through his symbolic sayings and actions he means to create insiders and outsiders with radically different appreciations of him. And indeed, the communities who witness his signs read him in incompatible ways. In fact, as Jesus is crucified and buried, no group's perception prevails. Only one community is clearly defeated: his own. Having supposedly lived a life of wisdom, he suffers the fate of the fool. Having supposedly obeyed the law, he dies a felon. Jesus' insiders desert him, and his vision of Tanakh and of himself dies and is buried with him.

Then comes a judgment from outside. Jesus is raised, the tables are turned, the defeat of Jesus' school of interpretation is declared victory. Like Job, Jesus is vindicated over against his companions — not through a rhetorical *coup de grâce* or brilliant argument, but through abject surrender to the God whose judgment alone really matters. An event external to the Christian hermeneutical tradition sets into motion Christian interpretation's most massive transformation.

This is the claim of early Church preaching (Acts 2:23-24; 13:27-41). It is carried through in contemporary theology most thoroughly in the Christology of Wolfhart Pannenberg. Pannenberg clearly sees the need for an authority external to Scripture, who is God himself. Like Juel his fellow Lutheran, Pannenberg places the entire weight of Christology on the Resurrection in such a way that apart from it there would be no grounds whatsoever for Chris-

---

144. Juel, *Messianic Exegesis,* pp. 175-76, critiquing Schillebeeckx.

tian confession of faith in Jesus Christ.[145] The only clarification to the ambiguity inherent in Jesus' own ministry can come "from above" and from afterward, in God's proleptic eschatological inbreaking.

Pannenberg's argument is attractive. But how well does his exclusive emphasis on resurrection fit the critical and biblical pictures of Jesus' career? Were it right, Jesus' irritation at the imperceptivity of those around him would be unreasonable, his high expectations entirely unjustified. Others, even Jesus himself, could hardly know his true status.

Furthermore, Jesus' resurrection is not presented as the only moment of clarity in his career. There are others. The first is the *bath qol* that proclaims Jesus' sonship at his baptism and again at his transfiguration. Whatever form it took, God's baptismal affirmation of Jesus is affirmed in every Gospel and in the apostolic preaching preserved in Acts (10:36-38). It is universally portrayed as the moment when Jesus' ministry is divinely authorized and empowered. The second moment of clarity is really *moments:* all the miraculous feedings, healings, exorcisms, water miracles, and moments of powerful teaching to which his disciples are exposed. These are unveilings, however partial, of Jesus' significance. Jesus himself expresses incredulity that people do not comprehend his signs. The third means of clarity is the holy texts that Jesus considers such obvious heralds of his Gospel.

If Pannenberg is right, the Scriptures are not only liable to misinterpretation; they are impotent to communicate the one message that the early Church consistently finds in them. But in spite of his own apocalyptic worldview, Jesus does not share Pannenberg's assumption that God's future vindication is the only grounds for other people's trust in him.[146] Jesus' self-assurance explains the frustration he feels towards his own followers, the criticism he levels against his opponents, the hostility his attitude meets, and the post-Easter Christians' bitter polemic against the Jews who do not share their hindsight. Nowhere in the New Testament witness is it suggested that the crowds or authorities act reasonably when they reject and condemn Jesus.[147]

We are thus presented with two apparently contradictory facts: First, despite Jesus' two-level discourse, he expects his followers to understand and believe in him according to what they read in Scripture and see in his career, and he judges those who express disbelief. Second, neither the Tanakh's mes-

---

145. Wolfhart Pannenberg, *Jesus — God and Man* (Philadelphia: Westminster, 1968), p. 66.

146. Pannenberg, *Jesus — God and Man*, pp. 58-65.

147. Even when it comes close to doing so (Acts 3:17; 13:27; 17:30), the apostolic *kerygma* explains the Jewish authorities' complicity in Jesus' execution as ignorance that still demands repentance (Acts 3:18; 13:40-41; 17:30-31).

sianic testimonies nor the events of Jesus' career are enough to establish lasting confidence in his status as an interpreter of Scripture, let alone his status as Israel's Messiah. It takes God's massive reversal at the tomb to establish his status, even among Jesus' closest companions, just as Pannenberg and Juel insist.

These two facts conflict only in a Pelagian world where human agents are free and able on their own power to discern and acknowledge God's evidences. Jesus' expectation of faith and the world's inability to exercise faith are reconcilable according to the categories of sin and grace. God's real presence in Israel and its Tanakh, and in the signs and texts of Jesus' ministry, makes it reasonable for Jesus to expect the impossible from his witnesses. Yet human depravity makes the Ethiopian eunuch's reply to Philip equally reasonable: "How can I [understand what I am reading], unless some one guides me?" (Acts 8:30).

Once we can properly distinguish between the character of Scripture and the sinfulness of its context, we can appreciate its mission and the role it plays as a witness to Jesus Christ. The further grace of God's vindicating signs does not bring a clarity to creation, Scripture, and the signs of Jesus' ministry that these things had previously lacked. They are not unstable texts that depend upon their readers for their meaning, but *perspicuous* texts, just as Athanasius and Augustine claim, and the psalmist before them (Ps. 19:1-4). They are not powerless, but pneumatically empowered and effective (Eph. 6:17; Heb. 4:12). Their failings are contextual, not textual.

Yet the Bible does not work entirely on its own, nor on the power of unaided human reason, in creating and maintaining the community of God's faithful. Its efficacy turns on its cooperation with God's other saving works. As a means of grace, Scripture works as both an agent accomplishing God's saving will and as an *object* of God's saving will. It is a message of grace at which God's further clarifying grace is directed, so that its blessings and curses will be appropriated by God's elect for the salvation of the world.

God's vindicating and clarifying grace brings clarity not to the text, but to the *audience,* like sight to the blind, allowing them to see what Jesus has seen all along. The eunuch's request is graciously met in the good news of Philip's reply. Furthermore, their exchange is preserved for our benefit in the texts of the New Testament. So in hindsight, Augustine can state that the New Testament lies in the Old concealed, the Old in the New revealed.[148] The charismatic gifts of discernment, teaching, and interpretation are graces upon grace, further divine gifts that overcome the sins of God's people and allow

---

148. Augustine, *Quaestiones in Heptateuchem*, 2.73 (PL 34.623).

them to appropriate his earlier gifts of Scripture and sign. This is how both Athanasius and Augustine describe God's repeated descents into the created order: not as momentary invasions in which God begins anew, but as interventions that reinforce and build upon God's earlier interventions, pushing back the powers again to affirm, restore, and sometimes add to the lingering signs in the original creation. Jesus' story further subverts the old royal prosperity gospels that misread Scripture's wisdom and promises, revealing a wisdom *sub contrario* that honors the old wisdom and promises while revealing God's character and purpose in a new way (cf. 1 Cor. 1:17-31, quoting Isa. 29:14). Like Jesus, God's biblical signs enter a world of human division and exacerbate its divisions. But all the time, they are performing Jesus' work of uniting (Col. 1:20).

Scripture as a Means of the Atonement

To suggest that the Bible performs Jesus' work of uniting suggests a further, bolder claim: that Scripture plays a role in his work of atonement, even that one of the dimensions of its relationship to Jesus might be called a *means of atonement*. Can it? The answer is as complex as the soteriological category of atonement. Since multiple visions of the atonement (the classical term is "theories," the postmodern favorite "metaphors")[149] have arisen in the Christian tradition to appreciate the once-for-all saving work of Christ, the question might better be asked, "What roles does Scripture play in the various Christian visions of Christ's atonement?"

One short answer is that the best of these visions have drawn deeply on the raw material of Scripture for their images. New Testament reflection casts Jesus' career in an astonishing variety of Old Testament imagery:[150] as Isaiah's Suffering Servant and Daniel's apocalyptic Son of Man and the Psalms' Messiah-King; as an eternal Melchizedek interceding in the heavenly tabernacle's Holy of Holies; as the slain lamb reigning in eternal victory over death and Hades; as the prophet like Moses who delivers God's saving revelation with unparalleled clarity and authority; as Wisdom, co-creator and redeemer of the world. It is not just as a historical and cultural backdrop that the Tanakh

---

149. "Vision" is meant to play on the meaning of *theoria*, suggesting a creative description of something one already sees. It tries to avoid the possible impression that the metaphorist is doing too much of the work, projecting atoning significance *onto* an otherwise neutral event. In other respects the meanings are compatible.

150. See McClendon, *Doctrine*, p. 216.

acts to make Jesus intelligible, but ultimately as a guide and interpreter of his mysteries.

But Scripture does more than provide resources for soteriology and an authoritative storehouse of its images. Neither of these functions really describes the Bible as a *means* of atonement. Theologians have often grouped the many different visions into groups or types, and what must be demonstrated is that the Bible plays a role *intrinsic to each*. We will put the question to three major groups of atonement theories.[151] What role does Scripture play in Jesus' saving sacrifice? In his victory? In the moral influence wrought by his passion? This is the place not to explicate each vision in detail, defend one against the others, or draw out a comprehensive soteriology, but simply to explore in general the way in which Scripture participates in each vision.

Christ the Sacrifice

We have already seen that throughout Jesus' career he obeys the Father's will as Scripture expresses it to him. The Lord of the Law is born and dies under the Law, a member of the people Scripture has brought into being, a party to its commands and promises, in order to secure its blessings and freedom from its curses "only by enduring the law's full weight" (Gal. 3:6-29).[152] There is no limit to the soteriological variations on this theme. But several scriptural features belong to *any* vision of Jesus' death "for our sins": First, the role of Law in making sin known (Rom. 7:7ff.) and magnifying the sins of the fallen

---

151. The threefold typology is common, and what it gives up in detail it more than makes up in clarity, economy, and theological insight. See F. W. Dillistone, *The Christian Understanding of Atonement* (Philadelphia: Westminster, 1968); McClendon, *Doctrine*, pp. 199-213, who describes *Godward, evilward,* and *manward* metaphors; Trevor Hart, in Colin E. Gunton, ed., *The Cambridge Companion to Christian Doctrine* (New York: Cambridge University Press, 1997), pp. 194-95, who speaks of metaphors of release, transformation, and access; and Colin Gunton, *The Actuality of Atonement* (Edinburgh: T. & T. Clark, 1988), who speaks of battlefield victory, God's justice, and Christ the sacrifice (none of which includes Abelard). Cf. Alister McGrath, *Christian Theology: An Introduction*, 2nd ed. (Cambridge, Mass.: Blackwell, 1997), pp. 390-412, who distinguishes between "the cross as a sacrifice" and "the cross and forgiveness" to arrive at four groups, but is otherwise similar. These different schemes overlap only roughly, but they all demonstrate a kind of inner logic among the main visions of atonement. On the other hand, John McIntyre's *The Shape of Soteriology* (Edinburgh: T. & T. Clark, 1992) represents the opposite tendency, distinguishing among thirteen main groups (pp. 29-52). His lesson for the practice of soteriology is that oversimplification inevitably accompanies any typology of atonement.

152. McClendon, *Doctrine*, p. 217. See also Hart, in Gunton, ed., *The Cambridge Companion*, p. 195.

world (Rom. 5:20). Second, the Law's inability to justify on its own power (Rom. 3:20). Third, the legal demands of blood sacrifice for sin that make Jesus' blood the seal of a new covenant (1 Cor. 11:25). Fourth, the Law's curse upon Jesus' death on a tree, making him sin for us (Gal. 3:13 on Deut. 27:26; 2 Cor. 5:21). Fifth, the role of Isaiah 53's Suffering Servant in unmasking the injustice of Jesus' death and thereby revealing its atoning significance (1 Pet. 2:19-25). Sixth, the scriptural blessings and freedom from the Law's curses that Jesus secures through his righteous life and death (Col. 2:13-14), and shares with his adopted brothers and sisters (Gal. 3:22).[153]

Scripture surrounds the cross of Christ on all sides. The climax of Jesus' fulfillment of Scripture is his personal appropriation of its provisions and consequences in his baptized, Spirit-filled, crucified body. The Tanakh defines the saving significance of his sacrifice. It is Calvary's world. Without it, Jesus' sacrifice would not only be unintelligible, it would be unsacrificial.

Christus Victor

Chapter 1 explores the investment of God's own character in the biblical words of story, law, promise, and prayer. Insofar as the Son's incarnate life fulfills Scripture and his baptism in repentance for Israel's sins is found acceptable by the One who sent him, it is not only Jesus and his school of interpretation left defeated on the cross. The whole Godhead is implicated, and all of God's testifying signs. In the absence of Jesus' resurrection, the Father's promises are broken, the Son's integrity ashamed, the Spirit's power surrendered, Scripture's inspiration impugned, the signs and wonders a grand fraud. Alone and abandoned, there is nothing left for Jesus to do but use Scripture against itself: "O God, O God, why have you forsaken me?"

Easter's reversal, the climactic act of what Gustaf Aulén calls "the drama of redemption,"[154] vindicates the Son at the expense of the principalities and powers. They, not he, become the public example (Col. 2:15). Yet Easter's reversal is more than the Son's vindication: It is also Scripture's, and therefore God's.[155] The Sanhedrin invoke *both* in order to sentence Jesus to Rome's punishment. If "corrupt justice interprets the deep meaning of the cross," as

---

153. Note Paul's striking use of "scripture" in 3:8 to refer to the gospel preached to Abraham. Its role in Jesus' sacrifice is much more than merely Law.

154. Gustaf Aulén, *Christus Victor* (New York: Collier, 1986), p. 66.

155. Here one may understand an element of the Father's compassion *(sympatheia)* on the Son's passion *(patheia)* that is not merely vicarious.

James McClendon says,[156] then Scripture is a co-conspirator as long as the sentence is allowed to stand. Neither God nor his words may be trusted. Indeed, they are more than defeated on the cross; their ruthlessness is unmasked. In their tyranny God and his Bible are really no different from the powers.[157] But with Easter's vindication, it is the myth of the scapegoat that is unmasked, and God's righteousness that is revealed.[158] Jesus' obedience to God's words has been rewarded, not betrayed. Scripture's trustworthiness is reinforced, and more: It now reveals God's *ethos* of justice and mercy in the new clarity of hindsight. Psalm 22:1 is not the last word after all, but the first line of a drama of redemption whose triumph will cover the world before the Last Day arrives (Ps. 22:25-31). The cross is revealed as God's ultimate victory, not hope's defeat. The prophecies *are* true! says the risen Jesus on the road to Emmaus. And they prophesy not just suffering, but glory (Luke 24:26-27).

At the empty tomb, Scripture's vindication is complete. The promises have not prevailed against the Law or the disciples against Israel, so as to yield a Marcionite "canon." The oracles of God are proven to be trustworthy in their entirety, so much so that Gentile as well as Jewish Christians take up the whole of the Tanakh as their Scripture, and as the one weapon with which they wage their spiritual warfare in the world (Eph. 6:17). "The Lion of the tribe of Judah, the Root of David, has conquered, so that he can open the scroll and its seven seals" (Rev. 5:5).

Moral Influence Theory

The soteriological tradition begun in Abelard and strengthened in liberal Protestantism sees the fruit of Jesus' "objective" saving work chiefly in its subjective effect on human hearts.[159] In Jesus' ministry of exorcism, healing, and

---

156. McClendon, *Doctrine*, p. 216.

157. Cf. Aulén, *Christus Victor*, p. 4.

158. On the Bible's unmasking of the myth of the scapegoat, see René Girard, *Things Hidden Since the Foundation of the World*, trans. S. Bann and M. Metteer (Stanford, Calif.: Stanford University Press, 1987). Girard is quoted in Miroslav Volf, *Exclusion and Embrace: A Theological Exploration of Identity, Otherness, and Reconciliation* (Grand Rapids: Eerdmans, 1996), pp. 292-93, and William C. Placher, *Narratives of a Vulnerable God: Christ, Theology, and Scripture* (Louisville: Westminster/John Knox, 1994), pp. 118-20.

159. See McClendon, *Doctrine*, p. 209. He says, paraphrasing Bushnell, "Forgiveness creates partners in the attitude of love for others, so the forgiven themselves become vicarious sacrificers in spirit" (p. 212).

reaching out to outsiders, God's saving compassion is enacted, and met by joyful human response. God's love reconciles the estranged relationships of sinful humanity. The two greatest moments in God's compassion for humanity occur at the beginning and ending of Jesus' road to Jerusalem: his baptism of solidarity with sinners outside the promised land, and his death between two criminals outside the city of David. At these two points and everywhere in between, Jesus draws new boundaries between insiders and outsiders, according not so much to the demands of the Law as to their loving relationships with him and with each other.

What roles has Scripture to play here? Two, both of which call into question the common criticism that moral influence theory is entirely "subjective" in nature. First, according to Ephesians 2:12 and 2:15, Scripture sets up the very divisions between insiders and outsiders that Jesus annihilates. Second, it mediates the Gospel, without whose texts the saving events of God's compassion would be forgotten. "God's love has been poured into our hearts through the Holy Spirit which has been given to us," Paul says. "God shows his love for us in that while we were yet sinners Christ died for us" (Rom. 5:5, 8; cf. Eph. 2:17). But this extraordinary gift of God's love must be mediated by the ministry of proclamation: "How are they to call upon him in whom they have not believed? And how are they to believe in him of whom they have never heard?" (Rom. 10:14). The Spirit-inspired preaching of Christ's witnesses, preserved in the inspired writings of the New Testament, is the only way for God's compassion to reach needy hearts. Moral influence theory describes the *pathos* that the Bible's divine rhetoric calls forth.[160] Without the Gospel's continued performance, there would be no moral influence.

Conversely, without the real referent of Jesus' ministry and death, the Gospel would be but a story. Its truth would be real, but entirely "intrasystematic."[161] The compassion it evoked would be real, but not a manifestation of God's love for us. The true power of Abelardian soteriology hangs on the dialogical nature of the conversation between Jesus and Scripture, between event and text.

Athanasius is commonly appreciated for his soteriology of divinization. Less commonly is it appreciated how his account of divinization depends upon the other visions of atonement presented here. One purpose of incarnation is Jesus' substitutionary sacrifice for all (*On the Incarnation*, §8). Another

160. This dimension of Scripture's role in atonement can equally well be applied to visions of salvation-by-revelation by which God saves simply by communicating knowledge of himself (cf. John 1:14 and 1:18).

161. See George Lindbeck, *The Nature of Doctrine* (Philadelphia: Westminster, 1984), p. 64.

is his victorious invasion and occupation of the devil's territory, like that of a warring king, in order to secure it and make it his own (§10). Yet as important as these are in Athanasius' argument, it is the moral influence of the *logos* that takes most of his attention. He describes Christian salvation in two steps, which today we would label objective and subjective:

> While he blotted out the death which had ensued by the offering of his own body, he corrected their neglect by his own teaching, restoring all that was man's by his own power. (§10)

Jesus' *teaching* is the second theater of God's war on corruption. The Word's sojourn in the world is not restricted to the time of the bodily Son's earthly tenure, but sojourns still by his teaching (§49). The Word's powerful persuasion of the world's darkened but still faintly wordly minds restores what they lost in the Fall, regenerates the idea of God that has vanished from them, and creates a new school, different even from Israel's "holy school for all the world" (§12). Christ preaches by means of his own disciples, carries persuasion to human minds, and teaches them to lay aside their idols, know him, worship the Father, and "come over to the school of Christ" (§51). So strong is Jesus' agency in Christian preaching that Athanasius says it is Jesus *by himself* who bears off all humanity from their errors (§53).

It is only here, at the climax of Athanasius' account of the Christ's moral influence on the disciples newly enrolled in his school, that he uses his famous phrase: "For he was made human that we might be made God; and he manifested himself by a body that we might receive the idea of the unseen Father; and he endured the insolence of men that we might inherit immortality" (§54). The *pathos* of Jesus' teaching is an indispensable part of the salvation the Eastern Church calls *theosis*. The one raised on Scripture's wisdom (Luke 2:52) is found to be Wisdom herself, the world's creator and savior (1 Cor. 1:24, 30; Col. 1:15-17).[162]

It has been necessary in treating atonement under the chronology of Jesus' own ministry to leap ahead conceptually to the time when his Gospel is preached. Salvation by moral influence anticipates dimensions of Jesus' relationship to Scripture that follow below. How is the preaching of Christ related to Israel's and the Church's Scriptures? What is the nature of the school of Christ? What does the *pathos* of Scripture look like in the human lives it transforms? A full description of the moral influence of Scripture is no less than an account of the Bible's role in the Christian *ordo salutis*,

---

162. A feminist appreciation of the Bible's wisdom Christologies can be found in Johnson, *She Who Is*, especially pp. 150-69.

which comprises part of the next chapter. We must postpone these questions until then.

It is possible to describe other clusters of atonement visions and develop Scripture's roles in them, but the overall conclusion is already clear: Israel's and the Church's Scriptures are crucial participants in Christ's atonement for the sins of the world. Like the wood of the cross, they neither take the place of Christ the Savior nor compromise from his centrality. But apart from them, it is really impossible to conceive of Christian salvation at all.

The Bible as Kerygma: *Jesus' Dialogue with Scripture*

Preaching the death and resurrection of Jesus emerges as a fundamental means of Jesus' reconciliation by moral example. Scripture is, as Barth observed, a collection of signs that point forward and especially backward to Jesus' ministry. Here our elusive dialectic between saving event and saving text resurfaces. Neither the events nor the texts stand on their own. This brings us to the next dimension of Scripture's relationship to Jesus: It is his *kerygma.*

The interdependence of event and text in Jesus' career should not mislead us into thinking of Christ and his witness as equal partners. Bibliology is neither biblicism nor bibliolatry. The *penultimate* signs of God's saving grace are Jesus, who made himself a sign by emphatically pointing beyond himself and his actions,[163] and the twin climaxes of his ministry: his crucifixion and his resurrection. The very word "sign" would seem inappropriate for them if it were not Jesus' own (Matt. 12:39-40). God's saving grace *is* the Messiah's death and resurrection.

Yet even the resurrection is not God's last word. Its inauguration of the eschatological age is only an inauguration. The resurrection brings Israel's Scriptures into a new eschatological setting. And because of sin's persistence in creation even after the resurrection, further interventions continue in the days and years that follow. They create authorities that communicate God's saving signs with a new level of forcefulness and clarity. Jesus' ministry and his witness are not identical, but they are so deeply interdependent that many Christians do not even sense a distinction. Athanasius calls *both* of them sojourns of the *logos* into the world, comparing "the foolishness of the word preached" (1 Cor. 1:21) to the condescension of a master teacher for the benefit of his pupils (§14).

163. Kasper, *Jesus the Christ*, p. 30.

Chief among these signs are the *kerygma* of Jesus' original disciples[164] and the New Testament Scripture itself. These build upon Jesus' life, death, and resurrection as a pearl's layers of nacre surround the grain of sand that provoked them. Further layers of Holy Tradition never cease to accumulate, but the pearl still owes its shape to the authoritative contours of Old and New Testament Scripture. Luke Timothy Johnson calls the New Testament Christianity's Talmud, its authoritative interpreter of the Old Testament, "not as the replacement of Torah, but as the indispensable prism through which Torah is to be read and understood."[165]

God's eschatological interventions continue to transform Christian biblical practices, but not as new *epiclēses* that turn Christian Scripture into something entirely new. Instead, they renew and extend Scripture's decisive, unrepeatable, messianic transformation, giving it a new inspired voice for a new time or place. (This is how fillings with the Holy Spirit work after Pentecost in Acts 4:8, 31, and so on.) So upon canonical Scripture rest the Church's magisterium (whether such a thing be conceived in terms of the *sensus fidelium,* the college of bishops, the Ecumenical Councils, local pastorates and presbyteries, or worshipers gathered to hear from and speak to their present Lord) and the Church's rule of faith (embodied in the Apostles' and Nicene-Constantinopolitan creeds and other "normed norms") that emerges from Scripture and in turn interprets it.

We will discuss Scripture's contested place in the hierarchy of God's authorities in the next chapter. This list of authorities is here to illustrate Scripture's dual role as the authoritative embodiment of the prophetic and apostolic confession, and as the authoritative basis for the Church's further reflection on Jesus Christ. Both roles are famously expressed in the Barthian category of *witness:*

> We think of John the Baptist in Grünewald's painting of the crucifixion, with his strangely pointing hand. It is this hand which is in evidence in the Bible. . . . Shall we dare turn our eyes in the direction of the pointing hand of Grünewald's John? We know whither it points. It points to Christ. But to Christ the sacrificed, we must immediately add.[166]

---

164. See C. H. Dodd, *The Apostolic Preaching.*

165. Luke Timothy Johnson, *The Writings of the New Testament: An Interpretation* (Philadelphia: Fortress, 1986), p. 548. Of course, the New Testament is itself canonical Scripture in a way the Talmud is not (see Childs, *Biblical Theology,* p. 76).

166. Karl Barth, "Biblical Questions, Insights, and Vistas," in Douglas Horton, trans., *The Word of God and the Word of Man* (New York: Harper, 1957), pp. 65, 76.

We only put Barth's insight in a somewhat different way in claiming that Scripture is also Jesus' *kerygma*.

Scripture's quality as witness to Jesus Christ is well trodden and often contested ground. What is the relationship between event and text at the Ground Zero of Christianity? Does the *kerygma* only originate after the first Easter, as Juel contends? Or is it to be found in Jesus' ministry? Or is it even perceived beforehand by the prophets themselves?

The answers are by and large semantic. The prophets foresee *something;* but exactly what they see and how clearly they see it are impossible to tell. The Last Supper and other passages in the Gospels (Mark 8:28-31 and parallels; Luke 11:8-9; Acts 10:36-39; John 2:18-22) suggest a call for a response that is decisive for one's relationship to Jesus during his ministry. But Jesus' witnesses — the ones who have responded to this call — claim that the full meaning of their own confession only hits home following Jesus' resurrection appearances and the witnesses' return to Scripture for their interpretation. In *this* sense, Juel's thesis is absolutely right that

> the confession of Jesus as the crucified and risen King of the Jews stands at the beginning of christological reflection and interpretation of the [Old Testament] Scriptures — at least the reflection and interpretation that form the substructure of NT Christianity.[167]

The entire field dedicated to exploring the New Testament's use of the Old Testament centers on this pivotal moment in Scripture's salvation-history. Where later Jewish hermeneutical practice remains centered on the Tanakh, Jesus' disciples re-read the ancient texts for their divine commentary on the Master's death and life, find the Messiah's career to have taken place "according to the Scriptures," and set Christian hermeneutics on its new course as a practice of interpreting Scripture and Jesus in each other's terms.[168]

The product is what C. H. Dodd calls "the apostolic preaching": the Je-

---

167. Juel, *Messianic Exegesis,* p. 171.

168. See Ellis, "Biblical Interpretation," in Mulder, ed., *Mikra,* pp. 704-5: "(1) While the rabbinic midrash seeks to discover some hidden element within the OT text itself, the NT midrash with its eschatological orientation applies the text theologically to some aspect of Jesus' life and ministry. (2) While for the rabbis the text is primary, the NT writers give primacy to Jesus and to the surrounding messianic events, or tradition of events, and only then use OT texts to explain or illuminate them." Ellis thinks this even holds true for the Matthean infancy narratives, which presuppose traditions such as Jesus' birth in Bethlehem. But it is much more difficult to apply this view to events like the flight into Egypt, which fit so perfectly into a Matthean Christology that sees Jesus as eschatologically recapitulating Israel's Egyptian slavery and Babylonian captivity.

rusalem Church's *kerygma* preserved in the Acts sermons, and the Pauline *kerygma* which is rooted in and deeply compatible with the Jerusalem *kerygma*.[169] The Jerusalem *kerygma* confesses (1) that the eschatological age of fulfillment has dawned (2) through the ministry, death, and resurrection of Jesus the son of David. (3) His resurrection has exalted him at the right hand of God as Israel's messianic king, and (4) his Church's experience of the Holy Spirit confirms his power and glory. (5) He will shortly return to end the messianic age. Therefore (6) through his preaching he calls for repentance unto salvation, the gift of the Holy Spirit, and membership in his community.[170]

Even if Jesus frames this message with his own preaching (as Mark 1:14-15 describes it), the Jerusalem and Pauline *kerygmata* are not mere repetitions of Jesus' words. Yet the Church still considers the performance of its *kerygma* to be "preaching the Kingdom of God."[171] To preach Jesus crucified and risen is to preach what Jesus preached.

Likewise, to preach Jesus is to preach Scripture. The witness of Israel's Scriptures is presupposed in Paul's *kerygma* (1 Cor. 15:3-4's "according to the Scriptures") and developed at length elsewhere in the Pauline and catholic Epistles, in the Gospel narratives, and in the apostolic preaching preserved in Acts. So deep is the New Testament Church's conviction that the Scriptures testify to Jesus' salvation that texts with no obvious messianic referent are subsequently seen to refer to events in Jesus' career. The *kerygma* reads the texts and Jesus' life in terms of each other as a dialogue of signs. Jesus is the occasion for revisiting God's words in Scripture, since God has drawn all the more near in Jesus. Incarnation sends God's biblical signs to the periphery; yet ironically, at the same time God's humanity now makes God's words all the more powerful. So Christ occupies the center position of a two-way conversation between event and text. The first sentence of Hebrews' intricate Christology, which it develops by juxtaposing Israel's salvation-history, scriptural testimonies, and the life of Jesus Christ, beautifully characterizes this dialogue: "In many and various ways God spoke of old to our fathers by the prophets; but in these last days he has spoken to us by a Son."

---

169. Dodd believes many of the Acts sermons represent a pre-Lukan Aramaic source that faithfully represents a very early confession of the Jerusalem Church; and Paul's *kerygma* is derived from the very early Palestinian tradition behind 1 Cor. 15:3-5 which is deeply similar to the Jerusalem *kerygma*. See *The Apostolic Preaching*, pp. 7-35.

170. Dodd, *The Apostolic Preaching*, pp. 21-24. Paul's preaching uses sonship language, the Jerusalem Church servanthood language; and Paul stresses his death *for our sins* and his present ministry of intercession (pp. 25-26). In other respects the two *kerygmata* are essentially similar.

171. Cf. Luke 4:43, 9:2, 16:16, Acts 8:12, 28:31. See Dodd, *The Apostolic Preaching*, p. 24.

Space permits only two specific examples of this kerygmatic dialogue at work within the New Testament itself: first, the use of Joel 2:28-32 and Psalms 16, 132, and 110 in Peter's Pentecost sermon; and second, the puzzling formula quotation in Matthew 2:15 on the fulfillment of Hosea 11:1, "Out of Egypt I have called my son." The former uses texts from the early Church's list of biblical "testimonies" in order to understand and preach not only Jesus' passion but the events on either side of it, in a way deeply typical of and influential for the Church's evangelistic and apologetic uses of Scripture. The latter is an example of the Matthean typological use of the Old Testament that, through the exegetical school of Antioch, profoundly influenced Christian biblical practice. These two texts are less different than they seem. Both show Scripture in its new role as eschatological missionary of the Gospel of Jesus Christ.

This Is That: The Pentecostal Fulfillment of Joel and the Psalms

If Dodd and others are right that Luke used a source for Peter's Pentecost sermon, we can consider up to three discrete stages in Old Testament interpretation in Acts 2: First, the application of Joel 2:30-32 to the events of Jesus' career, centrally his death and resurrection. Second, the Lukan Peter's midrashic discourse on Joel 2:32a, which draws upon Psalms 16:8-11, 132:11, and 110:1 to clarify the referent of its "name of the Lord." Third, Luke's own use of the sermon, concentrating on Joel 2:28-29 but applying the whole passage to the structure of Acts 2 as a bridge between Luke and Acts. We use "Peter" and "Luke" roughly to refer respectively to the apostolic preaching itself and to Luke's redactive appropriation of it in the framework of Luke-Acts. Whether these are occasionally conflated or artificially separated below is unimportant. It may be impossible to retrace the rich tradition-history of Acts 2 with complete confidence; but it is obviously there.

There is no particularly messianic reference in Joel 2:28-32. Nevertheless Peter applies the passage, which Dodd considers an "apocalyptic-eschatological text" in wide use in the earliest Church,[172] directly to Jesus. The Pentecost events prefigured in Joel 2:28-29 are evidence of Jesus' heavenly exaltation (Acts 2:33). Joel 2:30's "wonders above . . . and signs below" are the "mighty works and wonders and signs" of Jesus of Nazareth (Acts 2:22) that divinely attest to his character. Peter even glosses the Joel text, adding *semeia, ano,* and *kato* in Acts 2:19 to make it clearer that Joel speaks

---

172. Dodd, *According to the Scriptures,* pp. 46-48, 62-64.

of the specific events both before and after Jesus' ascension. Finally, with great rhetorical power Peter latches onto 2:32, cutting off the verse in midcourse in order to identify "the name of the Lord" in the next stage of his sermon.

The answer lies in the Psalms. Peter's exegesis of the Psalmic passages is characteristic of the early Church's practice of reading the Psalms in terms of Jesus. Psalms 110:1 and 16:8-11 are particular favorites: Psalm 16:10 appears again in Acts 13, and Psalm 110:1, the most often used Old Testament text in the New Testament, appears by quotation or allusion in Stephen's sermon, all three synoptic Gospels, Romans, 1 Corinthians, Hebrews, Ephesians, Colossians, and 1 Peter. This text in particular is kerygmatic bedrock. Peter refers these passages to Jesus' life-events thus: Psalm 16's "let your holy one see decay" refers to Jesus' death and resurrection, since King David himself remains dead and buried.[173] Psalm 16:8, "the Lord at my right hand," and Psalm 110:1, "sit at my right hand," in Acts 2:33 signify Jesus' ascension, exaltation, and eschatological rule as king. Psalm 132:11 is put to a similar purpose: God's oath that he will put a Davidic descendent upon David's throne forever is fulfilled in the Davidic Jesus' eschatological rule. Psalm 132:17, "I have prepared a lamp for *my anointed*," while out of direct view in Acts, brings further messianic significance to the text at the allusive level. This is consistent with Dodd's and Richard Hays's findings that contextual exegesis and echo are common characteristics of early Christian biblical practices.[174] Here they allude to Jesus' messiahship and to the inbreaking of the promised eschatological age.[175] Finally, Psalm 110, "until I make your enemies a footstool," refers to God's eschatological return to judge his enemies on the Day of the Lord, "the great and manifest day" (Joel 2:31 in Acts 2:20).

This last text does double duty in the Pentecost sermon. Peter uses it for a final homiletical lunge at his audience. In three psalmic prooftexts, his midrash has established that the "name of the Lord" in Joel 2:32 is "Jesus of Nazareth" (Acts 2:22). Now he thrusts: "God has made him both Lord and Christ, this Jesus *whom you crucified*." The crowd, cut to the heart — morally influ-

---

173. Peter assumes David foresaw this Christological fulfillment of his prophecy (Acts 2:30), a characteristically typological, Antiochian view of the intent of the Bible's own writers.

174. Dodd's *According to the Scriptures* is in part a refutation of Rendel Harris's hypothesis that the early Church was using a book of brief biblical testimonies rather than the canonical texts themselves (pp. 23-27). For an examination of Paul's use of allusion and echo see Richard Hays, *Echoes of Scripture*.

175. So Dodd (*According to the Scriptures*, p. 62) reads Joel's "call a trumpet" and "gather an assembly."

enced, Abelard would say — asks how possibly to respond, and Peter completes his kerygmatic coup by delivering the final phrase of the Joel text he has left hanging: "Repent, be baptized, receive the gift of the Spirit, for the promise is for you and your children" (Acts 2:39, on Joel 2:32b).

In this short, brilliant passage is rehearsed Dodd's entire Jerusalem *kerygma:* Jesus' Davidic descent, his ministry, his death, his resurrection, his exaltation, his return,[176] the Church's experience of (the gift of) the Holy Spirit, the invitation to repentance, and the eschatological setting that frames it all. All these events are tied to the whole of Jesus' life, read centrally through his death and resurrection, interpreted in terms of Israel's Scriptures, and applied to his continuing ministry through the Church in the Spirit.

It remains only for Luke to concentrate on Joel 2:28-29, using imagery from Sinai[177] to associate Joel's prophecy and the outpoured Spirit with the newly gathered men of Israel and with Peter's own prophetic speech,[178] and to order these events toward their ecclesial embodiment in 2:41-47. Acts 2 ends with a fulfilled Joel 2:32b: God is adding daily to those being saved. The next phase of Scripture's rhetorical mission is already unfolding under God's powerful agency. Its *pathos* gives rise to the *praxis* of the Church of Jesus Christ. Or, as Athanasius puts it,

> Christ alone, by ordinary language, and by men not clever with the tongue, has throughout the world persuaded whole churches full of men to despise death, and to mind the things of immortality; to overlook what is temporal; to think nothing of earthly glory and to strive only for the heavenly. (§47)

Typology Run Riot? Matthew's Vision of Biblical Fulfillment

Matthew's use of Hosea 11:1 ("out of Egypt I have called my son") is a far less straightforward example of the kerygmatic dialogue between Jesus' career and Israel's Scriptures. Not only is it less typical of New Testament exegesis of

176. Though Dodd himself does not cite this, Psalm 110 may be alluding to it.

177. Raymond Brown notes the first-century association of Pentecost and the events at Sinai. As Sinai came one-and-one-half months after the exodus, so Pentecost was timed appropriately for Jews to remember God's giving them the covenant and calling Israel to be God's own people (Raymond E. Brown, *An Introduction to the New Testament* [New York: Doubleday, 1997], p. 283). The first Christian Pentecost becomes another Sinai, a regathering of Israel in God's presence. The wind and fire of Acts 2:2-3 and 2:19 (Joel 2:30) perhaps echo the thunder and smoke of Exodus 19.

178. The latter is an example of Pentecostal tongues: Compare *apophthengesthai* (2:4) to *apephthegxato* (2:14).

the Old Testament, but it has left interpreters scratching their heads ever since. Its oddness has led in several directions: First, warranting what Robert Grant calls "typology run riot," a hermeneutic characteristic of early exegetes like Justin Martyr that has sometimes crossed the line between the use and abuse of Scripture.[179] Second, warranting a reaction *against* the practice of typological interpretation, either in fundamentalistic defenses of the literal historicity of the events portrayed in the formula quotations,[180] or in a scoffing repudiation of Matthew's hermeneutical method. R. Vernon McCasland, in "Matthew Twists the Scripture," represents the last school: Matthew "misunderstood" the Hosea text as being a predictive prophecy, which it obviously was not. His misunderstanding led him to look for a meaning "entirely foreign to the original" context of Hosea, and he felt "free to distort" it as his own hermeneutical assumptions required.[181] The implication of such reasoning is that we moderns know better and should shy away from such excesses, if not out of respect for rationality, certainly out of respect for the integrity of the Old Testament's own witness.

At stake in these kinds of debates is the nature of the dialogical relationship between Israel's Scriptures and Israel's Messiah. The issue goes to the very character of the apostolic *kerygma* and to the mission of Scripture. Are texts like these Bultmannian mythologizations of an ordinary life seen in light of the gift of faith? Are they Christian betrayals of Israel's Scriptures, which end up betraying Jesus' own historicity by fabricating a childhood out of whole cloth? Do they always depend on real events, as Ellis maintains, or does the Church's proclamation take greater liberties with what actually happened? In sum, what is the relationship between event and text? How exactly *does* Scripture participate in the divine economy of salvation?

The answer, that Matthew the Evangelist was a creative historian who knew what he was doing, does not quite fit in any of the above schools of interpretation. A contextual reading of Hosea 11:1 in light of Jesus' career can arrive at a reasonable explanation for this formula quotation: Matthew sees Hosea not so much fulfilled verse by verse as fulfilled in its entirety.

The obvious referent in Hosea 11:1 is not Jesus, but Israel. The narra-

---

179. Robert Grant and David Tracy, *A Short History of the Interpretation of the Bible,* 2nd ed. (Philadelphia: Fortress, 1984), p. 45. Note that Grant is impugning Justin, not Matthew!

180. For an interesting example that takes the historicity of Jesus' flight into Egypt for granted but goes on to explore the implications of Matthew's use of Hosea 11 for evangelical doctrines of Scripture, see Tracy L. Howard, "The Use of Hosea 11:1 in Matthew 2:15: An Alternative Solution," in *Bibliotheca Sacra* (1986): 314-28.

181. *JBL* 80 (June 1961): 143-48.

tive, however, does not stop at Israel the man; it concerns Israel *the nation*. God calls Israel (The man or the nation? The Masoretic Text is ambiguous, but the LXX renders *libni* as *ta techna autou*, "his children") out of Egypt because of his love. But idolatry leads them astray. So they shall "return to the land of Egypt" (11:5), this time under Assyrian rule. However, God's love will not let him wipe out his people: "How can I hand you over, O Israel" (11:8)! So he will call them back, and "his sons shall come trembling . . . like birds from Egypt," to return to their homes (11:11). Hosea 11:1 alone is in no way a predictive, messianic prophecy. But the verse in context provides a different picture. It is not about exodus, but return from exile. It is still not an explicitly messianic text, but it *is* an eschatological, predictive text, like Joel 2:28-32, in which Messiah naturally plays a part.

God's faithfulness and love in fulfilling his promise to Jacob is thwarted, first by the famine that sends Jacob's family into Egypt, then by the idolatry that exiles them. But both times God's mercy reverses the disaster and brings them home.

Matthew adds a third twist to the plot. Herod's jealousy (Matt. 2:7-8) puts the promise in jeopardy yet again, on the eve of its final fulfillment. So Jesus is sent away, exiled, back into Egypt. Will this exile of Israel's king frustrate God's promise? Will Herod's jealousy cut off Israel from God's messianic blessing, as the jealousy of Joseph's brothers had once threatened to do? Hosea 11, itself embodied in 11:1, has already answered. "*Out* of Egypt I have called my son."

The Matthean episode is usually referred to as "the flight into Egypt," but its real emphasis, like Hosea's, is *return* from Egypt. The flight into Egypt in 2:13-14 merely sets up the return in 2:19ff. that is fulfilled in 2:15.

Hosea 11 is eschatological, but it is not messianic. Nevertheless, Matthew can and should treat it *as* messianic — because Jesus embodies, leads, and represents returning Israel. Thus a text about Israel the nation's eschatological return should be read messianically. Other formula quotations allude to the role of "the shepherd" in Israel's eschatological return, but such a figure is missing from Hosea 11. What allows Matthew to make this hermeneutical leap is the Church's own prior dialogical reflection on Jesus' career and Israel's Scriptures (and perhaps on Jesus' own teaching). Jesus personifies Israel, and so Israel's salvation-history proleptically participates in Jesus' own.

This hermeneutical assumption is characteristic of Matthew's and Hebrews' typological treatment of the Old Testament, and also characteristic of the typological *theoria* of the school of Antioch it would inspire. In its particular exegetical *techniques,* it is worlds apart from Acts 2. There the kerygmatic reflection is particular, treating the events of Jesus' life discretely. But here in the formula quotations, the Christological reflection manifests itself in the broadest terms, as an account of events in Jesus' life in light of his overall significance as Israel's messianic representative.[182] The overarching hermeneutical similarities between the Acts and Matthew passages far outweigh all their technical differences. Both advance a dialogue between Jesus' career and his Scriptures that finds the ultimate significance of each in the other.

Matthew's use of Hosea is no more a willful distortion of biblical texts than the Lukan Peter's use of Joel. It is neither arbitrary nor capricious. Nor is it an esoteric example, unrepresentative of the Church's usual use of Scripture, for Dodd considers Hosea (not just 11:1, but the book in its entirety) one of the earliest Church's "testimonies," one of the foundational texts it drew on to understand and preach its Master.[183] It is a Matthean rendering of Paul's "according to the Scriptures," a way of confessing Jesus as the fulfiller of holy writ. It affirms that God's words are not fulfilled *here and there* in the life of Jesus so much as they are fulfilled *everywhere*. It is deeply informed by Christological and bibliological assumptions, a product of the *kerygma* as much as a producer; and its assumptions are both reasonable and representative of the New Testament Church. Echoing these convictions, Athanasius says that "the whole inspired Scripture cries aloud" concerning Christ (§33), and him only (§37).[184]

Confession as the Ultimate Exegetical "Technique"

Paying attention to the kerygmatic character of the dialogue between Jesus and Israel's Scriptures sheds light on the long-standing problem of how the later Church should regard the exegetical practices of the New Testament Church. Today's biblical interpreters belong to communities that calls them-

---

182. Of course, this still fails to answer the historiographical question of whether Jesus went to Egypt as a toddler. Since there is no external evidence of any kind regarding his travels as a child, there is simply no other source to which the historian can turn than to the Scriptures themselves. And so the question returns to Matthew's hermeneutical practices. One's conclusion on the modernistic historicity of the flight into Egypt is inevitably bibliological.

183. See Dodd, *According to the Scriptures,* pp. 74-78.

184. On the other hand, later interpreters who do not share or even understand Matthew's reading practices and miss its incredible hermeneutical subtlety often do violence to the Old Testament's sensibility in their attempts to imitate the New Testament's typologizing.

selves apostolic, but they generally hesitate to adopt the exegetical techniques of the apostles. They find it hard to reconcile themselves to a tradition built upon exegesis by means of methods deemed "unjustifiable with regard to normal, sober hermeneutical canons."[185]

But is the tradition really built upon such methods? In biblical studies the reigning approach to the New Testament's use of the Old has been *technical:* Scholars have painstakingly catalogued ancient examples of midrashim, pesher exegesis, Hillel's seven exegetical rules, and so on, in order to establish some kind of hermeneutical pattern with which to compare Christian schools of interpretation to those of the Talmud, the Qumran community, or Hellenistic Judaism.[186] On the other hand, as we have seen, the most striking consistency in the New Testament's use of Scripture is the priority given to *Christological and eschatological* assumptions rather than technical ones in choosing which texts to read and how to read them. The particular techniques ancient interpreters put to the text — Paul's *qal wahomer* in Romans 5–8 or his *pesher* in Romans 9:7-9 — are secondary, even dispensable. Augustine would put it this way: The *telos* to which God has pointed the texts in the service of salvation is the ultimate criterion of exegetical validity, not the reading techniques used to retrieve it. The previous chapter would say that because Christ is the content of Scripture, the confession of Christ is its only true hermeneutical canon.

When the early Church's reading practices are viewed primarily as functions of exegetical techniques, insoluble problems emerge that distance the contemporary Church from the tradition upon which it is built. For example, Richard Longenecker tries to overcome the problem by distinguishing between the inspiration and authority of the writers' *conclusions* and their flawed or inimitable exegetical *techniques.*[187] This distinction has proven to be problematic, for Longenecker's approach has already made their conclusions depend upon their techniques.[188]

The trouble with approaches like these is that they treat the New Testament writers as if they are working syllogistically, using exegetical techniques as their foundational hermeneutical assumptions. In fact, their most power-

185. Hays, *Echoes of Scripture,* p. 181, on Paul's use of Scripture.

186. Ellis's article ("Biblical Interpretation," in Mulder, ed., *Mikra,* pp. 691-725) is typical of the genre.

187. Richard Longenecker, *Biblical Exegesis in the Apostolic Period* (Grand Rapids: Eerdmans, 1975), p. 219.

188. Longenecker's other solution is to privilege the New Testament writings because of special revelation given to its writers, which may solve the problem of authority but reproduces the problem of inimitability. See Hays, *Echoes of Scripture,* pp. 180-81.

ful hermeneutical assumptions are the events of Jesus' own life and their own kerygmatic traditions. The ultimate cornerstone of early Church exegesis is Jesus, not *pesher* or allegory or literalism (Eph. 2:20). Exegetical techniques are the servants of the dialogue, not the masters. When they become the masters rather than servants of confession, as they too commonly have in the history of biblical interpretation, the result has usually been Christological marginalization, weakness, incoherence, or even heresy.[189]

If the most basic hermeneutical assumptions of Christianity's first generation lie in Jesus' life and the Church's faith, then critical and postcritical interpreters *can* use Scripture apostolically without having to return to techniques that neither the present-day Church nor the academy finds persuasive. Furthermore, the Church *can* apply such techniques if it wishes, as long as the ultimate criterion remains the apostolic *kerygma* and rule of faith. This is because the New Testament writers' central theological assumptions are still authoritative for the contemporary Church, and because Jesus is the same yesterday, today, and forever. The present-day Church truly imitates the apostles' and prophets' inner-biblical exegesis when it continues their dialogue of Jesus and his Scriptures according to the kerygmatic terms set down by Jesus himself and his appointed witnesses.

The Gospel's Reformation of the Canon

Kerygma remains the fundamental relationship between Jesus and Scripture in the eschatological age. It gives Scripture a new function in its mission: *euangelion*, proclamation of the Gospel of Christ.[190] The "Old Testamentization" of Tanakh begun in Jesus' ministry deepens as the kerygmatic community matures. Scripture's other roles take new positions relative to the Gospel. The promises, messianic or not, are swept up into their fulfillments and preached as Gospel. The psalms and other doxologies, which "made praise canonical,"[191] are adapted from Israel's worship to inspire the Church's

---

189. A fuller account of this relationship is developed in "The Confession of Christ as Hermeneutical Norm," a presentation for the 2001 Wheaton Theology Conference.

190. Here we do not use "Gospel" in the narrow sense of describing only some sections of the biblical witness as opposed to other sections, like "Law." While Käsemann characterizes this kind of "biblicistic" attitude as a new legalism (*New Testament Questions of Today* [Philadelphia: Fortress, 1969], p. 268), it need not be. All of Scripture is "Gospel" if it is presented in proper Christian perspective; none of it is Gospel if that perspective is distorted.

191. James L. Mays, *The Lord Reigns: A Theological Handbook to the Psalms* (Louisville: Westminster/John Knox, 1994), p. 62.

worship of Jesus and (somewhat later) the Holy Spirit along with God the Father.[192] Law and wisdom become *didachē*, regulators of the kerygmatic community, formally unchanged but now deeply dependent upon Jesus' narrative for their eschatological meaning.[193]

This canonical reordering around Jesus opens up a space for direct testimony on the Savior and his community, which is rapidly filled by the texts that make up the New Testament. These bring the *kerygma* itself, Christ's narrative and *didachē*, and the community's own regulations and exhortations into the authoritative corpus of God's words.[194] They form a kind of Christian Tanakh[195] (though one that naturally follows the Septuagintal sequence): a series of narrative histories of origins not unlike the Pentateuch and Former Prophets, and perhaps developed in the genre of Greco-Roman *bioi*; sayings traditions and a body of epistles akin to the Writings; and a Christian apocalyptic work that centers its "climax of prophecy" on the Lamb as the agent responsible for bringing about the very last of the last things.[196] These too are inspired by the Spirit of their Lord, who was breathed on the apostles (John 20:22) and poured out on those present at Pentecost.[197]

In terms of the Trinitarian economy of salvation, the Bible functions as

192. On the Church's worship of the Holy Spirit, see Basil of Caesarea, *On the Holy Spirit* (Crestwood, N.Y.: St. Vladimir's Seminary Press, 1980), and Alasdair I. C. Heron, *The Holy Spirit* (Philadelphia: Westminster, 1983), p. 80.

193. Relativized, not annulled. James's culturally conservative evaluation of the Torah's ceremonial and purity laws wins the day at the Council of Jerusalem; Peter's and Paul's more radical opinions prevail in churches outside Jerusalem's jurisdiction. All visions except for the legalistic doctrine of the circumcision party, the only one fully repudiated, adjust the requirements of the Law to the power of the *kerygma* and to Jesus' teaching (cf. Mark 7:19). See Brown, *Introduction*, pp. 307-8, on the various sides in the debate, canonically preserved in Gal. 2 and Acts 15.

194. See Dodd, *Apostolic Preaching*, pp. 7-8, on these different literatures in the New Testament.

195. "I myself fail to see the similarity," said Luther, in his "Preface to the New Testament."

196. For John as an intentional writer of prophetic Scripture, see Richard Bauckham, *The Climax of Prophecy: Studies on the Book of Revelation* (Edinburgh: T. & T. Clark, 1993), ch. 9. It is ironic that the New Testament work that most consciously imitates Scripture had the hardest time gaining acceptance as canonical!

197. Wolterstorff's vision of a historical defense of the Christian claim that the Bible is an instrument of divine discourse follows these lines (*Divine Discourse*, pp. 288-95). But Wolterstorff's neglect of the historical career of Jesus and his own concrete relationships to Scripture leaves him unable to develop a similar claim for the Old Testament, or explain the centrality of Jesus rather than Bible in Christian faith and practice (pp. 295-96).

Gospel in this way: The Church's *kerygma* is the death and resurrection of Jesus read through the Old Testament. Both testaments proclaim the cross, as the Father's will for the Son. And they proclaim the resurrection, as the Father's verdict on and vindication of the Son. This proclamation is "the Gospel of God" (Rom. 15:16), delivered and received in the power of the Holy Spirit (1 Thess. 1:5) and to the glory of the Father (Phil. 2:11). It is a participatory medium by which the saving work of Jesus Christ is extended to the world and appropriated in the lives of the saved.

This is not an entirely new trajectory for Scripture, but it does represent a shift in emphasis. So the old unevenness in the Tanakh's liturgical use, which is reflected in the synagogue's cycles of Torah and Haftarah readings, naturally gives way to a new unevenness in Christian use of the Bible. The psalms and prophets increase, the Law and the histories decrease. Texts like Dodd's testimonies and the contexts on which they depend become the Church's canon within the canon, and over time the New Testament texts displace even them. Above all, the kind of soteriological value once expressed for the Law in Psalm 119 is now reserved for the Messiah.[198]

The rise of Marcion and his more moderate descendants demonstrates the grave dangers to the unity of God, the coherence of the Gospel, and the safety of Israel when kerygmatic unevenness turns to kerygmatic repudiation of God's canonical words.[199] Yet the new unevenness of canonical use is by and large a healthy development. It is a function of Scripture's eschatological

---

198. "For the undisputed status of the Old Testament as Word of God did not alter the fact that, for the men of the New Testament, the Old Testament, though authoritative, was no longer the communicator of salvation, and in particular not the communicator of salvation to the Gentiles. Only the preaching of Jesus Christ as crucified and risen communicated salvation in the Christian sense. . . . The essential verbal authority was the kerygma of the Gospel . . ." (Barr, *Holy Scripture*, p. 14).

199. Here Lutherans in particular, for instance Adolf von Harnack, have often rightly been accused of neo-Marcionite tendencies in their habit of placing the *kerygma* on a bibliological pedestal. A more nuanced but still problematic attitude is found in Käsemann's "The Canon of the New Testament and the Unity of the Church" (*New Testament Questions*, pp. 95-107) and "Thoughts on the Present Controversy About Scriptural Interpretation" (pp. 260-85). For Käsemann the evangelical faith must maintain that "not everything that is in the Bible is God's Word," over against the superstition of a docetic reliquary of texts with magical powers detached from the will of the Father. "The Bible has, and preserves, its authority from the Gospel and is, for the rest, only one religious document among others" (pp. 272-73). Käsemann's doctrine is a Lutheran counterpart to Barth's dialectical Calvinism. By describing how Scripture's other roles take new places in Christian practice according to the *kerygma,* but do not thereby cease to be God's Word, this bibliology concludes that Käsemann's dilemma between the critical fracturing of the Christian canon and docetic superstition is an entirely false one.

transformation into the Bible of the Church of Jesus Christ. It reflects the eschatological phase of its saving mission. The Christian canon itself is a result of the kerygmatic conversation between Christ and Scripture, and an aspect of Jesus' saving work.

Texts of Triumph: The Canonical Shape of Holy Scriptures

It is in the Gospel's reformation of the canon that we can fruitfully appreciate the holiness of Scripture, even the holiness of the "texts of terror" that seem to betray rather than serve the love of God. There are many such scriptures — most of the canon might even qualify, depending on one's definition. These come in three varieties: the unholy words of the unholy (say, the "comforting" words of Job's friends), the holy words of the unholy (say, Isaiah's prophecies), and the holy words of the holy (say, Jesus' apocalyptic discourses).

We have already claimed that Mariology offers an account of the middle variety. Scripture's main and supporting characters, and even its apostles and prophets, may be sinners. Mariology helps us see that the Bible's holy texts (and their divine author) are not thereby impugned with human sinfulness. Nor does the holiness of the Bible's texts lift their human authors into divinity, or even sinless humanity. Mary is neither the sinful mother of a firstborn sinner, nor the sinless mother of a holy son of God.

It is important to distinguish this variety from the first. Consider, for instance, Peter's confession of Jesus' messiahship in Mark 8:28. Jesus sees the terror in Peter's triumphalism. It has sent many zealots, oppressors, and innocents to violent ends. So he silences Peter, and later rebukes him as a satan. Sin has fundamentally compromised the apostolic *kerygma* from its beginning! How can such words be holy?

They are holy in that they are *narrated* by an inspired narrator, who is *not* silenced as Peter is. "Meaning is use," claims Ludwig Wittgenstein. Peter is right not in what he means, but in what he says. The story itself rescues the reader from Peter's error, by redefining the category of Messiah according to Jesus rather than Peter. An originally defective Christology becomes the story's narrative turning point. Texts such as these are *canonical* — that is, they are framed in an overarching narrative context that alone can offer the rules of faith and charity by which they are properly understood. This means that Peter's confession must be understood not only in terms of the overall Markan narrative, but by the overall biblical metanarrative. "To discern what God is saying by way of the Bible," says Wolterstorff, "we have to take these sixty-six or so biblical books together."[200] Only in such a context can any confession of biblical infallibility be defended and any hermeneutic of trust be practiced.

Here McClendon offers wise advice for those who would renarrate biblical passages to advance the agendas of powers and principalities:

> The biblical narrator, the ultimate giver of the Scriptures of the Old and New Testaments, is God. . . . As theology this may offend some, but I mean it in the first place as literary truth: We can make *full sense* of biblical narrative only when we see its implied narrator not as the human author (who, to be sure, is fully involved at his or her own level), but as the very God of whom Scripture speaks. . . . Whenever it speaks, its story not only supports and conserves, but challenges, corrects, and sometimes flatly defeats the tales we tell ourselves about ourselves. God's Spirit who breathed upon the writers of Scripture breathes also on us, *sometimes harshly*. The consequence is that our stubborn wills are turned, our blind eyes opened, our arhythmic hearts set beating in tempo. This is not always immediate and is never without ugly exceptions; but it happens often enough to confirm our faith in the Author of the Book.[201]

Wolterstorff finds the claim of an implied narrator fatally flawed if it is taken to refer to an omniscient metanarrator providing historians inspired access to historical details that are beyond human discovery (such as Jesus' prayers in Gethsemane, perhaps).[202] But McClendon understands God to be narrating *everything* — even matters of historical record (Luke 1:1-4), and illocutionary devices like discrepancies, ambiguities, and poetic license. *All* Scripture is Spirit-breathed (2 Tim. 3:16). McClendon understands narrative not in terms of authorial epiphany, but in terms of canonicity. As a narrative orders and interprets discrete events, so the Christian canon orders and interprets — narrates — its own discrete speech-acts and act-speeches.

What about the third variety? What about the awful consequences that sometimes come through supposedly holy words — such as God's curses, military decrees, commandments, and even some of his blessings? We have

---

200. Wolterstorff, *Divine Discourse*, p. 205. Wolterstorff calls Augustine's rule of charity a "prior conviction" of canonical interpretation (p. 207).

201. McClendon, *Doctrine*, pp. 40-41.

202. For Meir Sternberg, this metanarrator is not simply another invisible human author, but an omniscient, non-self-referencing, implied narrator of the Bible (for Sternberg, for the Tanakh). Such a narrator, in the case of historical narrative, can then only be history's *creator*. Therefore "every such narrative is to be interpreted as if it carried the preface: 'And God said.'" And the human beings who shared this privileged perspective are to be understood as inspired. See Wolterstorff, *Divine Discourse*, pp. 246-48.

already appealed to the fact that God's self-committal to human speech introduces vulnerability to abuse in the mouths of sinners. Human beings are taking advantage of this vulnerability even in the Garden of Eden, and continue to do so today. Warriors, crusaders, persecutors, powers, and authorities have all drawn rhetorical power from the Church's holy book. But this does not say enough either, for in Scripture much of the pain is caused by God's words delivered in righteousness, in apparent conformity with his will. Where is the relief for an Egyptian master, a Canaanite slave, an Assyrian, a Greek, a Samaritan, a Roman, a woman, or even a Jew hardened to the Gospel (Acts 28:23-29)?[203] How can *these* texts be holy?

The Christian canon, like the Tanakh, answers: They are holy — jointly and severally holy — *in the context of Messiah*. The biblical story (which is not simply the biblical *stories*), when read in full messianic perspective, is not oppressive history, but liberated and liberating history. Jesus recapitulates Israel's history, doing right what has until now been done wrong, taking on the Law's curses and turning them into blessings, relieving the texts of their terror and creating a community in which a *holy* Israelite story might now be lived. His victory turns a sinful history into a history of sinners. The former can only drive further cycles of violence; the latter can become hagiography. Thus the New Testament pictures what the Tanakh promises: a community sharing in Israel's now victorious story.

Indeed, so full is the victory that the age of the Church is not merely a happy ending, but a happy renarration of the story in its entirety. In Christ, the Church lives as Israel refreshed (Luke 1:46-55; Acts 3:18-19; cf. Isa. 61:1-2), as nations at peace (Eph. 2:19), as exiles in hope (1 Pet. 1–2), as citizens and aliens in the land (Acts 15:12-29), as nonparticipants in the sins of Cain, Balaam, and Korah (Jude 11-12), as the end-times witnesses to the nations (Matt. 10:18; cf. Isa. 60:6 and Ps. 72:10-11), as nonviolent conquerors (Rev. 2-3), as a people cleansed by the Genesis flood (1 Pet. 3:19-22), as nations paying eschatological tribute to Israel (Rom. 15), as an Israel restored and regathering and nations judged and reconciled (Acts 2; cf. Joel 2:12–3:21; Rev. 7), as the Israel of God (Gal. 6:16), seeking the eternal city on the verge of its coming (Heb. 13:14). How can the Church live in such an astonishing, apparently contradictory variety of historical contexts — many of them terrible moments in Israel's history? It can live contentedly here because Jesus' righteousness has freed Israel's victims, judged its oppressors, and broken down the wall between them. In him, the story comes together in perfect fulfill-

---

203. See Delores S. Williams, *Sisters in the Wilderness: The Challenge of Womanist God-Talk* (Maryknoll, N.Y.: Orbis, 1993), for a particularly pointed challenge.

ment. In him (that is, in the revolutionary recontextualization of his messianic life), there are only texts of triumph.

Marcion's example shows us how texts of triumph become texts of terror: by divorcing them from their broader context in the divine economy of salvation. A holy thing can be polluted not simply by introducing impurity, but by taking away wholeness (Deut. 17:1). Stripped of the contexts of their holiness, the holy texts can be made to do enormous damage. However, the converse is equally true: Appreciated in messianic context, supposedly oppressive texts can do the liberating work God intends for them. Augustine's rule of clarity is the methodological norm that respects Wittgenstein's axiom. (The one Wittgenstein used as a foil turns out to be his champion!) Thus the Church was right to oppose Marcionism by asserting the apostolic authority of its canon.[204] Both testaments are clear that the world's hope lies in Messiah. And the transformative effect of Jesus' life shows how this is true. His faithfulness radically reframes the events of Israel's history. The conquest comes now from the oral sword of the Word of God (Rev. 2–3; 19:11-21); the wanderings and the exile are now times of mission to the nations (1 Pet. 2:12); Israel's human king is no longer a king after the nations whose rule rejects the rule of God (1 Sam. 8:4-22); the Law is now a guide to infinite mercy as well as perfect justice (Matt. 5); Noah's flood now washes away sin and brings all comers to God (1 Pet. 3:18); the humbling of the nations is now the fellowship of mutual submission (Gal. 3:27-29); the nations' tribute is not the booty of war but the charity of brothers and sisters (Rom. 15:15-19; 1 Cor. 16:1-4). Jesus is the living rule of charity, in whom the biblical texts align with the intention of the God who is love. Hagiography is an occasion to celebrate deliverance, not a license to live in bondage!

The use of "reformation" here must not be taken to imply that the Tanakh is compromised until the New Testament sanctifies it, because this restoration is already something promised and anticipated in the Tanakh, and because the texts of Tanakh are already framed canonically according to this expectation. (Again, otherwise Jesus would have redeemed or overthrown Tanakh rather than fulfilled it.) The Tanakh has its own wholeness, its own quality of canonical holiness. As the canon of Jesus Christ, it is a canon within the (Christian) canon. In fact, it is the only defensible one.

---

204. Hans von Campenhausen, *The Formation of the Christian Bible* (Philadelphia: Fortress, 1972). Wolterstorff cites this argument himself (*Divine Discourse*, p. 294).

Summary: The Language of the Messiah

As the New Testament era closes, Scripture's formation of Jesus and Jesus' transformation of Scripture are now substantially complete, as is our "salvation-history" of the mission of Scripture. There is perhaps no adequate way to condense even the few main dimensions of Scripture's relationship to Jesus Christ we have examined. But since twentieth-century philosophy's linguistic turn, the term *language* has acquired a richness that makes it an appropriate term. Scripture is Jesus' heritage, his horizon, his formation, his practice, his authority, his instrument, his medium, his teaching, his crisis and vindication, his witness, his confession, his community, and his glory. The Bible is the very language of the Messiah.

Biblical Community: Scripture in the Age of the Church

We have yet to explore the last items in that list: Scripture is Jesus' *community* and his *glory*. And our salvation-history of Scripture has trailed off at the close of the New Testament era (whenever that is). In both respects we have thus been brought to the theological present: the age of what Galatians 6:16 calls "the Israel of God," or what systematic theology calls the Church.[205] In describing the relationship between Scripture and Christ, we have all along also been describing the relationship between those *in* Scripture and Christ. Holy Scripture is also *the Church's* heritage, its horizon, its formation, its practice, its authority, its instrument, its medium, its teaching, its criterion, its witness, its confession, its community, and its glory.

This means the mission of Scripture is in no way over. In fact, in Paul's opinion, it has only just arrived.[206] The heart of Scripture's contemporary mission is the biblical practices of the churches of Jesus Christ.

So it is also in *On the Incarnation of the Word*. Athanasius concludes his Christology with a summary of the outcome of Scripture's mission so far: "Behold how the Savior's doctrine is everywhere increasing, . . . the darkness of the idols prevails no more, and all parts of the world in every direction are illumined by his teaching" (§55). Then comes his "altar call," in which this last dimension of his bibliology is finally revealed:

205. McClendon prefers Paul's description, as it is open to more ambiguity regarding the role of present-day Israel among God's communities. See *Doctrine*, p. 363.
206. See Rom. 10:8, on Deut. 40:14, treated in Hays, *Echoes of Scripture*, pp. 154-92.

But you, taking occasion by [this account], if you light upon the text of the Scriptures, by genuinely applying your mind to them, will learn from them more completely and clearly the exact detail of what we have said. For they are spoken and written by God, through men who spoke of God. (§56)

How is this to be done? Alone in a hotel room with a Gideons' Bible? Not according to Athanasius. Let the enquirer into God's biblical words purify him- or herself and live virtuously. Then let him or her "come to the place" of the saints in order to comprehend the words of the saints, and "associate with them in the conduct of a common life" (§57). In other words, the preached *kerygma* brings one to the threshold of the canon's divine knowledge. To cross this threshold is to be baptized, join the Church, and live among the saints in a common life glorifying God. Athanasius' program is a ladder of ascent like the one we will explore below in Augustine's *On Christian Doctrine*. The Church, says Athanasius, is the community of the Scriptures, of the saints, of Christ Jesus, and of the Holy Trinity (§57). Thus Athanasius takes us from soteriology to ecclesiology, and to Chapter 3's ecclesiology of Scripture.

This ladder of ascent works not only on the communal level but also on the personal. Scripture's one cosmic mission is also countless personal missions of salvation. It should be surprising, even troubling, that an entire chapter devoted to Scripture's role in the divine economy of salvation would neglect this crucial personal dimension. No evangelical soteriology of Scripture would be complete without an exploration of Scripture's mission in the life of a typical Christian. But the topic is most fitting within the broader discussion of Scripture's mission in the life of the gathered, worshiping, and evangelizing Church.[207] This is the next chapter's concern.

---

207. For a defense of this strategy, see Telford Work, "Reordering Salvation: Church as the Proper Context for the *Ordo Salutis*," in David Cunningham, Ralph del Colle, and Lucas Lamadrid, eds., *Ecumenical Theology in Worship, Doctrine, and Life: Essays in Honor of Geoffrey Wainwright* (New York: Oxford University Press, 1999), pp. 182-95.

Chapter 3

The End of Scripture:
God's Word in Faithful Practice

I. Church as the Bible's Community

Chapter 1's Trinitarian ontology of Scripture claims the Bible's words partici-. pate in the will of the Father, the *kenosis* of the Son, the power of the Holy Spirit, and the humanity of their authors and mediators. Chapter 2's Trinitarian mission of Scripture argues that Scripture plays an indispensable role in the Triune economy of salvation: It forms a people through whom all the families of the earth are blessed, then forms a Savior through whose work the blessing comes, then forms the Savior's blessed community of disciples. The chapter closes in the morning of the eschatological age of the Church, a time between Christ's ascension and his second advent, having left undeveloped the claims that Scripture is both "Jesus' community" and "Jesus' glory."

In other words, the Analogy of the Word grounds not only an ontology of biblical language, but a politics and ethics of linguistic and biblical practice for those incorporated into the *logos*.[1] Jesus' obedience to, fulfillment of, and transformation of Scripture open his followers' eyes to understand the Scrip-

---

1. Stephen E. Fowl follows and expands upon Nicholas Lash to connect the Analogy of the Word to the practice of the wordly community: "Word care [philology] is ultimately rooted in the character of God, the Word. Further, this word-care must be fostered within the common life of Christian communities." *Engaging Scripture: A Model for Theological Interpretation* (Malden, Mass.: Blackwell, 1998), p. 164, quoting Nicholas Lash, "Ministry of the Word or Comedy and Philology," *New Blackfriars* 68 (1987): 472-83.

215

tures in a new way (Luke 24:45; John 2:22; 12:16). Thus these two chapters together anticipate a third, in which we explore the Christian Bible's role in Jesus' eschatological community, as a means of divine presence to humanity and vice versa.

Jesus' community is threefold: his Triune *koinonia*, his nation Israel,[2] and his Church. Each of these locations is constitutive of the Christian Bible as such. Apart from all of them, the words simply would not be Holy Scripture. We have been focusing on each location in turn. With Chapter 2 the focus shifted from Trinity to Israel, and from the divine character of Scripture to its human formation in the ancient Near East. Then, on the descent of God the Son, the focus shifted from Israel to Jesus Christ, and to the Christological transformation of old Scripture and formation of new Scripture that accompanied his earthly career. On his ascension, the focus shifts again, now to the Church. As sharers in Jesus' body and ministry through the gift of the Spirit, the Church now enjoys relationships to Scripture rooted in (but not identical to) Jesus' own.[3] Thus the Messianic transformation of Israel's Scriptures and the formation of new Scriptures both continue, now along ecclesial lines, in the apostolic era.

Our ecclesiology of Scripture focuses on the Bible as a means of God's presence to his earthly, eschatological community, and as an instrument of the worshiping community when it is present before God. This chapter argues that in the ecclesial transformation of the Old Testament, in the new formation of Scripture within the apostolic Church, and in the Bible's continuing practice, Scripture both *confers* and *takes on* the characteristics of the Church. Therefore the categories of ecclesiology not only depend upon the data of Scripture, but also constructively inform bibliology.

As we have already said, through Christ and in the Holy Spirit, the Bible is now the Church's own heritage, horizon, formation, practice, authority, instrument, medium, teaching, criterion, witness, confession, community, and glory. This progression takes on Trinitarian shape in the life of the Church, as it does in Jesus' career. First, as Scripture was Jesus' heritage, horizon, and au-

---

2. *Is*, not *was*. Israel is still a primary context for the present and future role of Scripture in the divine economy of salvation, if Paul is to be believed (Rom. 11). There is no reason to think that Jews today do not experience God's presence when they perform the Scriptures (cf. 2 Cor. 3:7-18). Yet the Church is still Jesus' designated agent for spreading his Good News.

3. James B. Torrance sketches a threefold fellowship in the worshiping Church: In Christ, worshipers share in the communion between Father and Son, between the head and the body of Christ, and within the communion of saints. *Worship, Community & the Triune God of Grace* (Downers Grove, Ill.: InterVarsity, 1997), pp. 30-32.

thority as a first-century Galilean Jew, so it is for Jesus' disciples. The Church's obedience to Scripture is obedience to the God of Israel. Second, as the anointed Jesus is Lord of Scripture, so the Church's obedience to Scripture is also obedience to Christ, its sovereign Lord. Since Scripture is also Christ's pneumatic instrument, his teaching, his witness, and a means of his messianic work, the Church stands under Scripture as a beneficiary of Jesus Christ's saving grace. Third, because Jesus grants the Church a share in his own messianic power, the Spirit-indwelt Church enjoys a similar dialectic of "sovereign obedience" towards the Bible.

Chapter 1 closed with an appeal to Mary as the ultimate symbol for the humanity of Scripture, and she is an appropriate representative of the various relationships between Scripture and God's people. In Chapter 2 she could have stood in as a personification of the people of Israel (as she does in delivering the Magnificat), who mothered and reared the incarnate God, and as the first disciple in the incarnate God's restored Israel. Now in Chapter 3, as representative of the Church (which is clothed with the same power of the Most High that overshadows [Luke 24:49] and breathes upon [John 19:30] her), Mary personifies the *eschatological* human community's relationship to Scripture in all its complexity. She stands under the very texts she is partly credited for creating. Likewise, the Church, as the body of Christ, participates in Jesus' offices, and thus enjoys the gift of pneumatic freedom with regard to the biblical text as it accomplishes the will of the Father. Yet since Jesus is the head of the body, the Church still stands under the Bible's dominical voice. In order to build up the body of Christ, the Church must receive the same divine grace it dispenses. The various Christian traditions have worked out partially overlapping, partially compatible, partially incompatible accounts of this dialectic of "Scripture and tradition." As we shall see, the tensions among their accounts reflect the eschatological tension between the head and the maturing body of Christ.

The inaugurated eschaton thus frames this entire chapter. We begin by describing the sort of presence an ascended Lord has in a Church that has yet to experience its own ascension (1 Thess. 4:17). Next we explore the connections between revelation's divine descent and experience's human ascent, between the Bible's prevenient, divine character and its responsive, human characters, using Augustine's *On Christian Doctrine* to answer the opposing contentions of Karl Barth and James Barr. Then we delineate the qualities of the Bible's real and ideal human communities, drawing on Alasdair MacIntyre's theory of tradition-constituted enquiry to show that the Christian use of canonical Scripture resembles all human traditions, then using Scripture itself to explore what distinguishes the witnessing Church from traditions in general — *e.g.*, its unity, holiness, catholicity, and apostolicity. These distinguishing marks of the Church are distinguishing marks also of the Church's Scriptures. But the various Christian churches are deeply divided over the nature of each of these marks of the Church. Their disputes over the Church call into question the nature of the unity, holiness, catholicity, and apostolicity of the Church's Bible. This leads into the relationship among Scripture, Tradition, and traditions as the various Christian communities have envisioned it. There we find that biblical practice does not merely *reflect* the distinctions among Christians, but in some way *confers* them. Having described the character of the Church, we turn to the work of the Church, which centers on (but is in no way exhausted in) its formal liturgies. This work is appreciated in terms of the *telos* of Scripture (for which this chapter is named): the salvation of the world, and the restoration of divine-human relationships. This brings up the Bible's role in the *ordo salutis,* not only as it is developed in modern soteriology but as Augustine outlines it in *On Christian Doctrine* in terms of the soul's salvific movement into God's direct presence. As the chapter closes, another sense of *telos* arises: What is Scripture's role *after* the eschaton, if it plays any at all? Does the biblical vision survive the beatific vision?

Throughout the chapter, our goal is to appreciate how each of these areas contributes resources to bibliology — to show how the doctrine of the Church constructively informs the doctrine of Scripture.

Between Ascension and Return: Scripture's Eschatological Context

We begin with the eschatological setting that places the earthly Church in theological perspective. The "between-times" that Easter inaugurates is the age of the Church. Because Jesus' resurrection and appearances inevitably create the eschatological messianic community, the resurrection inaugurates an ecclesiological revolution in biblical interpretation that extends the Christological revolution that founded it.[4]

A good starting point for documenting the ecclesiological revolution of Scripture is Scripture itself — namely, the New Testament's ecclesiocentric interpretations of the Old Testament. The final chapter of Richard Hays's *Echoes of Scripture in the Letters of Paul*[5] concentrates on Paul's practice of

4. The Church's new way of reading Israel's Scriptures Christologically reinforces its habit of reading the Scriptures as referring to the community itself, and vice versa. There are still valid distinctions to be made between the Christological and the ecclesial transformations of Scripture. See above, p. 195.

5. New Haven: Yale University Press, 1989. "The Word Is Near You," pp. 154-92.

reading the Tanakh as addressed specifically to his eschatological communities. "He believes himself, along with his churches, to stand in a privileged moment in which the random clutter of past texts and experiences assumes a configuration of eschatological significance," says Hays, "because all has been ordered by God to proclaim the gospel to those who read what Paul writes."[6] An illustration is Paul's application of Deuteronomy 25:4 in 1 Corinthians 9:8-10 not to refer to the care of livestock, but to the care of Christ's apostolic messengers. How can Paul make this unprecedented hermeneutical leap? Not because the Torah teems with universal principles applicable across cultures, but because its words were written specifically for the Church of Jesus Christ at the turn of the ages. "Is it for oxen that God is concerned? Or does he not speak *entirely for our sake*" *(di' hēmas pantōs legei)?* This is not an exception to Paul's usual hermeneutical practice, but an example of the rule that "whatever things were written beforehand were written for *our* instruction" (Rom. 15:4).[7]

Texts like Deuteronomy 25:4 are not Christological texts — but through the work of Jesus Christ they have become ecclesiological texts. What Hays calls the "master hermeneutical trope" that governs Paul's use of them is itself grounded in Torah (and perhaps also in a creedal axiom of the ancient Church): "*The Word is near you,* on your lips and in your heart (that is, the word of faith which we preach); because, if you confessed with your lips that Jesus is Lord and believed in your heart that God raised him from the dead, you would be saved. For one believes with his heart and so is justified, and confesses with his lips and so is saved" (Rom. 10:8-10, quoting Deut. 30:14). The biblical word, Paul contends, is God's word *to us.* The full import of Tanakh only comes to the eschatological Church of Jesus Christ.

Paul's hermeneutic is grounded in Israel's earlier technique of reappropriating God's covenant with the ancients as God's covenant with his present-day assembly (Deut. 5:2-3).[8] Yet there is more to Paul's ecclesial hermeneutic than mere continuity with Israel's tradition of reappropriating God's words to its ancestors. Because Christ's death and resurrection have ushered in the new age, the community now participates in God's eschatological presence in a fundamentally new and revolutionary way. "Consequently," says Hays, "the eschatological perspective becomes the hermeneutical warrant for major shifts and revisions in the reading of Scripture. . . . God's word

---

6. Richard Hays, *Echoes of Scripture,* p. 165.

7. Hays, *Echoes of Scripture,* p. 166. In his *Interpretation* commentary on 1 Corinthians, Hays comments similarly on Paul's use of Deuteronomy to discipline the Corinthians in 1 Cor. 5:11. See *First Corinthians* (Louisville: Westminster/John Knox, 1997), pp. 87-92.

8. Hays, *Echoes of Scripture,* p. 167.

is alive and active in the present time, embodied in the community's Spirit-empowered life and proclamation."[9]

What Hays finds true of Paul's use of the Tanakh is equally true of the other New Testament writers, both when they are reading Tanakh as Christian Scripture and when they are writing the New Testament. The life of the Church is as pervasive a concern in the Christian Bible as the life of Israel is in the Tanakh. Ecclesiology can be overemphasized as a concern of parts of Scripture — for instance, the Gospels.[10] Yet it is prominent enough in the Christian canon to qualify as one of three "focal lenses" Hays finds focusing the ethics of every New Testament writing. The Church, claims Hays, is "a countercultural community of discipleship, and this community is the primary addressee of God's imperatives." It "embodies the power of the resurrection in the midst of a not-yet-redeemed world."[11]

The Christological and soteriological revolution in biblical practice therefore inevitably implies an ecclesial revolution as well. Because the Bible participates in the divine economy of salvation, one of its primary foci is the *object* of the divine economy — the body of God's redeemed. Thus texts that bear no direct relationship to the Messiah or to his death and resurrection are still read and heard in the worshiping Church. God is "alive and active" in them as much as in Isaiah 53 or Psalm 110. God is as present in the *Haustafeln* and Luther's epistle of straw as in the passion narratives and Romans 3:28. There is an irreducibly ecclesial dimension to Scripture's new eschatological status as God's Word. Like icons of the saints, which have become warranted through the new indwelling of the Holy Spirit in saints' bodies, the words of old and new prophets and apostles are transformed by the Spirit's outpouring and made into dwelling places for God.[12]

---

9. Hays, *Echoes of Scripture,* pp. 169 and 171, echoing Heb. 4:12.

10. See Richard Bauckham, "For Whom Were the Gospels Written?" in Richard Bauckham, ed., *The Gospels for All Christians* (Grand Rapids: Eerdmans, 1998), pp. 9-48. Nevertheless, see below for an analysis of the various Christian traditions that evokes parallels with the Gospels' various ecclesiological tendencies.

11. See Richard Hays, *The Moral Vision of the New Testament* (San Francisco: HarperCollins, 1996), pp. 196-98. Hays's third "focal image" of the collective New Testament witness is, of course, the cross: "Jesus' death on a cross is the paradigm for faithfulness to God in the world."

12. See John of Damascus, *On the Divine Images,* Third Apology 33-39, esp. 34 and 35 (Crestwood, N.Y.: St. Vladimir's Seminary Press, 1980), pp. 85-87, on the relative respect due to the various media of God's presence and salvation, including both fellow Christians and Scripture.

Presence-in-Absence:
God's Eschatological Relationship to the Church

What is it about the rise of the Church that causes such a transformation of Scripture? We shall seek to describe the grounds of Scripture's ecclesial revolution in terms both compatible with the bibliology developed up to this point, and amenable to Christians of all the major ecclesial traditions (and particularly my own Pentecostal tradition).

Chapter 1 has already provided an ontological ground for a doctrine of the Church, in the economic immanence of the Triune God. And Chapter 2 has provided a historical and phenomenological ground for the Church, in Israel. The two converge in the ministries of Jesus Christ and of the Twelve he appointed to follow him as leaders of a restored Israel. So our ecclesiology of Scripture begins with Christ's eschatological presence in the Triune God's earthly community.

Perhaps the most profound feature of the Church is its experience of Christ's abiding presence (Matt. 18:20). Yet the time between Ascension and Return is defined by Christ's absence! The paradox is well captured at the close of the Gospel of Matthew, in the image of Jesus departing from the presence of his disciples, while simultaneously telling them he will be present *(meth' humōn)* until the end of the age (28:20). "Good-bye," Jesus tells his disciples. "I'm not leaving, and I'll be back." This is a defining characteristic of the Church's self-understanding. Jesus' disciples meet in his absence to remember his past presence with them, to anticipate their future presence in his realized kingdom, and to enjoy his continuing presence in their midst.

To use more heavily loaded terms, the worshiping Church celebrates both God's *real absence* and his *real presence*. It does not dissolve hope into realized eschatology by denying Christ's absence (Rev. 22:17). Nor does it ignore its own real experience of Jesus in its midst (Rev. 1:12-13) by denying his presence. Instead, the Church affirms both — thus affirming the inaugurated new creation that constitutes it, as a community in eschatological fellowship with God, with Christ, and with itself. The Church's worship practice embodies a complex awareness of two simultaneous, mutually qualifying dimensions of Jesus' relationship to the Church — a reciprocal "presence-in-absence."[13]

Presence-in-absence does not merely characterize the Church's present-

---

13. A fuller account of the idea of "presence-in-absence" will appear in Work, *The Reason for the Season.*

day experience of God. It also describes and explains the role of the Bible, among other things, in Christ's eschatological fellowship. As we saw in the previous chapter, presence-in-absence is not immediate, face-to-face presence (cf. 1 Cor. 13:12; 2 Cor. 4:14), but *mediated* presence. In fact, Christ's presence in the world is twice mediated: first by the Holy Spirit, second by the Church itself.

A brief eucharistic illustration demonstrates the role these media play in making the ascended Christ present in the eschatological assembly. First, the Lord's Supper commemorates God's past presence and solidarity with the infirm. Second, it brings God's healing (or judgment) into the present-day Church through the *epiclēsis* of the Holy Spirit. Third, it looks forward in hope to the final banquet the faithful will enjoy in the Lord's direct presence. The character of the Lord's Supper as a sacramental means of grace is a function of God's presence-in-absence. In it the Father is mediated through the Son, in the Spirit, "in, with, and under" the elements, through and to the gathered earthly Church.

What can be said here about the Lord's Supper can also be said about the inspired Bible's illuminated performance in the Church. The various Christian traditions tend to characterize the Church in terms of episcopacy, or sacramental participation, or submission of the Word of God, or baptism in the Holy Spirit. All of these ways view the Father's priestly kingdom, the Messiah's body, the Spirit's Temple, in terms of the visible media of God's eschatological presence-in-absence in the world. Through the practice of Scripture, God makes himself present to the Church, and the Church finds itself present before the Father, Son, and Holy Spirit. The Bible supplies rungs of the liturgical Jacob's Ladder on which God and God's people descend and ascend in eschatological fellowship.

The Church as Eschatological Gathering

Rather than explicitly favoring one of these specific ways of characterizing the Church as the various "denominations" have done, this chapter will rely on a category both more common and more directly indebted to the experience of eschatological, reciprocal presence-in-absence. Rather than delineating the Church in terms of "apostolic succession" as magisterial traditions understand it, or in terms of sacramental participation as many high and low traditions understand it, or in terms of confessional or ecstatic response to the proclaimed Word as the evangelical traditions understand it, we will simply consider the Church according to the category of *gathering*. God gathers the

Church around the pulpit, around the baptistry, around the table, around itself (my local church is a "church in the round"), and ultimately around the heavenly throne (Rev. 4:4).

This vision of the Church is wide enough to accommodate both high and low, Orthodox, Catholic, Protestant, and radical accounts of Church. But it is more than an ecclesiological umbrella. On the one hand, it respects the underlying Jewish category of "the assembly of Israel" (1 Kings 8:14 etc.: MT *qhal Israel*, LXX *ekklēsia Israēl*)[14] in which the Church originally saw itself. This roots the Church's gatherings in the context of Israel's gathering, for which the role of Scripture has already been documented. On the other hand, it respects the eschatological *regathering* of Israel that Christian Israel understood to be taking place in the last days.[15] *Ekklēsia*, "the gathering," honors both the eschatological fulfillment and the eschatological reserve of presence-in-absence. It locates the community that reads and hears Christian Scripture in "the commonwealth of Israel" (Eph. 2:12), within the communities of biblical interpretation with whom and for whom Jesus and his first disciples struggled, and whom Paul confidently predicts God will never abandon (Rom. 11:2, 11).

Gathering describes both the weekly worship life of the Church and its course in salvation-history. It also resonates with Augustine's narration of the Christian life together as an eschatological journey into the beatific vision (*On Christian Doctrine* 2.2.11; 1.38.42, and see below), which has been so influential for Western eschatology, ecclesiology, and biblical practice in both the Catholic and the Protestant traditions.

Furthermore, the category of gathering corrects ecclesiology's bad habit of defining the Church too exclusively in terms of its borders. To be sure, this bad habit arose for good reasons. Circumstances have often forced churches to concentrate on questions of their own boundaries — whether to admit into the assembly those baptized by Donatists, or those having apostatized during times of persecution; the status of believers outside of their own par-

---

14. The LXX also uses *ekklēsia* to refer to (among other things) the day of assembly (Deut. 4:10; 9:10; 18:16), the assembly of the sons of Israel (Josh. 9:2; Sir. 50:20), the assembly of the faithful (Ps. 149:1 [LXX], echoed in Rev. 14:3 for the heavenly gathering), the assembly of Yahweh (Deut. 23:2-9; 1 Chron. 28:8; Micah 2:5), the great assembly (1 Kings 8:65; 2 Chron. 7:8; Ps. 21:26; 25:12; 39:10), the assembly of the holy (Ps. 88:6, cf. Joel 2:16), the assembly of the people of God (Judges 20:2), the assembly of the exiles (Ezra 10:8), the assembly of God (Neh. 13:1; Ps. 67:27), and the assembly of the congregation *(synagōgēs)* (Lev. 8:3; Num. 20:8).

15. See, among others, Matt. 16:18; Acts 20:28; 1 Cor. 11:18; Eph. 1:22-23; 3:10; 1 Tim. 3:15; Heb. 12:22-24; Rev. 22:16, cf. Rev. 1–2, and especially James 1:1 and 1 Pet. 1:1, which use only the language of Dispersion to describe the churches to whom they write.

ticular communions; the ecclesial status of congregations with other confessions or polities; and so on. The idea of Church as gathering appreciates these needs (*i.e.*, who is being gathered and who is not?), but its eschatological perspective stresses the Church as a *developing* organism in the process of *becoming*. The Church is an ongoing process by which those at the margins — those who are "not my people" (Hos. 1:9) — are gathered into the children of the living God (Hos. 1:10, in Rom. 9:25-26). As important as its boundaries are, especially in critical moments in the Church's history, the gathered and gathering Church is ultimately confessed in terms of the center towards whom it moves, towards whom Scripture moves it.[16] This center — "Christ the Center" — defines, locates, empowers, and finally accomplishes the proclamation, confession, initiation, sacramental participation, and fellowship according to which the various Christian traditions understand themselves.

Finally, the category of gathering appreciates the dialectic of divine initiative and human response that characterizes the Church. Christians are gathered, but they also gather. Christian Scripture takes on this same double movement: Through God's Bible, God addresses the Church. And through the Church's Bible, the Church answers back. Christian Scripture is a two-way medium of fellowship for both God and humanity. To its double movement we now turn.

Word as Response: James Barr versus Karl Barth

God's presence in Scripture is a presence to a fallen and reclaimed world, which calls and gathers a community of hearers and conforms them back into God's image. Yet Scripture is far more than simply God's words to humanity. The Christian Bible is a fully human institution. The divine presence in Scripture in no way compromises its humanity. It depends on human authors, redactors, and bearers as completely as the incarnate Son depends upon his human mother, or the Holy Spirit's indwelling depends upon the one indwelt. The canonical words that form this community are the community's own products, their own responses to the divine initiative. Furthermore, the Bible's human community is more than a collective amanuensis with no say in the form or the content of the message. Humanity is an active participant in

---

16. The Nicene and Apostles' Creeds can therefore be confessed by Christians in mutually exclusive communions, who mean very different things by the common ecclesiological terms they are using. The centering function of the third articles of these creeds gives them considerable ecumenical promise for pointing different Christian traditions back towards full communion.

the formation and delivery of God's canonical words. The Bible resembles its authoring personalities and communities as Jesus resembles his mother Mary and talks like a Galilean.

We will use two figures in modern Protestant theology to represent these two insights. The early Barth is an obvious representative of those who affirm that God speaks to humanity in the Bible's performance. But Barth's lifelong war against liberal theology makes him far less useful for appreciating the positive theological significance of the Bible's humanity, beyond its role in the Bible's fallible "witness" to events of true revelation. So God has sent James Barr, our second figure, as a thorn in the sides of fundamentalists and Barthians alike, to remind them that much of the Christian Bible is in fact human words addressed not merely as witness to other human beings, but addressed as praise to God. "Scripture is answer as well as address," he says. "The finger of John the Baptist should be given a rest; he is simply not an adequate analogue for the whole range of biblical statement."[17]

For Barr, the human element of Scripture is not something merely to be overcome through God's act of revealing; it is the basic quality of holy writ. Describing Barr's thought, Paul Ronald Wells says that the Bible is the human *answer* to God, in which the divine act and the human response are already inextricably intertwined. Its words are those of Israel and the Church, and "should not be thought of merely in terms of the incarnation but also as related to the human obedience of Christ in his priestly mission and ascension."[18] Barr himself says that the Bible is "not revelation coming from God to humanity but the Church's . . . response to and interpretation of that revelation."[19]

These two partisans of divine descent and human ascent share much common ground. (For instance, Barth would grant much of what Barr emphasizes in his critique of the threefold form of the Word of God — for instance, that "there is much that is in the Bible that is not there because it is a word spoken by God . . . but is there because it was already public knowledge." Indeed, this feature of the Bible's humanity is crucial to Barth's entire account.)[20] Unfortunately, Barth and Barr stand on opposite sides of a modern theological divide that polarizes both. And from either side, the differences

17. James Barr, "J. K. S. Reid, 'The Authority of Scripture, 1957,'" *Scottish Journal of Theology* 11 (1958): 87, quoted in Paul R. Wells, *James Barr and the Bible: Critique of a New Liberalism* (Phillipsburg, N.J.: Presbyterian and Reformed, 1980), p. 26. To be fair to Barth, he too sees Scripture as human response (I.2.552).

18. Wells, *James Barr and the Bible*, p. 29.

19. James Barr, *Biblical Faith and Natural Theology* (Oxford: Clarendon, 1993), p. 197.

20. Barr, *Biblical Faith and Natural Theology*, p. 196.

seem irreconcilable. To Barr, the significance of the Bible's humanity calls for jettisoning not only Barth's particular use of the Christological analogy for Scripture but the Analogy of the Word itself, which has proven to be more trouble than it is worth.[21] In effect, Barr follows Barth's Antiochan reasoning to its opposite conclusion: If there is no true union between divine Word and human words, and no Barthian event of revelation, Scripture has a single, human nature. Therefore "the *human* character is the bearer of revelation, the *human* word is the word that has authority."[22] Bibliology thus belongs not under the doctrine of God, Christ, or even Holy Spirit (where it appears in the creeds), but under the doctrine of the Church. The Bible is a word of the Church, no more and no less fallible than its authors, and effective as such.[23]

This bibliology seeks to reconcile and correct the two positions and affirm the coherence of divinity and humanity, divine descent and human ascent, by stressing three things: first, the validity of the Analogy of the Word (developed as an identity-in-contrast in which the two mutually dependent terms, divine Word and human words, intersect in Jesus' career); second, Scripture's indispensable role in Jesus' human formation and messianic career; and now, third, its thoroughly human context in the life of the gathered Church. Like Athanasius and Augustine, it affirms what Barth affirms against liberalism *and* what Barr affirms against neo-orthodoxy. In fact, it claims that the Analogy of the Word (*i.e.,* the analogy as Chapter 1 develops it, particularly through the categories of Mariology and Spirit-Christology) is not only *compatible* with an affirmation of the humanity of Scripture as strong as Barr's, but *demands* it. A Trinitarian ontology of Scripture and a Trinitarian soteriology of Scripture call for a Trinitarian ecclesiology of Scripture.

The Divine Humanity of Christian Preaching

To heed this call, we return to Augustine's *On Christian Doctrine.* This homiletics text, an extended treatment of the Bible's divine character and intention, human formation and language, and churchly performance, has been formative for attitudes towards Scripture in the Western Church. We have seen how it is grounded in the Analogy of the Word, and uses semiotic and rhetorical categories to describe how the Athanasian transformation brought

21. Barr, *The Bible in the Modern World,* 2nd ed. (San Francisco: Harper & Row, 1990), p. 22.

22. Barr, *SJT* 11 (1958): 90, quoted in Wells, p. 30.

23. Barr, *Biblical Faith and Natural Theology,* pp. 197-98.

about by the incarnation of the Word comes to life in the Church's concrete study and proclamation of Scripture.

Athanasius constructs no less than a cosmic salvation-history of God's self-involvements in the fallen world. Augustine's scope is narrower: He only(!) wishes to describe and prescribe the proper practice of Scripture in the Church — "a way of discovering those things which are to be understood, and a way of teaching what we have learned" (1.1.1). So as Athanasius' description of the Law and Prophets as a school for all the world inspires Chapter 2's mission of Scripture, Augustine's teleology of divine-human Scripture in faithful performance informs this chapter's ecclesiology of Scripture.

For Augustine, signification is to be understood according to the fact of incarnation. Indeed, the point of the Bible's signification is like the point of the Son's incarnation. Scripture's work is to turn minds, hearts, and souls to the service of God — or in the rhetorical terms Augustine adapts from Cicero, to yield knowledge, willingness, and persuasion (4.26.56). Like all the creation, created Scripture begins and ends in the love of God. Its words are ordered toward the enjoyment of God (1.35.39) and the building up of Christ's body in virtue (1.16.15–1.19.18).

On Christian Doctrine begins with a discussion of biblical signs and their connection with the ultimate sign, Jesus Christ. This groundwork is complete as Book I closes, and in Books II-IV Augustine moves on to concentrate on biblical language in its humanity, with little further mention of the analogy. For this reason many commentators have mistaken his work for a mere synthesis of classical rhetoric and Christian hermeneutics.[24] But Book 1 is not forgotten. It continues to operate in the background for the remainder of Augustine's project, validating the critical use of humanities such as grammar, foreign languages, and history in clarifying the signs of Scripture, and encouraging the critical use of classical rhetoric as "Egyptian gold"[25] reclaimed for homiletic use in God's new Temple. If Augustine constructs "an astonishingly brilliant fulfillment of the best traditions of ancient philosophy as they extend from Pythagoras and Plato to Cicero and Varro,"[26] he does so only because the pagans had occasionally stumbled into God's truth, and Augustine is unwilling to let them monopolize what rightfully belongs to God's

---

24. See Mark D. Jordan, "Words and Word: Incarnation and Signification in Augustine's *De Doctrina Christiana*," *Augustinian Studies* 11 (1980): 177.

25. Or perhaps *kherem* (cf. Josh. 6:18-19)? Both Egyptian and Canaanite gold proved useful as well as dangerous to its new owners. Egyptian gold became a golden calf, and the victory at Jericho led to the defeat at Ai and the purge at Achor.

26. D. W. Robertson Jr. (trans.), in Augustine, *On Christian Doctrine,* 1.2.2 (New York: Macmillan, 1958), p. ix.

own people (2.18.28) when it can be reoriented toward its intended end (4.2.3). If Augustine's account of Scripture provides the deep structure of medieval and Reformation Christian rationality, it does so only because the epistemology of Books 2-4 is grounded thoroughly in the Christology and soteriology of Book 1.

The thousand-year reign of medieval Augustinianism created a West barely able to distinguish between Church and world. This too makes it easy to turn Augustine the teacher of homiletics into Augustine the architect of Christendom, and to forget that his intended reader of this "classic of Western culture"[27] is actually "the ecclesiastical orator" (4.13.29). *On Christian Doctrine*'s lengthy treatment of the human language and performance of Scripture is firmly located in the earthly Church.[28] R. A. Markus says that "Book 2 of *De doctrina* is nothing less — though it may be rather more — than an account of how communities are constituted by how they understand the symbolic systems . . . in use within them."[29]

27. Duane W. H. Arnold and Pamela Bright, eds., *De Doctrina Christiana: A Classic of Western Culture* (Notre Dame: University of Notre Dame Press, 1995).

28. For this reason Takeshi Kato defends Augustine against Wittgenstein's contention that Augustine's theory of language from *Confessions* I.8.13 is a naïve theory of correspondence, by pointing out the importance for Augustine of *context* in lending meaning to verbal signs and enabling their hearers to decipher them. Takeshi Kato, "Sonus et Verbum," in Arnold and Bright, eds., *De Doctrina Christiana*, pp. 91-92. Similarly, Nancey Murphy appeals to the passage as one "not so much about affixing labels to objects, but rather about speech acts and human interactions: teaching, learning, requesting." Nancey Murphy, *Beyond Liberalism and Fundamentalism: How Modern and Postmodern Philosophy Set the Theological Agenda* (Valley Forge, Pa.: Trinity Press International, 1996), p. 133. The passage reads (here trans. Henry Chadwick [New York: Oxford University Press, 1992], pp. 10-11):

> My grasp made use of memory: when people gave a name to an object and when, following the sound, they moved their body towards that object, I would see and retain the fact that that object received from them this sound which they pronounced when they intended to draw attention to it. Moreover, their intention was evident from the gestures which are, as it were, the natural vocabulary of all races. . . . Accordingly, I gradually gathered the meaning of words, occurring in their places in different sentences and frequently heard. . . . In this way I communicated the signs of my wishes to those around me, and entered more deeply into the stormy society of human life. I was dependent on the authority of my parents and the direction of adult people.

The later sentences describe not a naïve correspondence theory but one where words operate in human contextual communities. Likewise, David Dawson criticizes Wittgenstein for ignoring the importance of the motions of souls that give rise to languages and motivate their use ("Sign, Allegory, and the Motions of the Soul," in Arnold and Bright, eds., *De Doctrina Christiana*, pp. 137-38 n. 13).

29. This paragraph depends on R. A. Markus, "Signs, Communication, and Commu-

Of course, for Augustine the Church is more than just another human community. Augustine is not what George Lindbeck would call an "experiential expressivist." The world has many linguistic communities and many semiotic systems, in which the "society of demons" misleads and abuses the God-given power of speech through the sinful use of conventional signs. Because of the plurality of human semiotic systems, many signs are ambiguous, shared by more than one linguistic community. The Church is not simply one among these, but a community of hearers and speakers of the truth that has set them free. It is the community moving towards God rather than away from him. Superstition, magic, and idolatry represent alternative social accounts of reality that Christians are to repudiate thoroughly (2.22–2.26). Their intentionality is human *and not* divine, their community a world whose devices are coming to nothing. The community of Christ is necessary to true human understanding not just because it gives God's universally accessible signs a context they need to take human intellectual shape, but because only its intentionality fundamentally conforms to God's, and so only from its perspective are God's signs truly understood.

Though it shares its vocabulary with the languages of the world, Christian language, and especially the language of Christian Scripture, is inherently ecclesial. Signs can be brought over from worldly communities into the holy community, but any such transference is a transformation. While human beings may put Egyptian gold to holy use, they may only do so after "observing the Pasch" — *i.e.,* fully participating in the sacramental life of the body of Christ (2.41.62). And these foreign treasures, which many of Augustine's modern commentators find so impressive, the bishop sees as trifles compared to the Church's native graces (2.42.63).

Human, but Human Enough?

Augustine lays groundwork for a thorough appreciation both of the Bible's divine ordering and its location in the human linguistic communities that comprise the catholic Church. How helpful is Augustine's groundwork for our account of Scripture? Barr would probably see it as a less than promising start. He might claim that Augustine, like all Alexandrian exegetes, ultimately shortchanges the Bible's humanity and the relevance of the humanities in the act of "affirming" them. Like Barth, Augustine acknowledges and

nities," in Arnold and Bright, eds., *De Doctrina Christiana,* pp. 97-108. The quotation is from p. 103.

even catalogues the presence of human literary and rhetorical devices in the biblical writings; but then, also like Barth, he refuses to accept that rhetorical style is important to the truth or inspiration of these writings. The best guides for Christians who would be eloquent are the Scriptures themselves, not the great writers or orators (4.5.8). If the holy writings employ tropes like metaphor and catechresis, it is not because they seek to imitate the achievements of pagans, but because these are common devices, employed even in vulgar speech (3.29.40). Scripture's eloquence is on an entirely different level, and worldly eloquence does not become it (4.6.9).[30] Augustine puts the Bible on a superhuman pedestal when he explains Scripture's clarity as one variety of special eloquence, then explains away its obscurity as another (4.6.9). He is offended by the allegation that Jesus' wisdom is derivative of Plato's, and replies that Plato after all probably learned *his* ideas through Jeremiah.[31] He acknowledges the usefulness of history in uncovering biblical meaning, but then denies that the discipline of history is a human institution (2.27.41)! At every turn he lifts the biblical writers and Church Fathers above even the most exemplary of other human achievers. Their humanity seems always removed from common humanity. Most of all, the distinguishing features of Augustinian exegesis, the rules of faith and charity that norm biblical interpretation, all but wash away the literal meaning of Scripture in "charitable" allegories, and stand ready to "correct" any reading of Scripture that conflicts with the magisterial dogmas of the Catholic Church. Is this really a full affirmation of the Bible's humanity, or is it bibliological Apollinarianism? Barr's trenchant criticisms of fundamentalism[32] seem to apply at least as well to Augustine's hermeneutical vision as they apply to modernist doctrines of Scripture.

How might an imaginary Augustinian reply to Barr's imaginary criticisms? To be sure, if Alexandrian or neo-Alexandrian exegetes err, they tend to err towards underappreciating or denying humanity. And few scholars today would deny the humanity of history, or privilege the grammar or rhetoric of the biblical writers, or suggest that Plato plagiarized from Israel or Judah.

30. Augustine continues: "Those things in that eloquence which our authors have in common with pagan orators and poets do not greatly delight me; I am more astonished and amazed that they have used our eloquence in such a way through another eloquence of their own that it seems neither lacking in them nor ostentatious in them" (4.6.10).

31. "It becomes more credible that the Platonists took from our literature whatever they said that is good and truthful than that Our Lord Jesus Christ learned from them. To believe the latter view is the utmost madness" (2.28.43).

32. See James Barr, *Fundamentalism,* 2nd ed. (London: SCM, 1981); *Beyond Fundamentalism* (Philadelphia: Westminster, 1984).

But these observations correct Augustine without undermining his overall vision. On each point an Augustinian could provide a counterpoint.

First of all, some of Augustine's tendencies are explicable in terms of his times. In critically embracing Cicero in an age of bitter Christian-pagan rivalry, Augustine is penetrating deep into enemy territory. He is being strikingly affirming of the universal humanity of Scripture's language. *On Christian Doctrine* is a culturally acquisitive vision of Christian thought that follows in the footsteps of Judaism's earlier culturally acquisitive Wisdom tradition (a particularly influential tradition in Alexandrian Judaism).

Furthermore, *On Christian Doctrine*'s line of reasoning leads in many different directions, and Augustine's own groundwork cannot be blamed for all of their weaknesses. Augustinians like Luther, on Christological grounds, will even more thoroughly explore the humanity of Scripture and its connections with other human literatures, the threats of paganism and Arianism having receded. Others will stretch the rule of charity to its limits, and beyond — "allegorizing everything," Luther will later complain. Both of these paths lead from starting points in *On Christian Doctrine*. Some of their varieties do neglect or undermine Scripture's true humanity, but by no means all of them.

At other points, Augustine *does* make fruitful use of the humanity of Scripture, drawing on it to make important practical conclusions. He emphasizes throughout the work that the knowledge of God is humanly mediated. This grounds the necessity of the Church's charismatic teaching practice. Human beings *must* teach inspired Scripture to other human beings — even to Paul, Timothy, and Titus (Prologue, 6, 4.16.33). The knowledge of human language is basic to the understanding of Scripture, so students should learn from the studies that are taught outside the Church. They simply should not confuse such studies with the learning that leads to eternal life (2.39.58).

Many Augustinians (including fundamentalist Augustinians) will also rightly protest that Augustine and they are not denying the humanity of Scripture, but showing rare appreciation for its *sanctified* humanity. To deny sin or error or duplicity in Scripture (which, again, is not to deny sin or error on the part of its human authors) is not to deny humanity. For Augustine, what taints rhetoric is not its human power to persuade, but the impure motives of pagan orators who use it to empower lies as well as truth (4.2.3, cf. 4.4.6). In the Church's preaching, rhetoric's power is put to its proper, intended use. And Augustine's point about history is not that it has *no* human dimension. It is that history is not *merely* human, for God is its first cause. Because God is Lord over creation, the human arts are ultimately divine institutions, grounded in the coherence of creation and therefore appropriate to its understanding. Incarnation creates a new continuity between God and humanity that demands both the affirmation of human institutions and the discernment of what needs to be redeemed and rejected in them.

Finally, do Augustine's rule of charity and the rule of faith clarify the biblical message, or do they impose other messages upon it? When abused, they do the latter. But these kinds of rules are themselves grounded in the biblical witness, so they cannot by nature be foreign intrusions into the Christian canon, or patristic innovations. Indeed, they have biblical precedents. Some rules of faith are already operating in New Testament churches (Gal. 1:8; 1 John 4:1-3). These hermeneutical rules are not meant to be *a priori* constructions derived from presuppositions of divine humanity or God's purposes, and therefore privileged over the canon. They represent theological conclusions emerging from the biblical faith itself. Barr's criticisms help remind interpreters that because rules comprise only part of a hermeneutical circle, they always remain open to critique, even radical critique, from the biblical texts they seek to interpret. Thus to endorse the idea of a rule of faith is not necessarily to endorse a *particular* rule of faith. With John Henry Newman, one might see the *Regula Fidei* as a continually developing criterion that guides subsequent interpretation through the course of Holy Tradition. Or one might obey the Lutheran rule of faith, which is simply justification by grace through faith; or even the Five Fundamentals of American fundamentalism; or the feminist hermeneutic of suspicion. A rule of faith can have either conservative or radical results, and can either silence biblical voices or bring them out.

Regarding the rule of charity, Augustine himself pleads that it is not a license to interpret Scripture idiosyncratically. It does not excuse the neglect of any of the skills, practices, and virtues he discusses throughout his work. In fact, charitable misinterpretations are to be corrected, lest they lead to bad habits (1.36.41). The rule of charity is really no more than an affirmation of the Bible's divine intentionality in terms of Paul's instructions in 1 Corinthians 12–14 regarding the edification of the Church (to which we will return below). Nor is it privileged above the biblical text. Like the rule of faith, it is informed by the very biblical texts it interprets, is open to critique, and is susceptible to a wide variety of applications. In cultures that demand critical precision in the treatment of Scripture, charity may even call for paying *more* rather than less care to exegetical accuracy, lest hermeneutical sloppiness become a stumbling block (cf. 1 Cor. 8:9). Stephen Fowl is right that the end of Scripture, expressed in the rules of faith and charity, should guide how Christians appropriate the exegesis of professional biblical scholars. But this is no less true of professional theologians, pastors, and lay people, many of whom engage in "theological interpretation" of Scripture that is neither charitable nor faithful to the Bible's divine humanity.[33]

These criticisms might be summarized in a worry, often expressed by biblical critics, that theology "from above" so constrains theology "from below" that it predetermines its conclusions. Undoubtedly this has often happened in the strained history of biblical interpretation. Theological and anthropological languages have often stifled rather than supported each other. However, rather than letting the abuses stifle fruitful exchange between the two, here we heed the words of John McIntyre, who affirms the *normative* and *theologically definitive,* but not *prescriptive,* nature of Chalcedonian Christology. That is, while its categories may not be breached, they define the problem of Christology so firmly yet lightly as to offer subsequent interpreters both unlimited guidance, and unlimited variety of expression.[34] Theologians need not impose their dialects on biblical scholars, nor vice versa, and Aristotelian metaphysics need not encroach on all others, for Chalcedon is an umbrella under which vastly dissimilar dialects are capable of speaking the common language of Christian faith.[35] By analogy, the same would be true of Chalcedonian hermeneutics.

So Barr's anticipated criticisms do not necessarily foreclose an Alexandrian, Augustinian account of either the Bible's human character or its human performance. But they correct Augustine on several points, and raise important cautions for ecclesiologies of Scripture. When the presuppositions of divine humanity swamp the realities, Alexandrian orthodoxy gives way to Alexandrian heresy. Divine priority championed too ideologically can effectively compromise the humanity of Scripture just as it can compromise the humanity of Christ. An Alexandrian affirmation of divine priority calls for an Antiochian share of attention to Scripture's human location and phenomenology. Pursuing this already led us on a grand tour of Israel's and Jesus' human histories. Now it brings us to the concrete communities calling themselves churches of Jesus Christ. We will develop a phenomenology of churchly biblical interpretation that is theologically oriented, yet sensitive to the acute historiographical and philosophical problems of human Christian communities and scriptural traditions.

33. Fowl, *Engaging Scripture,* pp. 179-80.

34. John McIntyre, *The Shape of Christology,* 2nd ed. (Edinburgh: T. & T. Clark, 1998), pp. 312-20.

35. McIntyre, *The Shape of Christology,* pp. 331-36.

II. Beyond Argument:
The Humanity of Churchly Biblical Interpretation

What Is the Church?
The Historical Problem of Christian Diversity

Such a phenomenology turns out to be a tall order — and not just because of the different confessional camps into which the Christian traditions have divided themselves. When historians of Christianity turn to the first few centuries of Christian biblical practice, what they see seems to undermine the integrity of nearly all the significant ecclesiological categories mentioned so far in this chapter. Among many orthodox Christian theologians, "orthodoxy," "heresy," "Bible," and "Church" have all gained connotations of settled normativeness (or at least stable areas of disagreement) that historians of ancient Christianity find largely absent during Christianity's first few centuries. Even more than they are today, all these ideas were essentially contested concepts among the different groups that claim the label "Christian." Even in the late fourth century, Augustine the bishop felt the need to articulate the contents of the canon (2.8.13), and to deprecate the rival biblical practices of Donatists (3.30.42). As unsettled as his times were, the centuries preceding him were far more fluid. It is not until Athanasius' festal letter of 367 that we find a list of New Testament books that matches ours, and even then its order is somewhat different. Circumcisers, Gnostics, Marcionites, Montanists, Arians, and Catholics are only the most famous groupings of the innumerable rival traditions that were equally emphatic about the authenticity of their mutually exclusive fellowships, textual and personal authorities, and doctrines. It is an open question in historical scholarship how appropriate it is to label "orthodox" or even "proto-orthodox" any early tradition that would later emerge as Nicene-Chalcedonian orthodoxy.[36] This fluidity and ambiguity threaten to end our ecclesiology of Scripture before it even really begins. How can we examine Christian biblical phenomenology without a clearly defined Christian community?

Historians and theologians following in the wake of Walter Bauer are not the first to encounter the problem. A much better candidate for that honor is Paul the church planter, who faced at least one community fractured

---

36. See Bart D. Ehrman's introduction to *The Orthodox Corruption of Scripture: The Effect of Early Christological Controversies on the Text of the New Testament* (New York: Oxford University Press, 1993), pp. 9-15. He accepts the terms "proto-orthodoxy" and "incipient orthodoxy" for the forefathers of orthodoxy (p. 25).

by divisive practices and schismatic leaders before many of the New Testament writings were even created (1 Cor. 1). Centuries of historical and theological consensus have lulled many commentators into overestimating the ease with which the first Christians distinguished true from false belief, but Paul is under no such illusions. He must defend his apostleship, the integrity of his own writings against the work of forgers,[37] even the validity of his *own* earlier work in the very congregations that receive his letters!

In Paul we have not only a principal architect of the Christian church network that emerges in the Mediterranean *oikoumene,* but a principal writer and interpreter of canonical Christian Scripture. No matter how problematic the historical picture is, Paul remains an appropriate authority on the ecclesial humanity of Scripture. Ecclesiologians need not (in fact, cannot) choose between the messy historical picture of early Christianity and later Christianity's own normative self-understanding. We can appreciate the theological significance of Christian biblical interpretation in light of the historical problem of Christian diversity and division, by paying close attention to Paul's account of both.

What Is Truth? The Philosophical Problem of Christian Diversity

Yet a phenomenology of Christian Scripture faces more than historiographical problems. It faces a vexing philosophical question: What is Christian biblical interpretation? How are we to appreciate the practice in an intellectual atmosphere where some hold to the concept of fixed, timeless truths, some deny the very existence of truth, and some affirm truth only at the communal or personal level? When truth itself is an essentially contested concept, how can we appreciate what Christians are doing when they interpret the Bible, and how should we understand the differences and conflicts between their rival interpretations?

The question is interesting for philosophers, but critical for a Church that confesses biblical authority, enjoys a multicultural character, suffers from long-standing divisions, and wrestles with modern accounts of unity and diversity in interpretation. The following answer appeals to a particularly helpful account of communal textual interpretation: Alasdair MacIntyre's theory of the rationality of traditions, and his description of a tradition of enquiry as an ongoing argument. MacIntyre's approach opens up the possibility of ap-

---

37. See 2 Thess. 2:1, 3:17, which illustrates the problem regardless of the letter's actual author.

preciating the insights of various biblical traditions while remaining open to their different, sometimes mutually exclusive claims. Yet while appreciating its strengths, we aim to improve it through a more thoroughly *theological* vision of diversity that arises principally from Paul's imagery of the body of Christ, in which all things are done decently and in good order for the edification of all.

Are Truth-Claims Even Defensible?

For centuries Western philosophers struggled to validate their convictions that "unaided" reason could establish objectively verifiable, universally accepted standards of truth. The increasing obviousness of the Enlightenment's failure to do this has left the Western world in disarray over the existence of truth, the relationship between communities and truth-claims, and the appreciation of rival claims. Biblical hermeneutics has of course been caught up in the confusion.

As the modernist vision of a universally accessible, objective criterion for truth-claims has faltered, two further conclusions have seemed to follow, which MacIntyre calls "relativism" and "perspectivism."[38] Relativism takes the Enlightenment project's failure to find a universal, self-evident truth as evidence that there *can be* no universal truth, or at least that the truthfulness of communities' competing claims can never be determined. Perspectivism (MacIntyre's understanding of which is not to be confused with other usages)[39] agrees that

---

38. Says MacIntyre: "The first [conclusion] is that at any fundamental level no rational debate between, rather than within, traditions can occur. The adherents of conflicting tendencies within a tradition may still share enough in the way of fundamental belief to conduct such debate, but the protagonists of rival traditions will be precluded at any fundamental level, not only from justifying their views to the members of any rival tradition, but even from learning from them how to modify their own tradition in any radical way.

"Yet if this is so, a second conclusion seems to be in order. Given that each tradition will frame its own standpoint in terms of its own idiosyncratic concepts, and given that no fundamental correction of its conceptual scheme from such external standpoint is possible, . . . a social universe composed exclusively of rival traditions, so it may seem, will be one in which there are a number of contending, incompatible, but only partially and inadequately communicating, overall views of that universe, each tradition within which is unable to justify its claims over against those of its rivals except to those who already accept them." Alasdair MacIntyre, *Whose Justice? Which Rationality?* (Notre Dame: University of Notre Dame Press, 1988), p. 348.

Subsequent citations to this work are given in the text in parentheses.

39. See, for instance, James Wm. McClendon, Jr. and James M. Smith, *Understanding*

any such truth is only available to enquirers mediated through their world-views; therefore, it claims, one community cannot legitimately make abso-lutizing claims against other communities' worldviews, which are very different but complementary perspectives on the same reality (pp. 352ff.).

These two rejections of modernist epistemology actually draw heavily on Enlightenment convictions of the universality of truth, so they appeal in societies formed by the Enlightenment project. Both locate truth in particular human communities, including Christian churches, and both argue for "plu-ralism" in biblical interpretation (provided of course that interpretations make no claims to absolute truth!). Neither renders biblical practice useless. But both effectively privatize Scripture's authority in the life of the Church. The Bible can still be a source of personal inspiration, guidance, and chal-lenge — chicken soup for the Christian soul.[40] It can wield great cultural and rhetorical power, even as an evangelistic text. But its authority is radically contingent on the approval of its audience.

This is the no-win situation in which modernity and postmodernity seem to place churchly biblical practice. Are old and new interpretations of the text only private interpretations? Is anything really at stake in arguments over the fidelity or superiority of an interpretation, if there is no neutral ground from which to judge? Are Christian interpreters even accurately con-veying their interpretations to others, given the different worlds in which Christians seem to live? Is the very idea of an ecclesiology of Scripture a pro-jection of an illusory category into a chaos of texts and eisegeting wills?

Overcoming the Postmodern Impasse: Exegesis as Argument

The intellectual atmosphere of late modernity has polarized Christians into two hostile camps: liberalism and fundamentalism.[41] These generally reflect the influences of experientialism and propositionalism that characterize modern theology. The former camp has been more comfortable (but by no means totally comfortable) with relativism and perspectivism. The latter camp has generally refused to abandon the Enlightenment project's search for absolute, objective truth, seeing in any alternative a fundamental compromise of the Gospel's claims. The open ends of Christianity's early history become

---

Religious Convictions (South Bend, Ind.: University of Notre Dame Press, 1975), which ar-gues for Wittgensteinian perspectivism.

40. Jack Canfield, *Chicken Soup for the Soul: 101 Stories to Open the Heart & Rekindle the Spirit* (Health Communications, 1993).

41. Murphy, *Beyond Liberalism and Fundamentalism*, pp. 1-7.

(for liberals) evidence of the arbitrariness of communal biblical interpretation, or (for fundamentalists) threats to the Bible's universal authority. But modernity has so shaped all parties in the debate that few can see beyond the impasse.

MacIntyre's vision of truth and intellectual enquiry claims to overcome modernity's dilemma of objectivity, relativism, and perspectivism. It situates practices like biblical interpretation firmly within human communities, yet it does not confine traditions to intellectual isolation. MacIntyre envisions traditions as ongoing *arguments* over the realities they seek to comprehend. Rational enquiry — for the purposes of bibliology, Christian enquiry into Scripture's meaning-as-use in the Church and its world — is itself inextricably embodied in a tradition of enquiry. When a church enquires into the Bible's meaning, it inevitably does so *as* a church. And a church, like any human community, inevitably features internal and external differences, conflicts, and incommensurabilities, which make it a living tradition of enquiry. A tradition is a kind of interminable argument over the nature of the tradition itself. Yet interminability does not mean futility, because "the standards of rational justification emerge from and are part of a history in which they are vindicated by the way in which they *transcend the limitations of* and *provide remedies for* the defects of their predecessors within the history of that same tradition" (p. 7, emphasis mine). In the Church's language, the communal practice of discernment guides the Church into God's truth. As it seeks, it finds.

MacIntyre's category of argument rejects the presuppositions that give absolutism, relativism, and perspectivism their plausibility. (His account reveals Barr not so much to be a champion of objective critical enquiry, as an absolutist who is fundamentally skeptical of "tradition," seeing it above all as a threat to proper understanding and a much abused warrant for flight into authoritarianism or relativism.)[42] It allows that empirical fact — what Lindbeck calls "extrasystematic truth" — *does* constrain and inform theologi-

---

42. James Barr, *Old and New in Interpretation: A Study of the Two Testaments* (New York: Harper & Row, 1966), p. 190: "This positive evaluation of the 'tradition' [as positive and negative body of prior interpretive practices] . . . nevertheless should not conceal from us the fact that this tradition can constitute the chief agency for the damaging and distorting of the meaning of the Bible." Despite its many good uses, tradition endorses the Church as it is rather than as it should be, and is thus sinful, "orthodoxist," and confining (pp. 191-96). In failing to see the reforming tradition in Protestantism as *itself* a tradition subject to canonical critique, Barr lifts criticism above (or, foundationalistically, sets it below) the rest of Christian tradition, free from its community and canon, and renders himself inconsistent. Below we shall see that MacIntyre's account, while Thomistic, still respects traditional Protestant accounts of biblical criticism.

cal and hermeneutical practice (p. 333). One may win an argument not merely because of one's intellect, consistency volume, rhetorical gifts, circumstance, or social power, but in part because one is right. Thus tradition-constituted enquiry is not relativistic. And while the partial disagreements over truth-claims between disputants hinder the resolution of arguments, they do not prevent it. Despite the incommensurability of different worldviews, arguments between them are still won and lost. Even in the absence of such resolution, the arguments serve to sharpen the traditions' skills of enquiry. Therefore tradition-constituted enquiry is not perspectivist. Yet tradition-constituted enquiry recognizes the radical contingency of hermeneutical practice on those who practice it. The meanings of Scripture do not exist in some disembodied state, waiting to be mined and refined into propositional truths that then no longer depend on the original texts or communities. Nor must they be freed from "bondage" to their communities by secular readers who can exercise Barr's "relative objectivity."[43] Without the interpreters and their horizons, there would be no harvests of the Bible's eternal surplus of meaning. Thus MacIntyre's account does not share the weaknesses of Enlightenment absolutisms.

A final strength of MacIntyre's account is its sensitivity to both the diversity and fluidity of traditions, and to the particularities of the Christian tradition of biblical interpretation. MacIntyre's account is itself a *Christian* account of rationality. It owes much to John Henry Newman's *Essay on the Development of Christian Doctrine,* which is perhaps the most highly regarded account of the history of interpretation in the Christian tradition (pp. 353-54). It derives from an extended exploration of Western intellectual history, centering on the *Summa* of Thomas Aquinas as a triumph over rival traditions of enquiry in the tradition of Augustinian Christianity. Yet it requires no precommitment to one particular community's privileged "orthodoxy." Orthodoxy is a matter of argument among the parties who contend for the label's authority. Thus it is profoundly sympathetic to the developmental and contested history and self-understanding of Christian intellectual enquiry.[44]

---

43. Barr, *Old and New in Interpretation,* p. 191.

44. One might object that despite the "massive debt" MacIntyre acknowledges owing Newman, his project "proceeds independently" as a generalized account of the rationality of traditions rather than a particular account of Christian doctrine (*Whose Justice?* p. 354). But to call MacIntyre's theory anything other than Christian is to abstract MacIntyre, a self-described "Augustinian Christian," from his project of describing what he calls "the history of my own tradition" (pp. 10-11).

One might then object for the opposite reason that using an account of rational enquiry informed by the categories of later Christian orthodoxy reintroduces the problems this

These are powerful reasons for considering MacIntyre's account of truth and diversity as a way to appreciate Christian biblical practices in their considerable development and diversity. The category of argument describes very well the historical data of actual Christian biblical practice, particularly during its formative centuries. Churches use the Bible to argue — meaning to discern together God's will for them — among themselves and against each other.

Locating Commonality and Difference in Canonical Practice

The problem of Christian diversity introduced our phenomenology of Scripture, and the category of argument holds promise for appreciating the extent of diversity in Christian uses of Scripture without abandoning the idea of "the Church" or its normative dogmatics. An adequate appreciation of difference is essential not just for a historically responsible or philosophically defensible phenomenology of Scripture, but also for a truly Christian doctrine of the Church, and of its hermeneutical practices — for theological reasons we are about to explore.

The category of argument respects the roles that both commonality and difference play in allowing friends as well as rivals to have productive exchanges (p. 351). Some commonality is required even to disagree; further commonality is required to resolve differences; but when commonality becomes identity, the result is only stagnant silence. Commonalities and differences are structuring forces within an argument/tradition. They relate diversity to unity in a way that neither imposes hegemony nor allows the chaos of unbounded pluralism. MacIntyre claims that "the problem of diversity is not abolished, but it is transformed in a way that renders it amenable of solution" (p. 10). Tradition-constituted enquiry shows why neither authoritarian nor anarchic exegetical practices are particularly fruitful, and goes a long way to explaining the confluence of unity and diversity of biblical interpretation that is so often felt within the Church.

Substantive arguments appeal to authorities, and literary traditions appeal to canonical authorities. In MacIntyre's account, a prerequisite of any sophisticated tradition of enquiry is a literary canon, a set of standard authori-

---

account was supposed to avoid. But if there is no neutral ground from which to describe Christian biblical practice, there is no alternative. Instead, one must accept that an account informed by the categories of Christian orthodoxy and friendly to them can afford a deeper insight into Christian biblical practice, so long as it remains open to fundamental revision.

tative texts. These texts go further than merely establishing constitutional boundaries for their community or containing and preserving their truth-claims. They are tradition's "poetry," its linguistic font, from which compe-tence in the tradition emerges and to which it constantly returns. Their surplus of meaning becomes a source of ever new applications, metaphors, multiple meanings, and modes of expression. They enable a community to "go on and go further" in its enquiry. Their sophisticated use requires the very linguistic competence that they provide. They are the textual embodiment of their tradi-tion, a library of fixed meanings that nevertheless creates a living tradition of their own critical rereading and reinterpretation according to the occasions of every new situation in which their community finds itself. They are their com-munity's "authoritative point of departure for tradition-constituted enquiry . . . essential points of reference for enquiry and activity, for argument, debate, and conflict within that tradition" (pp. 382-83).

This phenomenology well describes the Bible's role in Christian tradi-tion (so well, in fact, that here one senses the influence of *Christian* culture on the intellectual histories MacIntyre chronicles, and on the rationality with which he chronicles them). It even allows for the canonicity of *open* canons, as in literary traditions whose canons change over time, or in traditions like Christianity where the boundaries and center of the canon are controversial. We will nuance MacIntyre's description in important ways, but not until after we appreciate the relief it offers Christian interpreters of Scripture belea-guered by incompatible and inadequate accounts of truth and authority.

Naturally, it is the canon's community that generally knows best how to read its canon. MacIntyre's analysis recognizes who are the privileged inter-preters of the biblical text, and understands why. This is an area where Chris-tian practice has been threatened by both the rise and the crises of modernity. Modernists would claim hermeneutical privilege for any "rational" reader, Christian or not, because true rationality is universal, and the truthfulness of the biblical text does not depend on its own community of readers. One con-ducts and judges biblical interpretation according to universal, timeless stan-dards of truth that are independent of the Church. In opposition to modern-ists, relativists might continue to assign a kind of insurmountable privilege to Christian readers, by denying that Christians' insights into the biblical text carry rational weight for others. In fact, by extension, there would be no ra-tional way even for Christians themselves to evaluate the competing claims of Christian interpreters. The circularity of Christian rationality prevents ratio-nal criticism of biblical interpretations. It thus has no transcendent signifi-cance, and no prior or unconditional claim on readers or audiences. Finally, perspectivists would argue that the transcendent compatibility of all perspectives renders the comparative question of truth or falsehood meaningless; all biblical interpretations are different but ultimately complementary.

Given these alternatives, it is understandable that fundamentalists and others would continue to find the Enlightenment view of truth the most adequate. It comes closest to describing the Bible's universal and local claims to authority. Yet here too, tradition-constituted enquiry offers a superior view of biblical interpretation than even the Enlightenment account. Its great strength is that it appreciates that the adequacy of claims *can* truly be judged — not in spite of the fact, but *because of* the fact that they are judged according to the rationality internal to their own traditions. The circularity of Christian rationality is what enables it to judge biblical interpretations so well. Christians, with their distinctive rationalities, are the ultimate earthly arbiters of competing readings of Scripture. But Scripture itself is not at their mercy, for it is through the text that they receive the very competence they subsequently bring to it. The Bible norms Christian interpretation and argument, even in the absence of *a priori* criteria for settling hermeneutical questions. In fact, it norms them even in the absence of agreement over what constitutes either the canon or its authentic communities. So Christians with different canons — the Majority Text versus critical reconstructions, the Septuagint versus the Masoretic Text — can have productive, mutually enriching discussions over the extent of the canon, using the canonical texts themselves as primary authorities.[45] The standards of proper and improper interpretation of Scripture are not arbitrarily set by a tradition's institutional authorities; they are matters of sheer competence in the language of biblical Christianity. Thus a church needs no authoritative hermeneutic, prior teaching office, or even account of Scripture — not because these are unimportant or illegitimate, but because Scripture itself, and Scripture alone, can offer them.

Such an insight eases the considerable pressure put upon Christians to explain the endless and radical diversity in biblical interpretation. At least some diversity is evidence of the power and authority of Scripture in setting the agenda in Christian tradition, not evidence of Christianity's own failure, or of a relativistic absence of any criteria for ultimacy between competing interpretations.[46]

---

45. For very helpful background for and examples of this kind of discussion, see Siegfried Meurer, ed., *The Apocrypha in Ecumenical Perspective*, trans. Paul Ellingworth, UBS Monograph Series No. 6 (New York: United Bible Societies, 1991).

46. Here one cannot help comparing MacIntyre's account of traditions in general to the early Karl Barth's doctrine of Scripture, in *Church Dogmatics* I.

Is Life in Christ an Argument?

MacIntyre's account seems more acceptable to Christians than either the unsustainable Enlightenment vision of truth transcendent of all communities of enquiry, or the unsustainable objections of relativism and perspectivism. Its popularity at his own institution (Duke University) has won adherents to the claim that the Christian tradition is an ongoing argument over the essence and goods of the Christian life. Where matters of theological enquiry are concerned, they consider the Church an interminable debate over life in Christ. Just as an argument sustains a conversation and sharpens the thinking of all its participants, so Christianity's internal differences, especially those involving interpretation of its authoritative canon, sustain it as it meets the epistemological crises presented by rival traditions and rival claimants to interpretive authenticity within the Christian tradition. Argument is a function of unity in diversity, essential to the continuing life of the Church.[47] Indeed, it is so essential that a kind of sanctified dispute will continue even when Christians live eternally in God's full presence.

But is the Christian life really an *argument*? Or if it is, is it really supposed to be? One could plausibly claim this of rabbinic Judaism.[48] But such a description seems ill-fitting for a community Paul exhorted to "stand firm in one spirit, with one mind striving side by side for the faith of the gospel" (Phil. 1:27). This is the crucial difference between MacIntyre's Hegelian account and the self-understanding of the Pauline tradition, and the point on which ecclesiology proper begins to reframe Christian phenomenology.

To be fair to MacIntyre, his project is concerned with proving that rationalities and notions of justice are inevitably situated within competing traditions. It is not an attempt to define precisely what a tradition is, let alone the Christian tradition in particular. His concentration on the forces and personalities that challenge and enrich, and on the question of translatability between traditions, leads to an emphasis on *intertraditional* enquiry rather than on *intratraditional* enquiry. Thus he pays much attention to the role of "epistemological crises" that cause traditions to change violently. This has reinforced the wrong impression that MacIntyrean traditions

---

47. See also Fowl, *Engaging Scripture*, pp. 87, 97, and 161-62. Fowl follows MacIntyre to consider the absence of sustained disagreements about how to interpret and embody Scripture a sign of a community's ill health (p. 87).

48. Indeed, MacIntyre himself likens the Augustinian tradition on which he concentrates to the history of the development of Judaism, "within which the relationship of the devoted study of the Torah to philosophy engendered more than one tradition of enquiry" (*Whose Justice?* p. 10).

are *caused* and *maintained* by such crises. In fact, MacIntyre makes no such claim. He allows that traditions can exist, even coexist with rivals, for centuries while experiencing only minor epistemological crises (p. 366). He recognizes that not all change in a tradition is precipitated by epistemological crises (p. 354). Thus to treat a tradition as simply an argument is to caricature it, or at least to distort it.

Yet the shape of MacIntyre's project still lends itself to such a distortion of Christianity, because his case studies involve traditions at critical junctures in their histories. Christianity is a tradition full of such junctures, so it seems appropriate to treat it in these terms. This is precisely what Newman does in his theory of the development of doctrine, and in following the work of his fellow Catholic, MacIntyre reproduces Newman's reading of history. But a theory of enquiry that treats Christianity in terms of the actual history of Christian enquiry over the ages is liable to read it (or perhaps misread it) as an *endorsement* of the actual history of Christian enquiry, rather than merely an illustration of how enquiry historically proceeds from within a tradition. To read MacIntyre *prescriptively* is to adopt a view of crisis and argument as Holy Tradition itself. Rather than argument representing a *variety* of Christian rationality, or even a failure of it, argument is taken as the intellectual lifeblood of the Church. An ecclesial division becomes a *felix culpa,* a *necessary* epistemological crisis, without any of which the Church would wither and die from stagnation.

Now one can read the history of the Christian tradition (and of many non-Christian traditions) in this way. Arguments among Christians have indeed sustained and enriched Christianity in a variety of ways throughout the Church's history. Arianism and Docetism helped clarify the Church's confession of faith as the Nicene-Constantinopolitan Creed later expressed it, the most widely used confession in Christianity; and Apollinarianism and Nestorianism indirectly created the Chalcedonian Formula. Pelagius' and Augustine's debate sharpened the Christian categories of sin and grace, particularly at the Council of Orange and in the Reformation. The Iconoclastic controversy precipitated the Second Council of Nicea and led to what the Eastern Church celebrates as "the Triumph of Orthodoxy." It was so fruitful that we have used it as a paradigm for bibliology! But to admit that Christians argue is emphatically *not* to say that Christians are *called* to argue among themselves. Christians are not called to argue among themselves, but to agree (Matt. 18:19). If the Church is a tradition (*paradosis,* 1 Cor. 11:2), in this respect it is meant to be a peculiar one.

So MacIntyre's inductive, generalized account of enquiry and diversity must yield to a thoroughly Christian account in which the Church in its eschatological context is understood as categorically distinct from the world's other traditions.[49] A phenomenological account of Christian rationality as merely one example of human rationality will inevitably compromise the distinctiveness of Christian discourse, for "we impart a secret and hidden wisdom of God. . . . we have received not the spirit of the world, but the Spirit which is from God, that we might understand the gifts bestowed on us by God. And we impart this in words not taught by human wisdom but taught by the Spirit" (1 Cor. 2:6, 12-13).

The intellectual shape of Christian distinctiveness, and what it means for the Bible's ecclesial character and function, is thus our next topic. The doctrines of Trinity, Christology, and ecclesiology are our fundamental categories. And 1 Corinthians is our central text. In describing the distinctiveness of the Christian tradition, we will rely on the widely agreed upon (though still essentially contested) "marks" or "notes" of the Church. Likewise, in describing the distinctiveness of Christian canonical practice, we will find that Christian Scripture both confers and reflects the Church's unity, holiness, apostolicity, and catholicity. As a means of both God's descent into the created order and humanity's ascent into God's presence, biblical practice both shares in these qualities and creates them.

The Divine Shape of Christian Discourse

For Paul, the contrast between rationalities-in-general and Christian rationality could not be more dramatic. Human rationality, so-called, causes jealousy and strife, as it has among the Corinthian Church (1 Cor. 3:4). But truly Christian rationality produces a unity of mind and judgment that distinguishes it from the world's confusions (1 Cor. 1:10).

Like the High Priestly Prayer's "that they may be one, even as we are one" (John 17:11), the contrast in 1 Corinthians 2 between rationality-in-general and Christian rationality takes a Trinitarian shape.[50] The Spirit searches the depths of God, comprehends them, and teaches them to his indwelt Church, giving them the *nous christou* — "the mind of Christ," or in MacIntyrean idiom, "the Christian rationality" (1 Cor. 2:16). Christian distinctness models Trinitarian distinctness, which throughout the New Testa-

49. Incidentally, this is true for all canonical Christian traditions, even those (such as Roman Catholics, Protestants, Jehovah's Witnesses, Mormons, Christian Scientists, and so on) that other Christian traditions exclude from fellowship and even from their own definitions of "Christian."

50. See Leonardo Boff, *Trinity and Society* (Maryknoll, N.Y.: Orbis, 1988).

ment is always expressed as unity, and *never* expressed in terms of division, let alone actual argument. This is true even during the Passion, the Trinity's ultimate "epistemological crisis," where Jesus' anguished prayers in Gethsemane and his despondent cry on the cross (Matt. 27:46) end not with the vindication of one party over against the other, but through submission, obedience, and mutual vindication: "Not as I will, but as you will" (Matt. 26:39; cf. Heb. 5:7-8). The mind of God — and thus the mind of the Church — is neither undifferentiated nor divided. It is one of *perichoresis*.

This Christian rationality has immediate relevance for how the Church is to "argue." Paul knows that "Christian discourse" is often contentious — but to him this fact is scandalous. "For while there is jealousy and strife among you, are you not of the flesh, and behaving like ordinary humans? For when one says, 'I belong to Paul,' and another, 'I belong to Apollos,' are you not merely human?" (1 Cor. 3:3-4). To be divided into apostolic factions, to be "puffed up in favor of one against another" (1 Cor. 4:6) is to be merely human, *sarkikos* rather than *pneumatikos,* to fall short of the *synergeia* that characterizes the truly Christ-minded Church. It does not invigorate the community, but plagues it, for the Corinthian body's health depends on the harmonious contributions of all its members. "What then is Apollos? What is Paul? Servants through whom you believed, as the Lord assigned to each. . . . For we are God's fellow workers *(synergoi);* you are God's field, God's building *(oikodomē)*" (1 Cor. 3:5, 9).

Unity of God's Fellow Workers and Their Word

For Paul, such perichoretic unity is to mark the mind of the Church, as it marks the mind of Christ. His letter intends the reconciliation of the Corinthian body. His audience is God's edifice, his rhetorical goal their further edification. This is equally true elsewhere in the New Testament. In Romans 12, Paul applies the same logic to the churchly relations between Jew and Gentile. We find a similar concern in the Johannine literature in the High Priestly Prayer: "I have manifested your name to the people whom you gave me out of the world. . . . Holy Father, keep them in your name, which you have given me, that they may be one, just as we are one. . . . I do not pray for these only, but also for those who believe in me through their word, that they may all be one; even as you, Father, are in me, and I in you . . . that they may become perfectly one *(teteleiōmenoi eis hen),* so that the world may know that you have sent me and have loved them even as you have loved me" (John 17:6, 11, 20-23).

In all these texts, the unity of the Church's fellow workers is tied in directly with their word of the Gospel, with which the apostles were entrusted (1 Cor. 15:3), which the apostles model with their own lives (1 Cor. 4:14-20), and in whose hands the Church comes to belief, maturity, and perfect unity. The remembered, preached, and written Gospel confers and reflects the unity of the apostolic Church, centering it in its head and cornerstone so that its traditions of enquiry may never float free from their source.

This unity is not totalitarian uniformity. God's *synergoi* have different tasks and play different roles, but the same Spirit empowers their works. In first-century Corinth, this hermeneutical *synergeia* comes to expression in the distinctive works of Paul, Apollos, and the others. In the entire Church age, it comes to expression in the canon itself. The diversity of the Church's authoritative writings comprises *one* New Testament, and in its different ways proclaims *one* Gospel, for *one* Church.

The same is true in the New Testament's own preserved biblical practice: its unity comprehends the diversity of hermeneutical approaches to the Old Testament. The Scriptures treated independently in the different New Testament writings are canonical warrants and guides for diversity in biblical interpretation.[51] They demonstrate how interpretive diversity serves the unity of the Church and the Gospel it has received. These texts are not marginal to the Gospel; as the previous chapter demonstrates, they *are* the Gospel — the very "sub-structure of New Testament theology," in C. H. Dodd's words. The unity of Christian Scripture is God's unity, conferred on the Church that receives its one Gospel; and it is the Church's unity, reflected in the harmonies of its different messages and different contexts, both in the individual writings and in their later interrelationships in the Church's canon.

Diversity and Divisiveness in the Church: A Place for Both?

But is this so-called unity of the different New Testament writings, and of the so-called apostolic Church, not a construction of the later Church that canonized them? Is it fair to project onto "Paul and Apollos" the diversity of the biblical writings and the even greater diversity of their interpretation over the course of Christian history? Biblical scholarship has found radical open-

---

51. See C. H. Dodd's list of *testimonia* in *According to the Scriptures: The Substructure of New Testament Theology* (London: Nisbet, 1952), pp. 28ff., a valuable list of such texts and the roles they play in their various New Testament settings.

endedness in biblical interpretation within early Christianity that makes the Corinthian factions look trivial.[52] The relationships between rival interpreters and the settled orthodoxy of later traditions are also more ambiguous than had been commonly thought. Movements and Church leaders later distinguished by the labels "heretic" and "orthodox" mingled with surprising frequency in Christianity's first few centuries.[53] In their various factions (regardless of whether these were retroactively included in later Christian orthodoxy), insiders were "orthodox," outsiders "heretics." Later traditions projected their understanding of orthodoxy onto their favorite past interpreters, to suggest a smooth continuity over time that neither rivals nor third parties have been willing to acknowledge.

Then how does one define an interpretive "community" like the Christian Church? How does one tell its insiders from its outsiders? Does the "community" include or exclude dissenters? At what point? Or is the idea of *a* Church or *a* community of biblical interpreters simply indefensible?

The ambiguity leads some to conclude that biblical hermeneutics is a free-for-all, whose taboos and boundaries of legitimacy are entirely set by the interpretive community. MacIntyre's phenomenology of tradition-constituted enquiry too seems more comfortable with the ambiguous historical-critical picture of biblical interpretation than the clear lines drawn by later Christian orthodoxy. It offers no advice about what constitutes the unity of the Bible's interpretive community, because even the grounds and nature of that unity are occasions for argument within the tradition. Who are the tradition's insiders and outsiders is a matter of constant negotiation.

Paul's letter seems at first to confirm this vision of Christian biblical practice. It is an epistle addressed to a divided church, offering reinterpretations of that community's traditions (for instance, 1 Cor. 6:12-13; 7:1, 8:1, 4; 10:23-26) over against the interpretations of factions, arguing with fellow Christians over the essence and goods of life in the Christian tradition. But on closer examination, Paul's rhetorical strategy reveals a different emphasis. In 1 Corinthians he does not oppose *other* factions, but the very idea of factions.

---

52. The New Testament and patristic writings, as well as the heterodox literatures of Nag Hammadi, "demonstrate the existence of rival groups at every turn, in virtually every region of Christendom in which they, and we, have knowledge" (Ehrman, *Corruption of Scripture*, pp. 9-10).

53. Ehrman notes that Clement of Alexandria and Origen both held a docetic view of Jesus' body, and that Valentinus, Ptolemy, and Justin were all accepted as faithful fellow congregants at Rome, at or nearly at the same time (*Corruption of Scripture*, p. 10). Such fluidity among leaders was exceeded among laypeople, who were fond of devotional and polemical literature of dubious orthodoxy (p. 11).

His opponent is any opponent whatsoever who would compromise the unity of the Church.

Does this make Paul a John Hick-style pluralist, for whom the ultimate virtue of Christian community is unqualified tolerance?[54] It seems not, when the same Paul will later warn the same Corinthian body against those "superlative apostles" who preach a different gospel (2 Cor. 11:4-5). He will take a similar strategy in Galatians. The Church's unity is *apostolic* unity, grounded in the unity of those entrusted with the Word of the Gospel. A unity grounded elsewhere, for instance in partisan apostolic or pastoral favoritism, or in cultural homogeneity, is a false unity — a solidarity of hard-heartedness that destroys the divine edifice.

If arguing kills the Church, then why do Christians, including Paul, spend so much time at it? In the one place where Paul recognizes a legitimate place for divisions (*schismata*, 11:18) in the community, he attributes them to factions (*haireseis*, 11:19) that must arise in order for the *genuine* Christians at Corinth to be revealed. In other words, if heresies have a place in the Church, they are to identify the true Church within the historical phenomenon of Christianity. In the current and coming apocalyptic age, factions draw the line between the Spirit and the flesh, between the true Church and the world. (The line does not distinguish one true faction from others, but apostolic unity from faction*alism*.) Thus factions, though apocalyptic necessities, are still antithetical to the true communion of saints.

So given the eschatological tension between the communion of saints and the fading world around them, there may indeed be a place for division within "the Christian tradition." But the very eschatological tension that produces these heresies makes it clear that "the Christian tradition" cannot be identical to the Church of Jesus Christ. Division is not the well-being of the Church, let alone its being — certainly not in the age to come, and not even in the present age. The history of the Church and the texts of the New Testament both amply demonstrate that argument is a constant feature of Christian life in the present age. But such argument is to be directed *outside* the true fellowship: at divisive brothers and sisters, at enemies, at excommunicants, at those in need of redemption. When it is directed within the community, it is a sign of the community's immaturity (1 Cor. 3:2-3) and illness (1 Cor. 11:29-30) — the very opposite of the lifeblood of the Christian tradition!

54. See John Hick, *God and the Universe of Faiths* (London: Fount, 1977).

Diversity versus Discord

In Paul we find warrants for both diversity in apostolic interpretation, and divisions among those called Christians. But if divisions among Christians are antithetical to the health of the Christian community, and if apostolic diversity is not to be understood in terms of division, then how are Christians to tell the difference between diversity and divisiveness? How are interpreters to differ from each other without arguing? This is an urgent question for the vexed Corinthians. And Paul has an answer for them, which ecclesiology treats in terms of the *catholicity* of the Church. Catholic difference is never understood in terms of division or argument, but diversity of spiritual gifts.

Individual Christians are the organs in Christ's body. Their distinctives are not meant to estrange them from each other. The opposite is true: They are essential features of fellowship, bestowed by the Triune God, as "varieties of gifts, but the same Spirit; . . . varieties of service, but the same Lord; . . . varieties of working, but the same God who inspires them all in every one. To each is given the manifestation of the Spirit for the common good" (1 Cor. 12:4-7). Diversity is a necessary feature of the unity of the Church, as it is a necessary feature of incarnational Christology: "God arranged the organs in the body, each one of them, as he chose. If all were a single organ, where would the body be? As it is, there are many parts, yet one body. . . . Now you *(humeis)* are the body of Christ, and individually members of it" (1 Cor. 12:18-20, 27).

This is true of the local assembly, which anticipates and reflects the assembly that local churches together confess as *the* catholic Church.[55] Catholicity is not a later retrojection of Mediterranean hegemony over the isolated communities that received Paul's letters and preserved the Jesus traditions that would become each community's Gospels. "For all things are yours, whether Paul or Apollos or Cephas . . . ; and you are Christ's; and Christ is God's" (1 Cor. 3:22-23).

Living out this shared sense of catholicity, Christian communities throughout the ancient world quickly began transmitting Gospels and Epistles across great distances, and learned to read them synoptically. The early churches built a "holy internet," apparently with Rome as its "file server," to make available authentic Christian material, both Christological and ecclesi-

---

55. See Miroslav Volf, *After Our Likeness: The Church as the Image of the Trinity* (Grand Rapids: Eerdmans, 1997), pp. 270-72, on the catholicity of the local church. The concept is different in free church ecclesiology than it is in hierarchical ecclesiology.

ological, to the many member churches that were eager for it.[56] Indeed, Richard Bauckham persuasively argues that even the Gospels, so often assumed to be written only by and for particular communities, were in fact written *in order* to be distributed throughout the network of Christian communities that spread across the first-century Roman world. John's author apparently expected his Gospel to be read intertextually with the synoptic tradition, not as a replacement for it but as a supplement to it.[57] The catholicity of Christian Scripture has both conferred and reflected the catholicity of the Church from its first generation. The unity of Scripture's grand narrative, in all its diversity, has reflected the common witness of the Church's many different witnesses.[58]

Biblical interpretation plays a vital role in the local and universal life of Christ's body, which Paul has already referred to as God's building (*oikodomē,* 1 Cor. 3:9). The ongoing work of the Church builds upon *(epoikodomei)* the apostolic foundation, which is Jesus Christ (1 Cor. 3:11). Postliberal theology has recently worked to recover this insight to a Western Church that has sometimes forgotten it. Ellen Charry's *By the Renewing of Your Minds* examines the "aretegenic" (virtue-forming) nature of Christian theological tradition, a quality already rooted firmly in the New Testament writings. Good theology is, above all, *salutary,* because "God is good for us."[59] Texts like Matthew, Romans, and Galatians (and here, 1 Corinthians) are paradigmatic examples of aretegenic theology — projects of ecclesial edification. Inspired Scripture gathers the Church and creates it anew, conferring its ecclesial qualities through the Spirit's edifying work. Gifts of the Spirit produce first *apostles,* second *prophets,* third *teachers,* and so on (1 Cor. 12:28). All of these gifts

56. See Michael B. Thompson, "The Holy Internet: Communication Between Churches in the First Christian Generation," in Richard Bauckham, ed., *The Gospels for All Christians: Rethinking the Gospel Audiences* (Grand Rapids: Eerdmans, 1998), pp. 49-70.

57. See "John for Readers of Mark," in Bauckham, ed., *The Gospels for All Christians,* pp. 147-71.

58. See Gerard Loughlin's use of Gerard Gennette's *Narrative Discourse,* trans. Jane E. Lewin (Oxford: Basil Blackwell, 1980) in his own *Telling God's Story: Bible, Church, and Narrative Theology* (New York: Cambridge University Press, 1996), pp. 52-63, for a discussion of how multiple "conflicting" narratives can in fact tell a common story. Loughlin is arguing against Maurice Wiles's contention that the Bible has no unity of its own (pp. 43-45). Loughlin responds that the Bible's one story emerges from a "ruled reading of the Bible as Scripture . . . as constituting and constituted by the Church." It is an argument similar to the one presented here, except that here the unity of Scripture is not named as necessarily narrative in literary form.

59. Ellen Charry, *By the Renewing of Your Minds: The Pastoral Function of Christian Doctrine* (New York: Oxford University Press, 1997), pp. 233, 238.

are ordered not towards "vindicating [their tradition] as superior to their historical predecessors,"[60] or adequating one's mind to its objects,[61] but simply "building up the Church *(tēn oikodomēn tēs ekklēsias)*" (1 Cor. 12:5). Development is indeed God's object — but not the development of a tradition of enquiry.

All of Christ's members share in this task, performing their appointed roles according to the needs of all; or, as later Christian tradition puts it, *kath' holou*, according to the whole. Diversity in teaching and prophecy is a cause and function of the catholicity of the apostles' Church, a manifestation of the very wholeness of the body of Christ. Similarly, the Bible is Scripture because it serves the whole Church, even if it does so in different ways to different members. Catholicity orders and preserves — even bestows — diversity on God's people, producing the completion of unity (1 Cor. 1:10) rather than the immaturity of discord.

Holiness as the Divine Appointment of Difference

According to Paul, Christian identity is intimately bound up with the catholicity of the divine community. The distinctness of spiritual gifts sets individual saints apart first from the world, but then also from their fellow Christians. God puts them *(etheto,* 1 Cor. 12:28) where the Holy Spirit wills (1 Cor. 12:11) by bestowing upon them his various charisms. Christian distinctiveness on both the personal level and the communal level is thus *holy:* set apart for a divine purpose, marked out as distinct by the blood of Christ, and cleansed of the leaven of worldly vices (1 Cor. 5:6-8).[62] The holy Church is itself a fellowship of holy ones, a communion of saints, whose charismatic differences allow them to be and act as the body of Christ, accomplishing the will of the Father. Catholicity, then, is a manifestation of the Church's holiness, and vice versa. Catholicity sets the Christian community apart from the rest of humanity, making it not just another interpretive community or a tradition of enquiry, but a holy gathering. So Paul's letters

---

60. MacIntyre, *Whose Justice?* p. 360.

61. MacIntyre, *Whose Justice?* pp. 356f.

62. See Hays, *First Corinthians,* p. 83: Paul echoes Exod. 12:3-7 to highlight an unusual quality of the blood of Christ. "The blood of the lamb on the doorposts of the houses marks Israel out as a distinct people under God's protection, spared from the power of destruction at work in the world outside. In the same way, Paul's metaphor suggests, the blood of Christ marks the Corinthians as a distinct people."

to Corinth rightly concentrate on the maintenance and growth of the Corinthian Church's holiness.

It is fitting, then, that the holy Church should have as its canon a library of holy books, set apart from the other books of the world and even those of the saints, and each set apart from the others in order to honor its own purpose in God's economy. The harmonious practice of biblical interpretation in its proper variety is a function of the holiness of Scripture and of the divine gifts of interpreting it.

None of this is incompatible with the notion of rationality as constituted in and by a tradition of enquiry. But holiness *is* utterly incompatible with the notion of a tradition of "saints" at odds, one against another (*henos . . . kata tou heterou,* 1 Cor. 4:6) over the very goods of the Christian life. When catholicity fails and division sets in, the Church's holiness is compromised. Its people look once again like their former, unsanctified selves. No longer set apart from each other for their mutual edification, they cease to be set apart together from the world. When the Spirit's gifts are not exercised for the edification of all, but are reserved for the mere upbuilding of selves, outsiders perceive not the building up of God's own dwelling place, but the ravings of lunatics. They see a Church that looks no different from their world — just another tradition of enquiry in a state of epistemological crisis. In contrast, in a healthy, truly catholic fellowship these same outsiders see the edifying of others, through the deep sensibility of pneumatic interpretation. As a result they are convicted, worshiping the holy God they somehow have found in their midst (1 Cor. 14:23-25).

In this tight correspondence between edification and proclamation — *i.e.,* in the holiness of Scripture — lies the specific answer to the urgent question of how faithful Christians should test competing and even contradictory biblical interpretations. It is one thing to claim that competence in "the Christian language" is the prerequisite and standard for proper biblical interpretation; it is another thing to describe just what that competence looks like.

MacIntyre suggests one answer: Participants must have the proper kinds of commonality and difference needed to sustain a constructive argument. They must live within the catholic diversity of a living tradition of enquiry. Since fellow Christians will differ even about the nature and goods of Christian life, there is no *a priori* way of judging the superiority of an interpretation. The debate itself transforms the interpretive community, develops its linguistic competence, and may influence even its authoritative texts. Thus an argument is not merely evaluative of proper exegesis, but actually *constitutive* of it. The history of biblical interpretation and argument is then a kind of Holy Tradition.

One can appreciate the attractiveness of this view to Christians with progressive doctrines of tradition and commitments to the authority of ecumenical councils. And one would imagine that Paul the rabbi would share their enthusiasm. But here again, we see dramatically different pastoral advice from Paul the church planter: Proper interpretation is governed not by those who practice it, but by the sovereign Holy Spirit who inspires biblical practice from start to finish. Just as the Bible's voice is distorted or silenced by hermeneutical rules foreign to it, so the Bible's sovereignty, which is the sovereignty of the Holy Spirit, is quenched when its work is evaluated according to rules that fall short of fully respecting the work of the Holy Spirit, *even if they emerge from within the community itself.* The Church discerns the Spirit not so much by exercising its own intellectual resources in new situations as by observing the outcome of God's "fruits-test": the mutual upbuilding of the holy and sanctifying Church as it prefigures and prepares for Jesus' return.[63]

Lesslie Newbigin finds in Scripture only one comprehensive, "Pentecostal" test for biblical exegesis:

> The discernment of the Spirit can only come by living in the Spirit; . . . because there is in truth one Spirit who is Lord and God, He is able to make Himself known as one to those who earnestly seek Him; . . . all who have ever had any taste of His power to teach, convince, and subdue a gathering of Christians coming together with all their clashing wills and affections, know that this is true; and . . . whenever we try to seek some other sort of security against error and disunity, some criteria of judgment or rules of life which can be operated apart from this discernment of the Spirit in the Spirit, some ecclesiastical order in which we can be secure against error without constantly engaging in the risky adventure of seeking truth, secure against schism without constantly paying the price of unity in costly charity, we are in fact building not according to the Spirit but according to the

---

63. This is not to say that such discernment does not come through exercising the Church's intellect in new situations — for instance when the Council of Jerusalem discerns the Holy Spirit in responding to the crisis precipitated by the circumcision party (Acts 15:28). It is only to say that the Holy Spirit's agency can operate apart from a polemical or critical context, in the absence of people competent in the tradition, and without necessarily contributing to the intellectual resources of the tradition, at least not in a way MacIntyre would recognize.

Augustine was born again and Western literary culture transformed when he heeded an unidentified voice's *non sequitur,* turned to Rom. 13:13, and interpreted it in a naïve, reader-response fashion without regard to its biblical context. The rule of charity means an otherwise nonsensical reading of the Scriptures may build up a Christian community in a way that a more intellectually responsible reading may not.

flesh. We must take simply and seriously the truth that the Church is a communion in the Holy Spirit and that He is no cipher, no abstract noun, but living Lord.[64]

Such discernment of course means that some interpretations lie outside the bounds of authentic Christian exegesis of Scripture. We could describe these in MacIntyrean terms as arguments that failed to respect or serve the resources of the Christian tradition in the face of the epistemological crises facing it; and this description would not be unhelpful. Wrong interpretations of Scripture — even charitable ones, Augustine says — weaken rather than strengthen the Church, or strengthen the Church despite themselves. But a more theologically precise account sees these interpretive disputes, these competing rationalities within the broader interpretive "tradition," as fundamentally different Christian visions, which cannot be described in terms of the Church's catholicity. Unlike the cacophony of unqualified diversity, *catholic* diversity does not preclude the rejection of interpretations or even the excommunication of interpreters (1 Cor. 5:13). But neither does it subject interpreters to the tyranny of the community; for the ultimate criterion of judgment is no earthly human being, but only the Triune God whose Spirit blows where he wills.

Obviously the qualities of unity, holiness, catholicity, and apostolicity are mutually qualifying. Each depends on the others for its authenticity. "Catholicity" without apostolicity is empty pluralism, "unity" without holiness the society of demons, "holiness" without catholicity superapostolic elitism, "apostolicity" without unity the babble of "other gospels." Scripture's ecclesial properties cohere because under the Holy Spirit's agency, its many works cohere to build up the one Church in many different ways. Furthermore, while there are abundant reasons to affirm the validity of all four Nicene characteristics of the Church, we need not limit the marks of the Church to these four, or (as we will see below) to restrict ourselves to a particular tradition's understanding of any of them.

From MacIntyre to Paul: Beyond Argument

One of the most ironic qualities of MacIntyre's work is that its open-endedness provokes a radical re-examination of the Christian tradition of enquiry in terms of whatever resources are available for the project, while its re-

---

64. Lesslie Newbigin, *The Household of God* (New York: Friendship, 1954), p. 107.

spect for the traditional nature of all enquiry provokes an unapologetic return to the resources of Christianity's *particular* rationality to make the project worthwhile.[65] When we respond to both provocations, we gain much more than a helpful, general phenomenology of human rationality. We gain a fresh perspective from within on the Christian community's particularity. This is a great gift. It frees our culture's biblical interpreters from bondage to the acids of historiography and the lures of absolutism, relativism, and perspectivism, from having to defend their practices according to the world's expectations. They can then go on to see interpretation in truly Christian terms — ecclesiologically, pneumatologically, Christologically, soteriologically, and eschatologically.

Such a going on and going further reveals several crucial discontinuities between MacIntyre's category of argument and the nature of the Church. First, the exercise of spiritual gifts produces mutual upbuilding and harmony, not crisis and dialectical resolution; "you can all prophesy one by one, so that all may learn and all be encouraged . . . for God is not a God of confusion but of peace" (1 Cor. 14:31, 33). The history of the Church may be marked by crisis; but crisis is anything but necessary to the Church. Second, even the practice of the spiritual gifts of this age — including the Church's current biblical practices — is neither necessary to the body of Christ nor constitutive of it, for "as for prophecies, they will pass away; as for tongues, they will cease; as for knowledge, it will pass away" (1 Cor. 13:8). As important as biblical interpretation is — and it is very important! — its present form is marginal in the eternal life of the Church.

The common problem in these two discontinuities is that MacIntyre's Hegelian phenomenology, so well suited to recognizing the historical contingency of human traditions, is ill-suited to analyzing the Church in anything *but* historically contingent terms. Here MacIntyre's project stands in stark contrast to William J. Abraham's *Canon and Criterion in Christian Theology.* There Abraham chronicles a Western Christian tradition in decline through the debilitating effects of its arguing, rather than sustained or invigorated by them. He claims that the crisis of authority in Western Christianity stems from a long history, reaching well into the first millennium, of misinterpreting the Church's various canons (biblical and otherwise) as being epistemo-

---

65. MacIntyre senses this in *Whose Justice?* p. 401: "The point in the overall argument has been reached — it may indeed have been reached somewhat earlier — at which it is no longer possible to speak except out of one particular tradition in a way which will involve conflict with rival traditions. . . . It is here that we have to begin speaking as protagonists of one contending party or fall silent." Alas, MacIntyre the philosopher ends his account where a theologian would presumably begin it.

logical rather than soteriological in nature.[66] The differences between canons as means of grace and canons as epistemic norms are subtle enough, and the similarities natural enough, to have seduced Christians into inverting canon and criterion, making epistemic considerations primary and prior to the soteriological resources of canons, including the canon of Scripture.[67] In MacIntyre's terms, in the course of arguing, Christian apologetics were forced to appeal to epistemological warrants for their claims. The pressures outside and fissures among and inside Christian communities increasingly drove Christians to appeal to canonical institutions such as Bible and episcopate as epistemic norms. The most conspicuous moment in this transformation is the career of Thomas Aquinas (who is the hero of MacIntyre's analysis).[68] Over time, polemical theology tended to *reduce* these canons of the Church to their epistemic usefulness, and to pit them against each other in such a way that reinforced this reduction. Christian faith and practice became a high-stakes contest between rival traditions of enquiry, bent upon vindicating themselves over against opponents as epistemological crises called their validity into question.

From Abraham's perspective, MacIntyre's project itself is a manifesta-

---

66. William J. Abraham, *Canon and Criterion in Christian Theology* (Oxford: Clarendon, 1998), p. 1. Despite the apparent boldness of his claim, it is actually rather modest once he properly qualifies it: "The claim is that the epistemology of Christian belief is not the *primary* field nor the *primary* interest at stake for the Church in the creation of its canonical heritage" (p. 43, emphasis added). The force of Abraham's argument seems to lie in the word "primary." He does not dispute that the Church used canons such as the creeds, and above all the canon of Scripture, as criteria of truth. He simply disputes that they *are* criteria of truth: "To be sure, the Church believed the Creed to be true, and it readily used it to make judgements about other claims to truth within and outside the community. Believing the Creed to be true, teachers of the Church naturally rejected material which was incompatible with it. But this only shows such teachers to be intelligent and consistent; it does not show that the Creed is a criterion of truth" (p. 41). Nor is Abraham against the practice of epistemology, so long as one respects its nature and limits in the economy of faith (p. 479).

67. Abraham, *Canon and Criterion*, pp. 8, 471.

68. Abraham, *Canon and Criterion*, p. 471. While the Reformation doctrine of *sola scriptura* merely represents an alternative vision of Scripture as epistemic norm, Reformation *practice* of Scripture "borrowed lavishly from the full canonical heritage of the Church without there being any warrant in their canonical foundationalism to do so" (p. 472). The Protestant return to canon as means of saving grace was soon overshadowed by the peculiar foundationalism of the Enlightenment (p. 473). These Protestant weaknesses, according to Abraham, spurred the Pietist, Methodist, and Pentecostal movements that "represent a Protestant underworld of protest which has sought to return to a soteriological vision of the Scriptures" (p. 474). We can take Abraham's thesis as a long appeal to Newbigin's "Pentecostal" vision of biblical interpretation, in which the fruit of the Spirit is the final criterion of discernment (pp. 457-68).

tion of this impoverishment. The trajectory of the Western Christian tradition leads MacIntyre to reduce traditions in general to traditions of enquiry, and salvation to vindication. His account not only chronicles the inversion of canon and criterion in the course of history, but relies on that inversion for its persuasive power. His case rests on its plausibility structures. Like Newman's epistemology, MacIntyre tends to historicize the Church, ironically endorsing as realized eschaton what Paul opposes in the Corinthian Church, while pushing the truly realized eschaton of harmonious human community into the indefinite future.[69] Such an analysis confuses what is with what must be, for "the form of this world is passing away" (1 Cor. 7:31). The fleshly becomes normative, and the spiritual becomes unattainable.

Third, as important as canonical Scripture is in the Church, it is not its ultimate authority. That capacity belongs to *the* Word, the person of Jesus Christ, who is more than a text. The Christian "language" is comprehended not in its Bible, but in God's incarnate Son, who alone has made God known (John 1:18; cf. John 21:25). Here too, MacIntyre's generalized account of the role of canonical texts seems to fit some traditions (perhaps Islam and Judaism) better than it fits this one. While MacIntyre's generalized categories are better than those of absolutism, relativism, or perspectivism, in the end the specific qualities of the Church, its Lord, and its Bible simply explode them.

There is much to be learned from MacIntyre's insights into the nature of human rationality; and the logic of incarnation means that Christian rationality is a truly human rationality. But Christ's humanity is a *transformed* humanity, in which the Church participates and hopes. Likewise, Christian rationality is (except when it stumbles) transformed human rationality. The Christian tradition is a human community, transformed by grace to be the Church. Whatever epistemic norms its canons offer are judged according to their spiritual fruit. It should be no surprise that it is where the Church is distinct from other human communities — in its unity, holiness, catholicity, apostolicity, and so on — that MacIntyre's categories fail us. And thus, for all MacIntyre's insight into the human, tradition-constituted shape of biblical interpretation, it is the unity, the holiness, the catholicity, and the apostolicity of biblical interpretation that limit his analysis.

This does not mean that the history of biblical interpretation cannot be conveyed in terms of the development of a "Christian tradition" in conversa-

---

69. On the resolution of conflicts within and between traditions, MacIntyre can only say that "no one at any stage can ever rule out the future possibility of their present beliefs and judgments being shown to be inadequate in a variety of ways" (*Whose Justice?* p. 361).

tion with its canonical texts. The full humanity of the Church, its incarnate Lord, and its Scripture allows and even demands such projects. But any such projects will inevitably lump failures of interpretation together with successes; the tearing apart of the community together with its upbuilding; fleshly strife in with true spirituality. Paul wanted his readers to be gravely aware of the incidences of all of these within their community. But the last thing Paul wanted the arrogant, divided, impotent Corinthian Church to think was that it had already arrived at the genuine Christian life (cf. 1 Cor. 3:8-21). It would be just as tragic for Christian interpreters of Scripture to think the same thing of the Church in any other location or era. God came, comes, and will someday come again into the world to end the arguing, not to create more.

From the Church of History to the Church of Faith: The Bible as Transformer

While it may look as if Paul has given us an excuse to abandon a critical appreciation of Christianity for an idealized ecclesiology, in fact he has done no such thing. Paul's ecclesiology has one foot planted firmly on each side of the eschatological divide: "Cleanse out the old yeast so that you may be a new batch, as you really are unleavened" (1 Cor. 5:7). It negotiates the difference between the broken communities of Christians among whom God is at work, and the one, holy, catholic, apostolic Church God is building with them. Like any pastor, Paul is aware of the great disparity between the critical and the confessional pictures of his churches. His work as a fellow servant is to close the distance between the two — to realize the Christlikeness of the earthly Church.[70] The same is true of Scripture and all the Church's other sacramental means of grace. As a means through which God descends and the Church ascends into each other's loving presence, the primary eschatological functions of Scripture are to confer the Church's ecclesial qualities to the communities and persons who still lack them, and to reflect these qualities in those

---

70. Surprising support for this argument comes from Ernst Käsemann's essay, "Paul and Early Catholicism," in Käsemann, *New Testament Questions of Today* (Philadelphia: Fortress, 1979), pp. 236ff. Käsemann says, "Early Catholicism means that transition from earliest Christianity to the so-called ancient Church . . . a characteristic movement toward that great Church which understands itself as the *Una Sancta Apostolica*. . . . I propose the thesis, surely unusual for a Protestant, that from a purely historical viewpoint, Paul himself was a forerunner of early catholicism" (pp. 237-38). Käsemann argues for a consistent (if abused) theological trajectory from Paul's body of Christ language for the Church, in pp. 242ff.

who are being re-formed by them into Christ's image, as they worship their Lord and Savior and build up each other.

The realized eschatology of some Church traditions has led them to emphasize the marks of the Church as present qualities. The Church *is* one, holy, catholic, and apostolic; thus the true Church is not found where these qualities are lacking (cf. 1 Cor. 11:19). In reaction, the futurist eschatology of other Church traditions has led them to emphasize the marks of the Church as future qualities. The Church *will be* one, holy, catholic, and apostolic, and to claim these too strongly too early is to mistake present promise for future fulfillment. These qualities are not only lacking in present-day Christian communities, but they *must be* lacking, at least in part, as long as the gathering is away from the Lord (cf. 1 Cor. 13:10; 2 Cor. 5:8). We see that both positions, which we may roughly call "Catholic" and "Protestant," have canonical warrants even within the Corinthian correspondence. They are not so much idealist and realist visions of the Church as visions reflecting the two poles of dialectical eschatology. Catholics see a full chalice, Protestants a half-empty glass. Inaugurated eschatology tries to honor the truth of both by holding them together, as Paul himself seems to have done. The *gathering* Church is *becoming* one, holy, catholic, and apostolic.[71] So the Bible's inspired performance builds up the Church in gathering, growing, giving, and going to[72] the world's Christian believers. Scripture glorifies as it gathers. It speaks dominically as the husband of the Church, and ecclesially as the responsive bride of Christ — both conferring and reflecting the bride's preparedness for the final wedding day, as God's glory beheld transforms the beholder into its own reflection (2 Cor. 3:18).

Once Scripture's resemblances to the Church are appreciated, bibliology can benefit from a circular application of ecclesial categories back to Scripture. From the Church's unity we can analogically describe the Bible's unity, and so on. In this way we explore the holy, catholic, apostolic unity of Scripture through an analysis of the holy, catholic, apostolic unity of its Church. We gain resources for moving beyond both *a priori* definitions of the unity or holiness of Scripture, and descriptions that remain on the level of common phenomenology.

To do this appropriately requires a great deal of care. Inspired Scripture is not just another product of the Church, like a position paper or even a conciliar document. It is the canon, the ultimate authority for Christians, ex-

71. Cf. Newbigin, *The Household of God*, pp. 148-49, for a similar criticism of traditional denominational ecclesiologies.

72. My local church has adopted these four practices as "core values" constitutive of its being, without realizing their close correspondence with the four marks of Nicene ecclesiology.

cepting only God himself. While few should object to affirming a holiness in the Church after the holiness of Scripture, many would properly object to *reducing* the Bible's holiness to the Church's present holiness. Ecclesial categories are not enough to describe the Bible's ecclesiology, when the Bible *confers* as well as reflects them. When the Church's witness has been compromised, biblical practice has often done more than merely reflect the crisis; it has led the way back into right relationship with God. The Protestant tradition above all has refused to identify Scripture's role and authority in the Church with the Church's other roles and authorities. It has concluded that such a mistaken identity would hold Scripture captive to the Church who reads and hears it, to silence or falsify its prophetic voice, and to distort into an idol the God who inspires it.

In theological terms, despite their commonalities, different understandings of the relationships between Scripture and tradition (no longer used here in MacIntyre's technical sense) have sharply divided Christian traditions and distinguished their ecclesiologies of Scripture. It seems that reframing historical contingency in terms of ecclesiology has led us into yet another conundrum. Until we understand the issue, we will be unable fully to appreciate bibliology's family resemblances to ecclesiology.

III. The Bible's Life in the Church

Scripture as Process, Content, and Instances of Tradition

The Bible's "traditionedness" is a logical consequence of the ecclesiality of Christian Scripture. That Scripture itself is human tradition is uncontroversial among the various Christian traditions (though not always among those who, following Mark 7:8, would be uncomfortable with the sinful connotations of the adjective "human"). The 1963 Faith and Order Conference in Montreal tried to appreciate and clarify the multivalence of the Christian word "tradition" by distinguishing between three of its aspects. It defines tradition as "the process of transmission," which one might call "traditioning"; Tradition as "the content of what is transmitted," "*the* tradition"; and traditions as "the distinctive inheritance of separate churches or movements." All three of these dimensions of tradition apply directly to the Christian Bible.

First, Scripture is of course the fundamental Tradition that tradition transmits. Its words are the Church's authoritative witness. The Bible is the normative expression of Christian content — regardless of whether one understands its content in terms of philosophical or historical propositions, human experience, or the language of Christian life itself (to appeal again to Lindbeck's familiar categories).

However, to leave Scripture as this one form of tradition is to miss its dynamic dimension. This is an aspect powerfully recovered in Yves Congar's *Tradition and Traditions*,[73] from which draw both Montreal's threefold form of Christian tradition and *Dei Verbum*'s chapter 2, which helped set the stage for the revival in Catholic biblical practice that has followed Vatican II.[74] As the living and active Word of God, Scripture is *tradition* as well as Tradition, a transmitter as well as a transmission. The Bible does not wait passively to be passed along, but its prophetic words create the conditions for its preservation and spread to the ends of the earth. To alter the words but not the sense of the Second Helvetic Confession (Chapter 1), as the Word of God preached is the Word of God, so Scripture practiced is Scripture. One could sum up inspired tradition as the mutual breathing of life between the Christian community and the Christian canon. An ecclesiological bibliology can thus affirm a *twofold* inspiration of Scripture — by the Holy Spirit and by the Church — at every stage of the biblical tradition. The Church "traditions" Scripture by using it liturgically and devotionally, by translating, producing, and distributing Bibles; and by its catechesis, seminary, and ordination. Under and alongside the Spirit's agency, it breathes life into the Bible's silent words. Conversely, the transmitted canon of Scripture transmits and gathers the Church, breathing life into it through the same agency of the Holy Spirit. The lived Bible is the primary transmission of Christian faith within the communion of saints and to the ends of the earth, and an indispensable means of evangelism, salvation, and revival. One way or another, Scripture gives the Church's various activities for God, for itself, and for the world their Christian shape.

Finally, Scripture is *traditions:* a set of ever growing distinctive inheritances of the various churches — traditions — that share the body of Christ. Inasmuch as different churches have different Bible translations, traditions of interpretation, canons within the canon, prayers, hymnodies and liturgies, conceptions of preaching, and other uses for the Bible, they literally have different Scriptures. The American evangelical who declares "*My* Bible says . . ." with polemical flair against an opponent is speaking more truly than he or she may know — for the various Christian traditions are various biblical traditions, where the various Bibles of the Church do their work in various ways. Scripture has a different voice in my local Pentecostal church from the one it

---

73. Yves Congar, *Tradition and Traditions* (New York: Macmillan, 1967).

74. For a perceptive analysis see Avery Dulles, *The Craft of Theology: From Symbol to System* (New York: Crossroad, 1992), pp. 93-103.

has in the other communities of which I have been a part. Each is a different dialect of the Church's common biblical language.

But is it really so simple? When the Church of Jesus Christ of Latter Day Saints performs Scripture in worship, does it speak the common biblical language of the Trinitarian faiths, even in different terms? And how common is that ecumenical Trinitarian biblical language? Can the differences among the Roman Catholic, Eastern Orthodox, Lutheran, and Reformed uses of Scripture really be described properly as dialects of a common biblical language? The issue of the relationship between Scripture and tradition names far more than the mere fact that the Bible is itself a form of tradition. It names the painful issue of the uniqueness of the divine-human traditions that are Scripture proper, among the Church's other traditions.

All the major ecclesial traditions acknowledge the Bible's uniqueness in Christian Tradition. But they vary widely in how they conceive it. Each understands the Bible's character and purpose as the Church's canon in a different way. Often each has seen in the other not merely a different dialect, but another language, even "another gospel." Fortunately, from this chapter's eschatological perspective, these languages are more compatible than they usually appear to be, and each account can enrich an ecumenical ecclesiology of Scripture. We will briefly examine each major branch, choosing a contemporary theologian as a representative, then explore what the branches together say about Christian Scripture's eschatological work in its communities. The view they provide on the Bible's work in the gathering Church frames both the discussions on the liturgical practice of Scripture and its role in personal salvation with which the chapter closes.

While all the following theologians appreciate the three aspects of tradition enumerated above, not all make such precise technical distinctions as the WCC. So we will stay on safer ground, using the word "tradition" more generally and drawing out the above distinctions explicitly when necessary.

Dumitru Staniloae: Tradition Is Scripture

Shortly before his death in 1993, the Romanian Orthodox Dumitru Staniloae was referred to by Kallistos Ware as possibly " the greatest Orthodox theologian alive." Staniloae crafts a "pan-Orthodox" account of Scripture and tradition in *The Experience of God*.[75] His "neopatristic synthesis" (Georges

---

75. Ed. and trans. Ioan Ionita and Robert Barringer (Brookline, Mass.: Holy Cross Orthodox Press, 1994), pp. ix-x. The most relevant chapter is "Scripture and Tradition," pp. 37-52.

Florovsky's description) explores revelation in light of the favorite *loci* of Orthodox systematic theology: incarnational Christology, the soteriology of deification, Gregory Palamas's categories of the ineffable essence and uncreated energies of God, Cappadocian Trinitarianism, realized eschatology, and Cyprianic ecclesiology. The result is an elegant near-identity among Scripture, tradition, and the unfolding revelation of Jesus Christ in the Church through the Holy Spirit.

As one would expect, Staniloae's account is profoundly resonant with that of Athanasius. In a sense Staniloae's account continues where Athanasius leaves off. Athanasius' concern was the incarnation of the *logos*. Staniloae more explicitly follows the trajectory of the *logos* in creation forward in time to the present, to say that God's Word and Spirit cooperate "first of all, in revelation down to the time of its conclusion in Christ, and after that in the Church, in Scripture, and in Tradition."[76] "The revealed Christ remains and goes on working within creation. . . . To this end he makes use of three means which are concrete and unified: the Church, sacred Scripture, and holy Tradition."[77]

For Staniloae, Scripture is not just an instance of Tradition. Holy Tradition, all of it, *is* Scripture. Strong causal relationships run from Jesus, to the apostles, to apostolic Scripture, to apostolic tradition and Tradition, to the continuing life of the apostolic Church. All are forms of the same divine revelation. Through the Holy Spirit, each creates and empowers the next in the series. Scripture occupies a necessary middle ground between the definitive revelation of God, who is Jesus Christ, and the continuing work of the Holy Spirit in revealing God through the dynamic communal Christ that is the Church. Therefore Christ "is presented essentially" through Christian Scripture.[78] A strong ontological claim follows: that tradition transmits the *essential Jesus,* embodying him in the Church and, through the Church, witnessing to him in the world.

Staniloae denies that anything *new* is revealed in either Scripture or Holy Tradition, for "supernatural revelation came to its close in Christ." There is no means of greater intimacy with God or profounder knowledge of

---

76. Staniloae, *The Experience of God*, p. 29.

77. Staniloae, *The Experience of God*, p. 36.

78. Staniloae, *The Experience of God*, p. 40: "Sacred Scripture is the Son and Word of God who translated himself into words in his work of drawing close to men so that he might raise them up to himself, until the time of his incarnation, resurrection, and ascension as man. Through these words by which he is translated, Christ works upon us to bring us also to that state which he has reached." The strength of Staniloae's *is* is perhaps even stronger than the strength of Barth's.

him than Jesus Christ himself.[79] Yet the Church and its Holy Tradition are dynamic, not static. So the newness of the Church's pneumatic experience of God is nothing more than "the continuous deepening and unfolding of the content of Scripture."[80] Revelation is both continually unfolded and objectively unchanged in Scripture, Tradition, and Church.[81] The two indispensable mediators, Holy Spirit and Church, provide the power and the framework for this deepening of Christ's revelation in the world. So one can say of Staniloae's bibliology that Tradition *is* Scripture, extended over time into the world. The apostolicity of both Scripture and Tradition consists in the Spirit's ongoing amplification and interpretation of the unchanged content of Scripture.[82] Apostolicity then represents both the closed-ended and open-ended aspects of Scripture-Tradition. Scripture's open-endedness is a function of its plenitude of spiritual senses, for it reveals the uncircumscribable God. Its closed-endedness is a function of Jesus' concreteness, for it reveals the circumscribed God. The course of Scripture-Tradition in the Church of Christ is then a reflection of the continuing life of the Spirit-anointed Christ. Using Florovsky, Staniloae calls it not just "teaching" but the very grace of the Holy Spirit[83] — in effect, a *charisma* comprehending all the Church's other *charismata*, an *epiclēsis* invoking and receiving the Spirit's abiding presence in the Word and sacraments of the body of Christ.[84]

R. P. C. Hanson generalizes the Orthodox stand on Scripture and tradition in this way: "Tradition in [the Orthodox] view cannot either conflict with [so Protestant] or supplement [so Catholic] scripture, but must interpret it."[85] It is typically understood as a "one-source" account of tradition, rather than the "two-source" account we will see below in pre–Vatican II Catholicism. Staniloae fits Hanson's characterization closely. Even though he calls Scripture only "a part of revelation fixed in written form,"[86] he understands the content of Scripture and tradition to be essentially identical.[87] Thus he would not follow those Catholics who posit written Scripture and

79. Staniloae, *The Experience of God,* p. 37.

80. Staniloae, *The Experience of God,* p. 49.

81. Staniloae, *The Experience of God,* p. 39.

82. Staniloae, *The Experience of God,* p. 45.

83. Staniloae, *The Experience of God,* p. 48.

84. Staniloae, *The Experience of God,* pp. 48-49.

85. R. P. C. Hanson, "Tradition," in Alan Richardson and John Bowden, eds., *The Westminster Dictionary of Christian Theology* (Philadelphia: Westminster, 1983), p. 575.

86. Staniloae, *The Experience of God,* p. 58.

87. Staniloae, *The Experience of God,* p. 47: "In essence, the content of the apostolic tradition is nothing more than the content of Scripture applied to human life. . . ."

unwritten tradition as two *distinct* sources of revelation. Tradition interprets Scripture; it does not supplement it.

Staniloae's account is classically Orthodox in other ways as well. First, Staniloae constantly appeals to analogical coherence: Tradition is remembrance, like the eucharistic *anamnēsis;* tradition is *charisma,* like the eucharistic *epiclēsis;* tradition is interpreted and embodied Scripture. These tight metaphors read Church in terms of Trinity, tradition in terms of Scripture, all three in terms of the incarnate Christ, and so on. This is the same coherence that Aidan Nichols, an Eastern-minded Roman Catholic, finds elegant about the Analogy of the Word.[88] Like Balthasar, within a few paragraphs Staniloae effortlessly posits the connections this bibliology has been laboring to establish, offering no warrants to back up his assertions, as if none are needed. Second, the relentless coherence of Staniloae's model rests on a distinctively Orthodox ecclesiological idealism. The connections among God, Christ, Scripture, tradition, Tradition, and Church on which Staniloae's account depends are stipulated in the strongest and most general terms and nuanced by further similar stipulations, but never developed in terms of particular examples, and never troubled by potential problems and discontinuities. Staniloae leaves not only unanswered, but *unasked,* the question of what to do when tradition and Scripture conflict. They simply do not, any more than Jesus and the Spirit conflict. Misinterpretations of Scripture *are not* tradition, by definition. The Spirit-indwelt community of Christ cannot receive them. It will reject them just as the seven ecumenical councils rejected the classical heresies, and tradition will continue to unfold and deepen its unchanged revelation of Christ, a part of human history that is nonetheless essentially unaffected by its contingencies.

Protestantism: Is Tradition Scripture?

In light of the condition of the Western Church in the fifteenth and sixteenth centuries, the Reformers asked the question that Staniloae never entertains: What happens when traditions either crowd out the message of Scripture, or conflict with it? What happens when tradition fails its canon?

Whatever its other internal schisms, the Protestant Reformation answered, almost unanimously, that failed tradition was subject to the judgment of its own normative source: Holy Scripture. The insight is conveyed succinctly in the major creeds of the various Protestant traditions:

88. Aidan Nichols, *The Shape of Catholic Theology* (Collegeville, Minn.: Liturgical Press, 1991), p. 124.

Nothing is taught in our churches concerning articles of faith that is contrary to the Holy Scriptures or what is common to the Christian church. However, inasmuch as some abuses have been corrected (some of the abuses having crept in over the years and others of them having been introduced with violence), we are obliged by our circumstances to give an account of them and to indicate our reasons for permitting changes in these cases in order that Your Imperial Majesty may perceive that we have not acted in an unchristian and frivolous manner but have been compelled by God's command (which is rightly to be regarded as above all custom) to allow such changes.[89]

We do likewise reject human traditions, which, although they be set out with goodly titles, as though they were divine and apostolical, delivered to the Church by the lively voice of the apostles, and, as it were, by the hands of apostolical men, by means of bishops succeeding in their room, yet, being compared with the Scriptures, disagree with them; and that by their disagreement betray themselves in no wise to be apostolical.[90]

The Church hath power to decree Rites or Ceremonies, and authority in Controversies of Faith; and yet it is not lawful for the Church to ordain any thing that is contrary to God's Word written, neither may it so expound one place of Scripture, that it be repugnant to another. Wherefore, although the Church be a witness and a keeper of Holy Writ, as it ought not to decree any thing against the same, so besides the same ought it not to enforce any thing to be believed for necessity of Salvation.[91]

Hanson sums up Protestantism: "Tradition is to be accepted as a necessary part of the Christian faith, but tradition judged by and found agreeable to Scripture."[92]

In principle this is perhaps no different from the Orthodox position, once one grants that the two traditions define "tradition" in different ways. In practice, of course, the terminological difference makes all the difference in the world. The Protestant position puts Scripture in a fundamentally different position relative to the traditions of Christian communities. Two contem-

---

89. Preface to Article XXII of the Augsburg Confession, in John Leith, ed., *Creeds of the Churches: A Reader in Christian Doctrine from the Bible to the Present*, 3rd ed. (Louisville: John Knox, 1982), p. 79.

90. Chapter 2 of the Second Helvetic Confession, in Leith, ed., *Creeds of the Churches*, p. 136.

91. Article XX of the Thirty-Nine Articles of the Church of England, in Leith, ed., *Creeds of the Churches*, p. 273.

92. Hanson, "Tradition," p. 575.

porary continental theologians have brought the magisterial Reformation's protests into the twentieth century with particular vigor: Karl Barth, who represents modern Reformed Christianity in the pages that follow, and Ernst Käsemann, who represents modern Lutheranism.

Karl Barth: The Church under the Scriptures

We have already examined Karl Barth's ecclesiology of Scripture at length in Chapter 1. The fundamental point for Barth's Reformed ecclesiology is the sheer *priority* of Scripture in the Church's experience of God's saving presence. In *Church Dogmatics* the Church's experience of Scripture as the authoritative voice of its shepherd is the only possible grounds for its knowledge of the Bible's divinity, and the threefoldness of biblical phenomenology the only valid *vestigium trinitatis.* Scripture constitutes the Church (I.1.100) and continually impresses itself upon the Church (I.1.107). The Bible reveals God to the Church of Jesus Christ (§19), rules the Church as its dominical authority (§20), and empowers it with pneumatic sovereignty (§21). One can ground Scripture's authority in the Church, but only ultimately in Scripture and in the God who works through it (I.2.461-462). The Church and its divine qualities are utterly derivative of Scripture and subordinate to it. When the Church forgets this and seeks to establish an authority independent of Scripture, judging it rather than merely witnessing to it, it simply ceases to be the Church (I.2.481). Again, while attitudinally Barth and Staniloae are worlds apart, in principle here the Calvinist and Orthodox traditions agree. Both affirm that the Church enjoys the authority of Christ and the freedom of the Holy Spirit, but may never claim these gifts as possessions apart from their divine source or biblical mediation (I.2.670).

For Barth, (pre–Vatican II) Catholic and Neo-Protestant ecclesiologies make precisely this mistake, positing an authority that lies in the Church itself as the successor to the apostles and prophets, rather than in the Church as merely the trustee of the Scriptures. This means the Church has set itself up as its own authority, as its own Lord, and then cannot be called the Church of *Jesus Christ* (I.2.543). In order for the Church truly to be the Church of Jesus Christ, it cannot be its own authority; it must imitate the *original* apostles and prophets who, unlike their "successors," uniquely model faithful obedience in their roles as authentic apostles and prophets. They alone represent the "tradition which is older than Holy Scripture and on which Holy Scripture as such is founded" (I.2.552). Thus both the revelation and the model of obedience are available only in Scripture. In both senses the Bible is authentic witness — to the revelation that commands obedience, and to the obedient response to it (I.2.544).

Barth's treatment of Scripture and tradition radically counters the functional symmetry with which the two concepts are often treated in both Orthodox and Catholic ecclesiology. The Bible was and is so formative for the Church's traditions and practices that their development over the centuries is inconceivable without it. No other institution pervades Christian life like the Bible. The Church was never without Scripture: It always read the writings that became the Old Testament as inspired witnesses to God's culminating acts in Jesus Christ. Indeed, the "tradition which is older than Holy Scripture" is not the apostolic, but the Mosaic. Paul, perhaps the earliest New Testament writer, was a rabbi long before he was a Christian, and saw the Christological content of the Tanakh as soon as his eyes were reopened.

The most substantial difference between Barth's view of tradition and Staniloae's is in the exclusivity of Barth's claims. For Staniloae, "Sacred Scripture is one of the forms in which revelation keeps on being effective as God's continuous appeal."[93] For Barth, even this strong a claim compromises the Bible's sole authority as *the* second form of the Word of God. For Staniloae, Scripture comes alongside the Church's other divine institutions, norming them and sustaining them, but not creating them. For Barth, Scripture is simply without parallel. The Bible alone — say, falling from an airplane into a society with no Christians, translated but personally unaccompanied — could conceivably generate a more or less comprehensive Christian praxis and theology. Indeed, for Barth, merely hearing and receiving its Word would constitute any people in that hypothetical society as fully part of the Church (I.2.588). On the other hand, all the Church's other resources put together could never regenerate Holy Scripture. (Objecting that hymns, theologies, lectionaries, and so on would be more than adequate source material only proves how contingent their life is on the Bible's own.) Nor would the apostles' "successors" be in any position to reproduce an apostolic Bible; their successorship, as they themselves recognize, is apostleship on a fundamentally different order (I.2.592, and see Barth's exegesis of Eph. 2:20 and 3:5, I.2.580).

If Barth sees tradition differently from Staniloae, then what is it? According to Barth, when the Bible is heard and received, its authority conveys a subordinate and contingent authority in the Church. This is therefore a genuine ecclesiastical authority, even an authority within the Church for the Church (I.2.586, 590, 593). But this authority only comes while the Church stands obediently *under* the Word, never appealing directly to Jesus Christ or

93. Staniloae, *The Experience of God*, p. 40.

to the Holy Spirit (I.2.586-587). Thus confessions of faith, theologies, even delineations of the canon itself rest only on human authority. Ecclesiastical traditions are mere commentaries (I.2.621). Yet because of the existence of divine grace, they may still be accepted. For the human words of the Bible become the Word of God (only) through the work of the Holy Spirit, enabling the Church to find the prophetic and apostolic witness to Jesus (I.2.598-599). Again, underneath the differences lie profound similarities between the Reformed and Orthodox accounts. Both qualify as Holy Tradition: In Barth's scheme this is genuinely pneumatic transformation of the Bible, resting on the event of divine action he outlines in §19 whereby human words become the divine Word. In Switzerland as in Romania the Holy Spirit traditions the Scriptures, in ecclesial events that embody and participate in the divine economy of revelation and redemption.

The absoluteness of the Church's dependence on the Bible for its authority does not mean Barth adopts a crude *sola Scriptura* biblicism, for biblicism ignores the existence of those more experienced hearers of God's Word in Scripture in the past who help others hear the Word themselves. By ignoring God's effect on their fellow hearers, biblicists set themselves up to master the Bible in the name of having the Bible alone as their master (I.2.609). Thus the process of churchly discernment of the Scriptures — in other words, tradition — is an irreducibly social, ecclesiological, ecumenical exercise.

The uniqueness of the Bible's role in the Church means Holy Scripture confronts and radically relativizes all other subjects. The Bible's superiority is a "secret but decisive" one (I.2.677). Its victory, which is a part of Jesus' own victory, is no more obvious; it is a victory between the times, between ascension and return, while the defeated powers have yet to be destroyed (I.2.676). Thus Scripture works eschatologically, always struggling with the powers God has already defeated, always present only as both "already" and "not yet" (I.2.681). But its victory is truly victory. It does not just resist its would-be competitors, but puts them under its feet, "assimilating and making serviceable to itself the alien elements it encounters" (I.2.682). Such assimilation is *redemption*.[94] Here as elsewhere, Barth appreciates Scripture's triumph without qualification, understanding universalism to be a theoretically possible consequence of its work: "There is nothing which has of itself the power to escape the control exercised over it by Scripture" (I.2.682).

This eschatological unfolding of the Bible's freedom and supremacy has

---

94. It is perhaps even divinization, though Barth objects to the term even when applied to the humanity of Jesus himself. The objection may be merely a semantic one, for there are competing understandings of *theosis*.

features directly comparable with progressive eschatology, for it means the Bible may reveal "new," previously hidden meanings on its own part — not because of anything present in a new culture or brought to the text by its readers, but necessarily by the agency of its own eternally living content.[95]

Then is Tradition's ecclesial context dissolved into the cosmic work of the Triune God? It could be, according to Barth; but so far, it has not been. The divine subjectivity of Scripture determines both its universal sphere of action and its particular, primary sphere of action, which is the Church (I.2.685). Barth's formulation wisely avoids *identifying* the Bible's sphere of action with the Church, thereby silencing its witness outside it, yet still recognizes the privileged status of the Church as the community that hears and obeys it and that transmits it to the world. Scripture's ecclesiological dimension is thus, as it should be, a counterpart to its eschatological dimension: "His Word creates the Church first, and then by the ministry of the Church, it becomes a Word to the world" (I.2.686). This churchly role is thus subject to both poles of the eschatological dialectic: At any time it may move the boundaries between Church and world one way, even annihilating the Church entirely, or another way, until "God will be all in all" and the boundaries disappear entirely (I.2.686). The Word so determines the Church that "without Scripture [the Church] would inevitably dissolve into nothingness, perishing from the impossibility of the actuality and unity of faith" (I.2.688).

A Church without a Lord is logically impossible. This does not mean "an erroneous and deformed Christianity" could not exist apart from the Word; but it would have none of the Word's revelation, authority, or freedom. It would be Christianity as seen by comparative religious scholars, a merely human tradition, existing under the shadow of death by virtue of God's general (and only temporary) providence for all created things (I.2.689). While in fact "the Church *is* alive because it is the theatre of this life of the Word," Barth still means his description of a dead, Word-less Christianity to apply more than theoretically. All of Christianity's pious, well-meaning, even zealous efforts to be obedient to the Word of God but which restrict its freedom, even if only by trying to close the canon or make normative an exegesis of a biblical passage, amount to an exchange of life for death. The Catholicism and Neo-Protestantism of Barth's day are to him exactly such living dead,

---

95. I.2.683-684. This gives the practice of exegesis a radically Alexandrian, charismatic, "from above" direction: "What we call the investigation of Holy Scripture and its results is not at bottom our efforts and their conclusions, of which we usually think in this connexion, but rather the self-initiating movements of the Word of God Himself." History of exegesis "is quite inexplicable apart from the initiative which proceeded and still proceeds from the Bible itself." There emphatically *is* a text!

whose only hope for a return to life lies in their return to the radical freedom of the Word. God's Word is always prophetic, even to his own Church. His divine action in Scripture is not something the Church can effect itself, or possess on its own. The Bible is an eschatological document, and an ecclesiological one as well, and Barth's pneumatology of Scripture gives powerful explanations for how both of these qualities inform each other.

A last aspect of the pneumatic aspect of Scripture concerns its interpretation for others. A consequence of the freedom of the Word, of the Spirit's necessary role in biblical construction and interpretation, is illumination: the need to pray that God reveal anew through his written Word. Human understanding of God's revelation is "not a secure possession, or a merit, but a gift from the divine mercy, continually to be received as such, and only as such" (I.2.697). Nor is this merely a once-for-all gift. It is always on loan, radically contingent upon the Son's and Spirit's action.[96] A suggestive parallel here, following the analogy of the Lord's Supper proposed by Barth at the beginning of §4 but left undeveloped (and later abandoned), is the Spirit's *epiclēsis* at the Eucharist.[97] Prayer before and after proclamation, which amounts to interpretation in Reformed practice, is standard practice in Reformed worship. The Church can never assume God will work through a sermon or become present at the Lord's Supper, let alone force God to act. But through its faith in God's trustworthiness to fulfill his promise, "You will be my witnesses" and "I will be with you always" (I.2.671), the Church is right to believe and expect God will ever again become present through his Word.

Ernst Käsemann: Tradition over tradition

Lutheranism's fundamentally different appreciation of the canon produces a fundamentally different appreciation of Scripture's relationship to tradition. On the one hand, Luther's indifference towards *adiaphora* produces in Lutheranism a milder critique of Tradition, tradition, and traditions. These are innocuous as long as they do not interfere with the Gospel. On the other hand, the radical priority of the Gospel understood as Justification by Grace Through Faith can produce in Lutheranism a critique of even canonical Scriptures, wherever their traditions do not champion the article on which

96. "The Word of God comes to us only by the miraculous work of the Son and of the Holy Ghost" (I.2.701). "True interpretation and application of the divine Word is a real event . . ." (I.2.710).

97. The accompaniment of baptism in the Holy Spirit at one's baptism is analogous as well.

Luther's Church stands or falls. After all, they are creations of the Church![98] "What does not teach Christ is not apostolic, not even if taught by Peter or Paul," Luther writes in his preface to James. "On the other hand, what does preach Christ is apostolic, even if Judas, Annas, Pilate or Herod does it."[99] The result is a hierarchy within a canon, not (as commonly supposed) a "canon within the canon."[100] The latter phrase confuses the Reformed and Lutheran ideas of canonicity, which differ. Luther's criterion for apostolicity (which is not a criterion for canonicity) produces both traditions apparently unrelated to the Gospel, and a tradition prior to and potentially critical of Scripture. This drives a very different "two-source" picture from either the "one-source" visions of both Staniloae and Barth, or the "two-source" picture in Roman Catholicism.

The rise of the Enlightenment, a stepchild of the Reformation, gave rise to modern historical criticism. The practice of historical criticism takes a distinctive shape in the modern Lutheran tradition. While Barth embraces it formally but rarely puts it to constructive use except to stress God's sovereignty, modern Lutherans like Ernst Käsemann radically direct it at the canon in order to free the authentic divine voice within it. Luther, who "allegorized everything" as a Catholic monk, came to see in Scripture "one simple, solid [historical] sense."[101] In the spirit of Luther, Käsemann follows F. C. Baur, who put historical-critical principles to work in the service of differentiating "early Christianity" (that is, the Church's experience of Justification by Grace Through Faith) and "early Catholicism," its cultural accretions that are widely found even in the New Testament itself and that even there threaten to drown out the Gospel.[102] "Not everything that is in the Bible,"

---

98. Paul R. Hinlicky, "The Lutheran Dilemma," in *Pro Ecclesia* 8, no. 4 (Fall 1999): 393.

99. "Preface to the Epistles of St. James and St. Jude," in John Dillenberger, ed., *Martin Luther: Selections from His Writings* (New York: Doubleday, 1962), p. 36.

100. In the first edition to his preface to the New Testament, Luther speaks of a New Testament hierarchy with John at the top, followed by the Pauline Epistles and 1 Peter, then the synoptics, with James singled out as an "epistle of straw" by comparison, "because it contains nothing evangelical" (Dillenberger, ed., *Martin Luther*, pp. 18-19). Luther's New Testament table of contents (and later, Tyndale's) numbered 23 letters, and then — after a line to set them apart — listed Hebrews, James, Jude, and Revelation. F. F. Bruce, *The Canon of Scripture* (Downers Grove, Ill.: InterVarsity, 1988), pp. 243-46. Karlstadt had his own hierarchy (p. 245).

101. Martin Luther, *Tischreden*, Weimar edition, 1:136, quoted in Robert M. Grant and David Tracy, *A Short History of the Interpretation of the Bible*, 2nd ed. (Philadelphia: Fortress, 1984), p. 94.

102. Cf. Grant and Tracy, *A Short History*, p. 112. For Käsemann as a methodological disciple of Luther, see Käsemann, *New Testament Questions*, p. 274.

says Käsemann, "is God's Word. . . . The Bible . . . is only holy when, and to the extent that, the Lord speaks out of it, the Lord who does not allow himself to be taken possession of like a piece of loot."[103] To Käsemann, historical criticism's fruitful use in Christianity proves the Enlightenment to be a legitimate heir to the Reformation spirit and gives him confidence that its errors are self-correcting.[104]

Paul R. Hinlicky accuses Käsemann, Rudolf Bultmann, and other "radical Lutherans" of wielding criticism against tradition and the Church themselves.[105] But for Käsemann the work of discerning God's Word within the words of Scripture does not undermine the Church's canonical practice. In fact it honors the canon, in the same spirit that Matthew and Luke honor the Gospel of Mark by revising it, and the Bible's Christian scribes expressed their respect for Holy Scripture by glossing the texts with which they were entrusted.[106] The dialectical relationship between Christian Tradition and Lutheran tradition mirrors a dialectical relationship between Scripture and the Gospel.

In Barth, God's sovereignty finds expression in the eternal open-endedness of the canon: in its debated boundaries, its competing translations, and its unpredictability. This is true in a different way in Lutheranism. According to Käsemann, God's sovereignty finds expression in the canon's incoherent diversity. As simply a conglomeration of historical movements in the early Christian communities, as a collection of wheat and tares, the canon has no intrinsic unity. It can be neither the reflection nor the foundation of the Church's unity,[107] but only of Christianity in its concrete historical forms — that is, of the churches' diversities.[108] Scripture offers not one vision of the eternal Church but a series of incompatible ecclesiologies, each attempting to compensate for a Lord who left no "organizationally apprehensible and

103. Käsemann, *New Testament Questions,* p. 273.

104. Käsemann, *Essays on New Testament Themes* (Philadelphia: Fortress, 1982), p. 56.

105. Hinlicky, "The Lutheran Dilemma," pp. 392-93.

106. Ernst Käsemann, "Is the Gospel Objective?" in *Essays on New Testament Themes,* p. 54. Note that Käsemann and Ehrman each appreciate the tradition of biblical reproduction through the practice of historical criticism.

107. See "The Canon of the New Testament and the Unity of the Church," in Käsemann, *Essays on New Testament Themes,* pp. 95ff. Note that Käsemann begins his refutation of the canon's ecclesial unity with an analysis of the diversity of the Gospels. Bauckham takes the same data to understand the Gospels' intertextuality in terms of the catholic unity of the Church. Regardless of the authorial intentions of the Gospel writers, the Church at Rome and elsewhere preserved and read all the Gospels as testifying to a common Lord in a common community.

108. Käsemann, *New Testament Questions,* p. 275.

clearly defined" ecclesiology of his own.[109] Its many positions can only be the source of diversity and strife among the Christian communities.[110]

Therefore, to build an ecclesiology of Scripture that accords with the entire canon is to mistake the historical phenomenon of Christianity for the Church of Jesus Christ. Nevertheless, succumbing to the temptation to locate the source of God's authority somewhere on earth has led to innumerable failed experiments in relating God, Scripture, and tradition.

The most common form of bibliological error is of course early Catholicism,[111] the ecclesial "Esau" that idolizes Christian tradition itself. Early Catholicism was the primitive Church's response to the Gnostic threat. Beginning with Luke, it replaced eschatology with salvation-history and the *theologia crucis* with a *theologia gloriae,* in order to turn institutional Christianity into the ark of salvation.[112] Early Catholicism managed to prevail over its foe — but at the expense of the Gospel itself. With the catholic Epistles, says Käsemann,

> we have reached a stage when it is not enough for the Spirit to be effective in and through the process of tradition: the Spirit is now dissolved *into* tradition. The *ecclesia docens* has now acquired proprietary rights over the 'Spirit of Ministry'. Every unauthorized exegesis and interpretation of Scripture can now be prohibited; the *locus classicus* for this is II Peter 1.20. Ordination is now the expression of a principle of legitimacy and succession. In short, we have now crossed the border out of primitive Christianity and laid the foundations of early Catholicism. The time when it was possible to set up Scripture in its totality in its opposition to Catholicism has gone beyond recall.[113]

Yet there is *in* the canon the buried treasure of the Gospel itself — not *simply* an affirmation of God's Trinity or Christ's divine humanity, but a call to faith in God's work on behalf of sinners.[114] And its urgent voice drives

---

109. "Unity and Multiplicity in the New Testament Doctrine of the Church," Käsemann, *New Testament Questions*, pp. 252-59, quoted from p. 252.

110. Käsemann, *Essays on New Testament Themes*, p. 103. He offers as examples Luther's "quite right" discarding of James's theology; Paul's apostleship in Acts compared to that in Galatians; the eschatology of John and the eschatology of Revelation; and the "early Catholicism" of 2 Peter and charismatic Pauline ecclesiology (pp. 102-3).

111. See Käsemann's footnote to "Paul and Early Catholicism," in *New Testament Questions*, pp. 236-37, for an explanation of the term as he understands it.

112. Käsemann, *New Testament Questions*, pp. 21-22.

113. Käsemann, *Essays on New Testament Themes*, p. 103.

114. This helps explain how Luther can marginalize Hebrews, with its high Christol-

Christians to seek it within the Bible, testing Scripture's spirits in order to distinguish its authentic *bath qol* from its false prophets. "Only to such an attitude can the Word of God reveal itself in Scripture; and that Word, as biblical criticism makes plain, has no existence in the realm of the objective — that is, outside our act of decision."[115]

Ironically, Protestant Christianity has taken the same wrong turn as New Testament-era early Catholicism.[116] By identifying Scripture *itself* as the Church's ultimate authority, rather than God's Word spoken out of Scripture, the Protestant movement has yielded to another human institution and has fallen prey to another form of Catholic idolatry. By mistaking Tradition for tradition and letter for Spirit, they have surrendered to their own "defeated adversary" of Catholicism![117] For Käsemann, all forms of biblicism turn Scripture into a "reliquary," a source of superstition and bondage rather than of faith and freedom.[118] They leave God's Word a prisoner in his own medium.

Thus no authentically Christian theological or ecclesial system, even an ostensibly Protestant one, "can be based on the canon as such. Those who seek to maintain the identification of the canon with the Gospel are delivering Christendom over to syncretism, or, on the other wing, to the hopeless

---

ogy, along with James. While Hinlicky may accurately accuse Bultmann of undercutting the crucial Christological content of the *kerygma,* he unfairly accuses all "contemporary 'radical' Lutherans" of the same program ("The Lutheran Dilemma," p. 404).

115. Käsemann, *Essays on New Testament Themes,* p. 58.

116. Indeed, Hinlicky accuses Protestant orthodoxy of following *Trent* in affirming miraculous verbal dictation in biblical inspiration, while rejecting the role of ecclesiastical tradition in biblical interpretation. This set Protestantism on an incoherent trajectory, as well as a betrayal of the living Jesus' authority in the community, that inevitably self-destructed (pp. 394-98). Placing the wrong turn in later Catholicism allows Heiko Oberman to call Luther's doctrine of tradition a *return* to patristic tradition against the innovations of the medieval Latin West. What makes Käsemann more radically "Lutheran," then, is his rooting of the problem already in the New Testament-era Church rather than in medieval developments. See "Quo Vadis, Petre? Tradition from Irenaeus to Humani Generis," in Heiko Oberman, *The Dawn of the Reformation: Essays in Late Medieval and Early Reformation Thought* (Edinburgh: T. & T. Clark, 1986), p. 270, quoted in Hinlicky, "The Lutheran Dilemma," p. 399.

117. Käsemann, *Essays on New Testament Themes,* pp. 55, 62. Hinlicky distinguishes radical, anti-Church Lutherans like Käsemann from Luther, saying that "Luther's criticism is better called canonical than historical, since it is not based on a critically reconstructed history which tests the scriptural text, but on a christological-salvation history construal of the biblical narrative as a canonical whole" ("The Lutheran Dilemma," p. 393). But this appears to misunderstand Käsemann, for whom historical criticism is a new means of retrieving the authentic gospel of salvation history by faith, rather than a tool of objectivity.

118. Käsemann, *New Testament Questions,* pp. 264, 272.

conflict between the Confessions."[119] The false unity of both Catholic and biblicistic Christianity is the false objectivity of docetism.[120] It has directed Christians towards pious otherworldliness rather than to the world into which they are being called.[121] The Gospel, understood in terms of the faithful believer rather than the historian, is "the sole foundation of the one Church at all times and in all places."[122] Therefore the New Quest for the Historical Jesus is for Käsemann *pure* Christian tradition, which belongs over against both static orthodoxy and the false objectivity of the Enlightenment as the authentic modern expression of risk-taking Christian faith.[123]

The Christian Bible is (lowercase "t") tradition, and for Käsemann kerygmatic tradition always stands over and questions Tradition, so that Tradition may help the Church to hear the divine address that always comes from beyond it. Biblical criticism, modern as well as premodern, is the lifeblood of tradition.[124] Like Luther, Käsemann grounds it firmly in both Christology and soteriology.[125] (This makes his biblical criticism more theologically consistent and ecclesiologically coherent than Barr's.) The Christian practice of historical criticism fractures the Bible, as it fractures the Church. But this fracture is constructive, allowing the *kerygma* of Justification by Grace Through Faith to emerge from the text. It cuts away the Old Testament Law, the *Haustafeln* and other New Testament law, and the other clutter of early catholicism that crowd out and choke the voice of the *kerygma*. Through the practice of historical criticism, the Church gathers and learns to discern its shepherd's voice. Paradoxically, it allows a community to stand under the Word as the community's very creator, rather than to stand atop the Word as its possession and platform.[126] As for Barth, so for Käsemann this obedience to the shepherd's voice is the sole legitimate basis of churchly au-

---

119. Käsemann, *Essays on New Testament Themes*, pp. 56-57.

120. "New Testament Questions of Today," in Käsemann, *New Testament Questions,* p. 9.

121. Käsemann, *New Testament Questions*, pp. 283-85.

122. Käsemann, *Essays on New Testament Themes*, p. 106.

123. Käsemann, *Essays on New Testament Themes*, p. 62.

124. Käsemann's practice thus accords with Robert W. Bertram's argument that Scripture and Tradition are one sequential ecclesial "traditioning" of the gospel, even if he might adopt the polemical Protestant use of "tradition" in fundamentally negative terms. The difference seems semantic rather than essential.

125. Historical criticism is often portrayed as being merely a secular Enlightenment ideology, but in Käsemann it is not. Käsemann baptizes the historical-critical method in the same way that Origen baptized Philo — for Christological reasons and unto soteriological ends.

126. Käsemann, *New Testament Questions*, pp. 264-65.

thority.[127] Only when a community stands under the Word in this way is it the community of Jesus.[128]

James McClendon: Scripture Is tradition

Barth and Käsemann are not the last word on Protestantism. The Reformation cannot neatly be reduced to two camps, Lutheran and Reformed, nor can its visions of the relationship between Scripture and tradition. A third vision, or cluster of visions, exists. However, it is frequently forgotten in such discussions.[129] The Radical Reformation, it is said, adopted Zwingli's radical biblical methodology, and unlike the Calvinist traditions, took it to radical results. On such an account the Radical Reformation's bibliology should be reducible to Calvinism's.

Is it? James McClendon thinks not. He sees a "baptist vision" surfacing throughout Christian history that fundamentally distinguishes itself from the other major Christian ecclesial traditions, including Protestantism. The baptist vision has produced, among other things, the churches of the Radical Reformation, baptist denominations and communities in America, and the Holiness, Pentecostal, and some evangelical traditions in America and around the world. Yet it has largely failed to capture much theological attention, even among its own theologians, who have failed to see the resources that baptist distinctives offer Christian faith and practice.[130]

McClendon takes baptist biblical practice as the point of departure for understanding the distinctiveness of baptist Christianity.[131] "Scripture in [the

127. Käsemann, *New Testament Questions,* p. 258.

128. "Thoughts on the Present Controversy About Scriptural Interpretation," in Käsemann, *New Testament Questions,* pp. 260-85, quoting p. 261.

129. While Kenneth Hagen's typology of confessional biblical practices does widen the usual list to five ecclesial groups, its fifth group is "evangelical" rather than radical. Kenneth Hagen, ed., *The Bible in the Churches: How Various Christians Interpret the Scriptures* (Milwaukee: Marquette University Press, 1998).

130. "The baptists in all their variety and disunity failed to see in their own heritage, their own way of using Scripture, their own communal practices and patterns, *their own guiding vision,* a resource for theology unlike the prevailing scholasticism round about them." James Wm. McClendon Jr., *Systematic Theology,* vol. 1: *Ethics* (Nashville: Abingdon, 1986), p. 26.

131. McClendon names the baptist practice of Scripture "biblicism" (*Ethics,* p. 28), and finds it central to the practices of mission, liberty, discipleship, and community that together identify the [baptist-church] type" (*Ethics,* p. 29; also *Systematic Theology,* vol. 2: *Doctrine* [Nashville: Abingdon, 1994], p. 362).

baptist] vision effects a link between the church of the apostles and our own."[132] The distinctives of baptist Christianity grow from its biblical reading strategies. The performance of Scripture links the present baptist community with both the primitive community and the eschatological community. It overcomes whatever cultural or historical differences separate baptists across time and space, to bring them together under the cross, at each other's feet, and around the banquet table.

So baptist Christianity distinguishes itself from other varieties of Christianity primarily by its view of Scripture's relationship with tradition. Like an Eastern Orthodox icon whose inverted perspective invites the viewer into its scene as a participant, baptist hermeneutics bring all baptist communities into the mutual presence of God's people:

> The church now *is* the primitive church; *we* are Jesus' followers; the commands are addressed directly to *us*. And no rejoinder about the date of Jesus' earthly ministry versus today's date can refute that claim.

The fidelity of McClendon's claim to the baptist vision hangs on the meaning of *is* in the first sentence above. Today's baptist Church is not the *successor* of the primitive Church, nor its *development*, nor even its restoration. This Church is that Church in a "mystical and immediate" sense. The verb performs the strongest possible metaphorical work.[133]

The Church is not only connected mystically and immediately to itself, but the Church's times are extended throughout space and time into every one of its contexts. When Peter tells gathered Jerusalem, "*This is that* which was spoken through the prophet Joel," he is proclaiming the baptist vision. The aftermath of whatever ancient plague Joel was referring to *is* the first Pentecost after Jesus' ascension, when the Holy Spirit has been poured out anew onto God's people. The connection is stronger than even the typological historical vision of Eastern Orthodoxy. It marks out those who see and live by it as baptists — even if they would not recognize themselves as such.[134]

What is the warrant for such a radical collapse of spatial, temporal, de-

---

132. McClendon, *Ethics*, p. 31.

133. McClendon, *Ethics*, p. 33.

134. "My claim in brief is that just such an awareness of the Bible and especially of the New Testament setting in the present situation is characteristic of the baptist vision wherever we find it . . ." (McClendon, *Ethics*, p. 34). In his narrative ethics, McClendon finds it in Jonathan Edwards, perhaps America's most influential Calvinist; Dietrich Bonhoeffer, a Lutheran; and Dorothy Day, a Roman Catholic. One need not be a Baptist to catch the baptist vision. Its power straddles denominations as well as epochs.

nominational, and cultural distance? Scripture itself, or rather the practice of Scripture preserved in the very center of the Old Testament:

> When your son asks you in time to come, "What is the meaning of the testimonies and the statutes and the ordinances which Yahweh our God has commanded you?" then you shall say to your son, "*We* were Pharaoh's slaves in Egypt; and Yahweh brought us out of Egypt with a mighty hand. . . ." (Deut. 6:20-21)

The writers, editors, readers, and hearers of the Pentateuchal material know full well that no one speaking these lines, not even the original celebrants, will not have literally been Hebrew slaves. In fact, the very distance between them and the original Hebrews is precisely the point of the passage.[135] The apparent naïveté of Deuteronomy 6, Acts 2, and postmodern baptist hermeneutics is in fact sheer sacramental power. It rests upon *respect,* not disregard, for the historical and cultural distances that distinguish God's disciples, and God's ability to overcome them by bringing God's peoples into God's timeless presence. The baptist vision of Scripture's role in Christian tradition can be called a robust and sophisticated form of biblicism.[136]

Käsemann's so-called "canon within the canon" is clearly the uncontested Pauline Epistles. Baptist biblicism forbids the idea of a canon within the canon.[137] Nevertheless, the baptist canon has a *center:* the Gospel of Matthew, whose community of disciples *is* the baptist community. True to the Tradition, McClendon picks for his central illustration of baptist hermeneutics Clarence Jordan's *Sermon on the Mount,*[138] which puts the sermon in the terms of 1950s Georgia, obliterating the differences between the two (or more) contexts. Jordan illustrates not one but two hallmarks of baptist biblical practice, one being "this is that" identification, the other being the centrality of Jesus in Scripture and Tradition. Christocentrism (which is hardly the exclusive property of baptists) disciplines baptist reading practices, making the baptist vision a vision of Jesus Christ and not of biblical esoterica.[139]

McClendon's proposal enunciates the baptist vision for his own particular context. Yet it accurately conveys the vision of the Radical Reformation as others have seen it. Consider John Howard Yoder's claim against both contemporary theological ethics and contemporary New Testament studies:

135. McClendon, *Doctrine,* p. 468.
136. McClendon, *Ethics,* p. 29.
137. McClendon, *Doctrine,* p. 477.
138. Clarence Jordan, *Sermon on the Mount,* rev. ed. (Valley Forge, Pa.: Judson, 1970).
139. McClendon, *Doctrine,* p. 468.

> I will attempt to sketch an understanding of Jesus and his ministry of which it might be said that such a Jesus would be *of direct significance* for social ethics. . . . I will secondly state the case for considering Jesus, when thus understood, to be not only relevant but also *normative* for a contemporary Christian social ethic.[140]

In other words, *this is that:* What Jesus says and does applies directly to the ethics of his disciples, no matter how far removed they are from his historical context.

McClendon's and Yoder's projects make stronger use of historical criticism than many early and recent baptists might, but they never use it to undermine the canonical text, as Käsemann does. Their biblicism already implies a more positive appreciation of tradition than Käsemann's, because canonical Scripture is itself Tradition, tradition, and traditions. It is both a product of apostolic tradition and a transmitter of it.[141]

Yet Scripture is not *a* tradition to be placed alongside other authorities; it is *the* authority from which the Church's other authorities derive their authority. Its authority is universal in the Church of Jesus Christ, whereas the Church's other authorities are mere *monuments,* "trail-marks that indicate where the people of God have been on their journey through time. In this sense they tell us how Scripture has been (then and there) read, and invite us to read it that way if we can."[142] McClendon rejects the "two source" account of many Tridentine Catholics to which we will soon turn, in favor of the Reformed (and increasingly Catholic) view that the authority of truly holy tradition is only the authority of Scripture. Likewise, compared to Staniloae's one-source account, McClendon relates Scripture and tradition so asymmetrically that postbiblical tradition becomes merely a series of suggestions. These suggestions are often helpful, but even then only when they are heeded critically. Like other Protestants, he grounds biblical authority in the Bible itself, claiming that the Church's process of canonization was merely an exercise in acknowledging the prior divinity and intertextuality of some of the Church's books, an exercise open in principle to any local church at any time.[143] Indeed, for McClendon the practice of discerning the canon authenticates the *Church* rather than the canon, which needs no human assent to gain its divine voice.[144]

---

140. See John Howard Yoder, *The Politics of Jesus,* 2nd ed. (Grand Rapids: Eerdmans, 1994), p. 11 (emphasis added).

141. McClendon, *Doctrine,* p. 469.

142. McClendon, *Doctrine,* p. 471.

143. McClendon, *Doctrine,* p. 477.

144. McClendon, *Doctrine,* p. 476.

Is this a defensible stance? The radical relativization of all non-scriptural Tradition under Scripture raises a potential problem: *Why* is the Bible the only binding Tradition? Why do the books of Scripture, and only they, speak with such authority? McClendon offers "attributes of Scripture" as unique qualities that reflect the Bible's unique authority. But these qualities — "such attributes as being at once God's own story and a truly human story, as centering upon Jesus Christ, as evoking in their readers the prophetic or baptist vision" — surely belong to more than just biblical writings, and arguably do not all belong to every one of the canonical books! How do these attributes distinguish Esther and Proverbs from the Shepherd of Hermas, the Didache, and 1 and 2 Clement? Catholics might answer back that in fact, the Scriptures owe to Church Tradition not only their formal canonical status, but also their qualities *as* Scripture, that the ancient Church's criteria for canonicity were precisely McClendon's attributes and Barth's internal witness of the Holy Spirit — "a kind of superscripture defining scripture" according to ecclesial expectations of what Scripture looks like.[145] Like all biblicists, whether radical or Calvinist, McClendon is in the unstable position of privileging the Tradition that is Scripture, but not the tradition that created, canonized, and enlivened Scripture.

McClendon's vision at first seems to be Barth's own answer — that Scripture alone impresses itself upon the Church, and the Church can set up no authority even behind Scripture to validate it, save Jesus.[146] Yet the baptist vision actually has more to say about the matter. The fundamental baptist convictions that "this is that" and "then is now" are themselves endorsements of Holy Tradition. To recall McClendon's own example from Deuteronomy 6, the identity effected between Hebrews in Egypt, the Deuteronomist's own communities, and modern-day Jews and Christians is as powerful a process of tradition as the hierarchical apostolic tradition of Orthodoxy and Roman Catholicism. It *hands over* the identity of the people of God to whoever receives it obediently, whenever and wherever they may be. This process of identification is prior to Scripture, in that it is precisely the reason Scripture is created, preserved, and used — because in identifying *this* with *that* and *now* with *then*, God gathers his people from the ends of the earth.

Therefore the Bible's character and work are grounded in tradition — as Chapters 1 and 2 found them grounded in the Tanakh's role in forming Is-

145. Cf. McClendon, *Doctrine*, p. 476.

146. McClendon is consistent here in subjecting even his proposed "attributes of Scripture" to biblical critique, in circular fashion. He will not place the criteria for canonicity in a position prior to the Bible itself, with the exception of the centrality of Jesus: "The Bible is Scripture for us because Jesus Christ makes it so" (*Doctrine*, p. 472).

rael and its Messiah, in Jesus' concrete relationships with Israel's Scriptures, in his pneumatic speech, and in his gift of the Holy Spirit to his disciples and apostles. But because "this is *that*" and "*then* is now," because tradition is eschatological identification, the Bible's character and work are not grounded in tradition in such a way that tradition ever formally gains the upper hand over Scripture itself.[147] In the baptist vision, Scripture is tradition (it identifies its faithful hearers as the Church) and it is Tradition (it describes the Church with which its faithful hearers are identified). The sophisticated primitivism of the baptist vision, neither classically Catholic nor Protestant, finds in its particular form of biblicism its unique own way to relate Scripture and tradition.

Avery Dulles: Is Tradition More Than Scripture?

The Catholic answer is intentionally left until last, because it is as much a response to the sixteenth century as are Protestant answers, and arguably has undergone more development in the centuries since the Reformation era in response to Protestant arguments against it. *Both* Protestants and Catholics confronted and reformed a corrupt medieval Church. Their different responses developed distinct understandings of Tradition. Each in its own way took on what Avery Dulles, following the World Council of Churches at Montreal, quietly calls "the problem of distorting tradition."[148] So the Reformation sets the stage not only for the Protestant account of Scripture and tradition, but the Catholic account as well. We will use Dulles's account of Scripture and tradition in *The Craft of Theology* to represent Roman Catholicism. While Dulles is not a pioneer as John Henry Newman, Yves Congar, or Karl Rahner have been in Catholic thinking about Scripture and tradition, his work better represents post–Vatican II Catholicism, consolidating the work of the pioneers as it has been appreciated in the conciliar documents and practiced in the Church in the years since the council.

Dulles picks up his account before the Council of Trent. Catholics originally answered the Protestant challenge by appealing to the necessity of tradition and its claim to equal respect along with Scripture. Dulles accepts Tavard's classification of their views into three broad camps.[149] The first

---

147. This is not to say that baptist exegetes have always respected the priority of Scripture over their own local traditions!

148. Dulles, *The Craft of Theology*, p. 97.

149. Dulles, *The Craft of Theology*, p. 87, on George Tavard, *Holy Writ or Holy Church* (New York: Harper, 1959).

Dulles calls the "classical" view: All salvific truth is contained explicitly or implicitly in the canon of Scripture. The classical view, dominant in Aquinas, is also the closest to the Orthodox position. The second answer stressed the incompleteness of both Scripture and tradition as sources of revelation, and each one's resulting need for completion by the other. Revelation, they said, is *partly* contained in the canonical Scriptures and *partly* in oral and practical apostolic traditions. The third camp, which we might call the charismatic, held that the Church received new revelation over time through the Holy Spirit who abides in it. Therefore papal and conciliar decisions are binding, whether or not they are apostolic in the historical sense.

Trent judged revelation according to its traditional understanding of apostolicity, rejecting the "charismatic" account of Scripture and tradition for one affirming that the Church's deposit of faith, "received by the Apostles from the mouth of Christ himself, or from the Apostles themselves, the Holy Ghost dictating, [has] come down even unto us, transmitted as it were from hand to hand." Furthermore, Trent seemed to endorse the two-source view over the classical one-source view: "This truth and this discipline are contained in written books and in unwritten tradition," both of which the Church "receives and venerates with an equal affection of piety and reverence."[150]

Basil the Great is in a way responsible for the distinction between *dogmata,* meaning mainly unwritten gestural customs in the churches like the sign of the cross or prayer facing east, and *kerygmata,* the written traditions of Scripture. In his argument for the divinity of the Holy Spirit, he appealed to both, calling them "both sources."[151] *Dogmata* are best understood as practices that, while unwritten, were already normed by Scripture and by the other biblical practices of the Church. So Basil could not have meant a parallel source of doctrine that *stayed* parallel, independent of Scripture's norming influence.[152] In his view, Scripture and tradition are deeply interactive in the life of the Church. He saw the two as one Gospel. Appealing to one without the other would either "mutilate the Gospel" or "reduce the Gospel teachings to bare words."[153]

---

150. "Decree Concerning the Canonical Scriptures," Session 4, in Philip Schaff, *The Creeds of Christendom* (Grand Rapids: Baker, 1990), vol. 2, p. 80.

151. Basil the Great, *On the Holy Spirit* (Crestwood, N.Y.: St. Vladimir's Seminary Press), 27.66, pp. 98-99.

152. Hanson answers the Catholic interpretation of Basil by stressing that "significant, authentic oral tradition had virtually died out by about 250, unable to withstand the influence of the written tradition of the New Testament" ("Tradition," p. 576).

153. Basil, 27.66, pp. 98-99. Abraham maintains that Basil's statement refutes the Protestant claim of a patristic practice of *sola scriptura* (*Canon and Criterion,* pp. 37-38). But

Whatever Basil's original purposes, the distinction took on a life of its own in and after Trent. Like Basil, the council's decree affirms the necessity of tradition for the transmission of biblical revelation. But most of its Catholic and Protestant interpreters understood it to refer to two *distinct, static* apostolic sources of revelation. Such a scheme was perfect for opposing (and equally perfect for affirming) the Reformation's radical one-source account. However, the council was not as clear on the relationship between the two as most of its interpreters thought. In dropping the word "partly" *(partim)* from its final version, the council left ambiguous whether revelation properly has one source or two.

The two-source interpretation of Trent began to decline in popularity as Newman's and others' developmental accounts of dogmatic tradition found ways to respect both the fact of doctrinal development over time, and the supremacy and material sufficiency of primitive (biblical) apostolic revelation to warrant that development. The revolution Newman began was continued by Congar, author of *Tradition and Traditions*. In *Dei Verbum*, of which Congar was principal architect, Vatican II ratified the orthodoxy of the idea that tradition *does,* not only that Tradition *is,* and tried to account for the fact that Catholic doctrine has developed over time.

Vatican II preserved Trent's ambiguity over the objections of the two-source camp, strengthening the growing consensus within Catholicism on the material sufficiency of Scripture. In effect Vatican II's mandate to restore the reading of Scripture as a major element in Catholic piety and theology took Catholic theology in a one-source direction. Like Congar, *Dei Verbum* sees tradition not merely as verbal but also as practical, as a living reality that progresses pneumatically in the Church. While deliberately refusing to repudiate the two-source interpretation of Trent and the material insufficiency of Scripture, it nonetheless leads Roman Catholicism following Vatican II away from the Tridentine era's propositional, objective understanding of "traditions" into the more pneumatological, dynamic appreciation of "tradition" that Dulles himself endorses.[154] So Dulles follows *Dei Verbum* to call tradition "the mode in which the Church perpetuates its faith and its very existence," and "the total life and praxis of the Church."[155] Both Scripture and

---

Basil resorts to unwritten traditions only after appealing to written ones, in part because of the absence of clear biblical and liturgical prooftexts supporting his case. While he may not be practicing the crude form of *sola scriptura* that emerges later in Protestantism, he is practicing *prima scriptura*, which is a more accurate term for both Lutheran and Reformed biblical practices.

154. Dulles, *The Craft of Theology*, p. 94.
155. Dulles, *The Craft of Theology*, pp. 94, 95.

tradition are one Word of God, and both deserve equal respect. As the two work together, *Dei Verbum* explains, "the tradition that comes from the apostles *makes progress* in the Church, with the help of the Holy Spirit."[156]

Dulles endorses the one-source, dynamic interpretation of Trent and *Dei Verbum* not only in the conclusions his historical account reaches, but in its character as a historical account. Dulles reads Catholic history from before Trent to after Vatican II as doctrinal and practical *development* according to *Dei Verbum*'s categories. As many Tridentine Catholics found in the static two-source account of revelation the resources necessary to defend their practices against Protestant critiques, many contemporary Catholics have found in the dynamic one-source account the resources to answer unprecedented historical-critical assaults on their claim that modern Roman Catholic doctrine passes the Vincentian Canon's test, *quod ubique, quod semper, quod ab omnibus creditum est*.[157] Catholicism finds its theological justification in its own history. So history plays a far larger role in Dulles's account than in Staniloae's, Barth's, and even Käsemann's accounts. One might say that with the triumph of Newman's theory of the development of doctrine, the Roman Catholic doctrine of Scripture and tradition has become the Roman Catholic *history* of Scripture and tradition. The Holy Spirit's work has become historicized.[158] The Catholic answer to how the Holy Spirit relates Scripture and tradition is simply the unfolding history of the Church.

This sharply distinguishes the Catholic account from the Orthodox. Staniloae speaks of tradition as *deepening* Tradition precisely to avoid connotations of *Dei Verbum*-style development or progress. Where Staniloae em-

---

156. *Dei Verbum*, 8.

157. While "the problem of the historical Bible" poses the greatest threat to Protestant belief, the real threat for Roman Catholicism is the problem of the historical Church. So Dulles, *The Craft of Theology*, p. 99: "Vatican II's statement on tradition may be welcomed for helping Catholics to account for the dogmatic teaching of their own Church. It liberated them from the burden of feeling obliged to justify all their present beliefs as having come down unchanged from the apostles, or even as being logical deductions from what the apostles had taught. It thus made room for rather striking developments of dogma and practice. As a result of the council, Catholics can now cheerfully admit that some of their dogmas would have been unknown and even unintelligible to Christians of the early centuries. A new dogma such as the Immaculate Conception may emerge in the course of centuries with only the slenderest apostolic warrants and yet be 'traditional' insofar as it is inspired by the Holy Spirit, who remains continuously active in the Church." In other words, the issue of the historical legitimacy of a document like the Donation of Constantine becomes irrelevant when it is viewed in terms of pneumatology rather than historical apostolicity.

158. Cf. Newbigin's criticism of Catholicism: "The fundamental error into which Catholic doctrines of the Church are prone to fall is . . . the error of subordinating the eschatological to the historical" (*The Household of God*, p. 89).

phasizes dynamic *continuity,* Dulles emphasizes *dynamic* continuity. As a result, Dulles's account is both more complex than Staniloae's, and more accommodating toward historical contingencies.

Dulles's greater attention to concrete Church history also incorporates in his account a characteristically Catholic response to both traditions of *adiaphora* and to "the problem of distorting tradition." First, treating tradition in terms of pneumatology rather than simply Tradition and traditions makes possible the "renewal and reform" of Catholic practice that was at the heart of Vatican II.[159] It effectively lets the tradition criticize its own traditions. Ossified medievalism can be jettisoned because tradition equals not traditions, but the life of the Church in the Holy Spirit.[160] Therefore *Dei Verbum* opens up theological room for a Lutheran attitude towards *adiaphora* much harder to find in either classical two-source Catholicism or Eastern Orthodoxy.[161] Second, the very mention of corrupt tradition immediately distinguishes the more realistic tone of Dulles's review from the idealistic tone of Staniloae's Orthodox account. This too is part of the Reformation's legacy. The Orthodox Church acknowledges Apostolic Tradition and *ad hoc* ecumenical councils as resources with which the Church confronts error. But the Catholic model better accommodates the idea that error exists as a chronic problem within the Church itself. As Catholicism has built within its ecclesiology continuing, institutional measures for dealing with sin in the Church — for instance, penance and excommunication — so it has built continuing institutional measures for dealing with distorting tradition in the Church.

The central such institution is, of course, the Magisterium, which is the vicar of the teaching Christ as the priesthood is the vicar of the absolving Christ. "The task of giving an authentic interpretation of the Word of God, whether in its written form or in the form of Tradition, has been entrusted to the living teaching office of the Church alone," *Dei Verbum* 2.10 says. "Its authority in this matter is exercised in the name of Jesus Christ."

The Magisterium represents the center of tradition's dynamic work and the ultimate safeguard against corrupting tradition. For Protestants still nervous about the exclusivity of magisterial authority to interpret Scripture, *Dei Verbum* tries to offer words of reassurance: "Yet this Magisterium is not supe-

---

159. Dulles, *The Craft of Theology,* p. 99.

160. See Dulles, *The Craft of Theology,* pp. 100-101, on both the costs and benefits of this new relativism towards Catholic traditions.

161. Contrast Staniloae, *The Experience of God,* p. 56: "Tradition cannot be changed or rejected, because to change or to reject it would be tantamount to mutilating revelation and its full and authentic application, and this, in turn, would mean a mutilation of the Church."

rior to the Word of God, but is its servant. It teaches only what has been handed on to it. . . . All that it proposes for belief as being divinely revealed is drawn from this single deposit of faith." Of course, Protestants find the confident indicative verbs here anything but reassuring. *Dei Verbum* claims unqualified divine authority for *all* magisterial teaching, by definition, asserting only that the Magisterium never usurps power from its divine trustor. The Church itself is the answer to distorting tradition in the Church, just as the Church itself is the answer to its own sinfulness.[162]

Tradition and Eschaton

The Orthodox, Reformed, Lutheran, Radical, and Catholic accounts of how Scripture and tradition relate differ radically and incompatibly. John Paul II has identified their tensions as the top priority of further study in order that the dream of unity among believers may be realized.[163] But the plurality of proposals has a deeper significance than either the various traditions' distinctives or the barriers to their unity. The following comparison reveals

---

162. Dulles, *The Craft of Theology*, pp. 97-98.

163. *Ut Unum Sint*, paragraph 79 (emphasis added):

"It is already possible to identify the areas in need of fuller study before a true consensus of faith can be achieved: 1) the relationship between Sacred Scripture, as *the highest authority in matters of faith*, and Sacred Tradition, as *indispensable to the interpretation of the Word of God*; 2) the Eucharist, as the Sacrament of the Body and Blood of Christ, an offering of praise to the Father, the sacrificial memorial and Real Presence of Christ and the sanctifying outpouring of the Holy Spirit; 3) Ordination, as a Sacrament, to the threefold ministry of the episcopate, presbyterate and diaconate; 4) the Magisterium of the Church, entrusted to the Pope and the Bishops in communion with him, understood as a responsibility and an authority exercised in the name of Christ for teaching and safeguarding the faith; 5) the Virgin Mary, as Mother of God and Icon of the Church, the spiritual Mother who intercedes for Christ's disciples and for all humanity.

"In this courageous journey towards unity, the transparency and the prudence of faith require us to avoid both false irenicism and indifference to the Church's ordinances. Conversely, that same transparency and prudence urge us to reject a halfhearted commitment to unity and, even more, a prejudicial opposition or a defeatism which tends to see everything in negative terms.

"To uphold a vision of unity which takes account of all the demands of revealed truth does not mean to put a brake on the ecumenical movement. On the contrary, it means preventing it from settling for apparent solutions which would lead to no firm and solid results. The obligation to respect the truth is absolute. Is this not the law of the Gospel?"

ecclesial qualities of Scripture that go unappreciated in any one account alone, and offers a way to understand both the distinctives and the schisms that characterize the earthly body of Christ in terms of the work of Scripture.

It is common, and not unfair, to characterize Protestant ecclesiologies of Scripture in terms of divine transcendence, and the others in terms of divine immanence. For Staniloae and Dulles, the immanence of the incarnate Christ creates an immanent divine presence in the apostolic Tradition, at the center of which is apostolic Scripture; and this both reflects and creates a Church in which God is immanent through the Holy Spirit. For Barth, the transcendence of the ascended Christ creates a momentary divine immanence in the pneumatic event of biblical revelation, which alone momentarily creates a Church in which God otherwise remains transcendent. For Käsemann, God's transcendence is only overcome in the event of the Spirit through the faithful grasp of the Gospel, and neither Spirit nor Gospel can ever be contained in a New Testament canon.[164] Barth's and Käsemann's condemnations of fundamentalism rest in its quest to satisfy the hunger for immanence in a God eternally immanent in the Bible's revelation. (It is harder to characterize baptist bibliology in these terms. McClendon seems at different points more comfortable in each type.)

The category of causality offers another means of comparison. Paul McPartlan's eucharistic ecclesiology characterizes the patristic era by the conviction that "the Eucharist makes the Church," the Scholastic era by the conviction that "the Church makes the Eucharist," and modern Catholicism by a return to the patristic model, under the influence of Henri de Lubac.[165] So we might characterize the differences among these traditions according to the relative emphasis they place on the claims that "the Scripture makes the Church" and that "the Church makes the Scripture."[166] Both assertions are true, of course, and no Christian tradition denies either one. Yet each has a tendency to relate the two differently, and even to champion one over the other. Barth, for instance, famously spends most of *CD* I fighting the Tridentine overemphasis on the Church making the Scripture, by insisting that the Scripture makes the Church. And the course of Vatican II might be said to be a partial vindication of his claim from within Catholicism, or at least a fundamental Catholic rethinking of the lines of causality that run among God, Church, Scripture, and sacrament.

---

164. Käsemann, *Essays on New Testament Themes*, p. 106.

165. Paul McPartlan, *Sacrament of Salvation: An Introduction to Eucharistic Ecclesiology* (Edinburgh: T. & T. Clark, 1995). See especially ch. 3, "The Story of the New People of God: Two Thousand Years in Three Steps," pp. 30-44.

166. Loughlin makes the same claim in *Telling God's Story*, p. 36.

These are helpful ways to characterize the various types. But in follow-ing our eschatological framework for ecclesiology, we shall adopt a different perspective than either one. We begin by characterizing the various traditions explicitly according to their eschatologies. How each party sees tradition de-pends on how each tradition sees the past, present, and future Church in terms of God's eschatological *oikodomē*. On the whole, Orthodox accounts of tradition are more realized, Catholic accounts more inaugurated, Lutherans and Reformed decidedly futurist, and radicals more apocalyptic or dialecti-cal. Such an eschatological typology offers greater promise for appreciating the strengths, weaknesses, differences, and commonalities of each type.

Orthodox

For Staniloae, the Church *has become* the community of the Holy Spirit. There the revelation of Jesus Christ has been perfected.[167] This ecclesial per-fection is a function of the culmination of divine revelation in the finished earthly ministry of the incarnate Son and in the complete outpouring of the Holy Spirit.[168] The Church's experience of God deepens over time, but it does not travel in new directions from its foundation. It is charismatic yet conser-vative, because all it possesses is a gift it has possessed from the beginning. In Orthodoxy we see a "Johannine" Church — a body of Christ that is best de-scribed in the perfect tense.[169] This is no recent innovation in Eastern Ortho-doxy. Chapter 1 found these same characteristics in Athanasius' fourth-century eschatology, where the snowballing triumph of the Savior's doctrine and the declining powers of idols to deceive humanity are proof that Christ is the *logos* and power of God (§55).

167. Cf. Staniloae, *The Experience of God*, pp. 57-58 (emphasis added): "The Holy Spirit continues the revelation of Christ in this direction through the act of bringing the Church into existence and through the practical organization of her structures, that is, through the initial putting of them into practice. It is the same Spirit who afterwards main-tains the Church as a permanent milieu for the effective power of revelation once this has been brought to a close in Christ, or rather *perfected* as both content and way of being put into practice."

168. Staniloae, *The Experience of God*, p. 57.

169. Crucial statements about the Church are rendered in the perfect tense in the Fourth Gospel (*e.g.*, 3:18-19; 5:24; 17:22). But the tendency is pronounced throughout the Gospel. The Nestlé-Aland 27th edition counts 53 perfect verbs in Matthew, 48 in Mark, 61 in Luke, and 205 in John.

Catholic

Every tradition tends to see its own vision as the legitimate expression of *inaugurated* eschatology, since each in its own way appreciates both eschatological fulfillment and eschatological reserve in its present age.[170] Post–Vatican II Catholicism's emphasis on the dynamism of tradition can appropriately be called inaugurated eschatology. (Certainly it is too realized for Protestants, and not realized enough for the Orthodox.) Catholicism appreciates the inauguration of the eschaton in the present-day Church in a particularly Catholic fashion: "As the centuries advance, the Church constantly tends toward the fullness of divine truth, until the words of God reach their consummation in the Church."[171] Newman's ecclesiastical tree born from an apostolic seed is grown, but not yet *fully* grown. Contemporary Catholicism understands itself as rather a "Lukan" Church: one traveling along a trajectory from modest Palestinian origins to the ends of the earth (Acts 1:8; 28:30-31; cf. Luke 13:18-21). The radical changes it experiences over its history fulfill rather than betray its original message (Acts 1:1-2; *Dei Verbum* 5.19) and practice (Acts 2:42; *Dei Verbum* 2.10). Its growth is worldwide, yet normed by its apostolic center (Acts 8:14-17; Acts 15).

Protestant

What to do when the tree needs trimming? If Staniloae and Dulles appreciate the Church at its best, Käsemann and Barth fear the Church at its worst. For them the entire sanctification of the faithful and the full manifestation of the earthly kingdom of God lie profoundly in the future. They offer two versions of a "Markan" Church, elect yet hopelessly compromised, recognizing the *bath qol* in God's Word yet forever missing the point of Christ's actions and words, confessing his Messiahship yet sleeping in his presence and fleeing in his absence. For both Protestant ecclesiologians, the continuing, assured presence of divine revelation in the Church, even in canonical Scripture, is a docetic fantasy. Sinful hermeneutical practices always risk turning Scripture into an eisegeted "wax nose."[172] For Barth, God's presence-in-absence manifests itself precisely as *absence:* an open and flawed canon, a discontinuity be-

---

170. See Wainwright, *Doxology: The Praise of God in Worship, Doctrine, and Life* (New York: Oxford University Press, 1980), pp. 395-97, who applies inaugurated eschatology to describe the Church's relationship with its various wider cultures.

171. *Dei Verbum*, 8.

172. See Nicholas Wolterstorff, *Divine Discourse: Philosophical Reflections on the Claim That God Speaks* (New York: Cambridge University Press, 1995), p. 236.

tween events of divine revelation, a chronic need for human interpreters. Käsemann explicitly ties bibliology to futurist eschatology: "Like the Gospel, the unity of the Church is discerned not by saints already enjoying the beatific vision but by those struggling *in via*" (and by *in via* he means something quite different than either Staniloae or Dulles).[173] The doctrines and practices of Orthodox, Catholics, and Neo-Protestants imply a canon "fallen from heaven," which translates its performers into heaven, for "where on earth should we find a congregation composed only of believers, of those who were obedient, of those instructed purely by God, of the saints?"[174] In other words, they describe a bibliology of realized eschatology:

> The unity of the Church was, is and remains primarily an eschatological property, to be enjoyed only as a gift, never as an assured possession. The unity of the Church cannot be apprehended except by faith which hears the voice of the one Shepherd and obeys his call to form one flock, his flock.... The Church is the kingdom of Christ on earth, and this kingdom is always ahead of our earthly organizations, theologies and devotional practices.[175]

Käsemann explicitly ties the faulty eschatology of the "dubious" 2 Peter in with its early Catholic ecclesiology.[176] The primary distinction between primitive Christianity and early Catholicism, and the primary weakness of the latter, is that the imminent expectation of the former has been discarded in the latter. Early Catholicism represents a betrayal of the Lutheran Paul's *simul iustus et peccator* that dissolves hope into the smug, false assurance of a realized eschaton.[177]

---

173. Käsemann, *Essays on New Testament Themes*, p. 107. This difference was sharply expressed in Käsemann's debate with Raymond E. Brown at the 1963 WCC Congress in Montreal. Brown countered with his findings that a "unity of belief present in all stages of New Testament thought about the Church" can be found, though no straight line of progress towards later Catholic uniformity. See David M. Paton, "A Montreal Diary," in P. C. Rodger and Lukas Vischer, eds., *The Fourth World Conference on Faith and Order: Montreal 1963* (New York: Association Press, 1964), p. 17.

174. Käsemann, *New Testament Questions*, p. 277.

175. Käsemann, *New Testament Questions*, p. 257.

176. Käsemann, *Essays on New Testament Themes*, p. 195.

177. Indeed, all of the New Testament's theological partisans in Käsemann's analysis may be understood according to distinctive eschatologies: "Judaizers" who deny the newness of the *kerygma*, gnostic "enthusiasts" who deny the lingering claims of the present age upon themselves, early Catholics who realize the eschaton in the confines of the institutional Church, and the authentic Paulines and Johannines who appreciate the dialectical nature of kerygmatic Christian existence over against all the other camps. See, among others, "On the Subject of Primitive Christian Apocalyptic," in *New Testament Questions*, pp. 108-37, and

Baptist

Eschatology frames McClendon's entire dogmatics. He begins his theology "at the end," in the eschatological "rule of God" (translating *basileia tou theou*).[178] With Jesus' coming the kingdom is at hand, initiating a new community of "interactive love," membership in which costs one's own life.[179] Scripture plays a role in bringing this eschatological kingdom and its community of hope into the present. Its work of prophetic foreshortening collapses time and distance according to McClendon's dialectical eschatology. The Bible's pictures of the end-times burn themselves into the consciences of disciples and change their lives — not because the end-times remain the province of the future, but because the pictures bring them into the present. Scripture makes real the connection between contemporary "this" and primitive "that," eschatological "then" and contemporary "now" through which the Christian community is built. Its subjects learn to see the present according to both the biblical past and the prophetic future.[180]

So tradition is the baptist vision's connecting work, and Tradition is the baptist community it effects across space and time. Because of the revolutionary, universal, compelling character of the kingdom and its biblical pictures, tradition is neither the life story of a growing tree, nor the smooth continuity of deepening appreciation of God's mysteries, nor the tragic history of the Church's repeated failure. McClendon's eschatology is best described as dialectical, and his Church a "Matthean" fellowship of disciples, blessed with God's enduring presence and entrusted with the awesome power of binding presence-in-absence and loosing, yet subject to cruciform demands and strict discipline.[181]

"Unity and Multiplicity in the New Testament Doctrine of the Church," in *New Testament Questions*, pp. 254-55.

178. McClendon, *Doctrine*, pp. 64ff.

179. McClendon, *Doctrine*, p. 67.

180. McClendon, *Doctrine*, p. 92.

181. This account of Scripture and tradition is also reminiscent of the final chapter of Hays's *Echoes*, as well as his description of Matthew's ethics in *Moral Vision* ch. 4, pp. 93-110. Hays, a charismatic Methodist, calls the Wesleyan dialectic of grace and discipline a Matthean vision. McClendon himself draws out the connection between charismatic and Matthean Christianity from the other side, in claiming Newbigin's Pentecostal type (see below) as the baptist vision by another name (*Doctrine*, pp. 342-44).

Four Traditions, One Tradition?

We have arrived at a fourfold typology of visions of Scripture and tradition that surprisingly resembles the ecclesiological visions of the canonical Gospels.[182] Now one must not overextend the analogy between Gospels and ecclesiologies. Besides, one can offer a threefold (Troeltsch, Newbigin), five-fold (Niebuhr, Hagen), or manifold (Dulles) ecclesiological typology in which the Gospel parallels would no longer be so pronounced. Yet characterizing the various Christian polities in this way reframes the divisive issue of Scripture and tradition. If each vision is rooted in a legitimate vision of Christian life, the usual exercise of defending one camp over against the others becomes far less persuasive. One might as well argue Mark versus Luke![183] The question becomes one of the *interrelationships* of the various visions of tradition — or, if each distinctive vision reflects from valid aspects of the Church's canonical visions, a question of the interrelationships among the various canonical visions of Christian life upon which the separated Christian traditions are built.

To continue with the Gospels analogy, the answer in part reflects the interrelationships among the New Testament writings. Much biblical scholarship assumes that each Gospel is written by a discrete, even isolated community, largely to serve the particular present needs of that community. In this model, differences between Gospels represent differences, even incompatibilities, between Christian traditions. The Matthean and Lukan communities who redacted Mark would have done so to correct its flaws (as they often polish its grammar and nuance its christologically troublesome passages) and change it into Gospels truly their own. Therefore there would not necessarily be any fundamental compatibility or commensurability among these communities. Their intertextuality within the context of the canon would have been an imposition of the later, "catholic" Church. Furthermore, such an imposition from outside the texts themselves might well have introduced insoluble problems of how their theologies, hermeneutics, and polities can be reconciled. Insofar as today's Christian traditions faithfully follow the ecclesial visions of these original witnesses, the chronic schism their different tendencies has brought the Catholic Church would thus be canonically warranted

---

182. In defense of this typology, its resemblance to the Gospels came as a surprise emerging at the conclusion of the study rather than being planned (or forced) from its outset.

183. Käsemann, of course, would welcome such an exercise, and privilege Mark over the "early Catholic" Luke-Acts.

(just as Käsemann claims). There would be no escaping the dividedness of the Bible-believing churches.

On the other hand, if Bauckham and his fellow writers (and indeed, the early Christian Church) are right that the Gospels were written for the Church at large rather than simply for isolated communities, and were even intentionally intertextual from the outset, their interrelationship looks quite different. John, for instance, would not have been written to contradict or correct Mark, but to complement it for a readership already familiar with the first Gospel, not unlike the way 1 and 2 Chronicles would have been written for a readership familiar with 1 and 2 Kings and respectful of its authority.[184] The Gospels and their distinctives would have been committed to writing precisely for the purpose of the needs of the wider Church. In this case, the Gospels (and by analogy, the different ecclesiological tendencies of the various Christian traditions) would be intended to work together in the catholic Church, not to pit one community over against the others as "the one true Church." Literary dependence would be a sign of ecclesial dependence. In respecting the overall validity of other Gospels (not to mention the Pauline and catholic Epistles, many of which would already have been circulating widely), all these traditions would be respecting the overall truth of every Gospel's distinctive eschatological and ecclesiological vision. Formal canonicity would then not be an "early Catholic" imposition, but a natural outcome of the broad circulation and acceptance of the various New Testament writings. And to the extent that today's Christian traditions authentically reflect these writings' distinct visions, their ecclesiologies would be mutually supportive and capable of coexistence.

In other words, if there is room within the New Testament-era network of Christian churches for the Christological and ecclesiological distinctions we find in the New Testament writings they created and approved, then the catholicity of the New Testament Church presupposes a degree of political, theological, and hermeneutical diversity that resembles in some way the diversity of the later Church.

Of course, the canon of Scripture does not automatically endorse every subsequent vision of the Church that appeals to one or more of the canonical Gospels, any more than it endorsed every first-century Christology or ecclesiology. To the extent that the polities of the divided traditions deny or

---

184. See "John for Readers of Mark," in Bauckham, ed., *The Gospels for All Christians,* pp. 147-71. Bauckham argues for this reading of John (p. 170), while allowing that on a few particular details John may be correcting Mark (for instance, on the relative chronology of the Temple disturbance [p. 159]).

compromise what is true in the others, rather than simply affirming what is true in themselves, they compromise the implicit and explicit intertextuality of their own witness, and open themselves to critiques from themselves and the others.

Therefore, what seems at first to be an accommodating attitude towards the ecclesiological *status quo* is in fact a thorough critique of practically every Church polity. For most, if not all, of the Church's later ecclesiologies seem to fall short of the canonical picture, especially in their inability to honor what their rivals are best at honoring. In either their overexclusivity or in their underqualified pluralism, they miss the canon's delicate dialectic of diverse unity. And insofar as they cannot accommodate the full range of Scripture's work, they need fundamental correction.[185]

Of course, the canon does not proscribe particular churches from *preferring* one vision over others, so long as they remain open to legitimate alternatives. In canonizing multiple Gospel visions of Jesus and Christian community, *and refusing* to adopt a harmony like the *Diatessaron,* Christian churches thereby not only authorize but even commit themselves to political and theological diversity and favoritism among their communities.[186] Scripture offers both a permanent ground for the unity of Christ's assembled disciples, and a permanent ground for their diversity. It is a dialectic (but not a harmonization) of eschatologies — a synopsis of Gospels, so to speak — that best represents the relationship between Scripture and tradition, with all its built-in tensions, and the Bible's different roles as the Church's authority.

Thus there can be no simple answer to the question of Scripture and tradition. Indeed, it misleads even to speak of "Scripture" and "tradition" in the abstract, for Scripture is itself tradition (in all its dimensions), and neither is a monolithic institution. In a "Markan" church (*e.g.*, in a church

---

185. Cf. Lesslie Newbigin's complaint that the Protestant and Catholic traditions are wrong in denying the validity of the others' claims, and that their mutual exclusivity has led them each to a model of the Church "which can be identified by purely natural standards and categories" (*The Household of God,* p. 103). Newbigin might have quoted the passage from 1 Cor. that we have already cited: "For while there is jealousy and strife among you, are you not of the flesh, and behaving like ordinary humans? For when one says, 'I belong to Paul,' and another, 'I belong to Apollos,' are you not merely humans?" (1 Cor. 3:3-4).

186. Again, cf. Newbigin on the estranged ecclesiological traditions: "Each body is compelled to regard what it holds as of the *esse* of the Church. Yet no body can admit that what others hold apart from it, is of the *esse* of the Church, for that would destroy its own claim to be the Church. We are drawn to one another by a real working of the Holy Spirit which we dare not resist, but we are prevented from accepting one another as Churches by loyalty to the very truth upon which our existence as Churches seems to stand" (*The Household of God,* p. 123).

during Year B of the Revised Common Lectionary cycle), different Scriptures play different roles. Some establish Church traditions, others defend them, others critique and destroy them. Some loom large, others are silent. Some are used well, some are merely used, others may be abused. The same is true of a "Matthean" church — but in different ways, for there the various Scriptures play somewhat different roles (which by analogy could correspond to Matthew's distinctive hermeneutics of the Old Testament). Like a Swiss Army knife, the Bible offers a variety of resources for use in a variety of different settings. One day a sharp blade may be called for (Heb. 4:12), another day (Sunday morning?) a corkscrew. In the garage, some tools are in high demand; in the kitchen, others. If one of its tools can work adequately in a context for which it was not apparently intended, so much the better, for the value of a Swiss Army knife is its versatility. The point of its individual tools is to do the work of the owner, not simply according to the purposes for which each tool was originally designed, but according to the occasion and the owner's will. In Wittgensteinian terms, meaning is use. In Augustinian terms, the *telos* of Scripture is charity, and it finds innumerable ways to achieve its *telos*. In Pauline terms, the point of interpretation is the edification of God's *oikodomē*, however it happens.

Recalling Fishbane's categories of *traditum* and *traditio* in inner-biblical exegesis,[187] the relationship among *traditum, traditio,* and *tradent* reflects the relationship among Jesus Christ, the Church, and the Holy Spirit. The indwelt Church *is* the body of Christ, as Tradition *is* Scripture (1 Cor. 12:12). But Christ is also the body's head and its judge, and the content of Scripture. So Scripture critiques and norms Tradition, sometimes massively, as the Lord calls the Church to account for its own sins. Thus to build up the body of Christ (Eph. 4:11-16), sometimes inspired Scripture assumes the role of the head, speaking prophetically (as Protestants are fond of affirming[188]). Other times it assumes the role of the body itself, speaking responsively and intercessorily from within the midst of the faithful (as Catholics and Orthodox tend to stress[189]). Always it shapes communities into the primitive and final form of Christ (as baptists claim). Tradition sometimes preserves continuity with the apostolic witnesses; other times it brings a freshness to the witnesses; and still others it returns to the witnesses to refresh and criticize particular traditions. All these relationships *together* are constitutive of Scrip-

187. See Michael Fishbane, *Biblical Interpretation in Ancient Israel* (Oxford: Clarendon, 1985), p. 6.

188. See Käsemann, *New Testament Questions,* pp. 245ff., and especially p. 258.

189. For instance, in the bold Catholic claim that the Church is "the extension of the incarnation."

ture's status as the Church's Scripture.[190] They reflect the three strands of the divided Church that Newbigin brings out in his typology, and they depend on each other for their value in building up the body, as Newbigin's Catholic, Pentecostal, and Protestant types ultimately require and replicate each other's resources.[191] Scripture must be understood as both a manifestation and a means of the Church's organic unity. At the same time, it must critique the Church to which it is entrusted, as a manifestation and means of its brokenness. And the open-endedness of biblical interpretation in the Church *("tolle, lege")* respects the mysterious "Pentecostal" role of Scripture as evidence and agent of the powerful and sovereign Holy Spirit in guiding the Church into all truth and making all things new.

The coexistence of these different functions of Scripture in the life of the Church produces a complex ecclesiology that does not reduce neatly to one or another ecclesiological type. Disciples need Roman Catholic creativity and stability, as well as Orthodox continuity, analogical discipline, and aesthetics, as well as evangelical and radical respect for Scripture's power to critique, renew, and reform. The Church has rarely if ever attained more than a shadow of such a life-giving combination. When some of these functions of Scripture capture others, as they typically have in the Church's history, the resulting reductionism destroys the dialectic that enlivens and revives the Church. It fractures the delicate unity of Christ's maturing body. The Bible's building-up becomes a merely human tearing-down.

Tradition and Translation

It is under the heading of Scripture and tradition that we can appreciate the theological significance of textual and interpretive tradition in the Church. Ehrman's study of the relationship between scribal corruptions of New Testament manuscripts and the early Church's theological controversies illustrates the point well. The preservation of biblical texts is as much an exercise in tradition as preaching is. Both are new interpretations of canonical texts. The

190. Cf. Fishbane on inner-biblical exegesis within the Tanakh: "the older *traditum* is dependent upon the *traditio* for its ongoing life. The matter is paradoxical, for while the *traditio* culturally revitalizes the *traditum*, and gives new strength to the original revelation, it also potentially undermines it" (*Biblical Interpretation*, p. 15). "The inner-biblical dynamic of *traditum-traditio* is thus culturally constitutive and regenerative in the most profound sense" (p. 18).

191. Newbigin admits that his typology excludes Eastern Orthodoxy (*The Household of God*, p. xii).

very act of copying a text for oneself or for another is a handing down in space and time. Even an "exact" duplicate subtly changes both the status of the text (when it is appreciated as the common property of the various manuscripts) and the relationship between the text and those who receive it. Yet neither today nor in the Church's first centuries have the original New Testament texts ever been exactly duplicated.[192] Changes are wrought in the writing surface employed, calligraphy, versification, entitlement,[193] arrangement in codices,[194] and of course in textual variations introduced both accidentally and deliberately, by both orthodox and heterodox scribes and printers. The act of translating Scripture into a new language (or even of updating it as a culture's language evolves) is more obvious as an instance of tradition, but it is not a qualitatively different process than simple textual transmission.

Therefore the same tests that apply to the Church's other biblical practices — preaching, hymnody, prayer, and doctrine — apply to the duplication and translation of the biblical texts themselves. In every case, Scripture stands over the copyists and translators, and judges their efforts. In every case, the Bible's meaning may be conserved, or changed, or betrayed, or all of these at once. Because of this there can be no simple preference of textual primitiveness over textual emendation, or vice versa — even in the name of the Bible's "apostolicity" or "catholicity." The modern critical text is a tradition, and so is the Byzantine Majority text. The Masoretic Text, Septuagint, Vulgate, and King James are equally all textual traditions. The various Christian churches will tend to value some over others according to their eschatologies and ecclesiologies: Catholicism and Orthodoxy the scribal paraphrases and received translations that have taken root in the Church's practice, radical and magisterial Protestantism the critical texts and ancient languages that have critiqued abusive Church practices. These preferences arise from and reflect the theological, soteriological, ecclesiological, and eschatological categories of each tradition's bibliologies. The question of which texts and textual practices are privileged over which will inevitably appeal to them. (It is, however, both significant and discouraging how rarely the status of a particular text is defended with respect to its roles in the history of salvation that begins in Israel, *and* climaxes in the earthly life of Jesus, *and* continues in the Spirit-indwelt Church. Usually the appeal is to an abstract primitivism or developmentalism.)[195]

---

192. Ehrman, *Corruption of Scripture*, p. 27.

193. See Brevard Childs, "Psalm Titles in Midrashic Exegesis," *Journal of Semitic Studies* 16 (1971): 137-50.

194. See Graham Stanton, *Gospel Truth? New Light on Jesus and the Gospels* (Valley Forge, Pa.: Trinity Press International, 1995) on the codices of the Gospels.

195. In this analysis, the absence of direct relationships between Jesus and the

The effect of these appeals can, of course, be further division among the churches. It generally has been. But the Gospels analogy again suggests potential for a more inclusive attitude towards the churches' various textual traditions. The correlations between textual preferences, eschatologies, and the Gospels' ecclesial visions (not to mention the New Testament writers' different preferences for the MT, LXX, or their own translations of the Tanakh) suggest that a more theologically consistent outcome should be the growing ecumenical cooperation that has created many of the stronger biblical editions and translations that have emerged in the past century. These have improved relationships among the denominations, destabilized theological positions that had long polarized denominations, offered scholars and churches biblical texts of unprecedentedly high quality, and helped reform both the Protestant and Catholic lectionaries.[196]

Our long exploration of the relationships between the one, holy, catholic, apostolic Church, and its one, holy, catholic, and apostolic canon has yielded a picture that resembles the Christian canon's own diversity. The Bible confers and reflects both the divine and the human characteristics of Jesus Christ's communities. Its roles in the Church are as manifold as the gifts of the Holy Spirit. They cannot be reduced to one tradition's theological ac-

---

deuterocanonical/apocryphal writings yields a much weaker account of these writings. They were not Jesus' canon; nor were they the product of his apostolic Church. On the other hand, they enjoyed real relationships with both Israel and Church. The New Testament alludes to them, though without quoting them directly. Furthermore, the New Testament writers frequently rely on the LXX. Together, these call for more than flat rejection of their inspiration and authority. Their ambiguous and tenuous second-tier status within Scripture is theologically justifiable.

196. Countless recent translations of Scripture and even the United Bible Societies' *Greek New Testament* are evidence of the improvement in both the quality of Bibles available to the churches, and the relationships among those churches as denominations have cooperated to reproduce their common Scriptures. Not least among these are translations of Scripture in and for missionary environments. Lamin Sanneh finds Scripture in the vernacular tongues of Africa to have helped overcome many denominational differences that divided African missionaries. He quotes Tom Beetham as saying, "What has brought Protestant missions together more than anything else has been the fellowship in the work of translation of the Bible," and extends Beetham's insights to the increasing cooperation between Catholics and Protestants in missionary biblical practice. See Lamin Sanneh, *Translating the Message: The Missionary Impact on Culture* (Maryknoll, N.Y.: Orbis, 1989), p. 168, quoting T. A. Beetham, *Christianity and the New Africa* (New York: Praeger, 1967), pp. 55-56. For a discussion of the effect of denominationalism and ecumenical cooperation on the status of the Apocrypha in Bible editions, see Meurer, ed., *The Apocrypha in Ecumenical Perspective*, and in particular William Gundert, "The Bible Societies and the Deuterocanonical Writings," pp. 134-50.

count any more than the Gospel can be reduced to any one of its canonical enunciations. They finally lead us back to a now-thickened version of the same affirmation with which we started: That as a means through which God descends and the Church ascends into each other's loving presence, Scripture confers the Church's ecclesial qualities to those who lack them, and reflects these qualities in those who have received them and made them their own.

IV. Glorify God and Enjoy Him Forever: The End of Scripture

Scripture as Worship Leader

The discussion of Scripture and tradition has moved among the categories of ecclesiology, eschatology, and liturgy. These are appropriate combinations, since the gathered Church's worship practice is both constitutive of the various roles of Scriptures in the life of the Church and their most visible context.[197]

Every aspect of humanity's relationship with God's words has its fundamental application in worship. God's people use God's written words to worship at Sinai, at the tabernacle, in the Temple, in the synagogue, in the city and in the home, in Jesus' worship practice, and in the worship of his disciples.[198] Each section of this chapter has a fundamental application in the worship life of the Church. The gathering of the eschatological *ekklēsia* is symbolized in the regular gathering of local churches around the pulpit and table. The unity, holiness, catholicity, and apostolicity of the Christian Bible are revealed in macrocosm in the Church's tradition, *i.e.*, in the perpetuation, new creation, and reform of Christian Tradition and traditions. In microcosm, they are revealed centrally in the local churches' corporate worship.[199]

Seen from either perspective, Scripture manifests its divine-human

197. See Wainwright, *Doxology*, chs. 5 ("Scripture") and 6 ("Creeds and Hymns"). Wainwright summarizes his own exercise as an exploration of "the presence of the liturgy in the scriptures" and "the presence of the scriptures in the liturgy" (p. 150).

198. Old's history of the Bible's role in worship beautifully chronicles "the roots of the Christian Ministry of the Word" from ancient Israel to the New Testament era, particularly as it informs Reformed biblical practice and theology (*The Reading and the Preaching of the Scriptures in the Worship of the Church*, vol. 1: *The Biblical Period* [Grand Rapids: Eerdmans, 1998], pp. 19-250). In great detail he shows that later Christian biblical practice has deep roots in Hebrew, Israelite, Jewish, and apostolic biblical practice, and the biblical practices of all these groups are fundamentally doxological.

199. For a helpful account of this from a Reformed perspective see "The Search for a Fitting Word," in John P. Burgess, *Why Scripture Matters: Reading the Bible in a Time of Church Conflict* (Louisville: Westminster/John Knox, 1998), pp. 97-119.

qualities in a great variety of ways. In the gathering and gathered Church, Scripture prays, preaches, confesses, intercedes, forgives, remembers, and celebrates.[200] Scripture is the vocabulary of Christian worship, acting in different ways according to its various charismatic powers. In a healthy church's worship language, Scripture showers God with Spirit-driven gratitude. In an ailing Church, its dominical voice disciplines and restores the flock.[201] Remarkably, these different functions generally occur in the same liturgy, evoking something like the complex synopsis of eschatologies suggested above.[202]

Scripture summons the faithful to come. It supplies the metaphors of Christian hymnody. It moves sinners to repentance, offers words of contrition for penitents, assures their graceful pardon, and warns them to sin no more. It is the speech of baptism's and the Eucharist's speech-acts. Its teaching reveals the mysteries of God and God's work. It dismisses the worshipers with a benediction promising that God's words will remain in them and continue to work their grace throughout the time the believers are apart, and will soon regather them anew. In worship, verbal presence is sacramental pres-

200. While this is true of all Scripture, it was longest true of the Psalter. In medieval Europe, laypeople were allowed to voice only the psalms and the breviary (which was mainly psalms) in corporate worship, according to an eighth-century Frankish penitential, and the thirteenth-century Council of Toulouse (William Holladay, *The Psalms Through Three Thousand Years* [Minneapolis: Fortress, 1993], pp. 178-79). Luther expanded greatly on the congregation's hearing and singing of psalms (Holladay, p. 195). Calvin regarded the Psalter as "an anatomy of all the parts of the soul" (p. 196), and later Calvinists strongly appropriated the psalmists' words as the words of the elect (p. 198). Both traditions translated psalms metrically to enhance their use in corporate and personal worship. The Catholic breviary's Psalter became the Anglican Psalter in the *Book of Common Prayer* (p. 218), but liturgical psalms were said in Latin following Trent (pp. 222-24).

201. See Burgess, "The Life of the Church as Commentary on Scripture," in *Why Scripture Matters*, pp. 120-40, on the use and abuse of Scripture in the divided Church.

202. For the Psalms' power to speak for both Church and Christ, see Pius XII's *Mediator Dei*. Balthasar Fischer summarizes the patristic Church's perspective: "The early Church speaks the Psalms about or to Christ, or it hears Christ speak in them." He especially sees a liturgical ladder of divine descent and human ascent in Augustine's *Narrations on the Psalms*. It is there that Augustine hears in the voices of Christ and the Church one greater voice: "Psalmus vox totius Christi, capitis et corporis." See Balthasar Fischer, *Die Psalmen als Stimme der Kirche: Gesammelte Studien zur Christlichen Psalmenfrömmigkeit* (Trier: Paulinus-Verlag, 1982), pp. 22-23.

Thomas Merton claims that "Christ prays in us when we meditate on the Psalms" (*Praying the Psalms* [Collegeville, Minn.: Liturgical Press, 1956], p. 18). Joseph Gelineau's introduction to his translation of the Psalms states that "the psalms, expressing as they do man's attitude before God, find the fullness of their meaning in the new Adam. Henceforth we recognize in Christ the God of the psalms. Henceforth the voice of the psalmist is the voice of Christ" (*The Psalms: A New Translation* [New York: Paulist, 1968], p. 7).

ence, and vice versa. To adapt McPartlan's eucharistic categories again, virtually all ecclesial traditions affirm both the claim that Scripture makes the Eucharist (by supplying the words of institution that make it efficacious), and that Eucharist makes the Scripture (by supplying the context of worship in which the remembering believers hear and speak God's words).[203] A detailed description of even one of the Bible's common liturgical uses — Scripture in the sermon, the hymn, the eucharist, or any of the standard prayers — would be a project unto itself. But we need no extended analysis to establish that Christian worship would be inconceivable without the Bible — and conversely, that the rise, preservation, and canonization of Christian Scripture would have been inconceivable apart from the Bible's use in worship.[204]

This is not to suggest that the Bible is inert outside of the sanctuary! In Jesus' life as in the lives of his predecessors and followers, God's words are powerful wherever they issue: in evangelism, in polemic, in wandering, in war, in literature, in devotion. The Bible's impressive versatility is in line with the eschatological age in which the Church lives, in which God *continues* to build up the body of Christ from the raw materials of the old creation. The Word is effective at both the center and the margins of the eschatological gathering. So it is not surprising that all the Christian traditions (not least my own evangelical Protestantism) have found ingenious uses of Scripture in and out of church.

All of these innumerable biblical practices are ordered towards the common goal of the eschaton: the building up of the body of Christ. The Church receives its canonical heritage, in Abraham's words, "as gifts of the Holy Spirit."[205] They become intelligible according to the *telos* of God's self-involvement in the world, which, as the Westminster Shorter Catechism famously puts it, is for humanity "to glorify God and enjoy him forever." And so it is under the ecclesial end of Scripture that we finally attend to a fundamental dimension of any bibliology, evangelical or not: the Bible's role in the

203. Yet while these various Christian traditions *formally* recognize the mutual dependence of Word and sacrament, their enthusiasm for each varies remarkably. Generally it is one or the other that is made the ultimate criterion for authentic worship. This too is a tendency that can be plotted along an eschatological spectrum: Because Eucharist is a more "realized" moment in the Church's worship than many of the Word's different doxological moments, a eucharistically centered ecclesiology often represents a less futurist vision than a Word-centered ecclesiology.

204. Wainwright, *Doxology*, pp. 151-69, surveys the liturgical elements in the Old Testament, Gospels, Pauline Epistles, catholic Epistles, and Revelation to establish that both testaments of Christian Scripture are occasioned and deeply shaped by the Church's worship practice.

205. Abraham, *Canon and Criterion*, p. 467.

salvation of persons for the eternal glory and worshipful enjoyment of God. The practice of biblical interpretation means to fulfill this end.[206] To guard against the privatization of soteriology in both the Protestant and Catholic traditions, we choose to locate the salvation of persons within the doctrine of the Church that mediates and embodies it. By returning to Augustine's *On Christian Doctrine,* we will frame personal soteriology also within the teleology of salvation that Augustine developed so brilliantly that it has characterized Western theology ever since.

The Voyage Home: Scripture's Role in Personal Salvation

In Chapter 1 we briefly mentioned Augustine's seven steps to holiness through biblical practice. Augustine offers his list in the context of his treatment of textual ambiguities. He claims that these ambiguities are as much a part of the divine teleology of Scripture as its clear passages. The multiple meanings of Scripture are intended and ordered salvifically. His seven steps reveal a profound appreciation of the Bible's divine agency, character, purpose, and work with regard to bringing the lost out of condemnation and into God's full presence. Together they function as an Augustinian *ordo salutis* that was influential in the West long before Protestantism gave the term its technical meaning.

Chapter 1 rooted Scripture in the will of the Father. According to Augustine, Scripture's first job in a sinner's salvation is to impart the simple awareness that God *has* a will, and that the contours of that will are reflected in the Bible's commandments; for "the fear of the Lord is the beginning of wisdom" (Ps. 110:10, etc.). Fear leads to piety, to the humble submission of the sinner's will to the will of the Father (2.7.9). Then comes knowledge, in which "every student of the Divine Scriptures must exercise himself, having found nothing in them except, first, that God is to be loved for himself, and his neighbor for the sake of God." So Scripture reveals God's overriding purpose of love. This unveiling convicts the student of Scripture of his inordinate love for the world's temporalities, "a love far remote from the kind of love of God and of our neighbor which Scripture itself prescribes." Knowledge there-

---

206. Stephen E. Fowl puts it this way in his ethics of theological biblical interpretation: "Christian interpretation of scripture is not primarily an exercise in deploying theories of meaning to solve textual puzzles. Rather, Christian interpretation of scripture is primarily an activity of Christian communities in which they seek to generate and embody their interpretations of scripture so that they may fulfill their ends of worshipping and living faithfully before the triune God" (*Engaging Scripture,* p. 161).

fore yields lamentation, repentance, and prayer, which bear fruit in fortitude and a hunger and thirst for justice (2.7.10).

The striking resemblance between this statement and Matthew 5:6 is hardly coincidental: Augustine's order of salvation is a profound progression in holiness through the Beatitudes, imparting blessing upon blessing as the Bible moves its audience from poverty and meekness to hunger, justice, and mercy, then to purity and peace. The Bible is a medium for bestowing the numbered graces of the kingdom of heaven.

These middle steps impart a *metanoia* that turns the student of Scripture away from the entrapments of the temporal world and toward "the Trinity, glowing in the distance" (2.7.10-11, 39). This distant beatific vision gradually quenches the sin still warring against him, and so biblical meditation begins to confer holiness through the fifth step, the counsel of mercy (cf. Matt. 5:7). Mercy implies not just love of God and neighbor, but love of enemies ("Blessed are those who are persecuted for righteousness' sake," Matt. 5:10), and when the biblical seeker attains even this, he has passed to a state of holiness, a personal purity (cf. Matt. 5:8) that can now read signs properly and use things for the enjoyment of God.[207] And such a saint "ascends to wisdom, the seventh and last step, where he enjoys peace and tranquility" (2.7.11, cf. Matt. 5:9).

These steps not only resemble the Beatitudes, but also bear an equally striking resemblance to both Paul's teleology of virtues in 1 Corinthians 13, which form the corporate and personal character of his Corinthian children,[208] and modern systematic theology's *ordo salutis:* being called according to the Father's will, hearing in faith, repenting, being justified, then sanctified, and finally glorified.

Matt. 5	On Christian Doctrine 2.7	1 Cor. 13	*ordo salutis*
Blessed are the poor in spirit, for theirs is the kingdom of heaven.	Before all it is necessary that we be turned by the fear of God toward a recognition of his will.		Call
Blessed are those who mourn, for they shall be comforted.	Of necessity this *fear* will lead us to thought of our *mortality* and of our *future death* and will affix all our proud motions, as if they were fleshly members fastened with nails, to the wood of the cross.		Fear

---

207. "Therefore this holy one will be of such simple and clean heart that he will not turn away from the Truth either in a desire to please men or for the sake of avoiding any kind of adversities to himself which arise in this life" (2.7.11).

208. See Hays, *First Corinthians*, pp. 221-22.

Matt. 5	On Christian Doctrine 2.7	1 Cor. 13	*ordo salutis*
Blessed are the meek, for they shall inherit the earth (cf. Ps. 37:11, 22).	Then it is necessary that we become *meek* through piety so that we do not contradict Divine Scripture. . . . But we should rather *think and believe* that which is written to be better and more true than anything which we could think of by ourselves, even when it is obscure. After these two steps of fear and piety the third step of knowledge confronts us, which I now propose to treat.	Faith	Faith
Blessed are those who hunger and thirst for righteousness, for they shall be satisfied (cf. Ps. 37:28-29).	This knowledge of a good *hope* thrusts a man not into boasting but into lamentation. This attitude causes him to ask with constant prayers for the consolation of divine assistance lest he fall into despair, and he thus enters the fourth step of fortitude, in which he *hungers and thirsts for justice.*	Hope	Repentance
Blessed are the merciful, for they shall obtain mercy.	He will turn toward the *love of eternal things,* specifically toward that immutable unity which is the Trinity. . . . He purges his mind, which is rising up and protesting in the appetite for inferior things, of its contaminations, so that he comes to the fifth step, *the counsel of mercy.*	Love	Justification
Blessed are the pure in heart, for they shall see God (cf. Ps. 37:18).	On this step he so *cleanses the eye of his heart* that he neither prefers his neighbor to the Truth nor compares him with it, nor does he do this with himself because he does not so treat him whom he loves as himself.		Sanctification
Blessed are the peacemakers, for they shall be called sons of God (cf. Ps. 37:37).	Such a *son* ascends to wisdom, which is the seventh and last step, where he enjoys *peace and tranquility.*		Glorification
Blessed are those who are persecuted for righteousness' sake, for theirs is the kingdom of heaven (Ps. 37:39-40).			

The correspondences are not perfect (the absence of the last beatitude is puzzling, but perhaps less so in light of theological fondness for the number seven, and also possibly its popularity among Donatists!). But neither are they accidental. Augustine the homiletician skillfully and subtly weaves the Bible's performance into not one but two biblical schemes of personal salvation, whose "steps" happen to correspond nicely with the categories of Protestant and Catholic soteriology. For Augustine the performance of Scripture in Church is intended by God and empowered by the Holy Spirit to build communal and personal virtue and to accomplish personal salvation. It plays a role from start to finish in the conformation of a disciple into the image of Jesus Christ.[209] It moves its reader and hearer from idolatrous alienation into the direct presence of the Triune God.

Historical critics may object that the Sermon nowhere describes the Beatitudes as sequential steps.[210] Nor do its virtues have the interior, individualistic tone in Matthew that they have for Augustine. Nor (conveniently?) does Augustine note that the Sermon is a midrash on Psalm 37,[211] promising a persecuted Christian community divine vindication for the just and punishment for the unjust. Yet the contextual features of the Sermon still support Augustine's point that the Bible understands its own use to confer salvation and holiness. Certainly this was true in his own experience, and it has proven so throughout the Church's history. In fact, the Sermon's midrash illustrates exactly the teleological use of Scripture that Augustine is describing. Matthew's Jesus transforms Psalm 37 into an eschatological covenant that shapes the kingdom's community of salvation, both corporately and personally.

So as the categories of Trinity, Christology, corporate soteriology, Church, and eschatology inform bibliology, so the categories of personal soteriology inform it as well. The divine-human agency of Scripture makes it possible to trace a salvation of a sinner according to the Bible's varying roles in that person's life. Through the Bible's call, God truly calls out to the lost, and his voice is heard. The *logos* of Scripture effects the *pathos* of those the Holy Spirit moves to repentance. The Law convicts of sin, and the Gospel acquits. The good news, received in faith, justifies — creates a relational change between the new believer and God. Then as the Bible becomes the convert's new language, its words sanctify — they begin to effect a real change in the

---

209. See James L. Mays, *The Lord Reigns: A Theological Handbook to the Psalms* (Louisville: Westminster/John Knox, 1994), p. 50, for a similar Augustinian appreciation of the Church's practice of the Psalter.

210. See Glen Stassen and David Gushee, *Christian Ethics as Following Jesus* (Downers Grove, Ill.: InterVarsity, forthcoming).

211. Charry, *By the Renewing of Your Minds*, pp. 70-71.

new life into which the believer has been initiated through confession and baptism.[212] Scripture gradually becomes less of a disciplinarian and more of a tutor, less a Master and more a Counselor. Of course it is God working these changes, applying the once-for-all work of Father, Son, and Spirit that centers on the cross and at the tomb in the lives of those who receive its grace. And the human mediators of God's grace are not simply the inanimate pages of the Bible, but fellow disciples who mediate God's words through their own lives in a thousand ways. Yet again, just as worship is inconceivable apart from the practice of Scripture, so the Bible's use is woven so completely into the fabric of conversion and sanctification that bibliology and soteriology are inseparable, just as salvation is inseparable from its own verbal and sacramental signs. The Word is, along with the sacraments, a channel of God's saving grace. Working together, these mediate salvation, initiate outsiders into Christ's life, reorient them according to God's original will, create the mind of Christ, equip his body for the work of the Master, and accomplish the profound transformation of his new creation.[213] Each depends upon the others for its ultimate coherence, so there is no point in favoring one over another. (Nevertheless, it is worth noticing that the Bible plays a role throughout the course of personal salvation, something which even baptism and Eucharist do not [1 Thess. 2:13].)

Allegory as the Politics of Sanctification

Augustine's semiotics of Scripture presupposes a context in which biblical signs become intelligible; and that context is the Church, Scripture's reading community. Doctrine is salutary (in Charry's words) in cultivating virtues in the members of Christ's body. This is why for Augustine the movement from literal to spiritual interpretation of Scripture follows and facilitates the sanctification of pilgrims as they journey into the community of faith and journey together into God's presence. Scripture's unambiguous signs are shared even by the world. They build bridges over which people cross from death to life. On the other hand, the Bible's ambiguous signs yield their surplus of meaning only in the community in which their referents are truly identified. So their ultimate criteria are neither historical-critical "common sense" nor

---

212. While this order of salvation is ecumenical enough to comprehend both Catholic and Reformed soteriologies, it would have to be adjusted to accommodate the Lutheran *simul iustus et peccator*.

213. Abraham, *Canon and Criterion*, pp. 467-68.

the canonical text's literal sense, but the rule of *faith* (allegory), the living *hope* of the Second Advent (anagogy), and the rule of *charity* (tropology). The West's fourfold hermeneutic is grounded soteriologically and eschatologically, and therefore ecclesiologically.

Athanasius says essentially the same thing at the end of *On the Incarnation:* Those who apply their mind to the Scriptures will discover there a fuller and better account than Athanasius can offer (§56). But a *further* prerequisite for *true knowledge* of the Scriptures is an honorable life, a pure soul, Christlike virtue, and life in common with the Church to guide the intellect (§57). Both of these Alexandrians have inherited an allegorical method which, according to David Dawson, uses texts and their meanings to reinterpret, critique, and transform readers and their communities, and the worlds in which they live.[214] Their allegorical reading practices are transformative politics. Through them the community of Jesus Christ grows into conformity with his image, and ascends into his presence.

Are such praxes of Scripture still persuasive after the rise of critical hermeneutics? Many moderns simply assume that premodern allegorical methods can no longer be defended, while many postmoderns seek to unmask them as mere contests of human wills. But recall MacIntyre's postcritical description of a tradition's literary canon: It is a tradition's poetry, its epistemological wellspring, the source of its depth grammar, and the subject and object of its most profound enquiry. Its use yields a surplus of meaning for as long as its tradition lives. Its lessons attract and train novices, maturing them and granting them the expertise to "go on and go further" to explore the tradition's deepest wisdom.[215] In turn its masters train apprentices into the tradition's and its canon's core competencies.

MacIntyre's description is compatible in principle with Augustine's and Athanasius' hermeneutics of ascent. The fundamental difference is that the Church Fathers describe their reading strategies in explicitly theological (and theocentric) terms, rather than the generalized terms of MacIntyre's and Dawson's analyses. What MacIntyre would call tradition-constituted ratio-

---

214. David Dawson, *Allegorical Readers and Cultural Revision in Ancient Alexandria* (Berkeley: University of California Press, 1992), p. 236. Unfortunately, Dawson's analysis of Alexandria's reading practices in the first centuries of the Common Era draws out the commonalities among Philo, Valentinus, and Clement rather than emphasizing their differences. Like MacIntyre's generalized theory of enquiry, Dawson's final analysis stops short of a theological interpretation adequate to this bibliology. The differences among these interpreters are determinative in how one should appreciate their allegorical methods, as de Lubac's *Medieval Exegesis* demonstrates (on which see the Afterword).

215. MacIntyre, *Whose Justice?* pp. 382-83.

nality and Dawson would call a linguistic world, they would call "the mind of Christ." What MacIntyre would call expertise in the tradition and what Dawson would call the power for cultural revision, they would call ecclesial and personal sanctification.

Thus allegorical hermeneutics, whether in their earlier Alexandrian varieties or in the Catholic Church's later fourfold method, are not false on their face.[216] Rather, their plausibility is inextricably tied together with the roles of performed Scripture in the salvation of persons and the upbuilding of God's *oikodomē*. It is best evaluated not according to the common standards of either modernity or postmodernity, but according to the theological features that ground it.[217] There is no reason to accept every instance of allegorical medieval or even patristic exegesis of Scripture, and many reasons to reject many of them, as Henri de Lubac himself shows.[218] Yet there is also every reason to believe that Augustine's and Athanasius' accounts, adapted to reflect the development of critical and postcritical Christian tradition in the centuries between their times and ours, reflect the Church's present and future biblical practices at their best. To understand the Bible's work in the world is to understand it in terms of both the divine subject and the human objects of the Trinitarian economy of salvation.

The Bible after the End

We close Augustine's account with the Trinity in view, though still "through a glass in a dark manner, for we walk more by faith than by sight when we make our pilgrimage in this world, although our community is in heaven."[219] Given that the Christian Bible plays a pivotal role in that pilgrimage, mediating the dim view of Father, Son, and Holy Spirit that must suffice in this world, what is its role in the next? When the pilgrimage is over and the disciples are with

216. See Manlio Simonetti, *Biblical Interpretation in the Early Church: An Historical Introduction to Patristic Exegesis*, trans. John A. Hughes (Edinburgh: T & T Clark, 1994), on the wide variety of ancient allegorical proposals in the Greek and Latin Church.

217. See Geoffrey Wainwright, "Towards an Ecumenical Hermeneutic: How Can All Christians Read the Scriptures Together?" in *Gregorianum* 76, no. 4 (1995). There he recommends the fourfold hermeneutic of medieval exegesis, as jingled by Nicholas of Lyra (or Augustine of Denmark), as a promising foundation for an ecumenically promising biblical hermeneutic: *Littera gesta docet, quid credas allegoria, moralis quid agas, quo tendas anagogia*.

218. See the Afterword on Lubac's preference for Augustinian allegory over Origenist allegory.

219. *On Christian Doctrine* 2.7.11, quoting 1 Cor. 13:12, 2 Cor. 5:7, and Phil. 3:20 all in one sentence!

God, is the Bible dispensed with? Does the biblical vision survive the beatific vision? Despite the speculation involved, the answers go to both the character and the purpose of the Bible in Christian life.

Two senses of eschatology are often conflated (or the power of one crowds out the other): in McClendon's words, "what lasts" and "what comes last."[220] Here we mean to differentiate between them. God's sacramental presence through pulpit, font, and table is *eschaton*, what comes last, while full divine presence is the eternal *telos*, "for now we see in a mirror dimly, but then face to face" (1 Cor. 13:12). The force of 1 Corinthians 13 lies in the distinction between the two. *Eschaton* pertains to the imperfect, and *telos* to the perfect (13:8-10). Each depends on the other: The divine charity directs knowledge toward itself, and knowledge participates in the divine charity as it is present in the earthly Church, however imperfectly. Without the connection, there would either be no *telos*, or no efficacious Word and sacraments to bring people there.

The Gospel is the knowledge that moves the believer to God and not to any other object. Yet it is knowledge only in part, for "now I know in part; then I shall understand fully" (1 Cor. 13:12b). It is kataphatic and apophatic at the same time, provisional yet certain, incorruptible treasure in jars of clay (2 Cor. 4:7). It does not grow to perfection, but passes away, *replaced by* perfection (1 Cor. 13:10).

Furthermore, neither knowledge nor faith is the ordering principle in Christian rationality. That role belongs to charity. The teleological role of charity has already explained why MacIntyre's theory of the rationality of traditions, with its emphasis on academic philosophy and theology, can mislead when used to describe Christian rationality. It leads one to envision a Christianity whose center of gravity is intellectual and philosophical, not adorational and doxological. Newman's account is closer to the mark, but it still weights doctrine too heavily, making it too central to ecclesiology (his analysis of the *filioque* being a prime example). According to Paul, Christian rationality is ultimately a rationality not of *gnōsis* but of *agapē*. After the imperfect passes, "faith, hope, charity abide, these three: but the greatest of these is charity" (13:13). Charity is to be the Church's aim (14:1), its ethical and temporal *telos*. It is the end of Christian rationality and its material expressions. It orders and directs all these others to its own final end, and gives them what significance they have. Then what role does a sacramental institution like Scripture have in the next age, when sacraments have given way to unmediated presence?

220. McClendon, *Doctrine*, p. 79.

For Augustine it seems that Scripture, with its knowledge, prophecies, and tongues, fades away along with all else Paul calls imperfect. Indeed, Augustine goes farther than Paul is willing, claiming that even two of the *theological* virtues cease in God's presence: "But the vision we shall see will replace faith, and that blessedness to which we are to come will replace hope; and when these things are falling away, charity will be increased even more" (1.38.42)! In Augustine's thoroughgoing teleology, charity is the *one* thing that remains. It is hard to see Scripture playing a meaningful role in such a heaven — especially considering the fact that Augustine considers Scripture theoretically dispensable even in the present lives of the saints (1.39.43).

The eschatological discourse of Mark 13 offers a less Platonistic picture: "Heaven and earth will pass away, but my words will not pass away" (Mark 13:31). The apocalyptic Jesus may be warning those in future generations who are tempted to scoff (cf. 2 Peter 3:3). But whatever his intention, the implication is clear: God's purposes and actions are rooted in eternity, and so is the particular linguistic shape they take in the mouth of the incarnate and Spirit-anointed Savior. A consequence of the humanity of God and the incorporation of created humanity into the body of Christ is their participation in eternity. This gift confers eternity not only upon the saints themselves, but also upon their work that survives judgment (1 Cor. 3:14). John the Seer, a more Pauline theologian than many people realize,[221] calls these the righteous deeds of the saints, which follow them into God's presence (Rev. 14:13; 19:8).[222]

So not only the Church, but the Church's narratives — and this must include above all the Church's *canonical* narratives — are carried forward into the *telos*. What form they will take is impossible to tell. Certainly they will remain assimilated in the One who fulfilled them, and embodied in those conformed to his image. The living stories of Jesus and his saints forever narrate the Messiah- and Church-making words of Scripture. Let us consider this affirmation a narrative, Antiochian corrective to Augustine's sometimes overdetermining Platonism.

The earthly Eucharist anticipates an eternal banquet, not an eternal fast. Similarly, the *telos* of the Bible's eschatological imperfection is something like biblical consummation, not biblical annihilation. When the prophets and apostles toast at the final banquet, their words will remember the events that

---

221. See Elizabeth Schüssler-Fiorenza, *Revelation: Justice and Judgment* (Philadelphia: Fortress, 1985), especially "Apocalyptic and Gnosis in Revelation and in Paul," pp. 114-32.

222. Of course, the witness of *martyrdom* is immediately in view at least in Rev. 14:13 and perhaps also in Rev. 19:8. But martyrdom is by no means the only work of permanent value, given the content of the seven letters of Rev. 2-3.

led to the occasion. "And when, in scenes of glory, I sing the new, new song, 'Twill be the old, old story that I have loved so long."[223] God's "biblical" words will live and act in the gathered assembly of the new heavens and earth, as they lived and acted in the gathering assembly of the protological and eschatological ages. It is even possible that the eschatological transformation of Tanakh Paul describes in Romans 15:4 has only *begun*, rather than come to completion, in the age of the Church. Scripture's roles are not exhausted in salvation's preliminaries, but they continue to find places in God's economy "for ever and ever" (cf. Rev. 22:5).

Conclusion: The Church's Book

The point of this chapter has been to explore the ways eschatology and ecclesiology positively inform bibliology. The end-times gathering of God's people through Jesus' pneumatic presence-in-absence identifies the eschatological character of Christian Scripture. The Bible's performance makes the absent Lord present in the coalescing assembly of his disciples. Ecclesial phenomenology reveals the "public" side of Scripture's performance. Its roles as the canonical text of the traditions called Christian are as basic to its purpose as they are obvious to the careful casual observer. Yet sociological and historical categories are exhausted before they yield the most profound insights into the Bible's churchly practice, which come from the categories of theology itself. The notes of the Church tie Scripture's qualities to the qualities of the Church that bears it, shapes it, preserves it, and performs it. The relationships between Scripture and tradition locate the Bible's work within the great diversity of communities and contexts that somehow comprise (if not now, then someday) the one Church of Jesus Christ. Liturgy centers the power of Scripture in the *worshiping* Church, giving the Bible both a sacramental present as a means of the salvation and glorification of persons, and an eternal future as a means of God's praise. These theological categories offer accounts of biblical truth that correct and transcend, but never displace, common epistemological categories.

The Bible is an agent in the divine economy of salvation, whose terrestrial focus is the Church. It is not the Word *ad intra*, but the Word *ad extra* — in creation, redemption, and eschaton. This means that in the age of the Church, it is the Word of the Church. Its speech is God's words to himself, to the Church, and to the world; and the Church's words to God, to itself, and to

---

223. "I Love to Tell the Story," words by A. Catherine Hankey (cf. Rev. 5:9).

the world. Because Israel and the Church occupy the middle position in this divine-human verbal exchange, Scripture plays an instrumental role in all the Church's activities, from its worship and glorification of God to its evangelization of the world.

This chapter will have served its purpose if it does no more than establish the *promise* of a bibliology that could be thoroughly informed by ecclesial categories, without domesticating sovereign Scripture and imprisoning it in the churches' human traditions. Only such a thoroughly theological, soteriological, and ecclesiological account of Scripture truly appreciates how it is that humans can both authoritatively bear and interpret God's own words and still be utterly dependent upon and subject to them.

The Measure of Scripture: Evaluating Systematic Bibliology

Implanted Word, Fiery Tongue: The Indispensability of Scripture

This bibliology was framed in the context of an imaginary crisis of "biblioclasm," a scenario in which the very practice of Christian Scripture is called into question. In response, Chapter 1 demonstrates the relationships between Scripture and the Triune God who gives it its divine character; Chapter 2 recounts the crucial role of the Tanakh and New Testament in the cosmic history of salvation that centers in the ministry of Jesus Christ; and Chapter 3 locates the Christian Bible inextricably within the eschatological human community that is the Church of Jesus Christ. The message to biblioclasts is clear: Scripture is basic to the Christian faith. It is the language of the Triune God, the language of Israel, the language of Messiah, the language of the Church, and the language of salvation. It is "the implanted word" that is able to save (James 1:21), the fiery tongue (Acts 2:3, not James 3:6!) of Christianity.

How many biblioclasts are really there to heed the message? No emperor is pillaging churches and burning their Bibles in the name of Christian orthodoxy. While many Christians may not appreciate these affirmations so strongly and explicitly, all Christians do appreciate them in some sense. Even those who fracture the Bible to liberate the gospel within it are fracturing rather than destroying the Bible; and even if they tend to recover the convictions they brought to the texts, they are usually seeking to liberate the message of the *Bible* and not some other book. Even this most radical biblical criticism is not *quite* biblioclasm.

Bibliology's Answers to Liberalism, Evangelicalism, and Narcissism

On the other hand, some Christians appreciate these affirmations so strongly that Scripture has arguably displaced the Triune God as their most fundamental conviction (for instance, taking first place in many evangelical churches' and schools' articles of faith).[1] The lesson from bibliology to these bibliodules (who are not *quite* bibliolaters) is different: While the Bible is basic to Christianity, it is also marginal — in that God alone occupies the center of the faith, and that both belief in God and the believing community predate and will succeed Scripture's present form and roles.

Ann Monroe's anecdotal study of biblical religion in America offers a reporter's eye view on both the near-biblioclasts and the near-bibliolaters who wage their battles over the Bible. She begins with a tour of liberal institutions, then visits evangelical churches and parachurches. For liberals, the Bible "is a lot like a Rorschach test,"[2] a tool for exercises in reader-response hermeneutics. Indeed, when many liberals "read the Bible," Monroe thinks the Bible as such is no longer really there. They have remade it in their image, pointing the signs of the Bible's dark glass (which, like the one in 1 Cor. 13, is really a mirror) back on themselves, and cutting the shepherd's own voice out of the divine-human conversation.[3]

Monroe finds in conservatism a refreshing respect for the Bible's authority and a strong conviction that in it, God really speaks of matters of life and death in ways that transform its hearers. But along with these comes a preference for morality tales over parables, certainty over ambiguity, dogma over story — in sum, law over Gospel. "For conservatives, the Bible is a book of commands that leaves the reader only one choice: to follow or not to follow."[4] Every sermon ends with a list of rules for application. Jesus is nearly ignored, while the *Haustafeln* of his kingdom multiply. The transformation

---

1. Examples include the Second Helvetic Confession, the Westminster Confession, the Helvetic Consensus Formula, the New Hampshire Confession, and the Barmen Declaration. By contrast, the Augsburg Confession, Thirty-Nine Articles, and [Methodist] Articles of Religion begin with the doctrine of the Trinity.

2. Ann Monroe, *The Word: Imagining the Gospel in Modern America* (Louisville: Westminster/John Knox, 2000), p. 99.

3. Monroe, *The Word*, pp. 100-101.

4. Monroe, *The Word*, pp. 162-65.

seems to her less, or other, than the deep transformation that conforms communities into the image of Christ. (Monroe did not visit the Institute for Biblical Research, evangelicalism's equivalent to the SBL, but one suspects that she would have found similar scholarly resemblances to popular evangelicalism.)

Yet in both the liberal and conservative camps, the old hermeneutics are giving way to a loyalty to the Bible determined by its perceived ability to help people fulfill their own personal and social potential. The Bible is fodder for positive thinking, or rules for peace and prosperity, or a daily horoscope of customized divine promises. Or, it is not, in which case the Bible is ignored. Many liberals and conservatives alike, unpersuaded by the claims of pastors, professors, booksellers, and televangelists, turn into biblical *non*-readers, as they fail to find it helpful in advancing their personal agendas.

The weaknesses of both historical criticism and fundamentalistic legalism pale in comparison to the problems of the bibliology of self-improvement. A Trinitarian and Christocentric doctrine of Scripture is an even more urgent remedy for Christians who have learned to make *themselves* the thing to be enjoyed, and God the sacramental thing to be used in the service of their own adoration. In the end, Monroe finally abandons both these options for communities like her own church (and an A.M.E. church that is in many ways its polar opposite), where Christians "look at the Bible not as they want it to be, or not to be, or as they have always been taught it was, but as it is, in its rawness, there on the page in front of them." In these churches, the Bible remains undomesticated, the "lively oracles of God."[5]

The Place of Bibliology: Everywhere

We have already noted that in much of the evangelical tradition, systematic theology travels linearly, from Scripture to the Scripture principle to the other theological *loci*.[6] This follows Calvin of course, but it particularly follows the Calvinism of B. B. Warfield, evangelicalism's bibliological Church Father. For Warfield, the doctrine of inerrant Scripture or plenary inspiration "is *methodologically indispensable* for doing theology . . . but *logically dispensable* so far as the explication and defense of other doctrines is concerned."[7]

5. Monroe, *The Word*, pp. 213-14.
6. Cf. David Kelsey, *The Uses of Scripture in Recent Theology* (Philadelphia: Fortress, 1975), pp. 22-24.
7. See Kelsey, *The Uses of Scripture*, p. 21.

Were there no inspiration of Scripture, Warfield claims, Christianity would still be true and all its essential doctrines intact — and even still accessible through the normal traditions that would have kept alive Jesus' and his followers' teachings.[8] For Warfield, inspired Scripture is logically extrinsic to the Christian faith. But because plenary inspiration *is* a quality of Scripture, attested there and in the convictions of the Church, the doctrine of inerrancy becomes the fundamental guide for biblical interpretation, methodologically indispensable for Christian faith and practice.

Our approach of rooting Scripture in the Trinitarian economy, rather than merely in human epistemology, amounts to a surprising double rejection of Warfield's claims that such a doctrine of inerrancy is the best way to characterize the Bible's truth, and that the doctrine of Scripture is logically dispensable for other Christian doctrines. For Warfield, Scripture is acting *solely* as an inerrant witness to events and beliefs that are otherwise complete in themselves. But the Bible's beginning in the will of the Father, its participation in the *kenosis* of the Son, its empowerment as a means of the work of the Holy Spirit, and its work in Israel, on and in Jesus' career, and in the Church go far beyond the category of witness or the affirmations of propositional inerrancy. The Bible is no mere "store-house of facts"[9] on which theology draws for its work of systematization, but reaches into the characters of both God and God's people. Jesus' formation and career are inconceivable without it. One might as well say that Israel, Mary, and the Church are dispensable to the Christian story. All of these — their events, their texts, and Christ their Center — are interrelated, not simply as effects and cause, but as mutual causes and effects.

In traveling through the theological *loci* in order to develop bibliology, this project proves that an adequate doctrine of Scripture depends circularly on the very doctrines that Scripture helps establish. It fits equally well at the end of a systematic theology as at its beginning. Indeed, it arguably best fits throughout one's theological system, developing along with its other categories in order to inform them and be informed by them at every point. The Bible is a truly rich theological resource, as both a prophetic and apostolic foundation for Christian doctrine and a beneficiary of it.

Nevertheless, a truly systematic bibliology still supports both the basic claim of inerrancy that the *form* of the Bible (insofar as it is properly practiced) is true and trustworthy, and the basic claim of infallibility that the Bible

---

8. B. B. Warfield, *The Inspiration and Authority of the Bible* (Philadelphia: Presbyterian and Reformed, 1948), p. 210, quoted in Kelsey, *The Uses of Scripture.*

9. See Charles Hodge, *Systematic Theology* (New York: Scribner's Sons, 1891), vol. 1, pp. 9-15.

functions reliably in Christian faith and practice (again, insofar as it is properly practiced). Within the fundamentalist and evangelical movements, there is a dizzying variety of positions on the authority of Scripture (and no love lost among many of the partisans).[10] While some accounts of inerrancy and infallibility fall short of honoring the rich resources of the Bible and the stringent demands of a truly Christian doctrine of Scripture, the categories themselves do not. The Bible's truth is a reflection of and participation in God's very truth: Christian Scripture accomplishes the will of the Father, through the ministry of the Son, in the power of the Holy Spirit and the maternal humanity of God's people. The Bible — *i.e.*, the Church's Tradition, tradition, and traditions of Scripture — is the set of canonical textual, oral, practical practices created by and constitutive of the community of God's chosen people. As such, it is authored, used, and illuminated by God, and neither fails nor errs (since it thoroughly norms all Church traditions, including itself — even over the objections of communities whose biblical practices are corrupt).[11] Or, for those who like things simple, *the Bible is true.*

In drawing on the main systematic categories, this bibliology has also found space for a wide variety of "models" of Scripture. Without intending to, it has traversed the same ground as John Goldingay's typology in *Models of Scripture:* Scripture as witnessing tradition, authoritative canon, inspired Word, and experienced revelation.[12] It has also covered much common ground with Avery Dulles's typology of revelation: as divinely authoritative doctrine, manifestation of salvation-history, God's self-manifestation to the inner human spirit, God's address to those whom proclaimed Scripture encounters, and a breakthrough to a higher human level of consciousness and deeper participation in God's creativity.[13] This shows the superiority of a systematic bibliology over any one model of Scripture by itself.[14]

10. Gabriel Fackre offers a helpful taxonomy of evangelical and fundamentalist positions on Scripture in *The Christian Story: A Pastoral Systematics,* vol. 2: *Authority: Scripture in the Church for the World* (Grand Rapids: Eerdmans, 1987), pp. 62-73.

11. Among Fackre's types of inerrancy and infallibility, his "intentional inerrancy" and "Christocentric infallibility" types are most adequate to the doctrine of Scripture advanced here.

12. John Goldingay, *Models of Scripture* (Grand Rapids: Eerdmans, 1994).

13. It is true that for Dulles these are models of *revelation*, not *Scripture*. But Christian Scripture participates abundantly in each model, so the analogy is not unfair. For Dulles's own summary of the models see *Models of Revelation* (New York: Doubleday, 1983), p. 115.

14. While Kelsey's descriptions of seven uses of Scripture in theology might lend themselves to a similar comparison, Kelsey denies that he intends to construct a typology or comprehensive account of the Bible's uses, even those restricted to academic theology (p. 15).

Yet a systematic bibliology is not simply another set of models for Scripture, to be placed alongside Goldingay's and Dulles's arrangements. Rather than appropriating the various dimensions of Scripture as models, we have treated them as aspects of the Bible's character, purpose, and work in God's greater economy of salvation. They do not coexist in ambiguous relationship to each other, as typologies often do.[15] Systematic bibliology offers a principle of coherence and interdependence among these types that catalogues cannot offer by themselves. It orders the various dimensions of Scripture according to the divine economy of salvation: The Bible saves *because* of its divine character and agency. The Bible has a divine character and agency *in order to* form, reform, and govern God's chosen people. Scripture represents human consciousness *in* arising in the Spirit-indwelt prophets and the prophetic Church.

The rhetorical order of the Trinitarian economy makes Scripture's innumerable qualities and functions theoretically intelligible. In their different ways, they reflect both the *ethos* of God and the *ethos* of the redeemed humanity that speaks them. They arise in and fulfill the will of the Father. Their *logos* participates in the *kenosis* of the Son, both in terms of God's ethical investment in human *logoi*, and in terms of the human formation of the Messiah. Their power is the power of the Spirit, both in their rhetorical *pathos* on individuals, and in their formation of first Israel, then the Church of Jesus Christ, as God's earthly communities of *praxis*.

Hermeneutics: Bibliology's Ultimate Fruits-Test

The ultimate point of theological reflection is its application in the Church. As this bibliology closes, we should be ready to turn from the idea of Scripture back to the task of living biblically. One can apply to a proposed biblical reading strategy Newman's and MacIntyre's tests for any tradition's innovative responses to an epistemological crisis: Does the hermeneutic vindicate itself by proving itself superior to its predecessors? Does it solve the problems that have been plaguing the tradition? Does it explain how the crisis arose in the first place? Is it fundamentally continuous with the tradition? Does it develop the tradition's intellectual and practical resources constructively?[16]

---

15. For instance, Goldingay's models remain distinct as his account ends. No epilogue or further commentary relates them in any way.

16. See Alasdair MacIntyre, *Whose Justice? Which Rationality?* (Notre Dame: University of Notre Dame Press, 1988), p. 362.

Indeed, systematic bibliology further demands that such hermeneutical questions take specifically Christian forms. The circularity of the Christian doctrine of Scripture shows that old and new reading strategies are subject not only to the commonly appreciated rules of literal grammatical-historical exegesis, but also — indeed, first — to the gamut of churchly theological concerns: What are their Christologies? How do they relate the testaments? How do they respect the role of God's people? How do they understand salvation? How well do they honor both the "already" and "not yet" of the Bible's eschatological past, present, and future? Above all, how do they further the saving work of the Triune God? What fruit do they bear in the Church and the world? How do they glorify the name of their divine author and speaker?

The immediate point of the Iconodules' case for icons was to defend Church practice. Ultimately, however, their insights grounded, normed, and enhanced the Church's entire theology and praxis of images. Likewise, a systematic theology of Scripture can ground, norm, and enrich the Church's theology and practice of the Bible. Its most obvious application is in developing "biblical, theological hermeneutics" that Christians have widely and repeatedly called for.[17] With it Christians can develop and judge hermeneutical schemes and practices and aesthetics of Scripture.

Beyond the *kerygma* itself, there need be no explicit hermeneutical canons. Indeed, the Bible's inexhaustible versatility in God's plan of salvation suggests that explicit hermeneutical canons and casuistries would quickly outlive their usefulness. The most useful hermeneutical "canon" is simply an enriched appreciation for Christian Scripture among those who interpret it.

Testing hermeneutical practices is a project unto itself. Goldingay follows his account of Scripture with an entire volume on hermeneutics, in which he describes the hermeneutics of each of his models of Scripture.[18] A systematic hermeneutics along the lines of this bibliology would describe and evaluate not just preaching, but Scripture's part in all Christian ethics — what Geoffrey

17. Stephen E. Fowl's *Engaging Scripture: A Model for Theological Interpretation* (Malden, Mass.: Blackwell, 1998) is such a call and response, but the quoted words are Karl Barth's, in *CD* I.2.727. Barth calls the object of Scripture "this one thing — just this: the name of Jesus Christ, concealed under the name Israel in the Old Testament, revealed under His own name in the New Testament, which therefore can be understood only as it has understood itself, as a commentary on the Old Testament. The Bible becomes clear when it is clear that it says this one thing: that it proclaims the name Jesus Christ and therefore proclaims God in His richness and mercy, and man in his need and helplessness, yet living on what God's mercy has given and will give him" (I.2.720). Thus here we see that the only truly biblical hermeneutic is the Bible's own hermeneutic, which is the claim that "Jesus is Lord."

18. John Goldingay, *Models of the Interpretation of Scripture* (Grand Rapids: Eerdmans, 1995).

Wainwright calls "worship, doctrine, and life" — in light of the economy of Father, Son, and Spirit. Its promise is clear in at least three areas: hermeneutical schemes, proposed doctrines of Scripture, and the Church's biblical practices.

Wainwright has recently pointed out a substantial (though incomplete) ecumenical convergence among the major traditions, from Baptists to Eastern Orthodox, on the mutual reinforcement of Scripture and Tradition. Neither the Tridentine era's "two-source" theory nor a naïve *sola Scriptura* that pretends one can read Scripture without some kind of rule of faith has prevailed. The World Council of Churches has proposed that the most basic hermeneutical key to the Bible should be the Nicene-Constantinopolitan Creed, which as the most widely accepted expression of Christian faith is all but normative in defining the boundaries of the Christian community, even in free-church traditions.

Such a proposal resonates with our Trinitarian bibliology.[19] The creed considers Trinity, creation, Christology, pneumatology, ecclesiology, and eschatology, all of which we have seen play a part in the character, mission, and end of Scripture. The Nicene Creed both comes from and norms interpretation of Scripture. Therefore it is not only the most ecumenical but a deeply biblical tradition with which to interpret the Bible. Once one expands the creed systematically and appreciates its narrative movement from creation to eschaton, it unfolds into an outline quite like the structure our Trinitarian bibliology has intentionally pursued.

As it unfolds, its thickening categories suggest hermeneutical uses for the traditional theological *loci*. Here we can offer no more than suggestions that reflect on the material we have already covered. For instance, because of the unity, holiness, catholicity, and apostolicity of the Bible (bracketing marginal issues such as the status of the Apocrypha), Scripture's function is to be God's Word for the universal Church. Thus an ecclesial hermeneutic should honor rather than impede the Bible's conferral of unity, holiness, catholicity, and apostolicity on God's people. Its fruits-test is its power to do Christ's work of building up the Church. Similarly, because of Scripture's agency in the past, present, and future career of Jesus Christ, its work should reflect his threefold office: prophet, priest, and king. These might be taken to underline, say, the Bible's function as prophecy, as medium for divine-human restoration and communion, and as commandment, blessing, wisdom, praise, and curse. Finally, the mysteries it refuses to surrender even diligent readers are not merely failings of the text, or even puzzles put there to arouse curiosity (as Augustine

---

19. See Geoffrey Wainwright, "Towards an Ecumenical Hermeneutic," *Gregorianum* 76, no. 4 (1995): 639-62.

wondered), but reflect on the one hand the dark looking-glass perspective that is all the Church has until the next age, and on the other hand the eternal mystery of the Trinity that even then will remain beyond our comprehension. Dialectical eschatology and Trinitarian presence thus respect the inevitably apophatic results of exegesis, even exegesis done in a doxological context.

These kinds of categories offer theological grounds for multiple ways to read texts, including the spiritual exegetical techniques of the medieval Church. Yet the Analogy of the Word secures the *sensus literalis* in its primary position, so that it is neither neglected nor compromised by the availability of other readings. Indeed, the Analogy of the Word explains the spiritual potency of the literal sense (not to be confused with the *literalistic* sense) of Scripture, a property too often lost when readers oppose letter to spirit.

Theodore of Studium's critique of Iconoclast semiotics provides a compelling model for how systematic bibliology might scrutinize hermeneutical proposals. If his conviction is right that an objection to iconic practice can be heretical in its commitment to a flawed Christology or doctrine of the Trinity, then the Trinitarian dimensions of bibliology can help decide who is right, or at least who is wrong and why, when it comes to judging proposals for how to practice the Bible.

For instance, bibliology can issue "Nicene" criticisms of biblical hermeneutics such as those mentioned in the foreword: Naturalistic historical-criticism that denies God's direct supernatural action in the world is, at best, Ebionitic. Conversely, Origin's contrast between human words and the divine words of Scripture is docetic.[20] Likewise, some (but not all) varieties of fundamentalistic literalism and inerrantism deny the adequacy of normal human speech to accommodate the divine message. Such special categories for biblical discourse are docetic or Eutychian.[21]

Systematic bibliology can issue "Chalcedonian" criticisms as well: Treat-

---

20. Origen, *Contra Celsus,* 3.81, in *ANF* 4.496.

21. Most evangelicals have sufficiently nuanced doctrines of inerrancy to deny such a charge. Silva denies the very applicability of the label "docetism" to the evangelical doctrine of infallibility: "One wonders how the charge of docetism contributes to the discussion, other than by affecting the objectivity of the debate through the 'slur' factor." Yet he adopts precisely such a label in his next sentence, and quite appropriately: "Strangely, I have never heard anyone accused of *Arianism* in his or her view of Scripture, though it could be argued that, once we abandon the doctrine of infallibility, there is no meaningful way in which we can speak of the divine character of the Bible" (Moisés Silva, *Has the Church Misread the Bible? The History of Interpretation in Light of Current Issues* [Grand Rapids: Academie, 1987], p. 44).

ments of the "two natures" of Scripture that associate Scripture's humanity only with weaknesses in the text and its divinity only with transcendent spiritual meaning do not do justice to the coinherence of the two natures. Jesus' humanity is "divine humanity," and the Word speaks with two natures but one voice. Furthermore, readers who equate humanity with literalism and divinity with figuration do a disservice to the complexity of both human and divine language, and do violence to the verbal unity of the two. Allegorical proposals that fail to connect the literal sense with the allegorical are not just esoteric and arbitrary, but represent a dualistic Christology best expressed either as Gnosticism or Nestorianism, divorcing the saving work of God from the human career of Jesus.[22]

Other proposals call for theological considerations more subtle than Nicene or Chalcedonian categories, but no less theological. On the topic of soteriology, Henri de Lubac argues that the order of the *threefold* allegorical method (history, tropology, allegory), deriving as it does from Origen's tripartite "body-mind-spirit" anthropology, is defective and destructive, while a *fourfold*, Augustinian order (history, allegory, tropology, anagogy) where the allegorical sense directly follows the historical "expresses authentic doctrine in both its fullness and its purity."[23] According to Lubac, this latter order embodies the essence of the relationship between the old and new covenants and the testaments that testify to them — meaning the transforming work of Christ and the Holy Spirit in authoring faith, hope, and love.[24] The rule of chastity thus applies a soteriological test to allegorical proposals. Or, on the

22. Gnostics in fact enthusiastically adopted esoteric hermeneutics on the warrant that "the God who like them regarded the created world as a tragic mistake had given his revelation through Jesus only to them. They alone could understand the mysterious parables and enigmatic sayings in the gospels and other Christian documents, for they alone were 'spiritual' beings. . . . They then proceeded to claim that their meaning could be understood only in the light of the Gnostic myths about the spiritual world, man's fallen state, and the redemption of the 'divine spark.' This is to say that they separated Jesus from the church and removed his sayings from the contexts which the evangelists had supplied . . ." (Robert M. Grant and David Tracy, *A Short History of the Interpretation of the Bible*, 2nd ed. [Philadelphia: Fortress, 1984], p. 54). Contrast Grant's paraphrase of Clement of Alexandria: "What guiding principle is to govern [the reader's] interpretation? For one who was devoted to the church there could be only one answer: Faith in Christ in his person and in his work, is the key to scripture. The Logos who spoke in the Old Testament finally revealed himself in the New, and the Christian is better able to understand all scripture in the light of the knowledge which Christ has given" (p. 56).

23. See Henri de Lubac, *Medieval Exegesis*, vol. 1: *The Four Senses of Scripture*, trans. Mark Sebanc (Grand Rapids: Eerdmans, 1998), pp. 90, 114-15. The chapters that follow chronicle the fall and revival of Origenist exegesis in the West through the twentieth century.

24. Lubac, "The Unity of the Two Testaments," in *Medieval Exegesis*, pp. 225-67.

topic of ecclesiology, modernist hermeneutics that do not privilege churchly interpretation (or the strong use of the ecumenical rule of faith that this bibliology commends) fail to account for the power of Jesus' presence in the gathered Church as the head of his earthly body, or the ongoing sanctification of the Church in the Holy Spirit. Conversely, postmodern hermeneutics that radically restrict Scripture's perspicuity beyond the Church fail to account for the universality of Jesus' humanity, the Word's work in creation, the providence of God, the priority of God's prevenient grace, and the power of all human speech to signify, however incompletely. These are reflections of flawed eschatologies.

Theological criticism can affirm, not just oppose, hermeneutical proposals. The full humanity of Christ acquits historical-critical methods, as long as they do not deny at least the possibility of Trinitarian economy. It further encourages every other hermeneutical technique that sheds light on history and human discourse. Yet systematic bibliology locates and relativizes these various reading strategies, resisting any totalizing claims that any of them is *the* normative way to read Scripture. Bibliology respects the diversity of these techniques without sacrificing the ultimate unity of the message they help recover.

Canonical hermeneutics (*e.g.*, using Scripture to interpret Scripture) respect the unity of the Bible in God's single saving purpose through its hundreds of chapters — as long as they first respect those chapters' particularities. Allegorical and typological hermeneutics, when they follow the rules, respect the divine economy of salvation as we see it unfold over time in its complex unity. This is true of both the elaborate allegorical schemes of premodern Christianity, and the "application"-oriented allegorical hermeneutics that are popular today.

A second area of promise is in critiquing other bibliologies. Just as Theodore speaks not just about how images are interpreted but also what they actually are, bibliology directly addresses not just hermeneutics, but also doctrines of Scripture. For instance, a notion of authority that is ultimately grounded only in readers' or hearers' subjective responses to Scripture, or even the authors' original intentions or the historical events behind them, is church-denying in its individualism, and may even qualify as Gnostic.[25] Conversely, grounding authority in canonical status alone fails to respect the presence of grace, in the texts' history of mediating the prophetic prevenience of their divine author to an audience (which is not always a "community") that

---

25. See Stanley Hauerwas, *Unleashing the Scripture: Freeing the Bible from Captivity to America* (Nashville: Abingdon, 1993), for one form of this criticism.

may have forgotten or never known its canonicity (cf. 2 Kings 22:8–23:25). Positing a humanly generated body of literature that is then baptized by God is adoptionistic, while treating Scripture only in terms of the work of the Holy Spirit is modalistic.[26]

A third area concerns hermeneutics in the widest sense. Bibliology can help explain, evaluate, and enrich the full range of the Church's biblical practices, including its liturgical uses of the books themselves; the direct use of the Bible in evangelism and mission (for instance, by the Gideons); the development of lectionaries and the recitation of Scripture during worship services; small-group Bible study by those with and without formal ecclesial training; developing, marketing, and using paraphrases, commentaries, and new Bible translations; personal devotional and theological use of the Bible; Scripture in hymnody and prayer; and so on. A systematic bibliology can critique problematic practices, appreciate constructive ones, and suggest promising new ones.

If systematic bibliology involves hermeneutics in its widest sense, then it involves *academic* biblical practice as well. This project calls for rethinking how formal theological curricula use the Bible. Where biblical studies are reduced to historiography and critical methods, where Scripture is reduced to "Hebrew Bible" and "Early Christian Writings," where hermeneutics is reduced to the second-guessing of underlying events or original contextual meanings, where theology relegates the doctrine of Scripture to the doctrine of revelation, where the liturgical use of Scripture is reduced to homiletics — in short, wherever the reading practices are less than truly *biblical*, there systematic bibliology offers a sharp critique of how the Church mentors and catechizes, and also offers pointers to better approaches.

To illustrate how deeply a biblical "Triumph of Orthodoxy" could enrich theological education, consider how different Eastern Orthodox theological education and practice would be if icons were treated the way many semi-

---

26. As Alan Richardson has put it, "Most theologians today seem to agree that the non-biblical category of 'inspiration' is not adequate to the elucidation of the doctrine of biblical revelation. Whether in its conservative form of 'inspired words' or in its liberal form of 'inspired men,' it cannot adequately express the full biblical truth of God's self-communication to mankind." Alan Richardson, "The Rise of Modern Biblical Scholarship and Recent Discussion of the Authority of the Bible," in *The Cambridge History of the Bible* (Cambridge: Cambridge University Press, 1963), vol. 3, pp. 316-17, quoted in Thomas Hoffman, "Inspiration, Normativeness, Canonicity, and the Unique Sacred Character of the Bible," *Catholic Biblical Quarterly* 44 (1982): 447-69. The problem with rendering *theopneustos* in 2 Tim. 3:16 as "inspired" is that the Greek, "God-breathed," suggests not just the breath but the pneumatic Word *breathed*, and the Father who breathes him. Its Trinitarian implications are often ignored when it is treated simply as "inspiration" (Hoffman, p. 457).

naries and colleges treat the Bible. Orthodox iconology is understood to be as inseparable from the Church's practices, and never abstracted apart from the doctrines of Trinity, Christology, pneumatology, eschatology, ecclesiology, and soteriology. Above all, it is never merely studied. It is practiced, critically and faithfully. The Church's inspired human words of the Father's divine Word deserve at least as much respect.

In all three of these applications, a bibliology is most easily (and perhaps too quickly) used as a tool for critique. But tearing down is merely a preliminary step to building and planting. Bibliology's most profound uses are appreciative and constructive, rather than critical. Doxologies glorify God more powerfully than anathemas. Here the hermeneutical fruits-tests are not academic predictions or analyses, but disciples serving in the churches of Jesus Christ. Such exercises represent this project's ultimate measure of success, as that most popular bibliological prooftext suggests:

> Continue in what you have learned and firmly believed, knowing from whom you learned it, and how from childhood you have known the sacred writings that are able to instruct you for salvation through faith in Christ Jesus. All Scripture is inspired by God and is useful for teaching, for reproof, for correction, and for training in righteousness, so that everyone who belongs to God may be proficient, equipped for every good work. (2 Tim. 3:14-17)

References

Abraham, William J. *Canon and Criterion in Christian Theology*. Oxford: Clarendon, 1998.

Achtemeier, Paul J. *The Inspiration of Scripture: Problems and Proposals*. Philadelphia: Westminster, 1980.

Arkoun, Mohammed. *Rethinking Islam*. Boulder, Colo.: Westview, 1994.

Arnold, Duane W. H., and Pamela Bright, eds. *De Doctrina Christiana: A Classic of Western Culture*. Notre Dame: University of Notre Dame Press, 1995.

Athanasius. *Against the Arians*. In *Nicene and Post-Nicene Fathers* II.4. Peabody, Mass.: Hendrickson, 1994.

———. *On the Incarnation of the Word*. Crestwood, N.Y.: St. Vladimir's Seminary Press, 1993.

Augustine. *Confessions*. Translated by Henry Chadwick. New York: Oxford University Press, 1992.

———. *On Christian Doctrine*. Translated by D. W. Robertson, Jr. New York: Macmillan, 1958.

———. *On the Trinity*. In *Nicene and Post-Nicene Fathers* I.3. Peabody, Mass.: Hendrickson, 1994.

Aulén, Gustaf. *Christus Victor*. New York: Collier, 1986.

Balthasar, Hans Urs von. *Explorations in Theology I: The Word Made Flesh*. San Francisco: Ignatius, 1989.

———. *Mysterium Paschale*. Grand Rapids: Eerdmans, 1993.

Baptist Hymnal, 1975 ed. Nashville: Convention Press, 1975.

Barr, James. *Beyond Fundamentalism*. Philadelphia: Westminster, 1984.

———. *The Bible in the Modern World*. 2nd ed. San Francisco: Harper & Row, 1990.

———. *Biblical Faith and Natural Theology*. Oxford: Clarendon, 1993.

———. *Fundamentalism*. 2nd ed. London: SCM, 1981.

———. *Holy Scripture: Canon, Authority, Criticism*. Philadelphia: Westminster, 1983.

———. *Old and New in Interpretation: A Study of the Two Testaments*. New York: Harper & Row, 1966.

Barth, Karl. *Church Dogmatics*. Edinburgh: T. & T. Clark, 1935-1956.

———. *The Epistle to the Romans*. New York: Oxford University Press, 1968.

———. *The Humanity of God*. Richmond, Va.: John Knox, 1960.

———. *The Word of God and the Word of Man*. Translated by Douglas Horton. New York: Harper, 1957.

Barth, Markus. *Conversation with the Bible*. New York: Holt, Rinehart and Winston, 1964.

Basil of Caesarea. *On the Holy Spirit*. Crestwood, N.Y.: St. Vladimir's Seminary Press, 1980.

Bauckham, Richard. *The Climax of Prophecy: Studies on the Book of Revelation*. Edinburgh: T. & T. Clark, 1993.

———, ed. *The Gospels for All Christians: Rethinking the Gospel Audiences*. Grand Rapids: Eerdmans, 1998.

Boff, Leonardo. *Trinity and Society*. Maryknoll, N.Y.: Orbis, 1988.

Bozarth-Campbell, Alla. *The Word's Body: An Incarnational Aesthetic of Interpretation*. University, Ala.: University of Alabama Press, 1979.

Braaten, Carl. "A Chalcedonian Hermeneutic." *Pro Ecclesia* 3, no. 1 (Winter 1994): 18-22.

Braaten, Carl, and Robert W. Jenson, eds. *Reclaiming the Bible for the Church*. Grand Rapids: Eerdmans, 1995.

Breck, John. *The Power of the Word in the Worshiping Church*. Crestwood, N.Y.: St. Vladimir's Seminary Press, 1986.

Bright, John. *A History of Israel*. 3rd ed. Philadelphia: Westminster, 1981.

Brown, Raymond E. *Biblical Exegesis & Church Doctrine*. New York: Paulist, 1985.

———. *An Introduction to the New Testament*. New York: Doubleday, 1997.

Bruce, F. F. *The Canon of Scripture*. Downers Grove, Ill.: InterVarsity, 1988.

Burgess, John P. *Why Scripture Matters: Reading the Bible in a Time of Church Conflict*. Louisville: Westminster/John Knox, 1998.

Campenhausen, Hans von. *The Formation of the Christian Bible*. Philadelphia: Fortress, 1972.

Canfield, Jack. *Chicken Soup for the Soul: 101 Stories to Open the Heart & Rekindle the Spirit*. Deerfield Beach, Fla.: Health Communications, 1993.

Carson, D. A., and John D. Woodbridge, eds. *Scripture and Truth*. Grand Rapids: Zondervan, 1983.

Charry, Ellen. *By the Renewing of Your Minds: The Pastoral Function of Christian Doctrine*. New York: Oxford University Press, 1997.

Childs, Brevard. *Biblical Theology of the Old and New Testaments*. Minneapolis: Fortress, 1992.

———. "Psalm Titles in Midrashic Exegesis." *Journal of Semitic Studies* 16 (1971):137-50.

Collin, Brenda. "Incarnational Hermeneutics: The Brethren Approach to Scripture." *Brethren Life and Thought* 36 (Fall 1991): 246-70.

Congar, Yves. *Tradition and Traditions*. New York: Macmillan, 1967.

Cunningham, David. *Faithful Persuasion: In Aid of a Rhetoric of Christian Theology.* Notre Dame: University of Notre Dame Press, 1991.

Cuningham, David, Ralph del Colle, and Lucas Lamadrid, eds. *Ecumenical Theology in Worship, Doctrine, and Life: Essays in Honor of Geoffrey Wainwright.* New York: Oxford University Press, 1999.

Daniélou, Jean. *The Bible and the Liturgy.* Notre Dame: University of Notre Dame Press, 1956.

Dawson, David. *Allegorical Readers and Cultural Revision in Ancient Alexandria.* Berkeley: University of California Press, 1992.

Del Colle, Ralph. *Christ and the Spirit: Spirit-Christology in Trinitarian Perspective.* New York: Oxford University Press, 1994.

Dillenberger, John, ed. *Martin Luther: Selections from His Writings.* New York: Doubleday, 1962.

Dillistone, F. W. *The Christian Understanding of Atonement.* Philadelphia: Westminster Press, 1968.

Dodd, C. H. *According to the Scriptures: The Substructure of New Testament Theology.* London: Nisbet, 1952.

———. *The Apostolic Preaching and Its Developments.* 2nd ed. New York: Harper & Brothers, 1944.

Dulles, Avery. *The Craft of Theology: From Symbol to System.* New York: Crossroad, 1992.

———. *Models of Revelation.* New York: Doubleday, 1983.

Dunn, James D. G. *Christology in the Making: A New Testament Enquiry into the Origins of the Doctrine of the Incarnation.* Philadelphia: Westminster, 1980.

Ehrman, Bart D. *The Orthodox Corruption of Scripture: The Effect of Early Christological Controversies on the Text of the New Testament.* New York: Oxford University Press, 1993.

Eire, Carlos. *War Against the Idols.* New York: Cambridge, 1986.

Evdokimov, Paul. "Le Mystère de la Parole." In *Le Buisson Ardent.* Paris, 1981.

Fackre, Gabriel. *The Christian Story: A Narrative Interpretation of Basic Christian Doctrine.* Vol. 1. 3rd ed. Grand Rapids: Eerdmans, 1996.

———. *The Christian Story: A Pastoral Systematics.* Vol. 2: *Authority: Scripture in the Church for the World.* Grand Rapids: Eerdmans, 1987.

———. *The Doctrine of Revelation: A Narrative Interpretation.* Grand Rapids: Eerdmans, 1997.

Fischer, Balthasar. *Die Psalmen als Stimme der Kirche: Gesammelte Studien zur Christlichen Psalmenfrömmigkeit.* Trier: Paulinus-Verlag, 1982.

Fishbane, Michael. *Biblical Interpretation in Ancient Israel.* Oxford: Clarendon, 1985.

Fitzmyer, Joseph A. *Scripture, the Soul of Theology.* New York: Paulist, 1994.

Florovsky, Georges. *Creation and Redemption.* Collected Works. Vol. 3. Belmont, Mass.: Nordland, 1976.

Forstman, H. Jackson. *Word and Spirit: Calvin's Doctrine of Biblical Authority.* Stanford, Calif.: Stanford University Press, 1962.

Forte, Bruno. *The Trinity as History.* New York: Alba House, 1989.

Fowl, Stephen E. *Engaging Scripture: A Model for Theological Interpretation.* Malden, Mass.: Blackwell, 1998.

France, R. T. *Jesus and the Old Testament.* London: Tyndale, 1971.

Frei, Hans W. *The Eclipse of Biblical Narrative: A Study in Eighteenth and Nineteenth Century Hermeneutics.* New Haven: Yale University Press, 1974.

Freund, Nicholas T., et al., eds. *People's Mass Book.* Schiller Park, Ill.: World Library Publications, 1984.

Fry, C. George, and James R. King. *Islam: A Survey of the Muslim Faith.* Grand Rapids: Baker, 1982.

Gadamer, Hans-Georg. *Truth and Method.* New York: Continuum, 1995.

Geisler, Norman L. *Inerrancy.* Grand Rapids: Academie, 1980.

Gelineau, Joseph. *The Psalms: A New Translation.* New York: Paulist, 1968.

Giakalis, Ambrosios. *Images of the Divine: The Theology of Icons at the Seventh Ecumenical Council.* New York: E. J. Brill, 1994.

Girard, René. *Things Hidden Since the Foundation of the World.* Translated by S. Bann and M. Metteer. Stanford, Calif.: Stanford University Press, 1987.

Goldingay, John. *Models of Scripture.* Grand Rapids: Eerdmans, 1994.

———. *Models of the Interpretation of Scripture.* Grand Rapids: Eerdmans, 1995.

Grant, Robert M., and David Tracy. *A Short History of the Interpretation of the Bible.* 2nd ed. Philadelphia: Fortress, 1984.

Grenz, Stanley. *Theology for the Community of God.* Nashville: Broadman & Holman, 1994.

Gunton, Colin E. *The Actuality of Atonement.* Edinburgh: T. & T. Clark, 1988.

———, ed. *The Cambridge Companion to Christian Doctrine.* New York: Cambridge University Press, 1997.

Hagen, Kenneth, ed. *The Bible in the Churches: How Various Christians Interpret the Scriptures.* Milwaukee: Marquette University Press, 1998.

Hauerwas, Stanley. *Unleashing the Scripture: Freeing the Bible from Captivity to America.* Nashville: Abingdon, 1993.

Hays, Richard. *Echoes of Scripture in the Letters of Paul.* New Haven: Yale University Press, 1989.

———. *First Corinthians.* Louisville: Westminster/John Knox, 1997.

———. *The Moral Vision of the New Testament.* San Francisco: HarperCollins, 1996.

Heron, Alasdair I. C. *The Holy Spirit.* Philadelphia: Westminster, 1983.

Hick, John. *God and the Universe of Faiths.* London: Fount, 1977.

Hinlicky, Paul R. "The Lutheran Dilemma." *Pro Ecclesia* 8, no. 4 (Fall 1999): 391-422.

Hodge, Charles. *Systematic Theology.* 3 vols. New York: Scribner's Sons, 1891.

Hoffman, Thomas A. "Inspiration, Normativeness, Canonicity, and the Unique Sacred Character of the Bible." *Catholic Biblical Quarterly* 44 (1982): 447-69.

Holladay, William. *The Psalms Through Three Thousand Years.* Minneapolis: Fortress, 1993.

Howard, Tracy L. "The Use of Hosea 11:1 in Matthew 2:15: An Alternative Solution." *Bibliotheca Sacra* (1986): 314-25.

Hunsinger, George. *How to Read Karl Barth.* Ann Arbor, Mich.: University Microfilms International, 1989.

The Hymnal 1982. New York: Church Hymnal Corporation, 1982.

Jeremias, Joachim. "The Present Position in the Controversy Concerning the Problem of the Historical Jesus." *Expository Times* 69 (1958).

John of Damascus. *On the Divine Images*. Crestwood, N.Y.: St. Vladimir's Seminary Press, 1980.

John Paul II. *Ut Unum Sint*.

Johnson, Elizabeth A. *She Who Is: The Mystery of God in Feminist Theological Discourse*. New York: Crossroad, 1992.

Johnson, Luke Timothy. *The Writings of the New Testament: An Interpretation*. Philadelphia: Fortress, 1986.

Johnston, Robert K., ed. *The Use of the Bible in Theology/Evangelical Options*. Atlanta: John Knox, 1985.

Jones, L. Gregory, and Stephen E. Fowl, eds. *Rethinking Metaphysics: Directions in Modern Theology*. Cambridge, Mass.: Blackwell, 1995.

Jordan, Clarence. *Sermon on the Mount*. Rev. ed. Valley Forge, Pa.: Judson, 1970.

Jordan, Mark D. "Words and Word: Incarnation and Signification in Augustine's *De Doctrina Christiana*." *Augustinian Studies* 11 (1980): 177-96.

Juel, Donald. *Messianic Exegesis: Christological Interpretation of the Old Testament in Early Christianity*. Philadelphia: Fortress, 1988.

Jüngel, Eberhard. *Karl Barth: A Theological Legacy*. Philadelphia: Westminster, 1986.

Käsemann, Ernst. *Essays on New Testament Themes*. Philadelphia: Fortress, 1982.

————. *New Testament Questions of Today*. Philadelphia: Fortress, 1969.

————. *Perspectives on Paul*. Mifflintown, Pa.: Sigler, 1996.

Kasper, Walter. *Jesus the Christ*. Mahwah, N.J.: Paulist, 1977.

Kelsey, David. *The Uses of Scripture in Recent Theology*. Philadelphia: Fortress, 1975.

Kugel, James L., and Rowan A. Greer. *Early Biblical Interpretation*. Philadelphia: Westminster, 1986.

LaCugna, Catherine Mowry. *God For Us: The Trinity and Christian Life*. San Francisco: HarperCollins, 1991.

Leith, John, ed. *Creeds of the Churches: A Reader in Christian Doctrine from the Bible to the Present*. 3rd ed. Louisville: John Knox, 1982.

Leo XIII. *Providentissimus Deus*.

Levie, Jean. *The Bible, Word of God in Words of Men*. New York: P. J. Kennedy, 1981.

Lewis, C. S. *Reflections on the Psalms*. London: Geoffrey Bles, 1958.

Lindbeck, George. *The Nature of Doctrine*. Philadelphia: Westminster, 1984.

Lindsell, Harold. *The Battle for the Bible*. Grand Rapids: Zondervan, 1976.

Longenecker, Richard. *Biblical Exegesis in the Apostolic Period*. Grand Rapids: Eerdmans, 1975.

Loughlin, Gerard. *Telling God's Story: Bible, Church, and Narrative Theology*. New York: Cambridge University Press, 1996.

Lubac, Henri de. *Medieval Exegesis*. Vol. I: *The Four Senses of Scripture*. Translated by Mark Sebanc. Grand Rapids: Eerdmans, 1998.

Lutheran Book of Worship. Minneapolis: Augsburg, 1978.

MacIntyre, Alasdair. *Whose Justice? Which Rationality?* Notre Dame: University of Notre Dame Press, 1988.

REFERENCES

Macquarrie, John. *God-Talk: An Examination of the Language and Logic of Theology.* New York: Seabury, 1979.

Marsden, George, ed. *The Fundamentals.* New York: Garland Publishing, 1988.

Mascall, E. L. *Christ, the Christian and the Church: A Study of the Incarnation and Its Consequences.* New York: Longmans, Green, 1946.

Mays, James L. *The Lord Reigns: A Theological Handbook to the Psalms.* Louisville: Westminster/John Knox, 1994.

McCasland, R. Vernon. "Matthew Twists the Scripture." *JBL* 80 (June 1961): 143-48.

McClendon, James Wm. Jr. *Systematic Theology.* Vol. 1: *Ethics.* Nashville: Abingdon, 1986.

————. *Systematic Theology.* Vol. 2: *Doctrine.* Nashville: Abingdon, 1994.

McClendon, James Wm. Jr., and James M. Smith. *Understanding Religious Convictions.* South Bend, Ind.: University of Notre Dame Press, 1975.

McCormack, Bruce L. *Karl Barth's Critically Realistic Dialectical Theology: Its Genesis and Development.* Oxford: Clarendon, 1995.

McGrath, Alister. *Christian Theology: An Introduction.* 2nd ed. Cambridge, Mass.: Blackwell, 1997.

McIntyre, John. *The Shape of Soteriology.* Edinburgh: T. & T. Clark, 1992.

————. *The Shape of Christology: Studies in the Doctrine of the Person of Christ.* 2nd ed. Edinburgh: T. & T. Clark, 1998.

McKenzie, Steven L., and M. Patrick Graham, eds. *The Hebrew Bible Today: An Introduction to Critical Issues.* Louisville: Westminster/John Knox, 1998.

McPartlan, Paul. *Sacrament of Salvation: An Introduction to Eucharistic Ecclesiology.* Edinburgh: T. & T. Clark, 1995.

Merton, Thomas. *Praying the Psalms.* Collegeville, Minn.: Liturgical Press, 1956.

Meurer, Siegfried, ed. *The Apocrypha in Ecumenical Perspective.* Translated by Paul Ellingworth. UBS Monograph Series No. 6. New York: United Bible Societies, 1991.

Monroe, Ann. *The Word: Imagining the Gospel in Modern America.* Louisville: Westminster/John Knox, 2000.

Montague, George T. *Understanding the Bible: A Basic Introduction to Biblical Interpretation.* New York: Paulist, 1997.

Mulder, Martin Jan, ed. *Mikra: Text, Translation, Reading and Interpretation of the Hebrew Bible in Ancient Judaism and Early Christianity.* Minneapolis: Fortress, 1990.

Nasr, Seyyed Hossein. *Ideals and Realities of Islam.* San Francisco: HarperCollins Aquarian, 1994.

Neuhaus, Richard John, ed. *Biblical Interpretation in Crisis: The Ratzinger Conference on Bible and Church.* Grand Rapids: Eerdmans, 1989.

Newbigin, Lesslie. *The Household of God.* New York: Friendship, 1954.

Newman, John Henry. *An Essay on the Development of Christian Doctrine.* 3rd ed. London, 1878.

————. *On the Inspiration of Scripture.* London: Geoffrey Chapman, 1967.

Nichols, Aidan. *The Shape of Catholic Theology.* Collegeville, Minn.: Liturgical Press, 1991.

Nygren, Anders. *The Significance of the Bible for the Church*. Facet Books Biblical Series. Philadelphia: Fortress, 1963.

Oberman, Heiko. *The Dawn of the Reformation: Essays in Late Medieval and Early Reformation Thought*. Edinburgh: T & T Clark, 1986.

Old, Hughes Oliphant. *The Reading and Preaching of the Scriptures in the Worship of the Christian Church*. Vol. 1: *The Biblical Period*. Grand Rapids: Eerdmans, 1998.

Ouspensky, Leonid. *Theology of the Icon*. 2 vols. Crestwood, N.Y.: St. Vladimir's Seminary Press, 1992.

Packer, J. I. *Beyond the Battle for the Bible*. Westchester, Ill.: Cornerstone, 1980.

—————. *God Has Spoken*. Grand Rapids: Baker, 1979.

Pannenberg, Wolfhart. *Jesus — God and Man*. Philadelphia: Westminster, 1968.

Pelikan, Jaroslav. *Imago Dei: The Byzantine Apologia for Icons*. Princeton: Princeton University Press, 1990.

Pettersen, Alvyn. *Athanasius*. Ridgefield, Conn.: Morehouse, 1995.

Pinnock, Clark H. *Biblical Revelation: The Foundation for Christian Theology*. Chicago: Moody, 1971.

—————. *The Scripture Principle*. San Francisco: Harper & Row, 1984.

—————. *Flame of Love: A Theology of the Holy Spirit*. Downers Grove, Ill.: InterVarsity, 1996.

Pius XII. *Divino Afflante Spiritu*.

—————. *Mediator Dei*.

Placher, William C. *Narratives of a Vulnerable God: Christ, Theology, and Scripture*. Louisville: Westminster/John Knox, 1994.

Prickett, Stephen. *Reading the Text: Biblical Criticism and Literary Theory*. Cambridge, Mass.: Blackwell, 1991.

Rad, Gerhard von. *Old Testament Theology*. San Francisco: Harper & Row, 1965.

Rahner, Karl. *The Trinity*. New York: Crossroad, 1997.

Richardson, Alan, and John Bowden, eds. *The Westminster Dictionary of Christian Theology*. Philadelphia: Westminster, 1983.

Ricoeur, Paul. *Essays on Biblical Interpretation*. Philadelphia: Fortress, 1980.

—————. *The Symbolism of Evil*. Boston: Beacon Press, 1969.

Rodger, P. C., and Lukas Vischer, eds. *The Fourth World Conference on Faith and Order: Montreal 1963*. New York: Association Press, 1964.

Rogers, Jack B., ed. *Biblical Authority*. Waco: Word, 1977.

Rogers, Jack B., and Donald K. McKim, *The Authority and Inspiration of the Bible*. New York: Harper & Row, 1979.

Runia, Klaas. *Karl Barth's Doctrine of Holy Scripture*. Grand Rapids: Eerdmans, 1962.

Sanders, E. P. *The Historical Figure of Jesus*. New York: Penguin, 1993.

Sanneh, Lamin. *Translating the Message: The Missionary Impact on Culture*. Maryknoll, N.Y.: Orbis, 1989.

Schaff, Philip, ed. *The Creeds of Christendom*. Grand Rapids: Baker, 1990.

Schüssler-Fiorenza, Elizabeth. *Revelation: Justice and Judgment*. Philadelphia: Fortress, 1985.

REFERENCES

Silva, Moisés. *Has the Church Misread the Bible? The History of Interpretation in Light of Current Issues.* Grand Rapids: Academie, 1987.

Simonetti, Manlio. *Biblical Interpretation in the Early Church: An Historical Introduction to Patristic Exegesis.* Translated by John A. Hughes. Edinburgh: T. & T. Clark, 1994.

Staniloae, Dumitru. *The Experience of God.* Edited and translated by Ioan Ionita and Robert Barringer. Brookline, Mass.: Holy Cross Orthodox Press, 1994.

Stanton, Graham. *Gospel Truth? New Light on Jesus and the Gospels.* Valley Forge, Pa.: Trinity Press International, 1995.

Stassen, Glen, and David Gushee. *Christian Ethics as Following Jesus.* Downers Grove, Ill.: InterVarsity, forthcoming.

Tanner, Norman P., ed. *Decrees of the Ecumenical Councils.* Vol. 1. Washington, D.C.: Georgetown University Press, 1990.

Tarazi, Paul Nadim. *The Old Testament: An Introduction.* 3 vols. Crestwood, N.Y.: St. Vladimir's Seminary Press, 1991-1996.

Tavard, George H. *The Church, Community of Salvation: An Ecumenical Ecclesiology.* Collegeville, Minn.: Liturgical Press, 1992.

Terrien, Samuel. *The Elusive Presence.* San Francisco: Harper & Row, 1978.

Theodore of Studium. *On the Holy Icons.* Crestwood, N.Y.: St. Vladimir's Seminary Press, 1981.

Thomas Aquinas. *Summa Theologica.* Westminster, Md.: Christian Classics, 1981.

Thompson, John. *Modern Trinitarian Perspectives.* New York: Oxford University Press, 1994.

Torrance, James B. *Worship, Community & the Triune God of Grace.* Downers Grove, Ill.: InterVarsity, 1997.

Van Buren, Paul M. *According to the Scriptures: The Origins of the Gospel and of the Church's Old Testament.* Grand Rapids: Eerdmans, 1998.

Volf, Miroslav. *After Our Likeness: The Church as the Image of the Trinity.* Grand Rapids: Eerdmans, 1997.

——. *Exclusion and Embrace: A Theological Exploration of Identity, Otherness, and Reconciliation.* Grand Rapids: Eerdmans, 1996.

Wainwright, Geoffrey. *Doxology: The Praise of God in Worship, Doctrine, and Life.* New York: Oxford University Press, 1980.

——. *Eucharist and Eschatology.* New York: Oxford University Press, 1981.

——. *For Our Salvation: Two Approaches to the Work of Christ.* Grand Rapids: Eerdmans, 1997.

——. "Towards an Ecumenical Hermeneutic: How Can All Christians Read the Scriptures Together?" *Gregorianum* 76, no. 4 (1995): 639-62.

Wallace, Ronald S. *Calvin's Doctrine of the Word and Sacrament.* Tyler, Tex.: Geneva Divinity School Press, 1982.

Warfield, B. B. *The Inspiration and Authority of the Bible.* Philadelphia: Presbyterian and Reformed, 1948.

Watson, Francis. *Text and Truth: Redefining Biblical Theology.* Grand Rapids: Eerdmans, 1997.

———. *Text, Church, and World: Biblical Interpretation in Theological Perspective*. Edinburgh: T. & T. Clark, 1994.

Wells, Paul Ronald. *James Barr and the Bible: Critique of a New Liberalism*. Phillipsburg, N.J.: Presbyterian and Reformed, 1980.

Wenham, John. *Christ and the Bible*. London: Tyndale, 1972.

Williams, Delores S. *Sisters in the Wilderness: The Challenge of Womanist God-Talk*. Maryknoll, N.Y.: Orbis, 1993.

Wolterstorff, Nicholas. *Divine Discourse: Philosophical Reflections on the Claim That God Speaks*. New York: Cambridge University Press, 1995.

Work, Telford. *The Reason for the Season: Christology Through the Liturgical Year*. Lectures at Fuller Theological Seminary, 1997.

Wright, N. T. *Jesus and the Victory of God*. Minneapolis: Fortress, 1996.

Yoder, John Howard. *The Politics of Jesus*. 2nd ed. Grand Rapids: Eerdmans, 1994.

Youngblood, Ronald, ed. *Evangelicals and Inerrancy*. Nashville: Thomas Nelson, 1984.

Index

Abraham, William, 256-57

Absolutism, 236-42

Alexandria: interpretation in, 88n.82, 229, 230, 309; theological method of, 34-35, 50, 132, 233

Allegory, 51, 105, 230, 308-10, 324

Analogy of the Word: and Athanasius, 36-50, 92, 95, 107, 121n.149, 129, 132-36, 188, 194, 200, 203, 212-13, 264; and Augustine, 50-59, 64-67, 95, 96, 103, 112-13, 188, 226-33; durability of, 30-32; and epistemology, 47-50; equivocation in, 93-96, 102-6; explained, 15; and James Barr, 226; and James Wm. McClendon, Jr., 22-23, 23n.37; and Karl Barth, 18-21, 67-123, 225-26, 229-30; objections, 27-28; and Stephen Fowl, 215n.1; use among theologians, 19-25. *See also* Balthasar, Hans Urs von

Antioch: interpretation in, 199n.173, 202, 312; theological method of, 111, 132, 226, 233

Apocalyptic, 158-62

Apocrypha. *See* Deuterocanonical writings

Ark of the Covenant, 141-43. *See also* Priesthood

Athanasius: and biblical interpretation, 183, 309; eschatology of, 99-100; theory of atonement, 192-93. *See also* Analogy of the Word: and Athanasius

Atonement: Bible as means of, 188; as moral influence, 191-93; as sacrifice, 189-90; as victory, 190-91

Augustine: account of biblical misinterpretation, 183; and apocalyptic, 160; Augustinianism, 239; Bible as means of sanctification, 304-7; and Old Testament in the New Testament, 187, 204; Scripture interprets Scripture, 184; theory of signification, 51, 72, 92, 227. *See also* Analogy of the Word: and Augustine; Rhetoric; Rule of charity; Rule of faith

Authorial intent, 57, 157

Balthasar, Hans Urs von, 48, 63, 66, 78, 84, 89n.83, 100-106, 121n.151

"Baptist vision." *See* McClendon, James Wm., Jr.

Barr, James, 28-32, 41, 114, 115, 225-26, 229-33, 238

Barth, Karl: and *analogia entis*, 70, 72; and dialectical theology, 131-32; and Scripture and Tradition, 268-72, 291-